The Depository Firm and Industry
Theory, History, and Regulation

The Depository Firm and Industry
Theory, History, and Regulation

Lewis J. Spellman
Department of Finance
The University of Texas at Austin

ACADEMIC PRESS

A Subsidiary of Harcourt Brace Jovanovich, Publishers

New York   London
Paris   San Diego   San Francisco   São Paulo   Sydney   Tokyo   Toronto

ACADEMIC PRESS, INC.
111 Fifth Avenue, New York, New York 10003

United Kingdom Edition published by
ACADEMIC PRESS, INC. (LONDON) LTD.
24/28 Oval Road, London NW1   7DX

Library of Congress Cataloging in Publication Data

Spellman, Lewis J.
   The depository firm and industry.

   Includes bibliographies and index.
   1. Banks and banking. 2. Financial institutions.
3. Bank deposits. I. Title.
HG1601.S625 1982   332.1   82-8811
ISBN 0-12-656580-5   AACR2

PRINTED IN THE UNITED STATES OF AMERICA

82 83 84 85   9 8 7 6 5 4 3 2 1

To my mother

Contents

Part IV   Summary

Part V   Appendixes

Preface

The origin of this volume was a study of the savings–investment process. At some point, years back, the idea emerged that the processors are firms that, when stripped of folklore, legalisms, tradition, and money mechanics, are merely economic entities trying to survive in an industry that gathers and packages funds for the use of others. Although constrained by regulation, the depository firm responds to market signals and, in so doing, shapes the industry and affects the aggregate economy. This volume analyzes the firm and industry in the savings–investment process and the relationship of the industry to the performance of an economy.

The subject is treated at both an analytical and a historical level. The historical treatment is qualitative and quantitative, with some of the commercial bank data series extending back to the early 1920s and the thrift data to the mid-1930s. Regulation is treated in both the analytical and historical sections.

All that is required of the reader is some interest in financial institution and financial market developments and some intermediate training in micro- and macroeconomics. With these tools, one should have little difficulty in applying the same basic framework that is used to analyze the behavior of the production firm and industry to the depository firm and industry. The book is used in a graduate-level business school course entitled "The Depository Firm and Industry" at The University of Texas. It should be suitable for either the graduate or undergraduate student or for any reader with a reasonable background in economics.

Acknowledgments

The intellectual debts owed are numerous. Edward Shaw, who exemplified the Stanford monetary tradition from the 1950s through the mid-1970s, comes first to mind. He most clearly penetrated certain "monetary veils." He understood banks as firms, saw better than most people the similarities between thrifts and banks, and clearly realized that this industry was important because it was responsible for the accumulation of real capital rather than dollar-denominated deposits. Others to be thanked include Ron McKinnon, for convincing me of the importance of allocations as a response to relative prices, and Mordecai Kurz, for developing a framework to analyze economic growth. Dale Osborne of Oklahoma State University is to be thanked for instilling a healthy respect for microeconomic structures and a healthy irreverence for the motives of private and public institutions. This was in counterpoint to the reverence for public institutions and public policy that I drew from Herb Schwartz at the Federal Reserve Board, from Gardner Ackley at the Council of Economic Advisers, from Paul McCracken at the University of Michigan, and from G. L. Bach at Stanford University.

In addition, I worked with numerous colleagues on several papers that formed the basis for various chapters of this book. The ideas in Chapter 12 were developed along with Clark Reynolds of Stanford University in a yet-unpublished manuscript entitled "Financial Intermediation and Economic Development as Seen through the Flow of Fund Accounts." I worked with Professor Bill Rentz of the University of Ottawa on the theoretical structure of Chapter 6 in an unpublished paper entitled "Optimal Reserves and Deposit Rates of Financial Institutions: Some Theorems"; with Bob Schweitzer of the University of Delaware on a joint paper, "U.S. Commercial Bank Profits, 1969–1974," which was the basis of the empirical estimates of commercial bank efficiency and competition contained in Chapter 8; and with Al Osborne of University of California at Los Angeles and Bill Bradford of the University of Maryland to sort out some of the analytics regarding the measurement of nonrate competition that appear in Chapter 8. Other preliminary articles that contributed to the ideas in this volume are found in the bibliographies at the ends of chapters.

In addition to these colleagues and friends, numerous graduate students at The University of Texas contributed to this effort. Most notably, the historical statistics were processed and analyzed by Jose Volio; some regression runs in Chapter 8 were performed by Francis Lee; the analysis of market shares was pulled together by Bill Ashbaugh; and the analysis of the Latin American financial systems was performed by Julio Pflucker for Peru, Jaime Nino for Colombia, and Bob Deili for Mexico.

The writing of a volume such as this is costly. In addition to my own resources, I drew heavily from a variety of sources, including the Institute for Constructive Capitalism; the Dreibeelbis Fund for Banking Research; and the Banking Education and Research Fund supported by the First City National Bank of Houston, Texas Commerce Bancshares, Southwest Bancshares, Inc. of Houston, and Republic of Texas Corporation. In addition, support for research that is incorporated in this volume came from the Dean Witter Foundation, the Capital Markets Program of the Organization of American States, and the Latin American Institute of The University of Texas, as well as the research resources of the San Francisco Federal Home Loan Bank and the comptroller of the currency, United States Department of the Treasury. Among those helping me to procure these funds, I am especially grateful to Dean George Kozmetsky and Professor Lawrence Crum, both of The University of Texas.

In addition, I deeply appreciate the generosity extended by Herschel Moore and Margaret B. Moore, who made their office facilities available to me. Very special thanks go to Herschel for sharing with me revitalizing pauses in debate and reflection on some of America's finest golf courses. Joe Long also must be mentioned for unwittingly sparking an interest in the competitive effects from entry in the depository industry. The diligence of various editors at Academic Press in unifying an unwieldy manuscript is appreciated.

It has taken several years to produce this statement, which has required some enthusiastic support when my own enthusiasm wilted a bit. Among the cheerleaders was Conrad Doenges, who made some allowances within the purview of a department chairmanship. This volume was written within offices shared with attorneys-at-law, who seem to consider the toils of an academic to be a curiosity. Their sympathy for a self-imposed sentence of solitary confinement at hard labor was appreciated, and I drew strength as they cheered me onward. To the gang at 1302 West and at Katz's—Herschel, Gloria, Linda, Herb, Marc, Byron, and numerous other friends, among them Pat, John, and Jim—go my thanks for their tolerance, support, and understanding. Most of all I wish to thank Gloria Lawrence for being the chief factotum: typist, sparkplug, organizer, editor, disciplinarian, and treasurer. Without her this book simply would not have been completed.

The book is dedicated to my mother, Frieda, who asked merely that I do my best. I hope my best in this case is sufficient to provide the basis of an analytical framework for understanding the ever-changing complexity of financial intermediation and its regulation.

Introduction

This volume has a point of view. Commercial banks, savings and loan associations, mutual savings banks, and credit unions are dealt with much like firms in any other industry. They purchase resources, produce a product, and price that product. The firms operate in an environment constrained by competition and regulation. The frame of reference blurs old distinctions; banks are treated like any depository institution that accepts deposits and makes loans. Treating profit as a motive allows one to understand the depository firms' actions as market-induced, regulatory-constrained responses; decisions are not based on tradition or custom. The orientation is decidedly microeconomic, and the depository firm is not merely an incidental agent in the multiple expansion process of macromoney economics.

The analysis of the depository firm acting as a private entity, operating only under the restrictions imposed by the marketplace, is developed first. The neoclassical devices of firm cost and revenue curves and market supply and demand curves provide the structure for establishing an optimum deposit rate and the resulting rate spread, deposit and asset size, and levels of cost and profit. The depository firm is treated like any other microproducing unit.

In few industries has the workings of the market been as encroached upon by statute and the regulatory authority of supervisory agencies. This, in turn, has altered the behavior of the depository firm, reshaped the industry, and rechanneled financial flows. The economic effect of financial regulation is studied by adopting the neoclassical model to fit each regulatory constraint. The regulation of deposit and asset rates, of entry, merger, and branching, of asset and liability selection, and of cash and capital reserves, tends to impose constraints, alter elasticities, or introduce new variables to be considered.

In addition to the microeconomic model of the depository firm, an aggregate model is developed to study the economywide influences of a financial system. Here the variables of interest are the real capital, labor,

1

and output typical of growth theory. The depository sector is portrayed as using real resources that produce a service that can affect both per capita output and the growth rate of output. In this analysis, the depository industry becomes a distinctly separate sector in a two-sector growth model of the economy. The growth model traces how the regulation of that sector influences the output of the aggregate production sector. It is found that efficiency and competitiveness in the financial sector are of great importance because they affect the economy's growth rate, capital intensity, per capita output and consumption, as well as the distribution of resources and income between the real and financial sectors. The conditions shaping the size, instruments, and scope of a financial sector are also examined.

Another dimension of this study is historical. The process by which a labyrinth of both state and federal regulation became gradually imposed upon an industry is of interest. The concern is with the economic and political forces that caused financial regulation to be enacted, modified, or rescinded, and also with the comparative record of the depository industries in both a free and regulated market. While deposit growth is relevant, greater emphasis is placed on how the different eras of laissez faire or quasi-laissez faire influenced the portfolio earning rates, effective deposit rates, costs, profit margins, and distribution of the depository industry's revenues. All costs, revenues, and profits are measured as annual rates to facilitate comparisons among banks and thrifts, over time, and across countries.

PART I

Political Economy

The Political Environment and Competition in the Depository Industry, Past and Present

During the course of American history, several major changes in the political environment have affected the competitive environment of depository firms. As a result, the industry has been made to feel various combinations of pressures from both the invisible hand of the marketplace and the sometimes more visible hand of government.

With the adoption of the United States Constitution in 1787, the federal role in the banking or financial arena was not altogether clear. Though Congress had the constitutional power to provide for a national currency, the Constitution does not specifically spell out the authority to create a bank that could either issue a national currency or serve as the banking agent for the Treasury. Furthermore, a clear constitutional authority for Congress to charter commercial banks or other depository firms was also absent. Though definitive authority was lacking, the First Bank of the United States was chartered in 1791. Its charter permitted it to operate for 20 years as a private commercial bank with the government as a minority stockholder and the United States Treasury as its chief client. When its charter lapsed, the Second Bank of the United States was chartered in 1816. Since the power to create commercial banks did not have clear constitutional authority, it took a Supreme Court decision in *McCulloch* v. *Maryland* to uphold the power of Congress to incorporate the Second Bank. Like the First Bank, the Second not only performed banking services for private customers but also collected revenues and made disbursements for the Treasury. The Supreme Court decision legitimizing congressional bank chartering powers rested on the Second Bank's conduct as a Treasury fiscal agent, which was deemed to be a necessary and proper concomitant of Congress's power to levy and collect taxes and borrow money. While this Supreme Court decision of 1819 did not directly address the issue of Congress's power to charter private banks, there was an implied authority to do so. This authority, however, was not utilized after the charters of the First and Second Banks of the United States lapsed.

Resistance to these banks, though they served an important public purpose, was heightened by the feeling that banks operating with congressional authority possessed the potential to become a significant rival political force—a force as strong or even stronger than the fledgling central government of the 13 states. With this sentiment reigning, the federal government withdrew from the practice of chartering private commercial banks, even if they served the needs of the United States Treasury. The charter of the Second Bank of the United States lapsed in 1836, following an intense political debate on the subject of its continuity.[1]

Although Congress was now able to act in the banking arena, it chose not to do so. Of course, this was by design, since Congress implicitly preferred a fragmented banking system to one that was national in scope, with potential nationwide political power. The containment of political power through a series of checks and balances was extended to the banking and financial industry.

In this environment, the development of commercial banking in early American history reverted to the initiative provided by the states. On these matters, the states were also quite restrictive. Indeed, a state bank charter could be obtained only from a state legislature. Since the states did not delegate the chartering of commercial banks to state banking boards, commissions, or commissioners, but maintained these powers themselves, the granting of commercial bank charters was highly restricted and politically motivated. Thus, in the first few decades under the Constitution, entry by financial institutions was difficult at both the federal and state levels, and was subject to the close scrutiny of elected political bodies. Ironically, the desire to control political power created economic license for the few fortunate banks that enjoyed the virtual monopolistic protection of the government.

From the competitive extreme of near monopoly, the pendulum of market power swung dramatically in the direction of laissez faire. Because before 1837 a charter to form a bank could only be obtained through a special act of the state legislature, these legislatures were conferring a quasi-monopoly on a private entity at a price considerably below its market value. In this circumstance, there would obviously be an excess demand for bank charters that the legislators of that day had to somehow allocate. This, of course, led to many cases of capricious decision making

---

[1] An excellent discussion of political and social views regarding banking and finance is provided by Bray Hammond, *Banks and Politics in America from the Revolution to the Civil War* (Princeton: Princeton Univ. Press, 1957).

in which favoritism and bribes would often determine the award of a bank charter. Because of this, the state legislatures found it desirable to avoid the arbitrary act of bestowing bank charters on the fortunate few. They removed themselves from the decision-making process by allowing freedom of entry; and, in so doing, they moved from the competitive extreme of monopoly to the alternative extreme of perfect competition. With the elimination of barriers to entry, the state governments ushered in an era of free banking in the United States.

The first of the states to adopt this posture was Michigan. By the Michigan Act of 1837, anyone could obtain a bank charter by meeting certain minimal financial requirements. New York followed suit in 1838, and most other states followed soon thereafter. When free banking legislation was adopted by most states, this freedom to enter the market invited an explosion of new bank charters into the competitive vacuum of the late-1830s. Not only was freedom of entry through state charters the rule in commercial banking, but it also applied to newly developed mutual savings banks and building and loan associations. During this era, the discipline of market forces constituted the only regulator of the depository firms. This invited expansion when markets were uncrowded, and this expansion in turn increased competitive forces that eventually led to dwindling profit margins and meant either voluntary or forced liquidation for some firms. This normal process of the seesawing of entry and exit—common in any industry—was however, exacerbated, by the liquidity crises and financial panics of the late-nineteenth and early-twentieth centuries.

The general tone of laissez faire, free enterprise in commercial banking continued through the Civil War despite the National Banking Acts of 1863 and 1864. The system of national banks did not alter the environment of regulation by the market, as the newly formed Office of the Comptroller of the Currency in the Treasury Department perhaps even encouraged competition by providing an alternative chartering authority where free banking philosophies also prevailed. This did introduce, for the first time, the dual financial authorities: federal and state. These dual authorities affected competition at times as each sought control of the regulatory process. In fact, there was a period during the Civil War when Congress came very close to eliminating the state banking system. During the War, it imposed a tax of 10% on the circulating notes of state banks. The result, as intended, was a wave of conversions to the new national banking system, bringing state banking to the verge of extinction. The state banks, however, recovered when they found a means of avoiding the tax (demand deposits) and an asset market (collateralized mortgages and agricultural loans) from which national banks were excluded.

The introduction of the national banking system that brought the United States into an era of dual authority was eventually extended to the thrift institutions; the state and federal chartering agents for the thrifts could and often did have separate views regarding entry, regulation, and competition. The existence of a dual banking system raised the issue of whether state legislatures or state constitutions could impose requirements on national banks operating in their jurisdictions, or whether the federal banking authorities could relieve national banks of limitations imposed by states. It was not until 1927, with the McFadden Act, that these issues of dominance in the competitive environment of the dual banking system began to be addressed. This act ruled out interstate branching, but permitted each national bank, with the approval of the comptroller of the currency, to establish one or more branches in cities within its state of operation. The act, however, limited branching by national banks to those states having laws approving branching. That is, in issues of market structure, state law controlled at least the branching of national banks. Discretionary control over entry that was not exercised by the national banking authorities was also left undisturbed by the Federal Reserve Board, which began operations in 1914.

It was not until the depression of the 1930s that the competitive pendulum swung from laissez faire to regulatory control and protectionism. The depository industries experienced failure on a massive scale from both a liquidity and a solvency crisis in the 1930s. This invited a plethora of legislation to preserve the remaining depository institutions and remedy these problems. After almost a century of free banking, the pendulum could not have moved more dramatically toward regulation and control by statute and by the discretionary powers of the newly formed supervisory and insuring agencies of the federal government. The Federal Home Loan Bank Board closely supervised the newly chartered Federal Savings and Loan Association, and the Farm Credit Administration supervised the newly chartered federal credit unions. Discretionary power was also exercised through the supervision and the examination process of the new federal deposit insuring agencies: the Federal Deposit Insurance Corporation, the Federal Savings and Loan Insurance Corporation, and later the National Credit Union Share Insurance Fund. Deposit insurance at the federal level was the toehold for the extension of federal supervision over the state-chartered nonmember banks, mutual savings banks, savings and loan associations, and credit unions.

The regulation by market forces gave way to explicit regulation of deposit and asset rates; to the selection of financial assets; to the offering of liabilities; to minimum proportions of cash and capital reserves; and to other restrictions regarding asset and liability proportions, maturities, rates, collateral, and quality. Indeed, virtually every contractual term was subject to the possibility of control. Entry was restricted, and the expansion of existing firms was closely regulated. No new firm could be formed, nor could any firm expand its size through the acquisition of new capital or the formation of new branches, without the sanction of a public authority. Nor was any firm able to expand through the acquisition of other firms without the prior approval of government. In this highly protectionistic world of the 1930s, the depository industry had reverted to an environment that was highly restrictive and closely scrutinized by the political process. The thrust of the legislation was to reduce competition by carving out markets and by limiting asset and liability authority.

The motivations of both federal and state governments for this intervention grew out of a desire to protect depositors from the ravages of bank and thrift institution failure, while other market intervention was motivated by a desire to protect the depository firms and industry. Some regulations imposed on the depository industry were designed to give the federal government the power to deal with a depressed economy. Some were for the purpose of maintaining the economic integrity of the banks and thirfts, and others were designed to allow selective monetary controls over certain types of economic activity. In virtually every significant aspect, the structure of the depository industry became directly controlled by government.

Underlying this intercession of government into the business of the depository firm was a basic public policy decision that set this industry apart from others. The concern to safeguard the viability of the depository industry arose from the fact that financial failure had significant external effects that reached beyond the depositors and stockholders of the financial firm. The depository institutions played an important role as the chief conduit in both the payment process and the saving–investment process. Failures of individual firms in the depository industries led to widespread deposit runs that overflowed to other depository firms and businesses they financed. The losses of depository failure were not confined to depositors and the depository firms—the external effects were large. Indeed, the cumulative failure of the depository industry was blamed by some for the Great Depression of the 1930s.

The financial control that was initiated in the 1930s derived from law, which was translated into rules and regulations and was monitored by the reporting and the supervision and examination processes. This interdiction by government was myopically seen by the regulators to be directed toward seven social goals: (1) the preservation of a safe and sound financial system; (2) the preservation of competition; (3) consumer protection; (4) investor (stockholder) protection; (5) protection from fraud; (6) the desire to allocate credit; and (7) the desire to control monetary and financial markets. These goals were eventually often in conflict.

So it was in the panic of the mid-1930s that the state and federal governments interceded in a massive way in the affairs of the depository industries. This intercession continued through the depression, the war years, and the postwar period, with little resistance by the industry or the public. Indeed, it was welcomed by a desperate electorate hoping that Washington would restore the economy to its former vitality.

When the economy expanded in the postwar period of the late-1940s and 1950s, the depository institutions were still protected from competitive economic forces. In the postwar boom, these institutions grew not in numbers, but in prosperity. Profit margins per deposit dollar after the war were enviable. They reached peaks in the immediate postwar years for mutual savings banks, in 1950 for savings and loan associations and credit unions, and in the late-1950s for commercial banks. Regulators, unwilling to bestow excess windfall profits on the depository industry, began to allow entry in order to give competition a chance to control profit.

At this point, for a third time in 190 years, the competitive pendulum began to swing. The tilting of the pendulum back in the direction of a more competitive depository environment proceeded slowly. There was an increase in the number of new banks and savings and loan associations chartered and a substantial increase in the number of branches opened. The number of credit unions increased substantially. In competing for deposits with thrift institutions, commercial banks increased the rates paid on time and savings accounts to meet this competitive thrust. By 1966, competition for the savings deposit dollar among thrift institutions and competition between thrifts and commercial banks for over-the-counter savings caused deposit rates to increase sharply. These higher deposit rates in turn tended to substantially erode profit margins, and after the first credit crunch of the summer of 1966, deposit ceilings were extended to thrift institutions.

This extension of deposit ceilings was just a temporary backslide in the movement to a more competitive system. In fact, the ceiling rate on time and savings deposits merely altered the form of competition. The deposit ceilings forced the depository firms to engage in nonrate competition. This regulatory constraint served to increase profit margins for a time, but it proved to be a relatively short-lived reprieve from the growing competitive pressures of the marketplace. In fact, the protection afforded by deposit ceilings and the temporary restoration of healthy profit margins induced regulators to quicken the pace of entry. The number of commercial bank branches and savings and loan branches roughly doubled in the next 15 years. This competitive thrust tended to raise the costs of the saving–investment process without reaping equivalent benefits for depositors, who still faced controlled and depressed deposit rates. The higher costs were the result of the depository institutions having to compete for deposits using nonrate competition techniques that added to cost.

With the dual pressures of an inflationary environment and deposit rates constrained below market rates, depositors in the 1970s often faced negative real deposit rates. This, in turn, led to a politically potent outcry that caused a reexamination of financial regulation. This reexamination was also spurred by the increasing liquidity problems and earning problems thrifts faced in an inflationary environment in which rising market interest rates attracted away deposits that could not be held, since the institutions did not have either the earnings or the authority to pay higher deposit rates.

The reexamination of regulation began with the President's Commission of Financial Structure and Regulation (1972) and culminated in the Depository Institutions Deregulation and Monetary Control Act of 1980. This act (1) phased out deposit ceilings for all depository institutions over a 6-year period; (2) extended interest-bearing transaction accounts to all depository firms; (3) lifted usury ceilings on many asset categories unless overridden by states; (4) relaxed portfolio restrictions on savings and loan associations, mutual savings banks, and federal credit unions; and (5) required all depository institutions to maintain reserves at the Federal Reserve Banks and allowed them access to the services provided by the Federal Reserve.

This act was the culmination of a deregulatory movement that had accelerated in the decade of the 1970s. The thrust of the regulatory changes was to increase asset and liability flexibility by reducing restrictions relating to types of instruments, maturities, and rates—as well as removing geographic impediments to the seeking of deposits and the placing of assets. The inflationary pressures of the 1960s and 1970s resulted in a more competitive financial environment, since the protection market segmentation of both asset and liability markets was dismantled. While it is quite unlikely that the depository industry will ever return to the laissez faire environment of the nineteenth century, the competitive environment in which depository institutions find themselves is once again vigorous, as the discipline of the market takes over from the discipline of the regulator.

Thus, the political and regulatory pressures on American depository institutions have evolved through time. In 1787, with the ratification of the Constitution, there was substantial fear of economic and political power in the hands of bankers. To protect the nation from this potential power bloc, government at both the federal and state level opted to make bank charters quite scarce and localized. This ironically resulted in the formation of a small number of banks, but each enjoyed local monopoly power. The constraint of political power actually minimized the economic constraints normally exercised by the marketplace. After 1837, the control of the banking industry was taken out of the political arena and put into that of the free market. That is, control shifted from political to economic forces. As long as entry was free, competitive market forces prevented monopoly power in banking and allowed only normal profits. After 1933, control shifted again, since it was found that unfettered competition in the depository industries could produce significant adverse external effects. The external control mechanism over the industry derived from a combination of both economic and regulatory forces. The depository firms became quasi-monopolies that were to be protected from failure on the one hand, and were to be regulated from earning too much profit on the other hand. The quasi-monopoly position of the depository institutions was established through a segmentation of both asset and deposit markets by type, by maturity, and by geography. Banks, and later thrifts, were protected by deposit ceilings. The territories of the quasi-monopolies were protected by extreme limitations regarding entry and organizational form. And further, the quasi-monopolies were buffered against liquidity problems when the liquidity facilities of the Federal Reserve Banks, the Federal Home Loan Banks, and later the National Credit Union Administration were made available to their members.

The depository institutions that survived until these measures were put in place weathered the remaining storm of the Great Depression and the very low interest yields and revenues available through the war years. As the economy began to prosper in the postwar period, these quasi-monopolies, protected from competition, began to thrive. The regulating agencies sought to preserve and protect; but, at the same time, they could not sanction excess profits. They thus began to allow entry in the market in the postwar period. The regulatory barriers began to yield, and new branches and even de novo chartering resurfaced after an absence of almost 30 years.

The imposition of entry controls by requiring a public charter represents the most fundamental structural regulation of any industry. When freedom of entry exists, resources and enterprise will be committed to developing profitable opportunities. For prospering, regulated quasi-monopolies, the device of entry represents for the regulators a convenient mechanism that tends to reduce profits of existing firms and, at the same time, extends services to consumers and businesses. It simultaneously ensures that consumer needs will be met and that profit rates will be controlled. If, however, the pace of entry is too rapid, the deposit and asset markets become crowded, and the pressure becomes greater for more firms and branches to attract and place funds. Many offices begin to seek wider geographic markets, to seek new assets, to endeavor to have asset rate restrictions removed, and to compete for additional scarce deposits by inventing new instruments that will invade the deposit markets of others. Eventually, this competition for deposits even results in the evasion of deposit ceilings through the offer of goods and services in order to attract deposits.

This process of pushing at the asset and liability constraints and the imposed deposit and asset rate ceilings began to manifest itself in 1960. The negotiable certificate of deposit attempted to attract funds away from short-term money markets. Savings and loan associations conducted national campaigns to attract deposits and paid very competitive deposit rates. Eventually, the effort to raise funds extended not only across markets, across sectors, and across states, but reached deposit markets abroad as well. The savings and loan associations invaded traditional banking markets by offering an interest-bearing account from which transactions could be made, and credit unions offered equivalent share drafts. Commercial banks retaliated against these inroads by thrifts by offering automatic transfer services from savings to checkbook accounts to effectively circumvent Regulation Q, which had banned explicit deposit rates on demand deposits for over 40 years.

Asset selection changed as the regulatory constraints were bent and broken. Savings and loan associations offered graduated pay mortgages, variable rate mortgages, and renegotiable rate mortgages; and many states and finally Congress eliminated statutory and constitutional state usury ceilings. The nonmortgage investment portfolios of those institutions increased as their holdings of consumer credit and commercial paper increased. Mutual savings banks also entered the consumer credit market, and credit unions invaded the mortage market, which had been fairly well monopolized by the savings and loan associations. Furthermore, credit card services, once only available at commercial banks, became available at savings banks, savings and loan associations, and credit unions.

Documentation of the particular regulatory constraints and statues that were bent at any given time is of little importance. It is sufficient to point out that entry (even if achieved by branching) invades geographic territories in varying degrees and results in market penetration that increases competitive pressures. These increasing competitive pressures lead to demands—even by the competitors themselves—to break down the asset and liability restrictions. It is ironic that these very restrictions, which were set out to segment markets and establish a quasi-monopoly position for the depository institutions in the 1930s, were being trampled on in the 1970s by the very firms they were supposed to protect.

What might be in store for the depository firms in the 1980s and beyond? It is quite clear that the elimination of the segmentation of markets and the removal of the quasi-monopoly protection for the depository firms places them under the competitive pressures of the marketplace. It is likely to leave many firms with ever-narrowing profit margins. There will be an instinctive reaction by depository firms to cut costs and to merge where economies can be gained or where competitive forces would be lessened. There will be a high level of cooperation in these matters from the federal depository insuring agencies, since their risk exposure on insured deposits far exceeds their reserves for this contingency. In some ways, one can expect some reinstitution of devices to segment markets to reestablish quasi-monopolies if all existing firms are to remain in the market. Because of this federal commitment to insure deposits, devices will be found to protect the net income and asset position servicing these deposits.

During the 200 years of American financial history, regulation has been introduced to protect certain interests. Initially, entry into commercial banking was quite limited so that the power of the government would be protected from a concentration of economic interests. After almost a century of financial vicissitudes impinging on the banking system, regulation was introduced in the 1930s to simultaneously protect depositors and the existing depository firms and to insulate aggregate economic performance from financial collapse. In both instances, protectionism called for a reduction in the competitive level in the industry. In the 1950s and 1960s, when the depository institutions were again healthy, a more competitive environment was called for to protect depositor interests. By the late 1970s, depository markets had become quite competitive; but despite this, and because of growing inflationary forces, depositors found their claims deteriorating in real terms. Recently, the political power of the depositors has exceeded that of the industry, so that on balance, regulatory reform has been designed to recoup the real wealth of the depositor at the expense of the institutions. In this case, protectionism for the depositors has led to a more competitive market tone.

Adjusting the competitive environment has been a device successfully used to provide protection to those thought to be in the greatest need. It is quite likely that if the pendulum swings too far in the direction of competition, concern for the industry might once again be paramount. In any event, the depository industry, perhaps more than any other, has found itself at the crossroads of competing political and economic interests. This has been true in the past and will probably always be true in a capitalistic economy.

BIBLIOGRAPHY

Friedman, Milton and Schwartz, Anna. *A Monetary History of the United States, 1867–1960*. Princeton, N.J.: Princeton Univ. Press, 1963.

Hammond, Bray. *Banks and Politics in America from the Revolution to the Civil War*. Princeton, N.J.: Princeton Univ. Press, 1957.

Hunt, Reed, O. and Commission Members. *The Report of the President's Commission on Financial Structure and Regulation*. Washington, D.C.: U.S. Govt. Printing office, 1972.

Krooss, Herman E. and Blyn, Martin R. *A History of Financial Intermediaries*. New York: Random House, 1971.

Lapidus, Leonard, et al. *State and Federal Regulation of Commercial Banks*. vols. I and II. Federal Deposit Insurance Corporation, Washington, D.C., 1980.

U.S., Congress, House, Committee on Banking, Currency, and Housing. *Financial Institutions and the Nation's Economy (FINE), Discussion Principles, Hearing,* 94th Cong., 1st and 2nd sess., 1975.

West, Robert Craig. "The Depository Institutions Deregulation Act of 1980: A Historical Perspective," *Federal Reserve Bank of Kansas City. Economic Review,* February 1982.

CHAPTER 2

Market and Regulatory Forces That Shaped the United States Depository Industry

2.1 THE DEPOSITORY FIRM AND INDUSTRY IN A LAISSEZ FAIRE ENVIRONMENT

The intervention of government in the depository industry has taken many forms. Regulation has restricted the types, quantities, maturities, and credit ratings of assets available to depository institutions. It has restricted the types and maturities and rates of the liabilities they may offer. Regulation has dictated not only loan rates, but also many of the other contractual terms of the loans made by depository firms. Control has been exercised over all aspects of the industrial structure. Not only is expansion restricted, but both vertical and horizontal integration are subject to approval. Intervention has even been extended to the control of failure and withdrawal from the market. Ultimately, the form of enterprise and the risks and returns in the depository industries have been significantly shaped by regulatory forces.

It has not always been this way. Imagine a depository industry where the firms were treated like those in any other industry. In a laissez faire environment, all rates and quantities would be determined by market forces. Supplies and demands on asset markets could determine asset earnings rates; and those earning rates, along with the parameters of the firms' deposit demand curve and production costs curves, would dictate the configuration of gross and net rate spreads, of deposit rates, of profit margins, and of quantities of each asset and liability category. The intensity of competition would determine how much of the firms' earnings would be passed through to depositors. If competition were weak, a large share of revenues would be retained as profit; but with freedom of entry, high profit margins and high rates of return would tend to invite other competitors.

In the depository industry, as in any industry, a simultaneous relationship exists between competition and profit. Increasing profit attracts addi-

16

tional entrants to the market, and these additional competitors, in turn, tend to reduce profit. This adjustment process operates not only when profit is increasing, but when insufficient profit forces withdrawal and a contraction of the industry. Inadequate profit—compared to alternatives—leads to voluntary withdrawal, or forced liquidiation. One adjustment, short of failure, includes a contraction of the firms' scope to eliminate marginally profitable activities. Other adjustments could include the closing of branches or merger, if it would reduce competitive forces or if economies of scale in certain activities existed. Any of these responses might maintain profit levels for the surviving firms.

In this world free of government intervention, the firms would be regulated by the market. Equity accounts and capital–deposit ratios would be kept at a level that minimized the firms' cost of capital. This capital–deposit ratio would be chosen to add a buffer against asset losses and as an inducement to attract deposits. Temptations to reduce the level of capital would be tempered by a self-imposed constraint of an acceptable risk of insolvency. Not only would the capital account be subject to an internal optimization process, but cash reserves would also be optimally set by balancing off the cost of sterilizing cash in nonearning assets as compared to the expected illiquidity costs of having insufficient cash.

The structure of the industry—the numbers, types, and concentration of the firms—would be dictated by economic forces. Branches of financial institutions would exist in numbers and in locations that were economically viable. The concentration of these firms, their size, and the number of branches would be dictated by the technology on the cost side as well as the scale and scope of the market for deposits and assets. These forces would determine marginal revenue and marginal cost curves for attracting deposits. Then, given the firms' objective function—whether profit maximization or not—this would affect deposit rates, profit margins, and firm size.

In this search for the most desirable configuration, some firms might choose to vertically integrate production firms with financial firms, if their joint operation increased profit or reduced risk. Vertical integration would also exist among financial firms that specialized in different liabilities and asset markets. Horizontal integration by similar types of depository firms in different markets might also occur. Integration would be encouraged if there were gains to be made in cash management, economies of scale on the cost side, or risk reduction in portfolio selection. The workings of the invisible hand would not only determine the nature of the depository firms and industry, but would determine resource allocation within the industry and between the financial industry and the business sector.

While comparative advantage reigns, it does not imply that all financial firms would be homogeneous. Some might be large, with many offices serving a national clientele, while others might be smaller in size and scope, serving more specialized markets. In fact, comparative advantage might as likely result in a group of diverse firms, each tailored to the needs of a small submarket. Substantial overlap might exist so that each market—either asset or liability—could be served by a number of firms ensuring that their arbitrage among markets, over time and risks, and across geographic regions does not allow interest rate differentials to open.

The process of calculated commitment of capital and effort could backfire. There would be no explicit or implicit government guarantees. The depository industry would be exposed to the vicissitudes of fortune and misfortune from sources entirely beyond its control, which also could result in forced liquidations when depositors or other claimants pressed their legal remedies.

This adjustment process of product and firm is constantly in motion, although the adjustment process is perhaps more rapid at times of technological breakthroughs, at times of rapid intensive and extensive economic growth, and when the industry suffers the brunt of some external shock. Since the financial firms and industry tend to be vulnerable to external shocks, and because the adverse impacts from these shocks often reach beyond the depository firm, this industry is especially prone to government intervention and regulation.

At this point in a country's financial development, significant changes in the laissez faire environment occur. While business failure and the contraction of an industry are not uncommon, governmental attention directed at the depository industry results from the fact that failure of one firm has significant external impacts. The insolvency of one bank raises questions regarding the solvency of others, and when this cloud exists, deposit runs develop on what are otherwise solvent financial institutions. Since depositors have the right to demand cash, the depository firms are pressed to liquidate assets, as few hold sufficient cash reserves to withstand a general run. In a scramble to liquidate assets, loans are called, assets sold at distressed prices, and there is often insufficient time to liquidate even sound assets on reasonably favorable terms in order to meet the pressing cash withdrawals.

Steps are taken by depository firms to expand sources of liquidity in times of general deposit outflows. Correspondent relationships develop among financial institutions with prearranged lines of credit; secondary markets for assets develop; and private central banking or private gold or reserve asset pools with drawing rights for each contributing member emerge.

Despite these developments, many depository firms fail under a general run. Not only does the insolvency of one financial institution spread to others, but the failure of one financial firm in turn affects the business sector in which loans are called, credit extensions denied, and the liquidation of assets at distressed prices is forced in turn. Not only are the external effects of a single financial failure felt by other financial institutions and business firms, but depositors are also adversely affected when access to their funds is denied for a time or lost partly or wholly.

2.2   UNITED STATES DEPOSITORY INSTITUTIONS IN THE NINETEENTH CENTURY

As strange as this laissez faire scenario might seem today, the depository firms and industries operated in much this way in the United States until the 1930s. When the era of free banking began in 1837, anyone could obtain a bank charter by meeting certain minimum requirements. This led to a great expansion in the banking industry in a laissez faire environment. In 1836, the number of state banks was 500; by 1840, the number of banks had risen to 900.

Not only was this an era of growth in the commercial banking industry, but savings banks were actually the fastest growing financial institutions in this period of time. The mutual savings banks dated back to 1816, when two mutual savings banks, the Philadelphia Savings Fund Society of Philadelphia and the Provident Institution for Savings in Boston, began operations. The market niche for savings banks grew out of changing social and demographic conditions following the War of 1812. Population grew rapidly in the cities because of immigration and rising birth rates. Population growth was accompanied by expanding industrial and commercial activities that supported a large number of low-income wage earners. These individuals were faced with the problem of finding a place to store their savings, which in an agrarian economy would typically have been reinvested in a family farm. Commercial banks, while accepting large deposits, did not seek small individual accounts, which they felt were not profitable.

At the heart of the mutual savings bank movement were individuals apparently motivated by the desire to encourage thrift and provide an opportunity for wage earners to earn interest on their savings. For the new urban working class, savings were also the only source of funds to fall back on during periods of seasonal unemployment. Paternalistic motivations were apparent in the organizational structure of savings banks because all earnings of mutual savings banks accrued to the depositors, despite the fact that the depositors were creditors rather than holders of an equity position. However, since the depositors could not vote for either the trustees or managers and had no influence over how the mutuals invested their funds, handled their accounts, or paid interest, one suspects some self-interest motivated the organizers. In fact, some of the entrepreneurial organization for the mutuals was provided by the commercial banks. The motivation for this integration in the depository industries arose out of the banks' perception of the mutuals as a possible source of liquidity if a deposit run should occur.

While the mutual savings industry grew and prospered in the northeastern section of the United States, it did not, however, take hold in the other sections of the country. Since the South and West were primarily agricultural centers, these areas did not have a large number of nonproprietary wage earners as a potential deposit market. By the time wage earners were sufficiently prevalent in the South and West, commercial banks had begun to accept small savings accounts and thus preempted the deposit market of the mutual savings banks.

While commercial banks specialized in trade credits to the industrial and business sector, the early savings banks invested their funds in only federal or state securities and did not make commercial or consumer loans. This conservative portfolio allocation existed despite any investment restrictions in their charters.

After the initial rush to secure both commercial bank and savings bank charters in the later 1830s, there was at first a shakeout in which ineffective or fraudulent management quickly became exposed, especially in the great recession of 1837. By the 1840s, the savings banking industry underwent a fundamental transformation in management when businessmen who had become bankers came to understand the returns and risks involved in the financial industry. By the 1840s and 1850s, many savings banks became quite diversified in their asset selection. In addition to investing in federal and state bonds, they began to purchase corporate stock, make business loans, and enter the consumer credit markets by purchasing mortgages.

In addition to the increase in the number and diversity of commercial and savings banks, the first building and loan association, the Oxford Provident Building Association was organized in Frankford, Pennsylvania, at about this time. It was organized by a group of businessmen and wage earners for the specific purpose of pooling funds to purchase or build private homes. The idea, however, was not unique, as these institutions were replicas of existing financial firms in Europe. The market niche they found was one that catered not only to savers in general, but those who also desired aid in financing a homestead. This was an especially pressing problem because commercial banks, at that time, served business interests exclusively and would not extend credit to finance private housing.

It is interesting that the new building and loan associations were designed solely to finance the homes of their original members. When the home of every member was fully paid, the building association would terminate. In 1836, a second association was located in Brooklyn; a third, in South Carolina in 1843; and by 1849, the concept had reached Connecticut. By 1860, these limited-life organizations could be found in the major states along the eastern seaboard.

The limited life of the building and loans was a constraint on their development and growth. To alleviate this constraint, the Dayton Plan was introduced in Ohio in the 1880s. Depositors were permitted to withdraw their savings after meeting certain time constraints, and borrowers could accelerate payment schedules to reduce interest on their mortgage loans. This allowed for fluidity; new depositors and new borrowers could take the places of previous depositors and borrowers, so that it was not necessary to terminate the financial entity. The early savings and loan associations were mutual in form; depositors were both members and owners. Each depositor was eligible to vote for directors and other officers, and votes were weighted in proportion to savings in the association. With this organizational structure, the number of cooperative building and loan associations in the United States grew rapidly, so that by 1893 there were over 5000 associations. By the turn of the twentieth century, these associations only had approximately 3% of total deposits of all intermediaries, but held about 13% of the outstanding nonfarm residential mortgages in the United States. They have continued to specialize in this asset market.

Credit unions were depository institutions that emerged somewhat later, at the turn of the twentieth century. They were a mixture of early mutual savings banks, which encouraged thrift, and the early savings and loan associations organized for the purpose of making loans to depositors. Credit union charters were based on some common bond of organization, occupation, or residence. Initially, the market niche of the credit union was small consumer loans to its members. The need for credit unions grew out of the nearly complete absence of legal consumer lenders, which was partly due to the unrealistically low state usury ceilings that were common at the time. Both savings and loan associations and savings banks were prohibited by law from making unsecured personal loans, and commercial banks were not motivated to enter the consumer loan market. Thus, the development of credit unions, like savings and loan associations, grew out of an asset market gap rather than a deposit market gap.

2.3 THE NATIONAL BANKING ACT AND THE FEDERAL RESERVE ACT

The development of the United States depository institutions occurred at the time when both the federal and state governments were essentially following a hands-off policy. These institutions were the product of enterprising responses to a gap in the marketplace. The first federal intervention of any significance that was to control or shape the depository institutions occurred with the National Banking Acts of 1863 and 1864. The National Banking Acts were a response to the financial difficulties experienced by the Treasury during the Civil War. Without a federal income tax to offset the wartime expenses, and with limited supplies of gold reserves earned through import duties, the government turned at first to the sale of Treasury obligations and the printing of fiat paper currency to finance government expenditures. Each had its drawbacks. The large-scale sale of government bonds tended to elevate interest rates and increase debt service, and the printing of currency tended to cause inflation and high interest rates. In searching for other sources of finance, the federal government recognized the potential of inducing the commercial banking system to purchase its paper obligations. In 1863 Secretary of the Treasury Salmon P. Chase devised a scheme to establish a system of national banks. He proposed that Congress charter banks that would be required to hold government bonds and Treasury fiat money as required reserves against the issuance of bank notes. The intention of the legislation, of course, was to induce commercial banks to purchase both interest-bearing and noninterest-bearing Treasury debt with specie payment—creating a market for the Treasury's paper obligations and thus swapping paper obligations for gold. In order to make this attractive to commercial banks, the national bank notes that were printed by the Treasury were also redeemable at the Treasury. This feature tended to give these notes a competitive edge compared to state banking notes. Since few banks applied at first for national bank charters through the newly established Office of the Comptroller of the Currency in the Treasury Department, in 1865 Congress imposed a 10% tax on the notes of state banks in an attempt to make national bank notes and hence national bank charters more desirable when compared with state bank charters.

Of course, the tax was challenged in the courts as an unconstitutional attempt by the federal government to destroy a franchise that was the states' power to grant. The Supreme Court nonetheless upheld the tax, relying not only on the taxing power of the Congress, but also in part on the power of Congress to provide a national currency. With the legality of the tax temporarily established, banks in many states aplied for national bank charters. However, some state banks devised the demand deposit as an alternative liability instrument that would evade the tax. This financial innovation, born out of the necessity to avoid taxation, is the first of many examples of how the contours of the United States financial system were shaped by government policy rather than economic forces. As banks began to switch to demand deposits, they found they were able to operate profitably without bank notes. The state banking movement then began a strong comeback and, given the choice in the now dual banking system, most banks preferred state charters where capital and liquidity requirements were less stringent than those applied to national banks. Deposit banking then grew rapidly in the 1870s, and by 1890 there were again more state banks than national banks.

Although far from the primary motivation for the national banking act, federal regulation of depository institutions began as a concomitant of their chartering. Restrictions and limitations were placed on the type and amount of loans that national banks could make, and the act also set minimum cash reserve requirements against the banks' deposit liabilities. The cash reserves were set according to the location of a bank, with regional money center banks having higher cash reserve ratios than those of city banks or country banks. This classification of banks for the purpose of setting reserve requirements continued until the early 1970s.

Another feature of the National Banking Act was explicit capital requirements for new banks. The minimum capital requirements or the relationship of equity to deposits for new banks again depended on the size of the community. Although minimum capital requirements were established for new banks, the principle of free banking remained a part of national banking law.

Because the national banking system enforced both cash and capital reserves, this made the national banks more resistant to runs and resulted in greater banking stability for the national banks than the wildcat state banks of the free banking era. Stability was also thought to be built in, since the circulating notes of the national banks were printed by the federal government for the issuing bank and were almost perfect substitutes for other Treasury currency. Banks were allowed to issue these notes in proportion to their holdings of government bonds. However, this feature of the national banking system ironically built in a defect that threatened its survival. When the issuance of national bank notes was so directly and tightly controlled by the level of government debt outstanding, an expanding deposit and asset base for commercial banks would only be possible if the federal government ran deficits and sold bonds. Since monetary growth was tied to government deficits, and since this was an era when government bonds were being retired on balance, there was no provision for an expansion of the assets and liabilities of the national banks. Given those constraints on the national banking system, it was particularly vulnerable to liquidity crises, and these crises occurred with serious regularity. In 1873, 1884, 1893, and 1907 the scramble for liquidity spread across the country and descended upon the New York banks. The realization that liquidity crises were a national problem resulted in 1908 in the Aldrich–Vreeland Act, which called for a national monetary commission to investigate the banking system. After a relatively minor panic in 1911, the problem culminated to the point that public resistance to a central bank was finally overcome.

The major thrust of the Federal Reserve Act of 1913 was to solve the problem of a shrinking currency base for the money supply and to provide cash to the banking system when it was in need of instant liquidity to meet deposit outflows. The elasticity of the currency and the availability of liquidity were the paramount problems addressed by the act. Neither monetary control nor bank regulation was at the heart of the original central banking legislation in the United States. However, since a primary purpose of the Federal Reserve was to provide liquidity, it did regulate the cash reserve holdings of the commercial banks more directly by requiring cash reserves to be deposited at the central bank. It indirectly affected other asset holdings when commercial banks were induced to hold some "eligible" paper for the purposes of rediscounting at the Fed. The Federal Reserve Act, while affecting asset selection in a relatively minor way, did not change the principle of free banking, and the number of banks increased sharply during the early Federal Reserve years.

2.4 THE 1920s

The economic growth of the 1920s was paralleled by a substantial expansion of the entire financial sector. Of all the financial institutions, the investment banking houses especially prospered. In this period, the investment banking industry consisted of approximately 300 firms and was located mainly in New York and other major cities of the East and Midwest. The investment bankers were the conduit for the manufacturing firms to circumvent the banks and reach national capital markets. During this era, all depository firms, with the exception of the mutual savings banks, expanded as well. This growth included the newly organized state chartered credit unions.

Commercial banking growth, development, and innovation after the turn of the century were substantial. The number of commercial banks increased from 11,000 to almost 30,000 in the years between 1896 and 1920. Almost half of these banks were unincorporated partnerships. Growth in the number of banks reflected several elements. With the coming of the railroad, the population moved westward and spread itself thinly over agricultural areas of the Midwest and Far West. In addition, the somewhat restricted local transportation led to an explosive growth in the number of towns and cities with newly formed banks. This expanding banking market resulted in larger numbers of firms, since many states had unit bank rules. A great majority of these commercial banks were small banks in small towns with relatively small concentrations of the total commercial bank deposits.

These new banks, in violation of the prevailing orthodoxy of the real bills doctrine of self-liquidating short-term loans, began to provide longer-term capital to industry and agriculture by automatically renewing short-term loans. They also began providing longer-term capital when commercial banking became more involved in investment banking. Thus, with the most sizable private credit need of the day being the long-term corporate market, the commercial banking system marshalled the resources to be funneled to corporate capitalism by purchasing and placing corporate securities.

Innovations in commercial banking were not confined to the asset side of the balance sheet. Time deposits became an increasingly important source of funds to commercial banks. The growth of time and savings deposits had a distinct geographic pattern. Time and savings deposits were considerably more important as a source of funds for commercial banks in the South and West then they were in the industralized cities of the East, where there was greater competition for savings deposits from savings and loan associations, mutual savings banks, and credit unions.

While there was expansion in the commercial banking industry, there simultaneously was consolidation as the holding company movement, or chain banking, became prominent in the 1920s. The holding company was horizontal integration of depository firms. Other consolidation of deposits occurred from bank mergers. A bank branching movement occurred in the early twentieth century, when many states passed legislation permitting branching. Branching by national banks was somewhat expanded by the Consolidation Act of 1918, which permitted national banks to consolidate with state banks having branches and to retain these branch offices.

However, national banks were still restricted from branching in direct competition with state banks. Since this restriction on national banks would allow state banks a competitive edge, Congress passed the McFadden Act of 1927, which permitted national banks to have limited branching within the cities of their main offices, if branching was permitted by state banks in those states. The act also set the number of branches to be in proportion to the size of the population of the state. With this legislation, the 1920s saw over 3000 branches of commercial banks begin operations. Many of these were within the large urban areas, but in California and other western states where statewide branching was permitted, there developed large branch banking systems that were prohibited by states that maintained county or other geographic branching limitations.

A possible source of motivation for consolidation of bank deposits was a common statutory provision that limited the loan amount to any single customer to some ceiling percentage of the bank's capital and surplus. The merger movement and the holding company movement allowed the concentration of financial resources to match the size of loans needed by the industrial firms. The matching of the scale of the financial resources to the scale of industry needs has often been at the heart of efforts to consolidate financial resources, whether the form of consolidation is holding companies, branching, or merger. In addition to the motivation to concentrate deposits, mergers and holding company acquisitions surely stemmed from the desire to spread risks, provide complete lines of financial services, and possibly enjoy some economies of scale in production and cash management.

The 1920s was a time for growth for not only the commercial banking industry; the savings and loan industry prospered as well. The savings and loan industry benefited from the market pressure for housing construction and the substantial market for residential mortgages. At the same time, the industry's deposit activities benefited from the general economic prosperity.

Much the same could also be said of the mutual savings banks. Despite stagnation in the number of these institutions because of their confinement to the northeastern states, they did switch their asset selection from railroad bonds and other bonds associated with the economic expansion of the late nineteenth and early twentieth centuries to the high-yielding mortgage loans available because of the building boom. The growth of credit unions continued through the early part of the twentieth century; and, interestingly, their growth continued during the depression years, since they inherited the consumer small loan market when many commercial banks failed.

2.5 THE DEPRESSION AND FINANCIAL REGULATION

While the 1920s was a prosperous time for all the depository institu-(tions, the 1930s was a cataclysmic time for this industry. The orbituary list of depository institutions was awesome. The result was losses of wealth on many sides; the depositors, the borrowers, the stockholders, and the community were deprived of transaction services.

The result was overwhelming regulatory intervention in financial processes. The impact of the plethora of legislation was to impose upon the depository institutions a protected status quo. Deposit markets were to be protected by type and by territory, ceiling rates on deposits were imposed on commercial banks in order to relieve pressure on earnings, assets were to be judged for their riskiness, and sufficient quantities of cash and near-cash items were to be held in order to reduce risk and increase liquidity. Asset markets were to be divided up as each depository institution was to receive its own quasi-monopoly. Commercial banks were to specialize in collateralized business loans, the savings and loan associations were awarded the home mortgage market, and the credit unions received the consumer credit market.

By the mid-1930s, control of the financial industry was very much in the hands of federal regulators. Although state authorities continued to regulate state-chartered banks and savings institutions, the insurance of deposits at the federal level caused a regulatory overlap between federal and state agencies in both commercial and mutual banking and in the savings and loan industry. This resulted in a jurisdictional overlap and regulatory complexity that plagued the state-chartered depository institutions.

The thrust of the legislation and the charge placed in the hands of the newly created federal agencies was to replace competition by stability. The economic forces of competition were to be restrained. Indeed, the Glass–Steagall Act of 1932 forbade commercial banks to engage in competitive activities. Safety and soundness of the institutions, the deposits, and the loans had become the order of the day. In effect, the depository institutions had become privately owned and operated federal instrumentalities to provide financial and monetary stability. Entrepreneurship in the depository institutions both in the seeking of deposits and in placing those deposits in earning assets become constrained. The result was to maintain the status quo with respect to markets, types of asset and liability instruments, and geographic territories. All aspects of financial innovation came to a halt. The strategy of the anticompetitive policy was to reduce deposit and asset market elasticities that would tend to increase profit margins for the surviving depository institutions. In effect, the surviving institutions were granted quasi-monopolies and were provided with subsidized liquidity and insuring services. In return, they accepted the close scrutiny of their activities and severe restrictions on their risk taking. The longer term result of this anticompetitive move, unfortunately, was a hardening of the arteries of the depository firm and the financial system. It reduced the system's ability to direct funds to areas in which borrowers were willing to pay the going rate for credit, it restricted the ability of the depository institutions to raise funds, and it restricted their ability to finance enterprising economic activity. It also produced regulatory-induced specialization as opposed to market-induced specialization.

The straitjacket of financial regulation was probably considered a small price to pay to avert a reoccurance of the calamity of the 1930s. Indeed, the newly formed federal regulatory and insuring agencies were a source of considerable comfort to the depositing public. The Banking Act of 1933 established the Federal Deposit Insurance Corporation (FDIC). Federal deposit insurance became mandatory for national banks, but the act also brought state-chartered banks under federal bank supervision, as state banks were induced to join the FDIC so as not to be at a competitive disadvantage with their insured rivals.

The Emergency Banking Act of 1933 provided enough capital for most banks to reopen their doors. The Glass–Steagall Act, passed later that year, embodied reforms designed to limit the types of businesses that banks engage in and to restrain competition, which was thought to have caused a number of failures. The Glass–Steagall act strictly segregated investment and commercial banking by limiting commercial banks' investments in corporate stock, and severely limited banks' ability to underwrite securities.

The federal government came to the aid of the savings and loan industry first by providing direct assistance through the Reconstruction Finance Corporation, a subsidiary of the Treasury, which gave direct loans to troubled savings and loan associations. In addition, liquidity was provided to these associations when the newly formed Home Owners Loan Corporation was created to buy mortgages. In 1932, the Federal Home Loan Bank Act created the Federal Home Loan Bank Board, which was designed to roughly parallel the Federal Reserve Board. The Federal Home Loan Bank Board, like the Federal Reserve, was to provide liquidity to savings and loan associations, although the funds for these loans were borrowed in the capital markets. The bank board was also given the authority to charter and supervise federal savings and loan associations. Just as the FDIC had the power to supervise, examine, and hence, regulate, state chartered commercial banks, the Federal Savings and Loan

Insurance Corporation, established in 1934 and placed directly under the control of the Federal Home Loan Bank Board, similarly began to impose federal restraints on state chartered associations.

The dual system of federal and state charters also became extended to credit unions through the Federal Credit Union Act of 1934, which permitted federally chartered credit unions in all states. Federal credit unions grew quickly, increasing to over 3700 by 1940. The responsibility for administering federal credit unions was first given to the Farm Credit Administration. Then in 1942, administration of credit unions was transferred to the FDIC. In 1948, Congress created the Bureau of Credit Unions, an agency under the control of the Social Security Administration. Finally, in 1970 Congress created an independent agency, the National Credit Union Administration, which Congress charged with responsibility to administer federally chartered credit unions.

As for the mutual savings banks, no federal chartering emerged until 1980, and no separate supervisory agency was established. In the 1930s many states established their own insuring agencies for mutual savings banks, but in 1942 the FDIC lowered their insurance rates sufficiently to induce state chartered savings banks to join the FDIC system. In electing federal deposit insurance, the mutual savings banks were obliged to come under the regulatory influence and bank examination and supervision powers of the FDIC.

2.6 THE WAR AND POSTWAR DEPOSITORY ENVIRONMENT

Given the regulatory constaints on portfolio selection, the fate and fortunes of the depository institutions thereafter tended to react more sensitively to the effect of overall economic conditions on each credit sector of the economy. For example, in the 1930s and during the war years, there was a virtual cessation of activity in the markets for residential housing and consumer durables. This, of course, tended to adversely impact savings and loan associations and credit unions, since their loan portfolios derive from this activity. During the years of World War II, the most important debt-generating sector was the federal government. This was a market and a sector that all institutions could finance, and indeed they turned their attention to financing the war deficit not only for economic but also patriotic reasons. There was a risk, however, in purchasing government bonds, since the sale of large quantities of bonds could drive bond prices downward and rates upward. The risk was reduced when the Federal Reserve stepped in and made a commitment to purchase whatever amount of bonds was necessary to prevent a downward movement of bond prices. The depository institutions then entered the market, and by the war's end held almost 50% of outstanding public debt.

In the wartime period, the depository institutions contributed their efforts not only by directing funds into the government bond market, but they also administered the sale of Savings Bonds. This job was made easier by the high savings rate from disposable income and the absence of consumer durables or residential construction. These twin conditions led to relatively large inflows at the thrift institutions, and commercial bank deposits grew as a result of the monetization of the wartime debt by the Federal Reserve. With little or no expansion in their numbers, deposit inflows brought comparative prosperity to the members of the industry, despite the low interest rates.[1]

After World War II, the postponed housing needs, backlogged through the 1930s and the early 1940s, set the stage for a great expansion of residential construction. Because consumers held large quantities of liquid assets that enabled them to make down payments, and since the Veteran's Administration (VA) and Federal Housing Authority (FHA) insurance programs provided favorable financing terms, this generated a housing sector boom. The strong housing demand translated into high earnings, which allowed the savings and loan associations to pay competitive interest rates to attract funds for this market. Between 1946 and 1950, their assets almost doubled, compared to a 2% growth in commercial bank assets and a 20% growth in the assets of mutual savings banks. The comparative size rank of these two institutions changed as a result of the postwar boom in the mortgage markets and the isolation of the mutual savings banks in the northeastern states. In the mid-1950s, the deposit levels of savings associations surpassed those of mutual savings banks for the first time, and the gap has continued to increase. Comparative market shares also shifted against commercial banks, which were constrained by deposit ceilings and continue to lose ground to thrifts, as well as other types of financial intermediaries.

The changing asset market conditions, which were, in turn, a reflection of changes in production patterns in the postwar era, meant that commercial banks reduced their holdings of government bonds. This slack was taken up by increasing quantities of short-term business loans, state and local government securities, consumer loans, and even consumer mortgages. All these markets expanded in the postwar years.

With the healthy overall economic conditions of the postwar era and

---

[1] The historical data on which these observations are based are contained in Chapters 9, 10, and 11.

with severe limitations to entry, regulatory rent was generated in the form of growing profit margins for the existing depository institutions.[2] The regulatory agencies responded to high and growing profit margins at first gradually in the 1950s and then at a more accelerated pace in the 1960s and 1970s, by allowing entry by de novo branching and chartering.

The number of credit unions increased dramatically in the postwar era. De novo chartering of new banks began in the 1960s and continued in the 1970s. At the same time, a substantial increase in the number of branches took place in the savings and loan industry. In many cases, branching has a force equal to that of adding new firms, when branching is a territorial invasion into the domain of others. Offsetting this to a minor degree in the postwar era was the substantial number of mergers, especially by savings and loan associations and, to a lesser degree, by commercial banks. Further consolidation occurred as the result of the holding company movement in both the savings and loan and commercial banking industries. While these consolidations tended to reduce competition, there were nonetheless constraints imposed by the judiciary to ensure that the consolidations did not tend to substantially decrease it. In United States v. Philadelphia National Bank et al. (1963), the Supreme Court held that Section 7 of the Clayton Act, applies to bank mergers. This section makes unlawful any merger "in any line of commerce, in any section of the country, the effect of which may be substantially to lessen competition, or to tend to create a monopoly [p. 321]."[3]

Despite this antitrust constraint on consolidation, the market and regulatory agencies responded to the potential for economies of scale in production and the need for large, diversified portfolios of assets to meet growing postwar credit needs. Banking authorities began to approve branch and group (holding company) banking. A policy question debated at the time was whether the benefits of a branch or holding company system would outweigh the loss of the local responsiveness that is characteristic of unit banking. In addition, there was the classic concern that has occurred throughout our history over potential political and economic abuses resulting from the concentration of power in a few large entities.

In response to these conflicting concerns in the 1950s, many individual states adopted laws that varied widely in the handling of the branching and merging of banks. In order to standardize some of these laws, the Bank Holding Company Act, was enacted in 1956, gave the Federal Reserve the power to regulate multibank holding companies. In 1960, the Bank Merger Act, which split the responsibility for approving bank merg-

---

[2] Regulatory rent is more precisely defined in Chapter 7.
[3] United States v. Philadelphia National Bank et al., 374 U.S. 321 (1963).

ers among the three federal banking agencies, was passed. In 1970, one-bank holding companies were also added to the Federal Reserve's jurisdiction. As with branching and chartering, federal approval of bank mergers by the appropriate federal agency, as well as by the Justice Department, became necessary with passage of the Merger Act of 1960. Prior to that, bank mergers were subject to control almost exclusively through state agencies. The Bank Merger Act of 1966 specifically provided a justification for merging banks: The merger would be approved if the expected benefits to the community outweighed the anticompetitive effects. But this act merely defined the issue without resolving it. To the extent that economic tests were used, concentration ratios of deposits in a market were utilized. This, however, was a blunt test, as it did not directly measure the ex ante and ex post levels of competition.[4]

2.7 COMPETITIVE AND INTEREST RATE PRESSURES IN THE 1960s AND 1970s

The importance of competition for any industry is that it tends to pressure its firms. If competitive levels are increased because of entry, it stimulates a burst of creativity. It causes imaginative techniques to be used to attract deposits in a more crowded deposit market. It pushes the firms to find assets with greater yields or lower risks. It causes the entrepreneurs in the industry to push against the constraints imposed by regulation. The pressures that are created not only cause firms to seek out new deposit and asset markets; they also affect interest rates. Deposit rates increase when there are no regulatory constraints, and asset rates decline.

With the rapid advance in the number of depository offices competing for deposits, the thrift institutions operated in increasingly deposit-rate-sensitive markets; that is, markets in which the distribution of deposits became more sensitive to deposit rate differentials. These more highly competitive levels of the middle 1960s were to push deposit rates upward, which, in turn, resulted in diminishing profit margins. In March 1965, the Federal Home Loan Bank Board feared that rising deposit rates at savings and loan associations might seriously endanger the industry. The Board in its annual report of 1965 indicated that some savings and loan associations were increasing deposit rates in situations where aggressive competition for funds was not required. The Federal Home Loan Bank Board's solution to the problem of deteriorating earnings was to attempt to discipline the institutions that raised deposit rates by refusing to extend advances to

---

[4] For an excellent collection of papers regarding mergers and the public interest, see U.S., Treasury Department, *Studies in Banking Competition and the Banking Structure*, pt. 1.

those institutions. This act of cutting off liquidity services to institutions experiencing disintermediation was not dissimilar to the Federal Reserve's refusal to provide needed liquidity to the banking system in the early 1930s. In this case, however, large-scale failure was averted when the Board began to modify their restrictions on advances during the credit crunch summer of 1966. By late 1966, the Board terminated all restrictions on advances.

Since this heavy-handed attempt to discipline deposit rates downward was ineffective, the agency then went the legislative route. On September 21, 1966, the Interest Rate Control Act extended deposit ceilings to the thrift institutions. The Federal Home Loan Bank Board, after consulting the Board of Governors of the Federal Reserve System and the Board of Directors of the FDIC, was empowered to put ceilings on rates paid on deposits. At that time, a differential of .5% in favor of savings and loan associations and mutual savings banks over commercial banks was established. It was thought that this differential was sufficient to maintain relative market shares of deposits between banks and savings associations. In addition, credit union ceilings were set even higher for the same purpose.

The deposit ceiling legislation was only momentarily effective in controlling deposit rate competition, as the depository institutions responded by offering consumer-type certificates of deposit (CDs) at rates above ceiling rates. These were also quickly subjected to regulation, so the depository institutions turned to nonrate competition. While nonrate competition tends to generate income in kind for depositors, which adds to cost, it has, however, a considerably less cutting effect on profit margins than deposit rate competition.[5] Since the costs of nonrate competition are less than the reduction in deposit costs, they leave the depository institutions in relatively better condition. In the early 1970s, regulatory rent from deposit ceilings accrued. With the thrifts enjoying rising profit margins, regulatory authorities again quickened the pace of entry, particularly after 1971. This further fueled the drive by depository institutions to use more imaginative nonrate competitive techniques to attract deposits.

The growing nonrate competitive costs were not the only side effect of deposit ceilings. When restrictions are placed on deposit rates and when open-market rates increase, the depository institutions begin to operate at a competitive disadvantage to all other types of open market financial claims. Not only did the depository institutions receive a smaller share of the savings market, but they became vulnerable to net deposit outflows.

After the imposition of deposit ceilings, there began a series of episodes of disintermediation in which rising inflation rates translated into larger in-

---

[5] The impact on costs and profit from nonrate competition is developed in Chapter 8.

flation premiums in open-market rates, and these higher open-market rates were invariably higher than existing deposit ceilings. The rising inflation rates of the 1960s and 1970s created for the thrift institutions an inflation shock almost as significant to these industries as the growing competitive pressures from entry. With deposit ceilings compromising the ability of depository institutions to gather and retain deposits, and with an existing superstructure of asset restrictions, the thrifts were partially exposed to disintermediation and to deteriorating earnings. With many regulations restricting asset selection and with binding usury ceilings, the thrifts were vulnerable to rising inflation rates.

The most threatening interest rate realignments were the inversions of the yield curve structure that occurred in 1966, 1969–1970, 1974, and for a period of time beginning in 1979. Yield curve inversions in which short-term rates exceeded long-term rates put the thrift institutions into a highly vulnerable position, since they were borrowing their deposit funds in competition with short-term rates and placing these funds in long-term markets. Borrowing short and lending long pays off handsomely when there is a relative stability of inflation rates and interest rates. This was certainly the case in the 1940s, 1950s, and early 1960s, and it indeed contributed to the healthy earnings and explosive growth of the savings and loan industry at that time.

While yield curve inversions present extreme difficulties for the thrifts and especially the savings associations, the trend of rising inflation rates and rising market interest rates alone would have been sufficient to cause consternation in the industry. The depository institutions' market share declined when deposit ceilings prevented them from effectively competing for funds when rates on open-market instruments become more attractive to savers. When this occurred and disintermediation resulted, liquidity costs rose, since funds had to be borrowed at market rates to meet deposit outflows. Liquidity pressures on the industry became intense, especially since the market value of long-term securities declined during periods of rising interest rates. In fact, a better part of the industry became technically insolvent at times, and a wave of failures could have resulted had not the Federal Home Loan Bank System begun to vigorously advance loans to its members. The parallels to the liquidity crises facing commercial banking in the 1930s were all too apparent; however, in this case sufficient liquidity was advanced so that a similar conclusion was prevented.

In response to these liquidity pressures and in partial response to market pressures, there were some modest increases in deposit rates. However, most of the increase in deposit rates did not come as the result of changing existing ceilings but rather through the establishment of new deposit categories with higher ceilings. The mere recognition of the need to compete with the open market was not sufficient. Though the money market certificate, the ceilings of which floated at a differential with competing open-market instruments, was introduced in mid-1978; this deposit instrument might hold deposits, but it did not generate sufficient revenues to cover the higher interest costs.

One might wonder why, in an environment of rising market interest rates, the savings associations were not in a position to place funds at higher-yielding rates. The answer was simply that the new market interest rates could be earned only on net marginally attracted deposits. Since the major portion of the portfolios of savings and loan associations were locked into existing mortgages granted at earlier periods at considerably lower market rates, earnings were not sufficient to pay competitive rates to attract additional deposits as open-market interest rates continued to move upward over a 15-year period. Not only were the thrifts laboring under the legacy of earlier low-yielding mortgages, but in the late 1970s, the aggregate savings rate declined, so that the possibility of substantially increasing deposit levels and hence earnings was greatly diminished.

As a partial adjustment to cyclically rising interest rates and increasing depository competition, the pressure increased within the industry for the granting of broader authority for both asset and liability selection. The broader liability authority was sought to allow greater latitude for the firms to seek the marginal increases in deposits necessary to lower disintermediation costs and possibly lead to higher deposit levels. The expanded asset authority was to allow firms access to markets and instruments that might generate higher earnings. Furthermore, more flexible asset and liability authority would reduce vulnerability to a yield curve inversion. There was a conscious effect to shift assets to short-term markets and to extend the maturity of liabilities. Not only was there a movement toward lending in short-term markets, but an effort was made to introduce a mortgage that contained a long-term commitment of funds with an interest rate that varied with competing open-market rates. In addition to these adjustments to the problems presented by increasing and variable interest rates, the savings and loan associations began to seek expanded powers so that they might effectively operate as mortgage brokers and service entities. These increased services would generate income but would not incur the risk of interest rate fluctuations. Some savings and loan associations turned toward originating, bundling, selling, and then subsequently servicing mortgages.

The inflation shock of the 1970s also affected mutual savings banks and credit unions. While the federal credit unions were subject to deposit ceilings, their ceiling rates were higher than those applied to other thrifts and banks—granting them for a time a comparative rate advantage over the other depository institutions and less vulnerability to the drain of deposits to the open market. While the credit unions ran into relatively less resistance in their deposit activities, they did, however, ultimately experience earnings difficulties when rates continued to rise, since the Federal Credit Union Act set a ceiling interest rate on their loans at 1% per month of the outstanding balance. With this usury ceiling, credit union earnings began to deteriorate, and profit per deposit dollar in the late 1970s became negative.

The mutual savings banks also experienced difficulties during the 1970s. Their difficulties were the result of a combination of some similar and other unique problems. Since these banks operated in the highly competitive depository markets of the Northeast, their profit margins could be expected to be slimmer than those of other depository firms. The mutual savings banks were further plagued by the problem of location in a relatively slow-growing region of the United States that generated less savings. Furthermore, their asset portfolios contained assets of even older vintage and lower yields than those typical of savings and loan associations across the nation.

While the accelerating inflation rate of the 1970s had generally adverse effects on the thrift institutions, the commercial banks were not as badly affected by inflation. In fact, after 1974, the yield curve inversions caused their profit margins to actually increase, as they were able to escalate the effective yield on their portfolios more rapidly than the increase in their weighted average deposit rate. In general, the commercial banking industry was far better equipped to withstand the inflationary influence on financial markets. Broader lending authority to select desirable asset markets, and the ability to adjust rates on short-term business loans to current market rates meant that their earning rates held up well. On the liability side of their balance sheets, the sale of deposit certificates allowed the commercial banks to raise funds in needed quantities. This, however, added to interest costs, as did the declining proportions of demand accounts. At the beginning of the 1970s, approximately half of commercial bank deposits were demand accounts, whereas at the end of the 1970s only 30% were. Since some of the increase was in time accounts with fixed maturities, the commercial banks actually lengthened the maturity structure of their liabilities in the 1970s. On the other hand, the savings and loan associations' liability maturities were reduced, despite a desire to lengthen them, because of the shift of funds from CDs to the 6-month money market certificate and later into negotiable order of withdrawal (NOW) accounts.

While inflation caused the depository institutions to offer liability instruments to compete with the open market, the changes in the asset and liability instruments began in the 1960s when commercial banks sought to exploit several submarkets. The most significant market thrust was the negotiable certificate of deposit, aimed at the large corporate depositor. In offering the negotiable CD, commercial banks hoped to attract funds that would otherwise be invested in various money market instruments, such as commercial paper, Treasury bills, and banker's acceptances. This represented a significant break with the traditional practice of the commercial banking industry, which had formerly refused to court business time deposits. The certificate was not only aimed at a new submarket to increase deposits, but was an instrument that gave commercial banks the power to practice liquidity management in a more sophisticated and flexible manner than they were previously capable of. Although loans could be obtained through the growing Fed funds market and at the discount window of the Fed, the negotiable CD market provided commercial banks with an instrument that allowed them to more flexibly adjust their liquidity position for a longer time period.

There were other innovations as well. Commercial banks and, eventually, all thrifts introduced CDs for consumers that were nonnegotiable and issued in ever-smaller denominations. Such deposits carried higher interest rates than passbook accounts. The rates were regulated at first, but after 1978, the ceilings applicable to some of these accounts floated at a differential tied to money market instruments. On a smaller scale, some commercial banks and, eventually, savings and loan associations sought to expand sources of funds by selling subordinated debentures, capital notes, and unsecured short-term promissory notes. These means of raising funds sometimes had special advantages, as no reserve requirements were needed, and, in addition, some debt even satisfied capital account requirements. In another variety of financial innovation, the one-bank holding companies issued commercial paper through their nonbanking affiliates for use in participation loans sponsored by the banking affiliate. In addition to these sources of domestic funds, commercial banks, and later savings and loan associations began to compete for dollars abroad. The commercial banks, through their overseas branches, sought Eurodollars in a market that was beyond the control of deposit ceilings.

2.8 THE DEPOSITORY DEREGULATION ACT OF 1980

As for the thrift institutions, their entry into the market for transaction deposits actually began in the early 1970s and were permitted a gradual expansion of authority over the decade, until blanket authorization was granted in the Depository Deregulation Act of 1980.[6] These accounts are interest-bearing savings accounts on which checks can be written. Essentially, they are interest-bearing demand deposits. At first, NOW accounts were limited to two states, but NOW account authorization expanded in 1976 to include mutual savings banks, savings and loan associations, and commercial banks in all New England states. By the 1980 act, the NOW account, or some variation such as the credit unions' share draft account, may be offered by all institutions in all geographic areas. In addition, through electronic terminals called remote service units, depositor customers of thrift institutions are able to perform within seconds many of the transactions formerly conducted through demand deposit accounts, such as withdrawing cash, making charge account and loan payments, and transferring funds from one account to another. In addition, savings and loan associations, as well as mutual savings banks, have introduced telephone transfers to third parties and automatic payment services that allow customers to more easily utilize their savings accounts for transaction purposes.

On the asset side, there have also been significant developments. For the savings and loan associations, alternative instruments to the conventional mortgage have been developed. The variable-rate mortgage, the graduated pay mortgage and the renegotiable rate mortgage were among the first authorized. The adjustable mortgage loan essentially authorizes borrower and lender to negotiate any contract that is in their own best interests. In addition, the mortgage-backed bonds and the conventional pass-through securities have allowed the savings and loan associations to package new or existing mortgages for sale to the open market, a service for which they receive both origination and service fees. Savings and loan associations have also received authority to purchase other investment securities.

The 1980 Deregulation Act permits savings associations to invest in, redeem, or hold shares of certificates of open-ended investment companies and to invest up to an aggregate limit of 20% of assets in unsecured or secured consumer loans, commercial paper, and corporate debt securities.

---

[6] On May 2, 1972, the Massachusetts Supreme Court overturned a decision rendered by the Massachusetts Commission of Banks, and ruled that Consumers Saving Bank of Worcester (Massachusetts) could offer NOW accounts. The Court held that these accounts did not constitute transaction accounts, as the offering institution could delay third-party payment for up to 30 days. This decision was the key that opened the gates, as mutual savings banks and savings and loan institutions in Massachusetts and New Hampshire moved quickly to attract customers for these new accounts. After further conflict between banks and thrifts, subsequent legislation enabled all depository institutions in Massachusetts and New Hampshire to carry NOW accounts beginning in January 1974.

The act also allows federal savings and loan associations to invade another traditional commercial bank market by allowing them trust and fiduciary powers and to offer credit card services.

The act allows the federally chartered mutual savings banks to hold up to 5% of their assets in commercial, corporate, or business loans, provided such loans are made within the state in which the mutual savings bank is located or made within 75 miles of the home office. The act also permits federal mutual savings banks to accept demand deposits from any source.

Asset authority changes have also occurred with credit unions. The credit union's 10-year maturity ceiling on loans has been lifted, allowing them to venture into mortgage markets; and they now have the authority, along with other thrift institutions, to offer lines of credit to consumers when they were allowed overdraft checking. Credit card services also have been accorded increased importance by credit unions and other thrifts, which further cuts into a traditional banking domain.

An important regulatory change contained in the Deregulation Act of 1980 was the lifting of usury ceilings that had often been controlled for a very long time through either state constitutional provisions or state legislation. The federal enactment superseded state usury law ceilings, unless specifically overridden by the states within a 3-year period. This applies to mortgage loans made by any of the depository institutions. State usury ceilings on business and agricultural loans above $25,000 will be preempted for 3 years, subject to the right of affected states to override the preemption. A ceiling of 5 percentage points above the discount rate (including any surcharges) in the Federal Reserve district where the institution is located will apply to such loans. Not only were state and some federal usury ceilings lifted, but the 1% per month ceiling applicable to the loans of federal credit unions was increased to allow these institutions greater latitude when interest rates are affected by an inflationary surge.

Rate ceilings were not only lifted on the asset side of the ledger; deposit ceilings on all types of accounts were to be deregulated in a gradual phasing out process. In a provision of the act, authority to set ceilings rates on deposits was transferred from the Federal Reserve Board, FDIC, Federal Home Loan Bank Board, and National Credit Union Administration to a six-member Depository Institutions Deregulation Committee made up of the heads of those agencies plus the secretary of the Treasury, with the comptroller of the currency as a nonvoting member. Authority to control the rates paid on deposits by depository institutions was provided for a term of 6 years from the date of enactment of the legislation, in order to give thrift institutions time to incorporate the new powers granted to them; they may adjust their asset portfolios to increase their earnings and alter their asset maturity structure to be in a position to pay market interest rates on short-term deposits. During the 6-year period, the committee is directed to provide for a phaseout of deposit ceilings just as soon as possible by increasing the permissible rates paid to depositors on all accounts to open-market rates. Specific targets for increased deposit rates are set forth in the legislation. The legislation provides for a targeted increase of one-quarter percentage point in the permissible passbook rates within an 18-month period after enactment. Additional targets are set, and, while the committee is not bound by any target and may in fact exceed any target if economic conditions allow, at the end of the sixth year after date of enactment of the bill, all Regulation Q authority expires.

It was the intention of the act that the committee accomplish the phasing out of deposit ceilings in a way that ensures equity for depositors, especially those savers with small accounts, and ensures competitive equity among depository institutions and between depository and nondepository institutions that compete for the savings dollar. The conferees also are charged with handling the deregulation of deposit ceilings with due regard for the financial viability of the depository institutions. This implies not only a managed withdrawal of deposit ceilings as earnings allow, but a management of the deposit rate differentials so as to maintain market shares.

The act says little regarding entry, merger, and other matters of industrial structure. To some degree, the act, in a subtle way, obviates the need for additional branching. The NOW account authorization for thrift institutions is nationwide, and thus removes the necessity of opening bricks and mortar branches to attract deposits from a wider geographic area. The authorization for the remote service terminal further obviates the need for branching. In addition, there has been a further removal of geographic lending restrictions by the Home Owners Loan Act. Thus, the thrift institutions may attract deposits and place loans over wider geographic areas. While issues of interstate branching and merger and other matters of industrial structure are not specifically addressed, there are some provisions allowing the conversion of state stock charters to federal stock charters and the conversion of a state-chartered mutual savings bank to a new federally chartered mutual savings bank under the Federal Home Loan Bank Board. To further remove competitive differences between savings and loan associations and mutual savings banks, there is now a provision that allows the free conversion of the charters of the former to the latter and vice versa.

The overall impact of this loosening of deregulation is that the differences between thrifts and commercial banks have been blurred. In recognition of this, the monetary control title of the 1980 act requires that all depository institutions maintain reserves at the Federal Reserve and that all institutions have access to Fed services, including the discount window; and these services are to be priced on the basis of the costs of providing them.

The elimination of the differences between commercial banks and the thrifts extends beyond merely asset and liability authority. The traditional reason for distinguishing commercial banks from the nonbank financial institutions was the bank's ability to create deposits if adequate reserves existed. That difference has not been blurred. By the Deregulatory Act of 1980, not only can all federally chartered thrifts offer NOW accounts, but, in addition, these institutions will be able to offer extensions of credit that are linked to credit extensions in the depositors' NOW accounts. Although the authority for these extensions of credit has been delayed until the enactment of the Regulation Q phaseout, the act effectively grants all federally chartered thrifts power to operate essentially as commercial banks. In recognition of this expansion of monetary creation power by the thrifts, they in turn will be subject to the Federal Reserve's monetary management. The bill provides for required reserves to be deposited at the Federal Reserve on transaction accounts at the same time it provides these depository institutions with the privileges of Federal Reserve services. The most important of these services is, of course, the discount window, so that henceforth, the central bank could stand as a source of liquidity for all depository institutions. Thus, to some degree, the control of the central bank has been extended to nonmember commercial banks and federally insured depository institutions, thereby rendering the issue of Fed membership moot. Although nowhere specified in these acts the implicit effect is that the authority of the central bank has been strengthened, vis-à-vis the state and other federal regulatory authorities.

2.9 RECENT SOCIAL LEGISLATION AFFECTING THE DEPOSITORY INDUSTRY

Although the major thrust of regulation in the 1970s and 1980s was to loosen older restrictions, there was another set of legislative acts that tended to increase regulation and restrictions of the activities of the depository institutions. This legislation was directed at various social goals, including consumer protection, disclosure requirements, discrimination, and privacy. The sum total of this movement is the use of depository institutions to further social goals. The most dramatically expanding area of bank regulation over the past decade has been the enactment of federal disclosure requirements on consumer transactions. This legislation began with the passage of the Truth in Lending Act of 1968 and has since grown in length and complexity to require disclosure in all consumer credit transactions of, for instance, the amount financed, dollar finance charges, annual percentage rates, and payment schedules. Next came the Fair Credit Reporting Act of 1970 that further imposed disclosure requirements to include informing the consumer of investigative credit reports. The consumer must also be given access to the credit file information and its sources. Further disclosure aspects were addressed in the Fair Credit Billing Act of 1974. In addition, the Real Estate Settlement Procedures Act of 1974 required lenders to itemize, estimate, and disclose on a standard form the costs and charges incurred with the closing of residential real estate loans.

Federal legislation aimed at discrimination in lending really began with the Fair Housing Act of 1968, which prohibited lenders from denying real estate loans or making the terms more onerous because of the borrower's race, sex, color, religion, or national origin. The Equal Credit Opportunity Act of 1974 extended antidiscrimination clauses to all credit transactions.

The Home Mortgage Disclosure Act of 1975 and the Community Reinvestment Act of 1977 also added to the list of prohibitions. The Home Mortgage Disclosure Act requires depository institutions in metropolitan areas to compile and make available a breakdown of residential mortgage loans by location and type, with the purpose of revealing whether the lending institutions are (as they are sometimes accused of) "redlining" neighborhoods from obtaining mortgage credit. The Community Reinvestment Act of 1977 requires the appropriate federal supervisory agency to examine the record of depository institutions in "meeting the credit needs of its entire community" and to "take such record into account [p. 2901]"[7] in passing on an application for a branch or for an acquisition. While the act does not clearly indicate its purpose, the presumption is that the federal government wanted to force an allocation of credit on the depository institutions, an allocation not motivated by market incentives. If effective, the result of such legislation would be to force depository institutions to cause credit to flow to socially sensitive areas that might not meet the market test of risk and return. To some degree this direction of credit would act as a substitute for the use of federal, state and local monies to alleviate various perceived social and economic problems. Whatever its merits, if local deposits are to be directed only at local social and economic problems, the act has the effect of imposing rigidity on the financial system. While this act has not been extended, it establishes the precedent for credit allocation to meet social objectives.

---

[7] Community Reinvestment Act of 1977, P. L. 95-128 (12 U.S.C. 2901–2905).

2.10   COMPETITION IN THE 1980s

While there has been a tightening of restrictions in the areas of consumer protection, disclosure, discrimination, and privacy, the major thrust of regulatory change has been to liberate the depository institutions from regulatory constraints. The forces causing deregulation have been numerous. The rapid rate of entry into the protected domains of the depository institutions that began as a trickle in the 1950s and accelerated in the 1960s and 1970s ultimately unleashed competitive pressures within the industries, forcing each institution to reach for new techniques, means, and places to attract deposits and place them profitably. The segmentation of the asset and deposit markets instituted in the 1930s only served to delay, but could not deter, the razor edge of competitive forces from cutting away at protected profit margins.

Furthermore, in areas where depository industries were excluded from profitable markets, there were other entrepreneurs willing to provide financial services at competitive rates. As long as the economy provided the opportunity to profitably intermediate between savers and investors, and as long as there were no barriers to entry for near-banks, the depository institutions were forced to compete not only with one another but with the nonregulated competitors. Various near-banks such as the brokerage houses and retailers with national networks of offices have become a dynamic force in the consumer financial market. These near-banks assembled a financial supermarket for consumers by offering checking accounts, personal loans, savings-type instruments, and credit cards, and by selling millions of dollars worth of small-denomination notes. They became in effect a kind of financial institution, serving a national market, yet escaping the regulation of their activities. The chartered depository institutions and their regulatory agencies were helpless to deter this economic activity without major additional regulatory authority. Indeed, it was the segmentation of markets that restrained all the depository institutions, and the restrictions on interest rates that created the gap in the market that allowed these firms to compete savings away from the regulated depository industries.

Not only were growing competitive pressures and regulatory restrictions causing problems for the depository firms, but in addition, the rising inflation rates in the mid-1960s through the 1970s further added to the pressures, particularly on the thrifts. The rising inflation rates caused increasing market interest rates, but the thrift institutions had neither the earnings nor the regulatory authority to match these market rates. The result was either a slow growth in deposits or net disintermediation at times. The slow growth in deposits allowed limited opportunity to place funds at higher market rates, and the disintermediation caused high borrowing costs for the firms. Each firm now faced growing competitive pressures, not only from each other and the new nonregulated financial intermediaries, but also the open-market instruments and mutual funds.

The dismantling of the market segmentation was largely carried out under the banner of the need for flexible adaptation to changing market conditions, since the market segmentations and rate ceilings were designed for an economy with low and stable interest rates. Regulatory authorities acquiesced in this movement because of the liquidity and solvency problems faced by the industry.

The effect of this major deregulatory action was to substantially reduce the differences between the depository institutions. This has certainly been true on the liability side of the balance sheet, as all depository institutions now offer virtually the same depository instruments and are able to attract deposits without geographic limitation. While differences in regulatory authority still exist on the asset side of the balance sheet, the succession of deregulatory actions has substantially lessened these differences as well. Furthermore, if all depository firms become free to pay competitive deposit rates, this will force the existing asset barriers to erode, since all firms must have access to the same or at least similar asset markets in order to generate similar earnings.

Though an erosion of liability and asset barriers has taken place, there is no reason to expect that specialization in asset and liability instruments will not continue to exist. Market-induced specialization by comparative advantage will once again be the rule, as the depository institutions play more by the market rules of the 1920s than the regulatory rules of the 1930s.

While individual depository institutions might welcome the removal of restrictions that prohibited them from attracting deposits and placing these deposits in asset markets, the sum total of all the deregulation is that intense rate competition will again take place in highly competitive deposit and asset markets. The inevitable conclusion is a reduction in rate spreads and profit margins. This, in turn, could lead to a movement to restore regulatory constraints on competition.

In order to study these historical phenomena in a systematic way, we must develop first a model of the behavior of the depository firm. With this model in hand, it will be possible to judge the impacts of market forces and regulatory restrictions on the firm's deposit-setting activity, deposit size, profit margins, and levels of productive efficiency.

BIBLIOGRAPHY

U.S., Treasury Department, Administrator of the National Banks. *Studies in Banking Competition and the Banking Structure*. Washington, D.C.: U.S. Govt. Printing Office, 1966.

Ali, Mukhtar M., and Greenbaum, Stuart I. "The Regulatory Process in Commercial Banking," *Proceedings of a Conference on Bank Structure and Competition*. Federal Reserve Bank of Chicago, October 1972.

Auerbach, Ronald P. *Historical Overview of Financial Institutions in the United States*. Federal Deposit Insurance Corporation, Washington, D.C., 1978.

Benston, George J. "Discussion of The Hunt Commission Report," *Journal of Money, Credit and Banking*, **4**, November 1972.

Benston, George J. "Savings Banking and the Public Interest," *Journal of Money, Credit and Banking*, **4**, February, pt. 2, 1972.

Block, Ernest. "Two Decades of Evolution of Financial Institutions and Public Policy." *Journal of Money, Credit and Banking*, **1**, November 1969.

Board of Governors of the Federal Reserve System. *The Federal Reserve System: Purposes and Functions*. Washington, D.C., 1974.

Borts, George H. "Agenda for a Commission to Study Financial Markets, Their Structure and Regulation," *Journal of Money, Credit and Banking*, **3**, February 1971.

Borts, George H. "The Benston Paper," *Journal of Money, Credit and Banking*, **4**, May 1972.

Burns, A. F. "Maintaining the Soundness of Our Banking System," *Federal Reserve Bank of New York. Monthly Review*, **59**, November 1974.

Cameron, Rondo. *Banking in the Early Stages in Industrialization*. New York; Oxford Univ. Press, 1967.

Cassidy, Henry J., Marcis, Richard G., and Riordan, Dale P. "The Savings and Loan Industry in the 1980s," Research Working Paper No. 100, Federal Home Loan Bank Board, December 1980.

Citibank. *Credit Allocation: An Exercise in the Futility of Controls*. New York, 1976.

Commission on Financial Structure and Regulation. *Financial Structure and Regulation*. Washington, D.C.: U.S. Govt. Printing Office, 1972.

Croteau, John T. *The Economics of the Credit Union*. Detroit: Wayne State Univ. Press, 1963.

Dhrymes, Phoebus J., and Taubman, Paul J. "An Empirical Analysis of the Savings and Loan Industry." In *A Study of the Savings and Loan Industry*. Washington, D.C.: Federal Home Loan Bank Board, 1969.

Edwards, Franklin R. "Banks and Securities Activities: Legal and Economic Perspectives on the Glass–Steagall Act." In *The Deregulation of the Banking and Securities Industry*, eds. Lawrence G. Goldberg and Lawrence J. White. Lexington, Mass.: Lexington, 1979.

Ettin, Edward J. "The Implications for Federal Reserve Policy of Deregulation of the Thrift Industry: One View. In *Savings and Loan Asset Management Under Deregulation*. Federal Home Loan Bank Board of San Francisco, December 1980.

Ewalt, Josephine H. *A Business Reborn*. Chicago: American Savings & Loan Institute Press, 1962.

Federal Reserve Bank of Boston. *Policies for a More Competitive Financial System. A Review of the Report of the President's Commission on Financial Structure and Regulation*. June 1972.

Fisher, Gerald C. *American Banking Structure*. New York: Columbia Univ. Press, 1968.

Flannery, Mark J., and Guttentag, Jack M. "Problem Banks: Examination, Identification and Supervision." In *State and Federal Regulation of Commercial Banks*, vol. II. Washington, D.C.: Federal Deposit Insurance Corporation, 1980.

Friedman, Milton, and Schwartz, Anna J. *A Monetary History of the United States, 1867–1960*. Princeton, N.J.: Princeton Univ. Press, 1963.

Friend, Irwin. "Summary and Recommendations." In *Study of the Savings and Loan Industry*. Washington, D.C.: Federal Home Loan Bank Board, 1969.

Gambs, C. M. "Bank Failures: An Historical Perspective," *Federal Reserve Bank of Kansas City. Monthly Review,* **62,** June 1977.

Gibson, William E. "Deposit Demand, Hot Money, and the Viability of Thrift Institutions." In *Brookings Papers on Economic Activity 3,* edited by Arthur M. Okum and George L. Perry. Washington, D.C.: Brookings Institution, 1974.

Gibson, William E. "Improving the U.S. Financial System." In *Conference on Bank Structure and Competition.* Federal Reserve Bank of Chicago, March 1974.

Gilbert, Gary G. "The Potential Competition Doctrine in Commercial Banking: Theory and Policy." In *Conference on Bank Structure and Competition.* Federal Reserve Bank of Chicago, March 1974.

Goldberg, Lawrence G. "Bank Holding Company Acquisition, Competition, and Public Policy." In *The Deregulation of the Banking and Securities Industry,* eds. Lawrence G. Goldberg and Lawrence J. White. Lexington, Mass.: Lexington, 1979.

Goldberg, Lawrence G., and White, Lawrence J., *The Deregulation of the Banking and Securities Industry.* Lexington, Mass.: Lexington, 1979.

Goldsmith, Raymond W. *Financial Intermediaries in the American Economy Since 1900.* Princeton, N.J.: Princeton Univ. Press, 1958.

Goodman, Oscar. "A Review of Recent Legislative and Judicial Trends Affecting Banking Structure and Competition. Federal Reserve Bank of Chicago, March 1967.

Goodman, Oscar. "A Survey of Judicial and Regulatory Opinions Affecting Banking Competition Under the Bank Merger Acts of 1960 and 1966." In *Proceedings of a Conference on Bank Structure and Competition.* Federal Reserve Bank of Chicago, May 1969.

Grebler, Leo, and Brigham, Eugene F. *Savings and Mortgage Markets in California.* Pasadena, California Savings and Loan League, 1963.

Gurley, John, and Shaw, Edward S. "The Growth of Debt and Money in the United States: A Suggested Interpretation," *The Review of Economics and Statistics,* **39,** August 1957.

Heebner, A. Gilbert. "Negotiable Certificates of Deposit: The Development of a Money Market Instrument," *Bulletin,* New York University Institute of Finance, February 1969.

Heggenstad, Arnold A., and Mingo, John J., eds. *Public Regulation of Financial Services—Costs and Benefits to Consumers: Phase I, Interim Report,* Report No. 77-94-A, vol. I, National Science Foundation, 1977.

Hendershott, Patric H. "Model Simulations of the Impact of Selective Credit Policies and Financial Reforms: The Appropriate Monetary Policy Assumption," *Journal of Banking and Finance,* **1,** September 1977.

Hendershott, Patric H. "Deregulation and the Capital Markets: The Impact of Deposit Rate Ceilings and Restrictions Against Variable Rate Mortgages." In *The Deregulation of the Banking and Securities Industry,* eds. Lawrence G. Goldberg and Lawrence J. White. Lexington, Mass. Lexington, 1979.

Hendershott, Patric H., and Villani, Kevin E., *Savings and Loan Usage of the Authority to Invest in Corporate Bonds.* Federal Home Loan Bank of San Francisco, December 1980.

Hester, Donald D. "Financial Disintermediation and Policy," *Journal of Money, Credit and Banking,* **1,** August 1969.

Holland, R. C. "Bank Holding Companies and Financial Stability," *Journal of Financial and Quantitative Analysis,* **10,** November 1975.

Horvitz, Paul M. "Stimulating Bank Competition Through Regulatory Action," *Journal of Finance,* **20,** March 1965.

Horvitz, Paul M. *Monetary Policy and the Financial System.* Englewood Cliffs, N.J.: Prentice-Hall, 1979.

Hunt, Reed O., and Commission Members. *The Report of the President's Commission on Financial Structure and Regulation.* Washington, D.C.: U.S. Government Printing Office, 1975.

Jaffee, Dwight M. "The Asset–Liability Maturity Mix of S&Ls: Problems and Solutions. In *Change in the Savings and Loan Industry.* Federal Home Loan Bank Board of San Francisco, December 1976.

Kane, Edward J. "Short-Changing the Small Saver: Federal Government Discrimination Against Small Savers During the Vietnam War, A Comment," *Journal of Money, Credit and Banking,* **2,** November 1970.

Kane, Edward J. "Reregulation, Savings-and-Loan Diversification, and the Flow of Housing Finance." In *Savings and Loan Asset Management Under Deregulation.* Federal Home Loan Bank of San Francisco, December 1980.

Kaufman, George G. "The Thrift Institution Problem Reconsidered." In *Proceedings of a Conference on Bank Structure and Competition.* Federal Reserve Bank of Chicago, 1971.

Kendall, Leon T. *The Savings and Loan Business: Its Purposes, Functions, and Economic Justification.* Englewood Cliffs, N.J.: Prentice-Hall, 1962.

Krooss, Herman E., and Blyn, Martin R. *A History of Financial Intermediaries.* New York: Random House, 1971.

Lapidus, Leonard, et al. *State and Federal Regulation of Commercial Banks,* vols. I and II. Federal Deposit Insurance Corporation, Washington, D.C., 1980.

Laub, P. M. "The Deregulation of Banking." In *The Deregulation of the Banking and Securities Industry,* eds. Lawrence G. Goldberg and Lawrence J. White. Lexington, Mass.: Lexington, 1979.

Melvin, Donald J., et al. *Credit Unions and the Credit Union Industry.* New York: N.Y. Institute of Finance, 1977.

Mingo, John J. "Regulation of Financial Institutions: An Overview." In *Public Regulation of Financial Services—Costs and Benefits to Consumers: Phase I, Interim Report,* Report No. 77-94-A, edited by Arnold A. Heggenstad and John J. Mingo. National Science Foundation, 1977.

Motter, David C. "Comments on the Philadelphia–Girard Decision: Bank Mergers and Public Policy," *The National Banking Review,* **4,** January 1966.

Murphy, Neil B. "Removing Deposit Interest Ceiling: An Analysis of Deposit Flows, Portfolio Response, and Income Effects in Boston Cooperative Banks," *Conference on Bank Structure and Competition.* Federal Reserve Bank of Chicago, May 1976.

Murphy, Neil B. "Reforming the Structure and Regulation of Financial Institutions: The Evidence from the State of Maine," *Journal of Bank Research,* **9,** Winter 1979.

National Credit Union Administration. *Federal Credit Union Act,* Washington, D.C., June 1979.

Peltzman, Samuel. "The Costs of Competition: An Appraisal of the Hunt Commission Report," *Journal of Money, Credit and Banking,* **4,** November 1972.

President's Commission on Financial Structure and Regulation. *Report.* Washington, D.C.: U.S. Govt. Printing Office, 1972.

Rhoades, Stephen A. "Some Observations on Potential Competition in Banking." In *Proceedings of a Conference on Bank Structure and Competition.* Federal Reserve Bank of Chicago, October 1972.

Rockoff, Hugh. "The Free Banking Era: A Reexamination," *Journal of Money, Credit and Banking,* **6,** May 1974.

Saving, Thomas. "Toward a Competitive Financial Sector," *Journal of Money, Credit and Banking,* **4,** November 1972.

Scott, Kenneth E. "In Quest of Reason: The Licensing Decisions of the Federal Banking Agencies," *The University of Chicago Law Review,* **42,** Winter 1975.

Scott, Kenneth E. "The Dual Banking System: A Model of Competition in Regulation,' *Stanford Law Review,* **30,** 1, 1977.

Scott, Kenneth E. "Interrelationships Between Federal and State Bank Regulatory Statutes." *In State and Federal Regulation of Commercial Banks,* vol. I. Federal Deposit Insurance Corporation, Washington, D.C., 1980.

Shull, Bernard. "Commercial Banking as a 'Line of Commerce'," *The National Banking Review,* **1,** December 1963.

Shull, Bernard. "Federal and State Supervision of Bank Holding Companies." *State and Federal Regulation of Commercial Banks,* vol. II. Federal Deposit Insurance Corporation, Washington, DC., 1980.

Sinkey, Joseph, F., Jr. *Problem and Failed Institutions in the Commerical Banking Industry.* Greenwich, Conn.: JAI Press, 1979.

Spector, Louis E. "Entry, Branching, and Merging: How the State and Federal Bank Regulatory Systems Operate." In *State and Federal Regulation of Commercial Banks,* vol. I. Federal Deposit Insurance Corporation, Washington, D.C., 1980.

Stokes, Edwin. "Public Convenience and Advantage in Applications for New Banks and Branches," *The Banking Law Review,* **74,** November 1957.

U.S. Senate. "Depository Institutions Deregulation and Monetary Control Act of 1980." Report No. 96-640. Washington, D.C.: U.S. Govt. Printing Office, 1980.

U.S. Senate Committee on Banking, Housing, and Urban Affairs. *The Report of the Interagency Task Force on Thrift Institutions.* Washington, D.C.: U.S. Govt. Printing Office, July 1980.

U.S., Treasury Department, Office of the Comptroller of the Currency. *Comptroller's Manual for National Banks' Regulations.* Washington, D.C.: U.S. Govt. Printing Office, 1971.

PART II

The Depository Firm and Industry

CHAPTER 3

The Economics of the Financial Firm

3.1 THE PRODUCTION FIRM VERSUS THE FINANCIAL FIRM

The production firm purchases raw materials and employs capital and labor. The factors of production transform raw materials into final product, which is then sold on goods markets. The production firm makes a price or output decision based on the levels of marginal revenue and marginal cost. Its profit depends critically on the efficiency with which it produces and on the competitiveness of the markets for both inputs and output.

Similarly, the financial firm purchases raw materials and employs factors of production. What most distinguishes the financial firm from the production firm is the peculiarity surrounding the raw material and the final product. To the financial firm, the raw material is currency or funds; the financial firm transforms this raw material into earning assets with labor and capital. Pricing decisions are made more typically on the inputs, rather than the outputs, and these decisions, whether on rates or quantities, depend on marginal revenues and costs. As with the production firm, profit depends on the efficiency of production and the competitiveness of both the input and output markets.

Some financial firms generate revenues by selling final product, much as the production firm. Examples include the broker or underwriter of corporate stock, or a commercial bank brokering loans or savings association selling mortgages on a secondary market. More typically, the financial firm holds, rather than sells, the earning assets. This is generally true of the depository firm, a subset of all financial firms.

Another distinguishing feature of the financial firm is that those who supply raw materials to the firm usually have a continuing claim to the raw materials. This continuing claim, noted in the contractual terms of the liability instrument, implies that at some future time, the claimants will exercise their contractual right and request the return of the raw material in its

51

original form, currency. The contractual obligation of returning raw material in its original state incurs a cost and imposes a constraint on the operations of the financial firm that is not similarly experienced by the production firm. Probably the most costly of these contractual terms is the demand deposit where, as its name implies, the return of raw material is on demand without notice or forewarning. This cost of returning the raw material will be termed a liquidation cost and is analyzed in Chapter 6. The liquidation cost includes the cost of managing the liquidity position, but, more importantly, the costs of borrowing, the transaction costs from the sale of earning assets, and the opportunity cost from foregoing revenue when noninterest or low-interest assets are held in portfolios for this purpose.

In addition to a liquidation cost, the financial firm might experience another cost not ordinarily incurred by the production firm. If funds secured by deposits are transferable or negotiable to third parties, such as with a NOW or demand account, then there is also a transfer cost. Some instruments call for revenues to offset the costs of liquidation and transfer services, with the competitiveness of the market determining the balance of the revenues and costs between the depositor and the firm. These transfer and liquidation revenues are in the form of service fees or early withdrawal penalties. When transfer services exist, the financial firm provides monetary transaction services, which might alter its cost curve; but because the firm also provides monetary transfer services, it does not basically alter the structure of the model of the financial firm. Hence, commercial banks can be treated much the same as any other financial or depository firm.

Furthermore, though specialization in asset and liability selection has commonly been the basis for dichotomizing financial institutions, it will be argued here that the basic theoretical structure describing the financial firm is unaltered by specific asset and liability selection. This is particularly true among depository institutions. What might differ among these firms is the level of production costs incurred by gathering funds and transforming these funds into earning assets, as well as the costs of liquidation. For example, a mutual fund or a life insurance company might have relatively higher fund-gathering costs than a commercial bank. Fund gathering is more labor intensive for the insurance company compared to the multibranch commercial bank, which is relatively more capital intensive. The costs of transforming funds into earning assets is higher for loans than for securities, so that the consumer credit company would have higher costs than the typical pension fund. Since the average cost per loan is probably higher for unsecured personal and small business loans than a home mortgage, credit unions would have higher loan organization costs than the savings and loan association. These cost differences exist per loan, but they also translate into cost differences calculated as an annual rate per asset or deposit dollar. Another factor accounting for differences in cost per asset dollar is the loan maturity and servicing costs. Similarly, the maturity of the liability will affect the annual rate of liquidation costs.

The most common financial firm found in the financial systems of most countries is a depository institution in which funds are secured by a deposit obtained on a local deposit market. The terms of the deposit may vary as to the deposit rate, the maturity of the deposit, and its negotiability among other parties. Since the market is local and entry is often blocked, the market for deposits has been characterized as imperfectly competitive. When a deposit rate is set and a deposit is received, the depository firm can transform the funds into an array of possible earning assets. Without regulatory restrictions, specialization in the purchase of assets would be induced by consideration of revenues and costs, including the costs of default. With regulatory restrictions affecting asset and liability selection, further specialization is induced.

There are alternative modes by which the depository firm is able to raise funds. For example, the depository institution might desire to expand beyond local deposit markets by selling instruments on national capital markets. This mode of operation could be characterized by a bank selling negotiable CDs, a savings and loan association selling mortgage-backed bonds, or any depository institution selling debt obligations. With the local depository institution, the firm sets a rate, and the local market responds with a quantity. With the sale of negotiable CDs on national capital markets, the firm offers a quantity of securities, and the market responds with a rate by placing discounts or premiums on the debt offerings. If the depository firm sought to reach national capital markets as opposed to local deposit markets, it would not alter the structure of the model that described that firm. The firm would still purchase funds and incur production and interest costs for deposits; there would merely be a new configuration of the costs of production and deposit liquidation. The greater significance of this change in operating procedure would be the change in the competitive environment. Turning to national capital markets and away from local deposit markets would place the firm in a more highly competitive national and international capital market, with the usual implications for profit margins brought by greater competition.

A major difference among financial institutions and depository institutions is the competitiveness of the market in which they purchase assets. Regulation that limits a depository institution to purchasing a particular asset in a particular local market restricts its freedom to seek profitable opportunities; but, on the other hand, this restriction offers an opportunity to operate in a less competitive market. Just as regulatory change might liberate the scope of deposit activities from local to national markets, a regulatory change can likewise shift the scope of asset-seeking activities—but with the same implications for competition and profit.

There is a theory of the depository firm that is common to all. Many variations exist among depository institutions that do not require any essential alteration to the theory characterizing those institutions. Each depository firm has revenue-generating opportunities from holding earning assets, from the packaging and sale of earning assets, and from service charges for liquidation and transfer services; and each has its own cost relationship. The liability instruments might differ in name, contractual obligations, and cost; the firm decision variables could be rates or quantities; the asset and liability markets might differ in size, location, maturity, and competitiveness; but the basic analytical structure remains.

3.2 THE MICROECONOMICS OF THE SIMPLE
DEPOSITORY FIRM WITH FLEXIBLE DEPOSIT RATES

We shall begin with a simple depository firm operating in a local deposit market in which its discretion to set deposit rates is not subject to regulatory ceilings. But, because of regulatory imposed limitations to entry, depository firms generally operate in imperfectly competitive deposit markets. As a result, the community's demand for its deposits (or the schedule of the funds supplied by the public) is interest-elastic as deposit levels increase with the deposit rate.

In Eq. (3.1) D represents deposits, r is the deposit rate, m is the rate available on alternative market instruments, and y and w are the community's income and wealth:

$$D = D(r, m, y, w) \qquad \frac{\partial D}{\partial r} > 0. \qquad (3.1)$$

It is generally considered that *ceteris paribus*, the firm's deposit level is reduced with higher market rates and increases with higher levels of income and wealth.[1] In the local deposit market, the firm sets a rate. The community of wealth-owners responds by selecting a deposit level, giving consideration to the alternative market rates and its level of income and

---

[1] For a treatment of asset substitutability, income, and wealth effects, see for example, William Brainard and James Tobin, "Pitfalls in Financial Model Building," *American Economic Review* **58** (May 1968).

wealth. The deposit demand curve is upward-sloping, which indicates that deposit levels increase with higher rates. With its given deposit level, the firm then transforms that quantity of deposits into a similar quantity of earning assets. The asset selection is assumed to be simple, since the firm's portfolio selection is not presently at the forefront of our interest.[2] The depository firm could either purchase a homogeneous earning asset or purchase additions to a risk-diversified portfolio that could include cash reserves.

If the intermediary places its funds in local loan markets, it is assumed that secondary markets exist to resell loans across local loan markets, effectively making the loan market national in scope. Alternatively, we could assume that the firm is capable of participating in national or world markets for securities. It could do so exclusively or as a secondary reserve. In essence, the individual depository firm is sufficiently small relative to the national or world market that its demand for securities or loans does not run up security prices or reduce loan rates. Thus, under these conditions if the firm specializes in either loans or securities, or if they are substitutes in portfolios, the earning asset rate r_a does not decline as the firm increases the quantity of earning assets in its portfolio.[3] The intermediary is thus a rate taker and a quantity setter in asset markets. The annual revenues accruing to the depository firm are then equal to $r_a D$.

Concerning cost, the financial firm incurs production costs for factor inputs and various trivial intermediate products, such as supplies, in order to process both deposits and earning assets. These costs are assumed to depend upon these stock levels, since costs are incurred for both deposit gathering and management, as well as asset selection and management. Asset maturities and liability maturities effect turnover rates and hence production costs per unit of time, so that asset and liability maturities are reflected in the parameters of the annual production cost function. If the deposit carries with it transfer services, the cost of these services is also incorporated in the parameters of the cost curve. Annual production costs are C, and the production cost function is denoted $C = C(D)$. Marginal production cost $\partial C / \partial D$ is assumed to be positive. Average production cost per deposit dollar per annum C/D is denoted c. Average production costs c are stated as an annual rate and hence are denominated in the same dimension as earning and deposit rates. It shall be assumed, for now, that marginal costs are constant and equal to average costs per deposit dollar so that $\partial C / \partial D = c$.

[2] Portfolio allocations between earning and cash reserves are considered in Chapter 6.

[3] The rate r_a is assumed to be net of losses due to default. If the firm adds to its portfolio by making more risky loans, it will only do so by charging a rate that covers these expected costs.

In addition to production costs, the firm incurs interest cost for deposits. Interest accrues to all deposits at the annual rate r. The level of the deposit rate is a variable that increases with the deposit level. From the firm's point of view, the deposit rate is the average annual interest cost of a deposit or the average cost of deposit funds. [It is obtained by solving the deposit demand equation, Eq. (3.1), for r.] Total deposit costs per annum are rD. Considerations of liquidation cost will be discussed in Chapter 6.

The overall objective function of the depository intermediary is assumed to be the maximization of the present period's profit. The assumption of profit maximization is made, despite the mutual form of ownership of several contemporary financial intermediaries. If mutuals are in markets with firms the ownership of which rests in the hands of stockholders, the discipline of the market causes the depositor-owned firm to compete for deposits on similar terms.[4]

It is intended at the outset that the model be exceedingly simple, so as to make transparent some fundamental relationships. This requires the assumption of (1) certainty; (2) a single period; (3) a single liability class; (4) earning rates on assets that are exogenous to the firms; (5) the absence of expectations of the future that differ from those of the present; (6) the absence of taxes; and (7) the motive of profit maximization. Given these shortcomings, the usefulness of the model is to highlight the roles of competition and efficiency in determining deposit rates, rate spreads, profit margins, deposit size, and the depository firm's distribution of revenue. In later chapters, several of these assumptions will be relaxed.

3.3   THE DEPOSIT RATE, RATE SPREADS, PROFIT MARGINS, AND DEPOSIT SIZE

From the preceding assumptions, it follows that profit derived from the deposit activity consists of total revenues less the components of total cost:

$$P = r_a D - rD - C(D). \qquad (3.2)$$

[4] In a study of savings associations by Donald Hester ("Ownership and Behavior in the Savings and Loan Industry." In *Conversion of Mutual Savings & Loan Associations to Stock Form: Legal and Economic Issues,* Federal Home Loan Bank Board, 1967), it was found that there were relatively few differences in the behavior of stock and mutual savings associations. The primary differences concerned risk bearing and portfolio choice. At a minimum, the depository firms, whether stock or mutual, operate with a minimum profit constraint. The analysis of Chapter 5 translates a minimum profit constraint into maximum deposit rates.

The profit statement reflects income and expense or revenue and cost flows per annum.[5] These revenues and costs are associated with the deposit activity alone. In determining profit-maximizing deposit rates, the depository firm takes its deposit demand curve in its local market as given. The production technology, while presumably the most efficient available, is also taken as given, and in asset markets the depository firm is a rate taker. The financial firm then maximizes profit with respect to the deposit rate, as it is the only variable it can control directly in a free deposit rate environment.[6] With the value of D obtained from Eq. (3.1) and substituted into Eq. (3.2), the derivative of the profit function with respect to r is then set equal to zero:

$$\frac{\partial P}{\partial r} = r_a \frac{\partial D}{\partial r} - D - r \frac{\partial D}{\partial r} - \frac{\partial C}{\partial D} \frac{\partial D}{\partial r} = 0. \tag{3.3}$$

After dividing Eq. (3.3) by $\partial D / \partial r$ and rearranging terms, Eq. (3.4) can be more intuitively interpreted as the marginal revenue and the marginal cost derived from the last deposit dollar:

$$r_a = D \frac{\partial r}{\partial D} + r + \frac{\partial C}{\partial D}. \tag{3.4}$$

At the profit-maximizing deposit level, the marginal revenue from the last deposit dollar is just balanced against the sum of the marginal costs, where the marginal costs consist of the marginal interest and production cost. The marginal production cost is the term $\partial D / \partial C$. The marginal interest cost is represented by two terms: r is the deposit cost of the marginal deposit dollar, while $D(\partial r / \partial D)$ is the added deposit cost that results from paying a higher deposit rate $\partial r / \partial D$ to all existing depositors D. That is, in order to attract additional deposits by paying higher deposit rates, the interest cost to the depository firm increases because it must pay for the marginal deposit at the rate r, and also because it must pay the higher deposit rate to all existing intramarginal deposits.[7] Since average (and

[5] This profit statement implies a balance sheet in which assets are equal to deposits. Depository firms, in addition to raising deposits in the market place, can also resort to other forms of debt that generate both revenues and costs. These considerations will be discussed in Chapter 6. Capital contributions and retained earnings are sources of funds that are reflected in the net worth of the depository firm and could be used to purchase assets that generate revenues. This consideration is deferred until Chapter 5.

[6] The behavior of the depository firm under an imposed deposit ceiling is deferred until Chapter 7.

[7] There have been futile and costly attempts to avoid paying higher deposit rates to existing depositors; for example, awarding premiums only to new accounts. This merely induces a churning of deposit accounts among depository institutions.

marginal) deposit cost is an increasing function of the deposit level, by assumption, at some deposit size the added deposit costs exceed the added
revenues from an additional deposit dollar.

Though we wish to find the profit-maximizing deposit level, the rate setting depository firm determines that deposit level by setting the profit-
maximizing deposit rate. But since the magnitude of the term $\partial r/\partial D$ is
generally a variable that depends on the level of r, one then can only solve
Eq. (3.4) for r as an implicit mathematical function. This is because r
cannot be mathematically reduced to a separate term. However, if one is
willing to make the not unreasonable assumption that the firm's deposit
demand is characterized by a constant elasticity in r, then a great mathematical simplification is achieved. Where the marginal relationship of the
deposit level and the deposit rate is characterized by a constant deposit
elasticity ϵ, Eq. (3.4) can be rewritten and solved explicitly for the level of
the deposit rate consistent with profit maximization.[8] That is, since $\epsilon =$
$(\partial D/\partial r)(r/D)$ and thus $D(\partial r/\partial D) = r/\epsilon$, Eq. (3.4) can be rewritten as $r_a =$
$r/\epsilon + r + (\partial C/\partial D)$. Solving for the profit maximizing deposit rate r^* we
obtain[9]

$$r^* = \frac{\epsilon}{1 + \epsilon}\left(r_a - \frac{\partial C}{\partial D}\right). \tag{3.5}$$

The level of the deposit rate then depends essentially on two terms. The
term $(r_a - (\partial C/\partial D))$ will be designated net revenue per deposit dollar;
and the term $\epsilon/(1 + \epsilon)$, which contains the deposit response, will be designated the pass-through proportion. That is, the depository intermediary
earns gross revenues per deposit dollar, r_a, from which it then pays its
marginal production cost. Net revenue is the available funds per deposit
dollar that may be passed through to depositors in the form of a deposit
rate.

The level of the profit-maximizing deposit rate depends not only on the
level of net revenues, but also on the market's response to the deposit
rate. The deposit sensitivity of the market is measured by the level of
deposit elasticity. Given the net revenues, the proportion of these net rev-

---

[8] In general, the elasticity ϵ and the deposit rate r are jointly determined, so that we could
not write an explicit mathematical equation for r^*. However, if one is willing to assume the
constant elasticity deposit demand function, this assumption allows an explicit solution for
r^*. The log linear deposit demand function used in Section 3.5 is an example. In this functional form, the elasticity ϵ is a constant, and, furthermore, it is independent of the values of
m, y, and w. Since the constant elasticity deposit demand curve will be assumed, these variables will henceforth be omitted from the deposit demand curve.

[9] In this form, the marginal deposit response that triggers marginal increases in cost and
revenue is contained in the elasticity term, rather than in the $\partial D/\partial r$ term.

enues passing through to depositors depends on the value of the pass-through proportion $\epsilon/(1 + \epsilon)$ which, in turn, depends on the value of ϵ. The range of the deposit elasticity is $0 \le \epsilon < \infty$. At a zero elasticity, there is no deposit response to higher deposit rates. In this situation, there is no incentive to pay higher deposit rates because these higher rates add to cost but not to revenue or profit. At the other competitive extreme, an infinite deposit elasticity implies that increases in deposits overwhelm the depository firm when it raises deposit rates. This competitive extreme of infinite elasticities corresponds to what is understood to be perfect competition.

The range of the pass-through proportion is between 0 and 1. Hence, the share or proportion of net revenues that pass through to depositors is similarly between 0 and 1. When the depositors' response to the deposit rate is low, the term approaches 0; $\epsilon/(1 + \epsilon)$ approaches 0, and r^* also approaches 0. In a situation where the market's deposit response to higher deposit rate is great, the value of ϵ is larger, and the deposit rate will be higher. In the limit of perfect competition, when the deposit elasticity approaches infinity, $\epsilon/(1 + \epsilon)$ approaches a value of 1, and the deposit rate approaches net revenues. Thus, the effect of competition on deposit rates works through the elasticity of deposit demand in the local deposit market. The more elastic the intermediary's deposit demand, the greater is the deposit rate and the more nearly the deposit rate approaches the asset earning rate. As a numerical example, a deposit elasticity of 1 means that half of the net revenues are passed through to depositors, and a higher elasticity of 9 means that 90% of net revenues are passed through. Furthermore, at the margin, the extent to which higher earning rates are passed through to depositors depends upon the deposit elasticity:

$$\frac{\partial r^*}{\partial r_a} = \frac{\epsilon}{1 + \epsilon}. \tag{3.6}$$

Similarly, cost savings from greater technical efficiency are passed through to depositors in the same proportion:

$$\frac{\partial r^*}{\partial (\partial C/\partial D)} = -\frac{\epsilon}{1 + \epsilon}. \tag{3.7}$$

Just as the value of ϵ affects the level of the deposit rate, it also affects the spread s between asset and deposit rates:

$$s = r_a - r^* = \frac{1}{1 + \epsilon} r_a + \frac{\epsilon}{1 + \epsilon} \frac{\partial C}{\partial D}. \tag{3.8}$$

The rate spread is found to also depend on competition, as measured by the deposit elasticity and efficiency as measured by marginal costs.

Again, it is instructive to consider two extremes. In the case of a perfectly competitive market for the firm's deposits; that is, where ϵ approaches infinity, the deposit rate approaches

$$r^* = r_a - \frac{\partial C}{\partial D}. \tag{3.9}$$

In this case, the deposit rate approaches net revenues, and the spread between these rates approaches marginal production costs. Perfect competition could be contrasted with the case of a highly segmented monopolistic deposit market, where the elasticity of demand approaches 0. In this case, the monopolistic intermediary continues to maintain its captive deposit level irrespective of the deposit rate it offers, presumably because deposits are valued for security or other purposes. In such a circumstance, when ϵ approaches 0 the optimal deposit rate is 0, and the rate spread is equal to r_a. From this it is clear that the more deposit elasticities increase, the higher the deposit rate will be, and the smaller the rate spread will be. In the limit of perfect competition, rate spreads are forced down to marginal production cost.

A diagrammatic interpretation of the model is instructive.

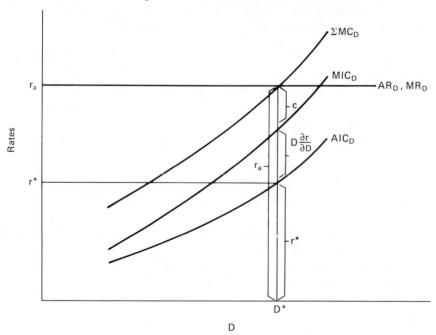

Figure 3.1   The profit-maximizing deposit rate.

From the firm's point of view, the deposit demand curve, Eq. (3.1), represents average interest cost of a deposit. Since average interest cost per deposit AIC_D rises with higher levels of D, the marginal interest cost curve per deposit MIC_D lies above it. To the marginal interest cost curve is added marginal production costs, which have been assumed to be constant, irrespective of the level of D, and equal to average production costs. The constant marginal production cost c is added to marginal interest cost, giving the sum of the marginal costs, ΣMC_D. Since average revenues r_a do not decline with D, revenues per deposit dollar AR_D are perfectly elastic and are represented by a horizontal line. Since average revenues are constant, marginal revenues MR_D are also constant and equal to average revenues.

The deposit level and deposit rate can be viewed from the perspective of the profit-maximizing condition of Eq. (3.4), where marginal revenue r_a equals the sum of marginal costs. As cost and revenues are measured on a per deposit dollar basis in the vertical direction, this intersection occurs at deposit level D^*. To induce this deposit level, r^* is set from the deposit demand curve. Thus, both deposit rates and deposit size are derived from the intersection of the marginal revenue and the sum of the marginal cost curve. Deposit rates in excess of r^* attract deposits in excess of D^*, but for these deposits the added cost exceeds the added revenues, causing the added deposits to be unprofitable.

3.4   COMPETITION AND INCOME DISTRIBUTION

Just as the competitive level as reflected by the value of ϵ affects the level of the deposit rate, it also influences the profit margin and the distribution of income between the depositor and the equity position. Substituting the profit maximizing value of r into the profit equation, Eq. (3.2), the profit level from the deposit activity can be stated

$$P = r_a D - \frac{\epsilon}{1 + \epsilon}\left(r_a - \frac{\partial C}{\partial D}\right) D - C(D), \tag{3.10}$$

where total profit P depends on net revenues, deposit level, the deposit rate elasticity and total production costs. The profit margin or profit per deposit dollar p is derived simply by dividing through by D. Recall that average cost $C/D \equiv c$, which by assumption is equal to marginal cost $\partial C/\partial D$. Hence,

$$p = (1/(1 + \epsilon))(r_a - c). \tag{3.11}$$

From this we can simply observe that profit per deposit dollar can be stated as a share of net revenues. That is, the ratio of the profit margin to net revenues is

$$p/(r_a - c) = 1/(1 + \epsilon),\qquad(3.12)$$

and this profit retention ratio depends completely on the deposit elasticity. The profit proportion or profit retention rate is that share of net revenues that have not been bid away in deposit rate competition.

Under the assumed conditions, the shares of income accruing to the depositor $(\epsilon/(1 + \epsilon))(r_a - c)$ and the equity position $(1/(1 + \epsilon))(r_a - c)$ fully exhaust net revenues:

$$r^* + p = r_a - c.\qquad(3.13)$$

Furthermore, the ratio of r^* to p via Eqs. (3.5) and (3.11) are found to be completely determined by the deposit elasticity

$$r^*/p = \epsilon.\qquad(3.14)$$

Thus, the greater the deposit response to the deposit rate typically found in more competitive markets, the greater will be the depositor's relative share.

The value of ϵ is obviously critical to distribution. This value can itself be measured in terms of interest rates and production cost rates from Eq. (3.5):

$$\epsilon = r^*/(r_a - r^* - c).\qquad(3.15)$$

One could depict revenue distribution graphically, as in Figure 3.2. Total revenue is the rectangular area $r_a D^*$. From these gross revenues total production cost is the rectangular area cD^*. Total interest payments are rD^* and by Eq. (3.13) the remaining revenues accrue to the equity position pD^*.

3.5 AN EXAMPLE

A hypothetical example would be instructive. A depository firm has a total production cost function per annum $C = .03D$, so that marginal and average production costs are .03. The firm invests its deposits at the weighted average asset rate .09 and can do so in any foreseeable quantity, so that average and marginal revenues per deposit dollar are .09. The firm's deposit level varies with its deposit rate, market rates m, and income and wealth y, w, so that $D = 3r^3 m^{-1} yw$; where D, y, and w are measured in millions of dollars, and r and m are expressed in decimal form. With a log linear deposit demand function, the constant deposit

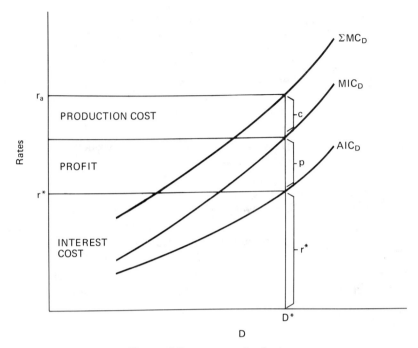

Figure 3.2 Revenue distribution.

elasticity $(\partial D/\partial r)(r/D)$ is equal to 3. This can be verified by calculating ϵ, which is $(\partial D/\partial r)(r/D)$ or $9r^2m^{-1}yw(r/3r^3m^{-1}yw) = 3$.

In these circumstances, from Eq. (3.5) the profit-maximizing deposit rate is $r^* = (3/4)(.09 - .03) = .045$ or 4.5%. Net revenues are .06 per deposit dollar per year, and the profit margin is 25% of net revenues, or .015. The depositor's share, or pass-through proportion, is 75% of net revenues. From the revenues per deposit dollar, .03 or 33% are distributed to factors of production, labor and capital, and for intermediate product.

Mathematical verification is obtained by the maximization of profit with respect to r:

$$P = (.09)3r^3m^{-1}yw - 3r^4m^{-1}yw - (.03)3r^3m^{-1}yw,$$

and

$$\frac{\partial P}{\partial r} = .81r^2m^{-1}yw - 12r^3m^{-1}yw - .27r^2m^{-1}yw = 0$$

Solving for r^*, we obtain .045 in decimal form or 4.5% per annum.

Assuming income and wealth levels of $100 and $400 million and a market interest rate of 6% (or .06 in decimal form), the deposit level corresponding to the deposit rate 4.5% is $182.250 million. At this deposit level, the total production cost is $5.467 million, and the total interest cost rD is $8.201 million.

Worth noting is the average cost of funds schedule. It is derived from the deposit demand curve by solving for r, which in this case is $r = (mD/3yw)^{1/3}$. With a constant deposit elasticity value of 3, the average interest cost schedule rises rather gently. With lower constant deposit elasticities, such as an ϵ value less than 1, the average cost of funds rises more steeply. That is, in a less competitive deposit market, higher deposit rates evoke a smaller proportionate increase in deposits. The shape of the curves of the average cost of funds schedule for different elasticities is shown in Figure 3.3.

The marginal interest cost is $(\partial rD/\partial D)$, which in this case is $1.33 \ (mD/3yw)^{1/3}$, so that the marginal cost of funds is 33% above the average cost of funds at all deposit levels.

The effect of disintermediation caused by higher market interest rates can also be analyzed by examining the deposit demand curve. The marginal effect on deposit levels from a higher market interest rate is

$$\frac{\partial D}{\partial m} = -\frac{3r^3 yw}{m^2},$$

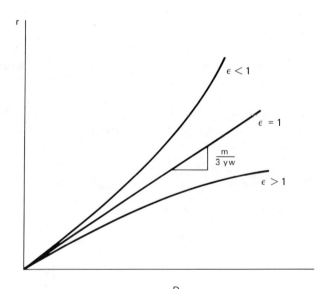

Figure 3.3   Average interest cost schedule and the deposit elasticity.

and the marginal impact on deposit levels from changes in income (and wealth) is

$$\frac{\partial D}{\partial y} = \frac{3r^3w}{m}.$$

BIBLIOGRAPHY

Baumol, William. *Economic Theory and Operations Analysis*. 3rd ed. Englewood Cliffs, N.J.: Prentice-Hall, 1972.

Benston, George J. "A Microeconomic Approach to Banking: Comment," *Journal of Finance*, **27**, June 1972.

Boyd, John H. "Deposit Rate Setting by Savings and Loan Associations, Comment and Reply," *Journal of Finance*, **26**, December 1971.

Boyd, John H. "Some Recent Developments in the Savings and Loan Deposit Market," *Journal of Money, Credit and Banking*, **5**, August 1973.

Brainard, William, and Tobin, James. "Pitfalls in Financial Model Building," *American Economic Review*, **58**, May 1968.

Bryan, William R. "The Determinants of Bank Profits," The American Bankers Association, Research Paper No. 8, 1972.

Chamberlain, E. H. *The Theory of Monopolistic Competition*. 7th ed. Cambridge, Mass.: Harvard Univ. Press, 1956.

Goldfeld, Stephen, and Jaffee, D. "The Determinants of Deposit-Rate Setting by Savings and Loan Associations," *Journal of Finance*, **25**, June 1970.

Goldfeld, Stephen, and Jaffee, D. "Reply," *Journal of Finance*, **26**, December 1971.

Graddy, Duane B., and Kyle, Reuben, III. "The Simultaneity of Bank Decision-Making, Market Structure, and Bank Performance," *Journal of Finance*, **34**, March 1979.

Gramlich, E., and Jaffee, D., eds. *Savings Deposits, Mortgages, and Housing*. Lexington, Mass.: Lexington, 1972.

Henderson, James M., and Quandt, Richard. *Microeconomic Theory: A Mathematical Approach*. New York: McGraw-Hill, 1958.

Hester, Donald. "Ownership and Behavior in the Savings and Loan Industry." In *Conversion of Mutual Savings & Loan Associations to Stock Form: Legal and Economic Issues*. Federal Home Loan Bank Board, 1967.

Klein, Michael. "A Theory of the Banking Firm," *Journal of Money, Credit and Banking*, **3**, May 1971.

Mangoletsis, I. D. "The Microeconomics of Indirect Finance," *Journal of Finance*, **30**, September 1975.

McKenzie, Joseph A. "Some Extensions of the Goldfeld–Jaffee Model of Savings and Loan Behavior," Federal Home Loan Bank Board, Research Working Paper No. 93, May 1980.

Meyer, Paul. "Comment," *Journal of Finance*, **33**, September 1967.

Miller, S. M. "A Theory of the Banking Firm: Comment," *Journal of Monetary Economics*, **1**, January 1975.

Mingo, John J. *An Imperfect Markets Model of the Banking Firm Under Regulation*. Board of Governors, Federal Reserve System, October 1977.

Mingo, John J., and Wolkowitz, B. "The Effects of Regulation on Bank Balance Sheet Decisions," *Journal of Finance*, **32**, December 1977.

Pringle, John J. "A Theory of the Banking Firm," *Journal of Money, Credit and Banking*, **5**, November 1973.

Pyle, David H. "On the Theory of Financial Intermediation," *Journal of Finance,* **26,** June 1971.

Pyle, David H. "Descriptive Theories of Financial Institutions Under Uncertainty," *Journal of Financial and Quantitative Analysis,* **7,** December 1972.

Sealey, C. W., Jr., and Lindley, J. T. "Inputs, Outputs, and a Theory of Production and Cost at Depository Financial Institutions," *Journal of Finance,* **32,** September 1977.

Slovin, M. B., and Sushka, M. E. *Interest Rates on Savings Deposits.* Lexington, Mass.: Lexington, 1975.

Smith, Paul F. *Economics of Financial Institutions and Markets.* Homewood, Ill. Richard D. Irwin, 1971.

Szego, G., and Shell, K., eds. *Mathematical Methods in Investment and Finance.* Amsterdam: North-Holland Publ., 1973.

Weber, Gerald. "Interest Rates on Mortgages and Dividend Rates of Savings and Loan Associations," *Journal of Finance,* **21,** September 1966.

CHAPTER 4

Some Extensions to the Microeconomic Theory of the Depository Firm

4.1 ECONOMIES AND DISECONOMIES OF SCALE IN PRODUCTION

In Chapter 3, the depository firm was analyzed under the condition that production costs were a constant proportion of the deposit level. With this assumed production cost structure, average costs and marginal costs were constant and equal. With a proportionality of costs and deposit levels, constant returns to scale are said to exist. Furthermore, the elasticity of production costs with respect to the deposit level is unity. This assumption had an important impact upon deposit rates, profit margins, deposit size, and income distribution. To demonstrate this, the cost structure will be scrutinized more carefully in this section. We will utilize a constant elasticity cost function and vary the value of the constant elasticity cost function in order to examine the impacts upon deposit rates, rate spreads, and income distribution from economies and diseconomies of scale in production.

When the production cost relationship has a constant elasticity of cost to the deposit level, this function takes the specific algebraic form

$$C = \gamma D^\eta, \tag{4.1}$$

where η represents the constant cost elasticity.

With this production cost function, marginal and average costs are

$$\frac{\partial C}{\partial D} = \gamma\eta D^{\eta-1} \tag{4.2}$$

and

$$c \equiv \frac{C}{D} = \gamma D^{\eta-1}, \tag{4.3}$$

and thus marginal costs are a multiplicative function of average production costs where the multiplicative factor is the cost elasticity

$$\frac{\partial C}{\partial D} = \eta c. \tag{4.4}$$

The cost elasticity could take values from 0 to infinity. If, for example, the constant elasticity is equal to unity, marginal and average costs are constant and equal, which was the assumption prevailing in Chapter 3. If economies of scale exist, total costs rise less than in proportion to the deposit level, and the cost elasticity is less than 1. In this case, economies of scale exist, as average costs decline with the deposit level and marginal costs also decline and lie below the average cost curve. For example, if $\eta = .9$, average costs decline with the deposit level and marginal costs are 90% of average costs at all deposit levels. Both economies and diseconomies of scale are shown in Figure 4.1.

When the production cost elasticity is greater than 1, diseconomies of scale exist, and average costs increase with the deposit level. In this case, marginal costs also increase, and the marginal cost curve always lies above the average cost curve.

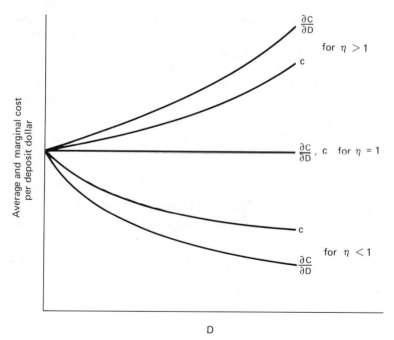

Figure 4.1   Economies and diseconomies of scale in production.

The value of the cost elasticity was the subject of substantial quantitative research during the 1960s. In general, the early pioneering work of Alhadeff[1] and Horvitz[2] found that for commercial banks, average costs were constant over a considerable range of deposit levels. This finding implied that the production cost elasticity was very close to unity. More recent work for savings and loan associations and commercial banks has found economies of scale when costs were analyzed for specific operating functions of the depository firm. For example, Benston found "consistent and significant" economies of scale for the demand deposit and real estate loan functions for these depository institutions.[3] Time deposit and installment loan production elasticities were closer to 1, whereas business loan cost elasticities could be greater than 1. Branching was generally found to increase costs, so that total production costs could have an elasticity greater than 1 with respect to the deposit level when financial institutions increase branches in proportion to the deposit level. The value of the cost elasticity with respect to the deposit level is an empirical issue. Whatever its value, we shall analyze the implications of economies or diseconomies of scale for the rates, profit margins, and deposit levels of the depository firm.

Proceeding as before with a profit statement consisting of total revenues less the components of total cost, we maximize profit with respect to the deposit rate. The first-order condition of Eq. (3.4) is still valid. Substituting Eq. (4.4) for marginal costs and solving for the profit maximizing deposit rate as in Eq. (3.5), we obtain

$$r^* = (\epsilon/(1 + \epsilon))(r_a - \eta c). \qquad (4.5)$$

Again, the profit-maximizing deposit rate depends on the deposit market elasticity, denoted ϵ, and net revenues. As before, the depository firm earns gross revenues per deposit dollar r_a, from which it then pays its marginal production costs. Since economies of scale in production affect marginal costs, scale economies in turn affect net revenues and ultimately deposit rates. Diseconomies of scale or a cost elasticity greater than 1 tend to reduce deposit rates, while economies of scale elevate deposit rates as these economies in cost are partially passed through to depositors.

[1] D. C. Alhadeff, *Monopoly and Competition in Banking* (Berkeley: Univ. of California Press, 1954).

[2] P. M. Horvitz, "Economies of Scale in Banking," in *Private Financial Institutions,* ed. P. M. Horvitz (Englewood Cliffs, N.J.: Prentice-Hall, 1962).

[3] George J. Benston, "Economies of Scale in Financial Institutions," *Journal of Money, Credit and Banking* **4** (May 1972).

Equation (4.4) could also be substituted into Eq. (3.8) in order to derive the equation for the rate spread, which in this case is

$$s = (1/(1 + \epsilon))r_a + (\epsilon/(1 + \epsilon))\eta c. \qquad (4.6)$$

From Eq. (4.6), diseconomies of scale also affect rate spreads. Diseconomies of scale in production tend to increase rate spreads because they have depressed deposit rates.

By the substitution of the profit-maximizing level of the deposit rate into the profit statement of Eq. (3.10), we obtain the profit margin equation (4.7):

$$p = (1/(1 + \epsilon))(r_a - c) + (\epsilon/(1 + \epsilon))(\eta c - c). \qquad (4.7)$$

Thus, profit margins or profit per deposit dollar also depend on the existence of economies of scale in production. The first term is the same as Eq. (3.11). Scale economies enter the second term alone as the divergence of marginal and average cost. As one would expect, rising marginal cost lowers deposit rates and tends to increase profit margins. Thus, when diseconomies of scale exist, the distribution of income is altered, which tends to increase the proportion of income accruing to the equity position. It is not clear, however, that higher profit margins will increase total profit. Since diseconomies of scale lower deposit rates, this will reduce the deposit level and will at least partially offset the higher margins per deposit dollar.

4.2   ASSET MARKET IMPERFECTIONS AND ASSET REGULATION

In Chapter 3, deposit rates and profit margins for the depository firm were derived when asset earning rates r_a were constant irrespective of the number of deposit dollars placed in asset markets. It was noted that as long as there were national markets from which loans and/or securities were available in perfectly elastic supply to the individual depository firm, firms could purchase ever-larger quantities of assets without driving up asset prices. In this circumstance, the individual firm was a price taker and quantity setter in asset markets, since the firm could expand its portfolio of assets and continue to earn the market earning rate r_a. Hence, average revenues and marginal revenues for the depository firm were constant and equal. An implication of constant average and marginal revenues is that the elasticity of the asset rate with respect to the quantity of earning assets is 0. Thus, as deposit dollars increase and more assets are purchased, asset earning rates remain constant.

There are circumstances, however, when it is not possible for the financial firm to gain access to broad national markets for loans or securities. The operational impact of barriers to national markets is that the depository firm could be locked into a specific asset market, and, as deposit funds increase in magnitude, these larger amounts of funds can only be loaned out at lower and lower loan rates. In this case, the perfectly elastic loan rate assumption of Chapter 3 would be violated. This could occur when there are regulatory restrictions placed on the lending activities of the depository firm. Indeed, many asset restrictions exist that result in the segmentation of asset markets. The very motivation for erecting asset market barriers has at times been the protection of the depository firms. At other times, the motivation for asset restrictions has been to force depository firms to channel loans to specific end users or to specific markets in order to encourage specific economic activity, such as housing. Many other asset restrictions were motivated by a desire to prohibit firms from undertaking what regulators considered to be undue risk. These restrictions are placed on all depository institutions as well as some nondepository financial firms and tends to limit them to a narrowly defined loan market. Restrictions could be placed on (1) the category of borrower (such as business or consumer); (2) the geographic area in which loans are made; (3) loan amounts; or (4) collateral, maturity, and other features of the loan, such as ceiling loan rates. In whatever manner loan restrictions are defined by regulatory agencies, they tend to limit asset selection. As firms are locked into a restricted set of qualified borrowers, an increase in deposit funds causes the firm to offer more attractive terms in order to place all the deposit inflow with these qualified borrowers. This tends to result in downward-sloping average revenue curves for the firm.

Another important circumstance that tends to cause asset segmentation is the absence of a secondary market for existing loans. Even when there is asset segmentation (e.g., by geographic area), if a secondary market existed for the resale of loans among financial institutions, the local firm would not be locked into its own local market. For example, prior to the 1970s, savings and loan associations were typically restricted to one geographic area in which they could originate loans. These geographic limits were sometimes defined as the state, the county, or a given number of miles from the home office. With this restriction, the savings and loan associations would be limited to originating loans of a specific type, to specific end users, of specific amounts, and with specific collateral. The effect of all these restrictions would be a downward-sloping average revenue curve for expanding loan portfolios.

However, in the late 1960s, the Federal National Mortgage Association (FNMA or Fanny Mae) began making a market for conventional mortgages originated by savings and loan associations. That is, the Fanny

Mae program purchased existing mortgages from the portfolio of savings institutions, either for its own portfolio or for resale to other financial institutions. The original intent of the program was to provide liquidity to savings and loan associations by providing a market for their assets, so that the associations could more easily meet deposit outflows; but the effect of this program was to enable savings and loan associations to purchase mortgages originated outside the geographical region in which they were authorized to make loans. The effect on the economy was a much smoother allocation of capital. Since that time, there has evolved a broad private market for existing mortgages. This market, conducted by mortgage brokers or mortgage bankers, has linked savings and loan associations of different areas. It has also linked the portfolios of savings associations with other financial institutions. Thus, whether the secondary market is conducted by the federal government or is privately motivated, the secondary market for assets links a geographically isolated firm with national markets. The operational impact of the secondary market is to make more elastic the supply of mortgage loans at the market rate, since the individual firm is able to purchase assets from other areas at the national rate rather than accept lower rates in its own area.

While the depository firm could be locked into highly segmented loan markets, the possibility of accessing national security markets still exists. That is, as rates on local loan markets become depressed, the financial firm may add securities to its portfolio. In many instances, however, limitations are placed upon the type and amount of open-market securities —either through regulation, charter restrictions, or contractual restrictions inherent in the liability instrument. For example, credit unions only lend to their members and real estate investment trusts only purchase real estate-related assets. Other causes of restrictions on asset selection could be a commitment to depositors to direct loan activity to local investment, or more recently, federal restrictions directing loans toward community redevelopment.

Regardless of the sources of resource misallocation from restricting the firms' portfolio activities, we shall examine the operational impact on deposit rates, rate spreads, profit margins, and income distribution. In these circumstances, the asset earning rate of a homogeneous risk class asset is a declining function of the quantity of loans, as loans increase in any given time period.

We shall analyze the circumstance in which the elasticity of the earning rate with respect to the quantity of loans is a constant elasticity ω. Since all deposits are assumed to be placed in the loan market, the earning rate in general is related to the deposit level. That is, higher deposit levels expand portfolios and depress the earning rate.

$$r_a = r_a(D) \qquad \frac{\partial r_a}{\partial D} < 0 \tag{4.8}$$

More specifically, the earning rate has a constant elasticity ω with respect to the deposit level.

$$\omega = \frac{\partial r_a}{\partial D} \frac{D}{r_a} \tag{4.9}$$

In this case, the asset earning rate depends on the deposit level, and the deposit level in turn depends on the deposit rate as per Eq. (3.1). Incorporating this assumption along with the constant elasticity production cost function (4.1) into the profit statement we obtain, in general,

$$P = r_a(D(r))D(r) - rD(r) - C(D(r)). \tag{4.10}$$

Then, maximizing profit with respect to the deposit rate, we obtain the first-order condition

$$\frac{\partial P}{\partial r} = \frac{\partial r_a}{\partial D} \frac{\partial D}{\partial r} D + r_a \frac{\partial D}{\partial r} - D - r \frac{\partial D}{\partial r} - \frac{\partial C}{\partial D} \frac{\partial D}{\partial r} = 0. \tag{4.11}$$

This first-order condition can be again simplified with marginal revenues for the last deposit dollar equaling the sum of marginal costs. In this case, marginal revenues per deposit dollar consist of r_a as before, but the declining revenues from portfolio expansion is indicated by the negative term $(\partial r_a / \partial D)D$:

$$r_a + \frac{\partial r_a}{\partial D} D = r + \frac{\partial r}{\partial D} D + \frac{\partial C}{\partial D} . \tag{4.12}$$

Substituting from Eqs. (4.9) and (4.4),

$$\frac{\partial r_a}{\partial D} D = \omega r_a \qquad \text{and} \qquad \frac{\partial C}{\partial D} = \eta c;$$

and since with a constant deposit elasticity

$$\frac{\partial r}{\partial D} D = \frac{r}{\epsilon},$$

the first-order condition can be restated in the following way:

$$r_a + \omega r_a = r + r/\epsilon + \eta c. \tag{4.13}$$

From this it is easy to solve for the profit maximizing deposit rate which is then equal to

$$r^* = (\epsilon/(1 + \epsilon))(r_a(1 + \omega) - \eta c). \tag{4.14}$$

It can be seen that the profit-maximizing deposit rate (4.14) reduces to Eq. (3.5), when $\eta = 1$ and $\omega = 0$. That is, with constant production costs and a perfectly elastic asset market (4.14) collapses to (3.5). As before, the influence of economies or diseconomies of scale in production is seen through the value of η. When this value is greater than 1, there are diseconomies of scale or increasing average costs, which will decrease deposit rates.

If the asset earning rate declines with a larger portfolio, and ω assumes a negative value between 0 and $-\infty$, such values tend to depress deposit rates. Lower deposit rates, in turn, reduce deposit levels. This is a familiar result of microeconomies. When the production firm has a downward-sloping average and, consequently, a marginal revenue curve, it tends to restrict output. It does this by increasing prices. With the depository firm, firm size or deposit levels are restricted by lower deposit rates when asset rates decline with portfolio size. Since profit maximization occurs when marginal revenues equal marginal costs, average revenues lie above marginal revenues, thus increasing profit margins.

A diagrammatic interpretation of the present model is presented in Figure 4.2. This figure is perhaps better understood by a restatement of (4.13), so that the earning rate adds up to the terms of the right-hand side of (4.15):

$$r_a = r^* + (r^*/\epsilon) + \eta c - \omega r_a. \tag{4.15}$$

In Figure 4.2, the deposit demand curve, or the average cost of funds to the depository firm, increases as before; and from the average cost, one derives the marginal cost of deposits. To the marginal interest costs are added the marginal production costs, which are drawn to increase with the deposit level so that the elasticity η is greater than 1. If average revenues decline with portfolio size, marginal revenues lie below average revenues and decline even more rapidly. The intersection of marginal revenue and marginal costs per deposit dollar satisfies the first-order condition of Eq. (4.15) and hence indicates the optimum deposit level and deposit rate.

Just as declining average revenues and increasing average costs of production limit the size of the production firm, these same factors also tend to reduce the depository firm's profit-maximizing deposit level. That is, values of the cost elasticity greater than 1 and values of the asset rate elasticity of less than 0 drive a wedge between the asset rate r_a and the deposit rate r. This wedge, of course, increases the rate spread:

$$s = (1/(1 + \epsilon))r_a + (\epsilon/(1 + \epsilon))(\eta c - \omega r_a). \tag{4.16}$$

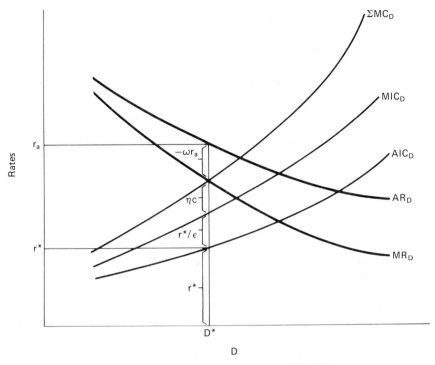

Figure 4.2   Deposit rates with diseconomies of scale and declining average revenues.

More importantly, diseconomies in production and declining average revenues increase the profit margin, which in this case is given by Eq. (4.17):

$$p = (1/(1 + \epsilon))(r_a - c) + (\epsilon/(1 + \epsilon))(\eta c - c) - (\epsilon/(1 + \epsilon))\omega r_a. \quad (4.17)$$

The combination of declining revenues and increasing costs per deposit dollar tends to reduce firm size by reducing deposit rates. Profit margins per deposit dollar are larger, and the distribution of revenue per deposit dollar is shifted to the equity position. Thus, regulatory-induced attempts to inhibit asset choice that result in declining average revenues tend to protect the profit position at the expense of the depositors. There have been times when this was the express intention of asset regulation. At other times, it has been an unexpected and unintended side effect of asset regulation, particularly when restrictions were designed to channel loanable funds back to a community or an industry.

4.3 LIABILITY DIVERSIFICATION AND THE DEPOSIT RATE STRUCTURE

In Chapter 3, the microeconomic theory of the depository firm was developed under the assumption that the depository firm offered only a single deposit class. While some single deposit class depository institutions do exist, in general there is always the potential for multiple sources and types of deposits. The firm with a single deposit class results from either an economic-induced specialization or a regulatory-imposed specialization.

Multiple deposit classes could come about in a number of ways. The depository firm could operate in more than one local market, either through branch offices or through individual entities in a holding company structure. The firm could sell its liability instruments on both a local and a national market. For example, banks and savings associations offer savings deposits in local markets and deposit certificates on national markets. Capital markets abroad can be reached with Eurodollar deposits. As another example, some savings and loan associations offer both savings deposits to local markets and mortgage-backed bonds to national capital markets.

A more common source of multiple deposit classes is the offering of different instruments within a given market. Deposit instruments could differ as to maturity, liquidity, transferability, tax treatment, or currency of denomination. Each of these factors acts on the cost structure of the depository firm, so that the marginal cost for each deposit class differs, which results in different profit-maximizing deposit rates for each deposit class.

In general, the profit-maximizing deposit rates and the resulting deposit mixture are the result of a marginal revenue and marginal cost evaluation for each deposit class. This evaluation of marginal revenues and cost is most easily made when there is perfect segmentation of deposit classes, such that higher deposit rates for one deposit class do not affect the deposit level of the other and where the marginal production cost for each deposit class is equal and independent of the other.

With these highly simplifying and unrealistic assumptions, the firm's two deposit classes do not compete in the market with each other, and furthermore, the mixture of induced deposit holdings do not affect production costs. These conditions are satisfied by a cost curve that is additive in its arguments; that is, $C = C(D_1 + D_2)$, so that $\partial C/\partial D_1 = \partial C/\partial D_2$. Additionally, with this cost curve, average costs are equal for the same deposit totals. The deposit demand curves that are independent of the rate offered by the other deposit class are simply

$$D_1 = D_1(r_1) \qquad \text{and} \qquad D_2 = D_2(r_2). \tag{4.18}$$

Profit when the deposits from each deposit class are invested in additions to the same asset portfolio is given by

$$P = r_a(D_1 + D_2) - r_1 D_1 - r_2 D_2 - C(D_1 + D_2). \qquad (4.19)$$

Maximizing P with respect to both deposit rates results in the following first-order conditions:

$$\frac{\partial P}{\partial r_1} = r_a \frac{\partial D_1}{\partial r_1} - D_1 - r_1 \frac{\partial D_1}{\partial r_1} - \frac{\partial C}{\partial D_1} \frac{\partial D_1}{\partial r_1} = 0$$

$$\frac{\partial P}{\partial r_2} = r_a \frac{\partial D_2}{\partial r_2} - D_2 - r_2 \frac{\partial D_2}{\partial r_2} - \frac{\partial C}{\partial D_2} \frac{\partial D_2}{\partial r_2} = 0. \qquad (4.20)$$

If we were to again assume that the deposit rate elasticities ϵ_1 and ϵ_2 are constant for each deposit class, the profit-maximizing deposit rates become

$$r_1^* = \frac{\epsilon_1}{1 + \epsilon_1} \left(r_a - \frac{\partial C}{\partial D_1} \right) \quad \text{and} \quad r_2^* = \frac{\epsilon_2}{1 + \epsilon_2} \left(r_a - \frac{\partial C}{\partial D_2} \right). \quad (4.21)$$

In this case, the deposit rate structure or deposit rate differentials $r_1^* - r_2^*$ depend solely on the deposit elasticities for each deposit class, as $\partial C/\partial D_1 = \partial C/\partial D_2$ by assumption:

$$r_1^* - r_2^* = \left(\frac{\epsilon_1}{1 + \epsilon_1} - \frac{\epsilon_2}{1 + \epsilon_2} \right) \left(r_a - \frac{\partial C}{\partial D} \right). \qquad (4.22)$$

Such complete segmentation of deposit classes, in which increases in the rate of one deposit class do not affect the level of the other deposit class, is extremely unlikely. Since alternative deposit classes of the same depository firm compete for the deposits of the same customers, increases in either rate should affect both deposit levels. In this case, there will be substitutability between the deposit classes. Furthermore, this substitutability between deposit classes need not be symmetric. Given this possibility, the deposit demand functions are

$$D_1 = D_1(r_1, r_2) \qquad \frac{\partial D_1}{\partial r_1} > 0, \qquad \frac{\partial D_1}{\partial r_2} < 0$$

$$D_2 = D_2(r_1, r_2) \qquad \frac{\partial D_2}{\partial r_2} > 0, \qquad \frac{\partial D_2}{\partial r_1} < 0 \qquad (4.23)$$

and

$$\frac{\partial D_1}{\partial r_2} \lessgtr \frac{\partial D_2}{\partial r_1}.$$

The first-order conditions for a profit maximum with marginal revenue equaling marginal cost for each deposit class are

$$r_a \left(\frac{\partial D_1}{\partial r_1} + \frac{\partial D_2}{\partial r_1} \right) = \frac{\partial D_1}{\partial r_1} r_1 + D_1 + r_2 \frac{\partial D_2}{\partial r_1} + \frac{\partial C}{\partial D} \left(\frac{\partial D_1}{\partial r_1} + \frac{\partial D_2}{\partial r_1} \right),$$

$$r_a \left(\frac{\partial D_2}{\partial r_2} + \frac{\partial D_1}{\partial r_2} \right) = \frac{\partial D_2}{\partial r_2} r_2 + D_2 + r_1 \frac{\partial D_1}{\partial r_2} + \frac{\partial C}{\partial D} \left(\frac{\partial D_1}{\partial r_2} + \frac{\partial D_2}{\partial r_2} \right).$$

(4.24)

In this case, marginal revenues from an increase in either deposit rate depend on the additional deposits for that deposit class less the loss of deposits from the other class. The net deposit gain or loss from an increase on the first deposit rate is the sum $\partial D_1/\partial r_1 + \partial D_2/\partial r_1$. It is possible, but would be unusual, that the sum of these terms might be 0. If they were, the deposit rate increase would have caused deposits to switch from one account to the other without affecting the total deposit level. If the sum of these terms is positive, a net deposit gain was made by the firm from other forms of wealth-owning or from competing depository firms.

In general, the switching of accounts by depositors is an important consideration for the depository firm. For example, when rates on money market or other certificate accounts increase, the switching of passbook deposits to certificates raises average deposit costs and can more than offset any gain in profits from a larger deposit total. Although it is difficult to accomplish, the segmentation of the firm's deposit accounts is desirable from the firm's point of view. Segmentation of accounts increases the possibility of attracting net new deposits instead of merely drawing from other existing accounts at higher deposit rates. Devices that attempt to freeze deposits are fixed maturities, early withdrawal penalties, and minimum deposit levels.

When less than perfect segmentation of deposit markets exists, the mathematical reduction of the first-order conditions to yield an explicit expression for the deposit rates becomes difficult, even assuming constant deposit elasticities as well as constant cross-deposit elasticities. While it is possible to solve for explicit deposit rates with explicit demand and cost curves, the general profit-maximizing conditions (4.24) can only be left in implicit mathematical form.

It is possible, however, to graphically analyze the deposit mix for the depository firm that offers more than a single deposit class. We can do so by examining a constant cost level for combinations of two deposit classes D_1 and D_2. We do this by drawing an isocost curve (as the sum of both interest and production costs) for the deposit mix shown in Figure 4.3.

In general, an isocost curve is the locus of all combinations of D_1 and

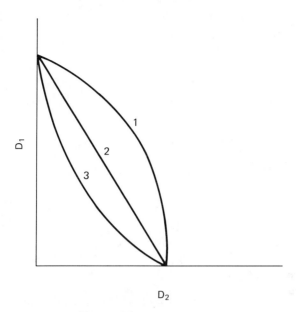

Figure 4.3 Isocost curves.

D_2, such that the total costs from the deposits of both classes are a constant amount. The isocost curve could take at least three typical shapes, which are numbered 1, 2, and 3. The question is, under what conditions would a depository firm wish to maintain positive quantities of both D_1 and D_2; or, on the other hand, which of these three possible cost interactions between D_1 and D_2 causes the firm to specialize in either D_1 and D_2? The answer to this depends not only on cost, but also on revenues. Since funds received from either deposit class are placed in additions to the same portfolio at the constant earning rate r_a, they generate the same amount of total revenues. Then, from the firm's point of view, the largest deposit total for any fixed amount of cost is the most desirable. Isocost curve 1 is preferable from the firm's point of view. This is because curve 1 yields the highest deposit level and thus the greatest revenues for the same total cost. This can be seen by starting at the upper intersection with the D_1 axis. As each dollar of D_1 is reduced ΔD_1, the firm adds ΔD_2. Since over a range each dollar loss of D_1 allows more than a dollar increase in D_2 without increasing cost, this adds revenue and profit. Continuing to substitute D_2 for D_1, the maximum total deposit level and revenue for the same total cost is at point a in Figure 4.4. With a cost structure typical of isocost curve 1, the firm will seek liability diversification of D_1 and D_2 rather than specialize in a single deposit class.

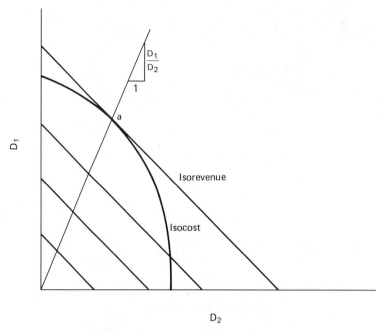

Figure 4.4 Optimal deposit combinations.

The geometric solution follows from the algebraic statement of total revenues TR which are

$$TR = r_a(D_1 + D_2).$$ (4.25)

When the total derivative of total revenues is set equal to 0,

$$dTR = r_a\, dD_1 + r_a\, dD_2 = 0.$$ (4.26)

The slope of the isorevenue curve is

$$\partial D_1/\partial D_2 = -1.$$ (4.27)

At the tangency point a where the firm maximizes revenue subject to maintaining a given total cost level, the slope of the isocost curve is equal to the slope of the isorevenue curve so that both slopes are equal to -1. When the total cost curve is concave to the origin there will be a mix of deposit classes, with the total deposit level measured at the axis of either D_1 or D_2. The deposit mix, or the proportions D_1/D_2, is measured by the slope of the ray from the origin.

For each total deposit level there will be an isocost curve, and the maximization of revenue for each cost level lies on an expansion path as shown

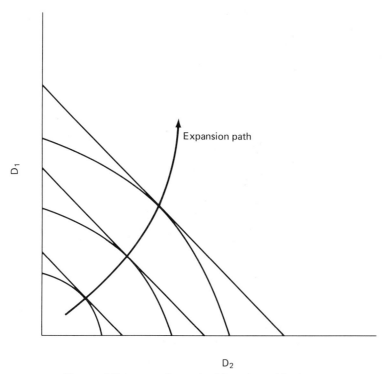

Figure 4.5   Expansion path of deposit combinations.

in Figure 4.5.[4] Each point on the expansion path is a deposit combination such that the ratio of the marginal costs is equal to -1.

With isocost curve 1 of Figure 4.3, the firm will select a deposit mix with positive quantities of each deposit class. It is possible, however, that if the total cost curve is either linear, as with isocost curve 2, or convex, as with isocost curve 3, specialization of either D_1 or D_2 will result. With the isocost curves 2 and 3, the maximization of revenue subject to a constant total cost produces a corner solution as at point b in Figure 4.6. That is, the highest deposit level and hence the highest level of revenues for a given level of cost would result from the specialization in D_1 for both isocost curves 2 and 3.

With the linear isocost curve, the ratio of the marginal costs of each deposit class is equal everywhere. This would, of course, occur if

---

[4] Somewhere along this expansion path lie the profit-maximizing deposit levels of D_1 and D_2. Profit maximization occurs when the absolute levels of marginal costs equal marginal revenues for each deposit class.

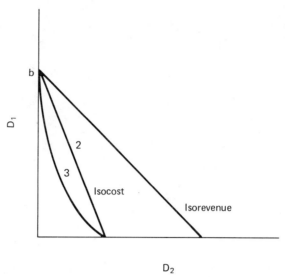

Figure 4.6   Induced specialization in D_1.

marginal production costs for each deposit class were constant and independent of each other. Furthermore, deposit or interest costs from each deposit class also need be constant and independent of each other.[5]

In the preceding analysis, costs were held constant as the deposit combination was varied. It is possible to examine economic-induced specialization by holding the total deposit level constant and allowing costs to vary as the deposit proportions change. In Figure 4.7, movement to the right indicates higher levels of D_2 and lower levels of D_1, with the total of these deposits held constant. The cost curve equivalent of isoquants 1, 2, and 3 are shown in Figure 4.7. Here the linear isocost curve 2 has a linear average deposit cost. This cost curve induces specialization in D_1. Isocost curve 3 also has a minimum average cost with specialization in D_1, with average cost rising as the portfolio proportions change. Isoquant 1 translates to an average cost curve that reaches a minimum with positive levels of both D_1 and D_2 inducing liability diversification.

The factors that tend to result in a diversified portfolio of liabilities are a declining average and marginal cost for each deposit class. That is, economies of scale for one or both deposit classes would lower average costs

[5] E. Baltensperger, in "Economies of Scale, Firm Size and Concentration in Banking," *Journal of Money, Credit and Banking* **4** (August 1972), analyzes liability diversification as the result of the minimization of interest costs and liquidation costs from deposit uncertainty. This later cost is analyzed in Chapter 6.

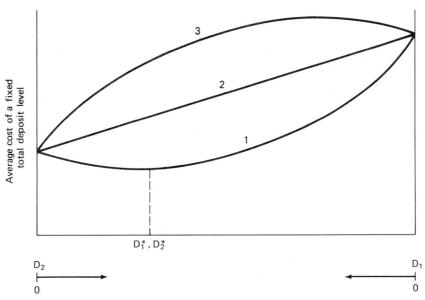

Figure 4.7 Average cost of deposit combinations.

with specialization. Furthermore, the interaction of costs between deposit classes should not negate these economies of scale. While economics of scale in production costs could enhance the possibility of a deposit mixture, it is not a necessary consequence. Even with increasing production costs for each deposit category, the average cost of a combination of deposits might be lower than from specialization. This is also true with interest costs. When imperfect locally competitive deposit markets exist, higher deposit levels are only reached with rising deposit rates. When this occurs, the average deposit cost in each deposit class increases with size. Again, it is possible that average costs of the deposit portfolio may increase more modestly when combinations of deposits are employed. This in turn depends very much on the cross-elasticities of the deposit levels for the alternate deposit rate. For example, the more sensitive the passbook level is to increases in *CD* deposit rates, the more likely average costs will rise with diversification.

BIBLIOGRAPHY

Adar, Zvi, Agmon, Tamir, and Orgler, Yair E. "Output Mix and Jointness in Production in the Banking Firm," *Journal of Money, Credit and Banking,* **7,** May 1975.

Alhadeff, D. C. *Monopoly and Competition in Banking.* Berkeley: Univ. of California Press, 1954.

Baltensperger, E. "Economies of Scale, Firm Size and Concentration in Banking," *Journal of Money, Credit and Banking* 4(August 1972).

Beighley, H. Prescott, and McCall, Alan S. "Market Power and Structure and Commercial Bank Installment Lending," Federal Deposit Insurance Corporation, Working Paper No. 72-18, 1972.

Bell, Frederick W., and Murphy, Neil B. "Economies of Scale and the Division of Labor in Commercial Banking," *Southern Economic Journal*, **35,** October 1968.

Bell, Frederick W., and Murphy, Neil B. "Returns to Scale in Commercial Banking." In *Bank Structure and Competition*, Federal Reserve Bank of Chicago, March 1967.

Benston, George J. "Economies of Scale and Marginal Costs in Banking Operations," *National Banking Review*, **2,** June 1965.

Benston, George J. "Cost of Operations and Economies of Scale in Savings and Loan Associations." In *A Study of the Savings and Loan Industry*, Federal Home Loan Bank Board, Washington, D.C., 1969.

Benston, George J. "Economies of Scale of Financial Institutions," *Journal of Money, Credit and Banking*, **4,** May 1972.

Blair, Roger and Heggenstad, Arnold. "Bank Portfolio Regulation and the Probability of Bank Failure," *Journal of Money, Credit and Banking*, **10,** February 1978.

Brigham, Eugene F., and Pettit, R. Richardson. "Effects of Structure on Performance in the Savings and Loan Industry." In *A Study of the Savings and Loan Industry*, Federal Home Loan Bank Board, Washington, D.C., 1969.

Burns, Joseph M. "An Examination of the Operating Efficiency of Three Financial Intermediaries," *Journal of Financial and Quantitative Analysis*, **4,** September 1969.

Burns, Joseph M. "On the Effects of Financial Innovations," *The Quarterly Review of Economics and Business*, **2,** Summer 1971.

Halpern, P. J., and Mathewson, G. F. "Economies in Scale in Financial Institutions: A General Model Applied to Insurance," *Journal of Monetary Economics*, **1,** April 1975.

Horvitz, P. M. "Economies of Scale in Banking." In *Private Financial Institutions, Commission on Money and Credit*. Englewood Cliffs, N.J.: Prentice-Hall, 1962.

Humphrey, David B. *Determinants of Commercial Bank Liability Structure: 1970–75.* Board of Governors, Federal Reserve System, July 1977.

Koot, Ronald S. "On Economies of Scale in Credit Unions," *Journal of Finance*, **33,** September 1978.

Longbrake, William A., and Haslen, John A. "Productive Efficiency in Commerical Banking: The Effects of Size and Legal Form of Organization on the Cost of Producing Demand Deposit Services," *Journal of Money, Credit and Banking*, **7,** August 1975.

Maisel, Sherman. "Some Relationships Betwen Assets and Liabilities of Thrift Institutions," *Journal of Finance*, **23,** June 1968.

Mullineaux, Donald J. "Economies of Scale in Financial Institutions: A Comment," *Journal of Monetary Economics*, **1,** April 1975.

Murphy, Neil B. "The Implications of Econometric Analysis of Bank Cost Functions for Bank Planning," *Journal of Bank Research*, **4,** Autumn 1973.

Powers, J. A. "Branch Versus Unit Banking: Bank Output and Cost Economies," *Southern Economic Journal*, **36,** October 1969.

Schweitzer, S. A. "Costs and Production in Banking: A Study of Scale Economics," *Southern Economic Journal*, **39,** October 1972.

Tucker, Donald P. *Financial Reform and Mortgage Lending by Thrift Institutions: Stability for Thrifts Through Liability Management*. Board of Governors, Federal Reserve System, January 1977.

Wood, J. H. *Commercial Bank Loan and Investment Behavior*. New York: Wiley, 1975.

CHAPTER 5

Alternative Objectives of the Depository Firm: Considerations of Equity Capital and Taxation

5.1 DEPOSIT MAXIMIZATION, RATES OF RETURN, AND OTHER MOTIVES OF THE FIRM

Profit maximization of the deposit activity has thus far been assumed to be the depository firm's objective. With profit maximization, there is an optimum deposit rate, and that deposit rate determines an optimum deposit level. The firm restrains itself in bidding up deposit rates because any higher deposit rate would attract additional deposits that would yield negative profits at the margin. These additional deposits, having negative yields, reduce total profit.

To see the implications of a profit-maximizing deposit rate more clearly, we refer to Figure 5.1. In this figure, average costs are portrayed as having the classic U shape. This could arise when there are some fixed production costs associated with the operation of the depository firm. Since these fixed production costs are quickly spread over a larger deposit base, average production costs quickly approach a constant level, assuming constant marginal costs. Since the average cost curve for the depository firm depends on both production and interest costs, the average cost curve as the summation of these costs most decidedly rises, with marginal costs exceeding average costs because interest costs increase with the deposit level. In Figure 5.1 a projection is made to the lower frame to indicate the corresponding profit margin (or profit per deposit dollar) at each deposit level. Maximum total profit exists where marginal revenues equal marginal costs. A projection is made to that deposit level, which is denoted D^*. Notice that the deposit level corresponding to maximum total profit does not correspond to the maximum profit margin. At the profit-maximizing deposit level, marginal revenues per deposit dollar are equal to marginal costs per deposit dollar, resulting in a 0 profit margin for that last deposit dollar. At lower deposit levels, additional deposits con-

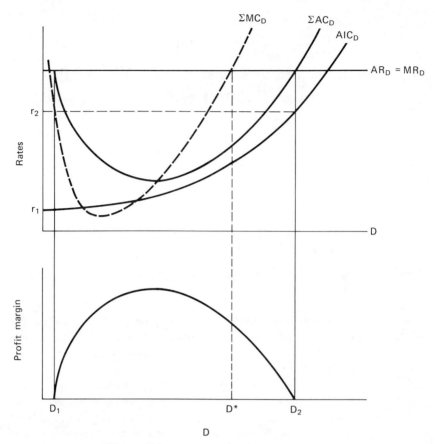

Figure 5.1 Deposit levels and profit margins.

tribute positive profit, whereas expansion beyond D^* results in additional deposits that generate negative contributions to profit, though total profit continues to be positive over a range.

From this it can be seen that if the depository firm strays from the profit-maximizing deposit level, there is still a range over which it can continue to operate profitably. In fact, the firm can operate with positive profit levels between the deposit levels D_1 and D_2, at which average revenues equal the sum of average costs. To attain these break-even deposit levels, the firm merely sets its deposit rate at either r_1 or r_2 to attract deposit levels D_1 and D_2. Since these are the deposit limits that produce positive profit levels, it is unlikely that the firm would operate outside these limits (except in the short run), as the depository firm would incur current losses. Current losses need to be confronted, since they must be covered with borrowed funds, corresponding reductions in assets and capital accounts, or capital contributions from the stockholders. This last option is, of course, not available to the thrift institutions that are mutual in ownership, but even for stock firms it is unlikely that the deposit insuring agencies would tolerate losses for long.[1]

Within the limits D_1 and D_2 of current profitability, the firm then would appear to have some operating discretion without incurring current losses. Reasons or motivations for selecting a deposit level between D_1 and D_2 have generally been rationalized by alternative motives or goals to profit maximization. These alternative goals of the depository firm have been prescribed to either the manager of the financial firm or to its owners. In one hypothesis, usually associated with the work of Baumol,[2] the firm is portrayed as having a large number of decentralized stockholders, each with a small minority position, so that the employee-managers are left relatively free to administer the activities of the firm. This freedom to employ discretion exists as long as a degree of profitability is maintained. In this view, it is in the interest of the employee-managers to increase deposit size, subject to maintaining positive profit levels, since executive salaries are often based on firm size. Other motivations for attaining a deposit size in excess of profit maximization have been expressed as the maximization of market share or the maximization of deposit growth. Though local deposit markets have often been characterized by high concentration ratios, with few firms having relatively large proportions of the deposits in the market, there is little systematic evidence that large market shares have brought with them market power to alter profit performances.[3] Yet the drive for higher market shares appeals to the intuition of many, if only because it provides measurable evidence that allows one to establish a pecking order among peers. Much the same could be said for a deposit growth motivation, which in this static analysis can only be interpreted as attaining deposit levels in excess of profit maximization in each period.

Whether a firm seeks to increase its deposit level or size because of self-serving motivations by managers, a drive for higher market shares, or deposit growth, the latitude for larger size while remaining profitable de-

[1] Current losses are likely to shift the deposit demand curve and require that risk premiums be paid on uninsured deposits and possibly on insured deposits. The effect of current losses on the deposit demand curve is discussed in Section 5.2.

[2] William Baumol, *Business Behavior, Value, and Growth* (New York: Harcourt, 1967).

[3] For a summary of the literature relating the market structure of depository firms and the performance of those firms, see George J. Benston, "The Optimal Banking Structure," *Journal of Bank Research* **4** (March 1973).

pends on how quickly the marginal and average cost curves rise. Since the average cost curve is the summation of both production and interest costs, and since average production costs are reasonably close to remaining constant, most of the increase in average costs is due to rising interest costs.[4] The prime determinate of how much a firm can expand beyond profit maximization and still show positive profit levels depends largely on the elasticity of the deposit demand curve. It is of interest that in deposit markets characterized by relatively little competition and a low deposit elasticity, the firm's average interest costs rise steeply, which tends to constrain the firm from operating much beyond profit maximization. Thus the monopolists, or the oligopolists, with a relatively lower deposit rate elasticity in their deposit demand curves, will find that their average and marginal interest costs rise rapidly; they would actually tend to have less latitude to operate profitably beyond the profit maximization deposit level. On the other hand, in a more competitive deposit market where the firm faces a greater elasticity in deposit demand, the average interest costs would tend to rise less sharply with higher deposit levels, and the financial firm would tend to have more latitude to exceed the profit maximization deposit level and still maintain a profitable operation.

Regardless of the range of profitable opportunities facing the depository firm, if the firm knowingly strays from profit maximization, it is at least implicitly, if not explicitly, making a utility trade-off of deposit size for profit. The utility loss from a lower level of profit must be balanced against the utility gain from greater deposit size. In this framework of utility trade-offs of size for profit one must also consider what has been called satisficing behavior. Satisficing behavior perhaps could be interpreted as the desire for a limited deposit level that still yields positive profit levels—though not maximum profit. In this particular case the utility gain from smaller size or perhaps leisure, is balanced against the utility of foregone profit.

There is an alternative hypothesis regarding the objectives of the depository firm that also leads to a compromising of current profit. This hypothesis is characterized as expense preference behavior.[5] Expense preferencing, which has been attributed to both the financial and the production firm, describes management as having a utility preference for higher staff levels and a desire to pay higher salaries than the profit-maximizing

---

[4] Reference is made to George J. Benston "Economies of Scale of Financial Institutions," *Journal of Money, Credit and Banking* 4 (May 1972), which summarizes the findings regarding economies of scale of depository institutions.

[5] Refer to O. Williamson, "Managerial Discretion and Business Behavior," *American Economic Review* 53 (December 1963) for alternative behavior when managerial discretion exists.

firm. Management is often able to do so as the result of the separation of ownership and control, which places considerable latitude in the hands of employee-managers. In this view, the average production costs of the firm are altered so that they are higher than they would ordinarily be if the firm operated efficiently. The motivation for expense preferencing could arise from a desire to justify higher executive salaries, when the firm has large staffs at high salaries. In some instances, higher earnings enjoyed by management and staff derive from implicit payments, such as various benefits that substitute for consumption expenditures or other fringe benefits that improve the working environment.

The susceptibility of the financial firm to expense preference behavior may be greater than that of the production firm because many financial firms are mutual in form. In the mutual form of organization, the depositors are the owners, and there is an even greater potential for the separation of management from ownership to lead to excess expenditures for staff. While it is difficult to indicate precisely how expense preferencing might affect the cost structure (as some of these excess costs are fixed and some are variable), it is safe to imply that they result in higher average cost schedules that reduce profit margins at all deposit levels. In fact, one motivation for expense preferencing on the part of managers might be to create some inefficiencies in production that could be removed, if need be, when the pressure for additional profit becomes apparent. In this way, expense preferencing could be explained as risk minimization by employee-managers that allows them some latitude in selecting a level of profitability.[6]

Beyond these motivations, there is yet another reason to question profit maximization as the firm's objective. Many financial firms are mutual in their form of organization, and the depositors are the owners. In these cases the deposit rate includes some distribution of profit to the depositor-owners. That is, the deposit rate might include both the returns to the depositor and a distribution of profit to the depositor-owners. This, of course, would elevate deposit rates and tend to increase deposit size.[7]

While the logic of this behavior for mutually-owned firms has appeal, Hester,[8] in a study of the differences between stock and mutual savings

[6] While expense preferencing is seen by some as an alternative motive to profit maximization, it is quite conceivable that some of these excess expenditures are a form of profit maximizing, nonrate competition, a subject that will be developed in Chapters 7 and 8.

[7] In addition to making an implicit distribution of profit in the deposit rate, some mutuals, such as credit unions, explicitly distribute profit to borrowers.

[8] Donald D. Hester, "Ownership and Behavior in the Savings and Loan Industry," in *Conversion of Mutual Savings and Loan Associations to Stock Form: Legal and Economic Issues*, (Washington, D.C.: Federal Home Loan Bank Board, 1967).

and loan associations, has shown that there are relatively few significant differences in the behavior of savings and loan associations when the ownership lies in the hands of the depositors. Where differences in behavior did exist between stock and mutual firms, they were primarily concerned with the willingness on the part of stock companies to assume greater risk in portfolio selection.

Some evidence regarding the relative deposit rates of mutual firms and stock firms is provided by comparing weighted average deposit rates for savings and loan associations, mutual savings banks, and credit unions.[9] Both the mutual savings banks and credit unions are mutuals, whereas the savings and loan associations are mixed. While differences in the deposit rates among these thrifts exist, they are relatively small and are better explained by differences in net revenues and in the competitive forces facing each type of thrift institution. Even though the credit unions had the highest deposit rates, they did not result from high pass-through proportions. These high deposit rates accrued from the highest net revenues, despite the smallest pass-through proportion of any of the depository industries. This small pass-through proportion is consistent with their less competitive deposit environment and completely inconsistent with the notion that mutuals pass through a distribution of profit to depositors. From an examination of deposit rate figures, there seems to be little cause to assert that the mutuals tend to pay more than profit-maximizing deposit rates and expand beyond profit-maximizing deposit levels.

Beyond all these hypotheses regarding alternative objective functions of the firm, there is still one self-imposed constraint that should affect the choice of deposit rate, deposit size, and profit margin. The most likely constraint narrowing the range of operations for the financial firm arises when the owners require a minimum rate of return on their invested equity capital. If ownership imposes on the employee-manager a lower limit on the acceptable rate of return on equity capital, this will in turn define a deposit range for the employee-manager. The minimum rate of return on equity capital could be translated into minimum acceptable profit margins that ultimately define the limits of the deposit rate and the deposit level.

To determine the effect of minimum rates of return on profit margins, the analysis must be expanded to include revenues associated with the investment of equity funds in earning assets. The total profit from the depository firm's activities includes not only the profit from the deposit activity (which was the centerpiece of Chapter 3), but the additional revenues that accrue through the investment of a portion of the equity capital

---

[9] Deposit rates are shown in Table 9.2. Historical relationships among thrifts are discussed in Chapters 9, 10, and 11.

and retained earnings. Equity funds are not all invested in earning assets, since a portion of them is allocated to the physical plant of the depository firm. The balance of equity funds is allocated to the portfolio of earning assets and is probably invested similarly to funds derived from deposits or from other forms of debt. Table 5.1 contains industrywide proportions of the equity capital allocation to the physical plant and equipment of the depository industries. At no time between 1919 and 1978 was more than 25% of equity capital committed to physical plant and equipment for any of the depository industries. This means that the balance committed to financial assets was never less than 75%.

If the proportion of equity capital not committed to fixed plant and equipment is invested in the portfolios of the depository firm at the average asset earning rate r_a, and b is the proportion of equity capital E invested in financial assets, the revenues per period from invested equity capital are

$$r_a bE. \tag{5.1}$$

To these revenues we add the profit from the deposit activity pD where p is the profit margin, and we obtain the shareholders' total net revenues from both deposits and invested capital. This total profit we shall designate P'.

$$P' = pD + r_a bE \tag{5.2}$$

If the rate of return on equity capital is the ratio of this total profit relative to the equity base, the rate of return then becomes

$$(P'/E) = (pD/E) + r_a b. \tag{5.3}$$

The rate of return on equity is then equated to a minimum required average rate of return $\bar{q}$

$$(pD/E) + r_a b = \bar{q}. \tag{5.4}$$

When a is defined as the equity–deposit ratio or E/D for the depository firm, the average return per equity dollar from both the deposit activity and invested equity capital is

$$(p/a) + r_a b = \bar{q}. \tag{5.5}$$

These values of a are shown in Table 5.2 for the depository industries. Solving Eq. (5.5) for the minimum acceptable profit margin called p_{min} we obtain

$$p_{min} = a(\bar{q} - r_a b). \tag{5.6}$$

Hence, if the stockholders of the depository firm require a minimum rate of return commensurate with their perceived risk, this translates into a minimum profit margin. The more the stockholders wish to increase the

TABLE 5.1

Percentage of Equity Capital Invested in Physical Plant and Equipment $(1 - b)^a$

Year	Federal Reserve members	FDIC members	Mutual savings banks	Savings and loan associations
1919	13.6	—	—	—
1920	13.7	—	—	—
1921	15.7	—	—	—
1922	16.3	—	—	—
1923	17.9	—	—	—
1924	18.9	—	—	—
1925	19.8	—	—	—
1926	20.1	—	—	—
1927	19.9	—	—	—
1928	18.7	—	—	—
1929	17.7	—	—	—
1930	18.8	—	—	—
1931	19.5	—	—	—
1932	21.2	—	—	—
1933	19.7	—	—	—
1934	19.8	19.4	—	—
1935	19.2	19.1	9.5	—
1936	18.6	18.5	8.3	—
1937	18.0	18.0	8.2	—
1938	17.4	17.3	9.0	—
1940	16.0	16.0	15.5	—
1941	15.4	15.4	14.6	—
1942	14.8	14.8	13.4	8.2
1943	13.2	13.2	9.5	8.1
1944	11.7	11.5	8.5	8.5
1945	10.3	10.1	6.8	8.9
1946	9.7	9.6	5.9	9.0
1947	9.6	9.6	6.2	9.4
1948	9.9	9.8	6.1	9.7
1949	9.8	9.8	5.7	10.3
1950	9.8	9.8	5.8	10.6
1951	10.0	10.0	5.5	11.6
1952	10.2	10.2	5.9	12.6
1953	10.4	10.4	6.2	13.7
1954	10.5	10.6	6.7	14.3
1955	11.2	11.3	6.9	14.9
1956	11.7	11.8	7.1	15.9
1957	12.1	12.2	7.2	16.8
1958	12.6	12.7	7.4	17.2
1959	13.5	13.6	7.5	17.4
1960	13.0	13.6	7.5	17.7

TABLE 5.1 (*Continued*)

Year	Federal Reserve members	FDIC members	Mutual savings banks	Savings and loan associations
1961	13.9	14.0	7.7	18.1
1962	14.2	14.3	8.0	18.3
1963	15.7	15.5	8.1	19.6
1964	17.3	17.3	9.1	19.5
1965	17.1	17.2	9.6	19.2
1966	17.7	17.7	10.0	18.9
1967	17.6	18.4	10.1	18.7
1968	18.2	19.0	10.4	18.1
1969	20.5	20.3	10.5	17.6
1970	21.5	21.4	10.8	17.8
1971	22.7	21.9	10.9	18.2
1972	22.6	34.1	11.1	18.6
1973	22.7	22.1	11.8	19.3
1974	23.5	22.5	12.8	20.9
1975	25.0	23.6	13.4	23.5
1976	—	23.1	13.3	23.4
1977	—	23.1	13.1	22.2
1978	—	23.5	13.1	21.0

[a] Source: Appendix tables A9.1–A9.13.

spread between $\bar{q}$ and the earning rate of their own capital $r_a b$, the higher they must push the profit margin of the deposit activity. The unique profit margin consistent with a target rate of return is also consistent with two deposit levels D_3 and D_4 in Figure 5.2. In this case the manager-employee would have discretion to operate at either deposit level.

An important observation is that if the target rate of return is increased, it might become so high that the corresponding deposit levels would exclude the profit-maximizing deposit level D^*. If the target rate of return were pushed to a maximum, the profit margin would be pushed to a maximum at D^{**}. The maximization of the rate of return could also be equivalent to the maximization of earnings per share and hence stock prices, if the depository firm chooses to maintain a fixed equity–deposit ratio. This is because although there are profitable deposits that can be added beyond D^{**} up to D^*, if these added deposits necessitate a fixed proportionate increase in the equity base, the new deposits with declining profit margins per deposit and equity dollar dilute earnings per share. Unless the profit margin on the additional deposits beyond D^{**} is as great as those at D^{**}, the new deposits reduce earnings per share and therefore the stock

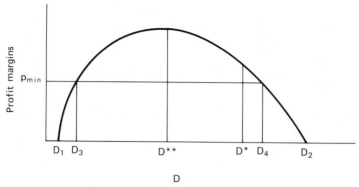

Figure 5.2   Target rates of return and profit margins.

price.[10] The equivalence of the maximum profit margin, earnings per share, and stock price would occur if the depository firm were subject to a regulatory-imposed capital constraint, a subject we now consider.

5.2   PRIVATE AND SOCIAL ASPECTS OF
THE EQUITY CAPITAL CONSTRAINT

All firms, whether financial or nonfinancial, use equity capital and various types of debt instruments in their capital structure. The blending of debt and equity in the firm's liability structure or the ratio of debt to equity has been the subject of extensive analysis for the nonfinancial firm. The issue has been often cast in terms of what degrees of leverage, if any, will reduce the weighted cost of funds to a minimum. Thus, an optimal capital structure in this sense is said to exist if the firm has minimized its cost of funds.

In addition to affecting the cost of funds, there are other reasons to maintain equity capital in the firm's liability structure, as it directly yields benefits to the equity holders. If there are current operating losses, they are effectively financed by equivalent reductions of assets and equity capital. The firm thus maintains the option to continue to operate despite short-run losses. It is in this way that equity capital serves as a buffer to

[10] The equivalence of the maximization of the profit margin and stock price are a result of the fact that there is a fixed relationship between output (deposits) and equity. This fixed relationship between output levels and the equity base do not exist for the production firm. Since production can increase without an equivalent or proportionate increase in a production firm's equity, no such rigid relationship exists between profit margins, earnings per share, and stock prices.

maintain the option of continuity of operations. Not only does the stock-holder derive benefit from this short-run insulation from bankruptcy, but those who supplied debt also derive benefits because the probability that income payments will continue on the debt instruments despite short-run adversities is higher. Furthermore, if current losses were not contained, the debtors would have a higher claim in the event of a forced liquidation of assets. With equity capital serving as an insulating buffer against current losses and forced liquidation or reorganization, the larger the amount of capital, the lower the risk premiums that firm must pay for its other funds. Thus the amount or proportion of equity capital in the firm's financial structure has a direct and important effect on the terms at which the firm is able to raise debt. The quantity of capital, *ceteris paribus*, shifts the demand curve for the firm's debt instruments, including deposits, so that the debt could either be raised in larger quantities and/or at lower rates (i.e., the market requires a smaller risk premium for the same quantity of deposits). This is shown in Figure 5.3 as the deposit demand curve or the average interest cost AIC_D shifts to AIC_D' with additional equity capital.

While some of the considerations for the capital structure for the depository financial firm are similar to the nonfinancial firm, there are, however, some differences. One conceivable motivation for providing equity capital for the financial firm in either original stock issue or retained earnings

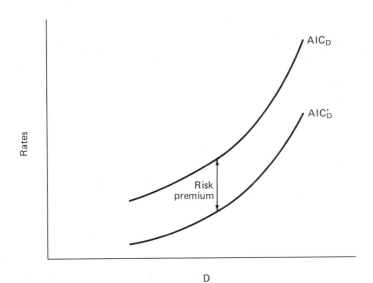

Figure 5.3 Equity capital and risk premiums.

is the ability to place these funds in financial assets and markets that might not otherwise be available to an individual investor. That is, by obtaining a charter and supplying equity capital to the firm, the individual investor gains access to certain otherwise restricted asset markets. An example is the savings association, in which the individual may purchase federally insured mortgages through the corporate entity. For the commercial bank, substantial amounts of equity capital are also invested in bank loans, a market and an instrument not otherwise readily available to the individual.

The desirability of investing equity funds through the financial firm rather than directly in the open market is enhanced if the rate of return is higher or the risk is less than the instruments available to the individual investor on the open market. Furthermore, investing through the financial entity might be more desirable when the advantages of portfolio diversification to reduce the risk per asset dollar are enhanced with a larger portfolio in which cost indivisibilities exist. In addition, when there are economies of scale in production or information costs, the advantages of the corporate conduit to financial markets are enhanced.

If accessing markets, however, were the only motivation for supplying equity capital to a financial firm, the unlevered mutual fund would be a sufficient vehicle to reach financial markets where scale economies in production could be exploited. To maintain incentive for leveraging the financial firm, there must be a positive rate spread, after all costs associated with borrowed funds. For the depository firm, the capital account serves as an inducement to attract deposits on favorable terms, much as the presence of equity affects the demand for the debt of the production firm.

It is of interest to examine the capital structure of the depository firms in a period during which the market operated free of government regulation and insurance guarantees. In such a free market, one would expect the deposit demand curve and the deposit level to be quite sensitive to the amount of capital the depository firm held as a buffer against potential losses in its earning assets. The importance of equity capital in an unregulated and uninsured market is evidenced by examining the capital account experience of commercial banks in the early history of American banking. Figure 5.4 shows the very high levels of equity capital relative to deposits beginning in 1803. There has been a long-run trend of an almost continuous decline from then to the present. This trend is evidenced whether one examines the ratio of capital to deposits, total assets, or risk assets. In the early nineteenth century, capital as a ratio to total assets was above 60%. There were several erratic movements over time, but it took nearly 140 years for the ratio of bank capital to total assets to decline to the present approximately 6%. The ratio of capital to deposits in the 1880s was as high

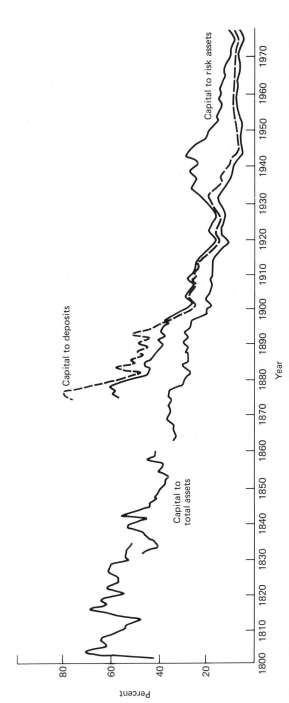

Figure 5.4 Bank capital as a percentage of assets and deposits 1803–1976. Source: Adapted from Wesley Lindow, "Bank Capital and Risk Assets," *The National Banking Review*, September 1963, p. 2; updated from 1963–1976. Derived from data (as of June 30): (1) 1803–1835 for Massachusetts banks—1876 *Report of the Comptroller of the Currency*, p. 98. (2) 1834–1862 for all banks in the United States—*Historical Statistics of the United States*, 1949, p. 263. (3) 1865–1962 for all commercial banks in the United States—*Annual Reports of the Comptroller of the Currency*, 1865–1974; *Journal of Political Economy*, December 1974, p. 559; *Historical Statistics of the United States*, 1957, pp. 631–62; *Banking and Monetary Statistics*, Board of Governors of Federal Reserve System, 1962 Supplement, p. 28; *Federal Reserve Bulletin*, March 1962, p. 346. (4) 1963–1970—*Banking and Monetary Statistics* 1941–1970, Board of Governors of the Federal Reserve System, pp. 29–31. (5) 1971–1975 —*Annual Statistical Digest*, Board of Governors of the Federal Reserve System, p. 61. (6) 1976—FDIC *Annual Report* Table 106. Reprinted by permission of the publisher from Lawrence G. Goldberg and Lawrence J. White, eds., *The Deregulation of the Banking and Securities Industry* (Lexington, Mass.: Lexington Books, D. C. Heath and Company). Copyright 1979, D. C. Heath and Company.

as 80% and declined erratically through the 1920s to a level of just under 20%. The ratio of capital to risk assets, which was close to 60% in the 1880s, also tended to decline in a similar fashion to under 20% in the late 1920s. This down-drift in the capital ratios evidently reflected a growing willingness on the part of depositors to supply deposits to commercial banks with less equity bufer as the confidence in the private banking system tended to increase through time. At the beginning of the 1930s, the capital ratios for commercial banks were relatively low by historic standards; and after the great wave of bank failures, federal deposit insurance was initiated, and capital ratios continued to fall ever since. There was one exception however: The ratio of capital to risk assets increased in the 1930s and World War II period, mainly because portfolios of commercial banks contained lower proportions of business loans and correspondingly greater proportions of government bonds and cash.

An overview of capital levels for thrifts as well as banks is provided in Tables 5.2 and 5.3. Following World War II, in the late 1940s the

TABLE 5.2

Ratio of the Capital Account to Average Deposits E/D[a]

Year	Commercial banks		Mutual savings banks	Savings and loan associations
	Federal Reserve members	FDIC members		
1919	14.8	—	—	—
1920	16.3	—	—	—
1921	17.2	—	—	—
1922	17.2	—	—	—
1923	15.6	—	—	—
1924	14.8	—	—	—
1925	14.0	—	—	—
1926	14.3	—	—	—
1927	15.0	—	—	—
1928	15.5	—	—	—
1929	17.4	—	—	—
1930	17.5	—	—	—
1931	17.7	—	—	—
1932	18.2	—	—	—
1933	17.7	—	—	—
1934	16.5	15.9	—	—
1935	14.2	14.1	12.4	—
1936	12.9	12.9	13.3	—
1937	12.8	13.6	13.2	—
1938	12.8	12.9	12.1	—

TABLE 5.2 (*Continued*)

Year	Commercial banks		Mutual savings banks	Savings and loan associations
	Federal Reserve members	FDIC members		
1939	11.9	11.6	12.6	—
1940	10.7	10.5	9.9	—
1941	9.9	9.8	9.0	—
1942	8.7	8.0	10.4	8.9
1943	7.5	7.2	16.8	9.5
1944	6.8	6.4	10.8	9.8
1945	6.3	6.0	10.7	9.7
1946	6.5	6.8	10.7	9.4
1947	7.0	6.8	10.5	9.2
1948	7.2	7.1	10.4	9.2
1949	7.4	7.5	10.4	9.3
1950	7.5	7.6	10.5	9.6
1951	7.4	7.5	10.9	9.7
1952	7.4	7.5	10.3	9.4
1953	7.6	7.6	10.3	9.0
1954	7.9	7.9	9.6	8.7
1955	7.9	8.0	9.4	8.6
1956	8.2	8.2	9.3	8.5
1957	8.5	8.6	9.2	8.5
1958	8.7	8.7	9.0	8.5
1959	8.8	8.8	9.2	8.6
1960	9.2	9.2	9.5	8.5
1961	9.2	9.2	9.5	8.6
1962	9.2	9.3	9.2	8.7
1963	9.3	9.4	9.2	8.4
1964	9.4	9.4	8.7	8.3
1965	9.3	9.3	8.6	8.3
1966	9.2	9.2	8.5	8.3
1967	9.0	9.0	8.0	8.2
1968	8.7	8.6	7.8	8.2
1969	9.0	8.8	7.9	8.6
1970	9.2	9.2	6.7	8.7
1971	9.1	9.1	6.6	8.3
1972	9.0	5.8	6.4	7.9
1973	8.8	8.9	6.6	7.8
1974	8.7	8.8	6.7	7.8
1975	8.9	8.4	6.5	7.4
1976	—	8.6	6.8	7.0
1977	—	8.5	6.8	6.9
1978	—	8.6	7.0	7.0

[a] Calculated as the ratio of the capital account to average deposits, and expressed as a percentage. Source: Appendix tables A9.1–A9.13.

TABLE 5.3

Ratio of Equity to Risk Assets[a]

| Year | Commercial banks | | Mutual savings banks | Savings and loan associations |
	Federal Reserve members	FDIC members		
1919	15.3	—	—	—
1920	16.6	—	—	—
1921	18.2	—	—	—
1922	18.5	—	—	—
1923	17.7	—	—	—
1924	16.8	—	—	—
1925	15.9	—	—	—
1926	16.2	—	—	—
1927	16.3	—	—	—
1928	17.2	—	—	—
1929	19.0	—	—	—
1930	19.4	—	—	—
1931	21.5	—	—	—
1932	23.2	—	—	—
1933	24.4	—	—	—
1934	26.0	26.1	13.3	—
1935	26.2	26.0	14.6	—
1936	24.7	24.5	16.0	—
1937	25.4	25.0	16.2	—
1938	26.2	25.6	15.5	—
1939	25.9	25.3	15.1	—
1940	24.9	24.3	13.0	—
1941	23.1	22.8	13.9	—
1942	26.4	25.9	15.9	9.2
1943	28.5	28.2	20.3	10.5
1944	27.6	27.5	22.7	11.4
1945	25.1	29.5	26.9	11.7
1946	23.3	23.1	28.7	10.0
1947	20.4	20.3	26.8	9.3
1948	19.5	19.2	23.5	9.1
1949	19.8	19.6	21.6	9.3
1950	17.0	17.1	19.3	9.2
1951	16.3	16.4	17.6	9.3
1952	15.6	15.7	15.3	8.9
1953	15.7	15.7	13.9	8.6
1954	13.9	16.0	12.7	8.3
1955	15.2	14.7	11.9	8.1
1956	16.5	14.5	11.1	8.2
1957	16.2	14.7	10.7	8.3

TABLE 5.3 (*Continued*)

| | Commercial banks | | Mutual savings banks | Savings and loan associations |
| | Federal Reserve members | FDIC members | | |
Year				
1958	14.8	14.8	10.2	8.4
1959	17.3	14.1	10.1	8.3
1960	17.0	14.3	10.1	8.3
1961	13.9	14.2	10.1	8.3
1962	13.3	13.4	9.6	8.3
1963	12.6	12.7	9.4	7.9
1964	12.6	12.3	8.8	7.9
1965	11.4	11.6	8.6	8.0
1966	12.6	11.3	8.4	8.2
1967	11.7	10.9	7.8	8.1
1968	12.8	10.3	7.6	8.1
1969	14.6	10.2	7.6	8.2
1970	13.2	10.0	6.4	8.2
1971	9.9	9.8	6.3	7.7
1972	9.8	6.0	6.1	7.3
1973	12.9	8.7	6.2	7.2
1974	16.6	8.6	6.3	7.3
1975	10.5	9.0	6.2	7.0
1976	—	9.2	6.3	6.7
1977	—	8.9	6.4	6.5
1978	—	8.6	6.7	6.6

[a] Expressed as a percentage. Equity is the capital account and includes common stock, preferred stock, surplus, undivided profits, and reserves for contingencies. Risk assets are total assets minus cash and treasury items. Source: Appendix tables A9.1–A9.13.

equity–deposit ratios for the thrifts were somewhat higher than those of the commercial banks, with capital to deposit ratios between 9 and 10%; banks were somewhat lower at approximately 7.5%. Since that time there was a down-drift in the ratio of capital to deposits for all these depository institutions to approximately 7%. This reduction in the equity–deposit ratio of course indicates there is greater leverage, since a 7% equity–deposit ratio corresponds to a debt–equity ratio of 14.[11] Not only has there been a down-drift in the equity to deposit ratio, but there has also

[11] It should be noted that for depository institutions, the capital account is broadly defined to include preferred stock as well as subordinated notes and debentures. While this latter source of capital is debt in nature, it is nontheless subordinated to the depositors' claims and thus constitutes a buffer to protect the depositors' position.

been a down-drift in the equity to risk asset ratios. Table 5.3 indicates this trend has occurred for the thrift institutions as well as the commercial banks. Again, for all the depository institutions there tended to be a convergence of equity as a percentage of risk assets in the late 1970s, with a slightly higher ratio for FDIC commercial banks of 8.6% as compared to 6.7 and 6.6% for mutual banks and savings and loan associations, respectively, by 1978.

During much of the long-term history of the nineteenth and early twentieth centuries, financial firms were free of regulatory constraints regarding their capital position by either state or federal agencies. The first national intrusions affecting capital requirements occurred through the National Banking Act of 1863 and the Federal Reserve Act of 1913. The latter act fixed minimum capital requirements for member commercial banks based on the population of a proposed bank service area. The requirements of the Federal Reserve Act based capital requirements upon the population of the city in which the bank was located. The act initially set a minimum of $50,000 for banks in towns of 6000 or less, which increased to a $200,000 minimum in cities with a population of 50,000 or more. However, since static legal minimums could not reasonably be expected to effectively assure capital adequacy for banks, especially as banks grew and economic conditions changed, various rules of thumb for capital adequacy evolved over time.

One of the first and most familiar of these capital adequacy tests is the ratio of capital to total deposits. It was usually stated as a concrete 1:10 minimum ratio, with little basis for this particular proportion. The California State Banking Act of 1909 contains an early citation of the 1:10 minimum ratio, and in 1914 the comptroller of the currency recommended that Congress enact legislation prohibiting national banks from holding deposits in excess of 10 times unimpaired capital and surplus. Although this particular recommendation did not become part of federal law, several states enacted similar legislation in the early 1920s. The use of the 1:10 standard by federal authorities was not adopted until after the Bank Holiday in 1933. This capital–deposit ratio was then used as a condition of membership in the Federal Reserve System, in the reexamination of banks applying for deposit insurance, and in reviewing bank dividend policies.

Criticism of the logic of relating capital needs to deposits increased in the late 1930s and early 1940s and led to other suggestions for measuring capital adequacy. Most of the literature of that period proposed a switch in emphasis from deposits to risk assets as the balance sheet items against which capital should be measured. It was argued that since the loans and investments purchased with deposit funds are a source of potential loss to banks, these assets alone must be protected by adequate capital. To further strengthen the concept of relating capital to risk assets, the 1939 annual report of the FDIC stated that the corporation's policy with regard to capital would be to urge each bank to maintain a minimum capital account equal to at least 10% of the appraised value of its assets. By relating capital to appraised value, capital requirements were strengthened, as appraised values of assets in recessions or high interest rate periods would often fall below book values.[12] This in turn would wipe out some of the book value of equity, requiring capital contributions or high levels of retained earnings to rebuild the capital position.

While the rules of thumb regarding capital adequacy employed by regulators were to change over time, they would often be changed dramatically in response to economic circumstances. For example, the use of capital adequacy ratios was suspended for a time during World War II. Total deposits expanded rapidly, and banks increased their holdings of United States government obligations. To avoid constraining banks from helping to finance the war deficit, capital adequacy requirements were suspended to allow banks to increase their purchases of United States government bonds. Obviously, bank supervisors felt that government securities, whose prices at the time were "pegged" by the Federal Reserve, were virtually riskless and that the relatively lower level of capital was sufficient to protect depositors. When in 1946 banks began to sell off their holdings of United States government securities and shifted to commercial loans, an environment was created in which the capital accounts of some banks were disproportionately low relative to risk assets. As the proportion of capital relative to risk assets and deposits continued to decline, the board of governors resumed a capital–risk asset ratio test.

Not only has the measure of capital adequacy changed both in terms of concept and to meet the expediencies of economic events, but the test of the capital adequacy of commercial banks has come under the often conflicting positions of the Federal Reserve System, the Office of the Comptroller of the Currency, and the Federal Deposit Insurance Corporation. Recently these three agencies announced an adoption of a uniform system for rating the condition of the nation's commercial banks. Although the system is continually changing, it is of interest to note some of its features.

[12] See, for example, Sherman J. Maisel and Robert Jacobson, "Interest Rate Changes and Commercial Bank Revenues and Costs," (Paper presented to the Western Finance Association, June 1978, Honolulu, Hawaii) for estimates of the reduction in the market value of assets of commercial banks as the result of interest rate changes.

A uniform interagency bank rating system will help insure consistency in the way the federal bank supervisors view individual banks within the banking system. The rating system has two main elements: (1) An assessment by federal bank examiners or analysts of five critical aspects of a bank's operations and conditions. These are adequacy of the bank's capital, the quality of the bank's assets (primarily its loans and investments), the ability of the bank's management and administration, the quantity and quality of the bank's earnings, and the level of its liquidity. (2) An overall judgment incorporating these basic factors and other factors considered significant by the examiners or analysts, expressed as a single composite rating of the bank's condition and soundness. Banks will be placed in one of five groups ranging from banks that are sound in almost every respect to those with excessive weakness requiring urgent aid.

Capital requirements for savings and loan associations, which are also continually changing, are governed primarily by the Federal Savings and Loan Insurance Corporation rules. Each insured association is required to establish a reserve account labeled *Federal Insurance Reserve* (FIR), and its purpose is solely for the absorption of losses. It is required that a savings and loan association must hold Federal Insurance Reserves in an amount equal to 5% of its total checking and savings account balances after reaching the 26th consecutive year of coverage. Newly covered associations must have a Federal Insurance Reserve of at least .5% of checking and savings account balances on the second anniversary of coverage, and this amount must be increased by at least .25% in each successive year. Once the minimum level of 5% has been attained, a savings association may, at its option, compute the required reserves as an average of balances covering the most recent closing date and the four immediately preceding closing dates.

In addition to the Federal Insurance Reserve requirement, an insured association must meet a net worth requirement. The net worth requirement represents an attempt to ensure that net worth is proportional to the riskiness of assets. Each asset classification is assigned a weight. Riskier asset classifications carry higher weights, with the result that an increase in riskiness will necessitate higher net worth levels.

It is evident from a review of bank capital ratios prior to the regulation of the capital adequacy of the depository firm that the aversion to risk by both the depositors and the firms served as an effective discipline to maintain equity capital in liability structures. With the advent of federal deposit insurance in the mid-1930s, the necessity for the depositor to closely scrutinize the quality of the depository firms' assets had diminished, since the federal regulatory agency insured the deposits. This assumption of the risk of failure by the federal insuring agency had the effect of shifting the deposit demand curves for the individual depository firms to the right. The depository firms then enjoyed lower deposit rates at the same deposit levels than would otherwise be available. In return for this reduction in risk premiums, the depository firms paid insurance premiums on their deposits and accepted the regulation of their assets, capital position, and overall supervision.

From the firm's point of view, the reduction in the risk premiums it must pay for deposits exceeds insurance premiums, so deposit insurance adds to profit. This is obviously the case, since the state chartered banks, mutual savings banks, and savings associations voluntarily applied for insurance of accounts that was not required of them.

The cost of public provision for deposit insurance undoubtedly could not be matched by a private insurer; not only does the insurance reserve fund back the deposits, but the full faith and resources of the federal government, including the Federal Reserve, are on the line in the event of massive depository failure. As the depositor views the risks, the deposit–equity ratios of the individual depository firms do not appear to have become low enough to deter depositors, except temporarily at times surrounding a notable depository failure. The influence of the individual firm's asset quality and leveraged position does, however, creep into the structure of risk premiums on uninsured negotiable CDs.

With deposit insurance, deposits became relatively more plentiful to the firm, without the need to maintain large capital balances. The depository firm then finds it to be in its best interests to hold low levels of capital so as to increase the rate of return on equity. That is, there are economic incentives for the depository firm to hold little capital, since deposit insurance reserves are seen by depositors as augmenting firm capital and protecting their claims. This makes deposits more freely available without the necessity to commit large amounts of equity capital. With the earnings of the deposit activity spread over a smaller capital base, this in turn raises rates of return to equity capital. A further motivation to maintain relatively little equity capital arises from the fact that the deposit insurance premiums and the protection afforded by the deposit reserve fund are unrelated to the firm's debt structure. Furthermore, the insurance premium is assessed on deposits and is unrelated to the riskiness of the portfolio. Since the pricing of the insurance premium is unrelated to either leverage or asset risk, regulatory requirements, rather than the pricing of insurance premiums, serves to constrain firms. When the pricing of insurance is unrelated to risk, a conflict between the insurer and the financial firm occurs, since the insurer has been put in the position of bearing risks with no commensurate return. The federal insurer then minimizes its own risk exposure by intervening in the affairs of the depository firm; it limits the riskiness of assets by maintaining "sound" management and by seeing that the financial institutions maintain "adequate" capital.

While the incentive for the depository firm is to hold less capital, the federal depository insurance agencies are motivated by both a concern for their own economic viability and the social cost of financial institution failure. The federal deposit insurance agencies are independent agencies of government and receive no appropriations from Congress. They charge the financial firm a fixed fee per deposit dollar and with these revenues hold portfolios of assets against contingent liability payments as a result of depository failure. In order to maintain their own economic viability, it is in the interest of the depository insurance agencies to increase bank capital to reduce the risk exposure of the agency to large-scale failure.

The ability of federal deposit insurance to prevent financial failure of depository institutions and in particular their cumulative effect is impressive. In the post-World War II period, for example, in only 2 years did more than 10 of the 14,000 banks in the United States fail. When bank failure did result, the failed banks generally had sufficient asset values to cover the payments to depositors. The actual losses incurred by the FDIC between 1934 and 1978 were only $349 million. Table 5.4 contains a

TABLE 5.4

Insured Deposits and the Deposit Insurance Fund, 1934–1978[a]

Year-end	Ratio of deposit insurance fund to	
	Total deposits (%)	Insured deposits (%)
1934	.73	1.61
1935	.68	1.52
1936	.68	1.54
1937	.79	1.70
1938	.83	1.82
1939	.79	1.84
1940	.76	1.86
1941	.78	1.96
1942	.69	1.88
1943	.63	1.45
1944	.60	1.43
1945	.59	1.39
1946	.71	1.44
1947	.65	1.32
1948	.69	1.42
1949	.77	1.57
1950	.74	1.36

TABLE 5.4 (*Continued*)

Year-end	Ratio of deposit insurance fund to	
	Total deposits (%)	Insured deposits (%)
1951	.72	1.33
1952	.72	1.34
1953	.75	1.37
1954	.76	1.39
1955	.77	1.41
1956	.79	1.44
1957	.82	1.46
1958	.81	1.43
1959	.84	1.47
1960	.85	1.48
1961	.84	1.47[b]
1962	.84	1.47[b]
1963	.85	1.50
1964	.82	1.48
1965	.80	1.45
1966	.81	1.39
1967	.78	1.33
1968	.76	1.26
1969	.82	1.29
1970	.80	1.25
1971	.78	1.27[b]
1972	.74	1.23
1973	.73	1.21
1974	.73	1.18
1975	.77	1.18
1976	.77	1.16
1977	.76	1.15
1978	.77	1.16

[a] Source: FDIC, *Annual Report*, 1978, p. 192.

[b] Figures estimated by applying, to the deposits in the various types of account at the regular call dates, the percentages insured as determined from special reports secured from insured banks, revised.

long-term record of FDIC insurance funds and deposit exposure. Though the deposit insurance fund was only slightly more than 1% of insured deposits throughout its entire history, this relatively small deposit insurance fund was sufficient to deter a loss of confidence that might result in depository failure from a domino effect.

To maintain their own integrity, the deposit insuring agencies seek to reduce their own risk. In this way, the insuring agency behaves much like a private insurer. This inherent conflict between the position of the depository firm wishing to reduce capital and the interests of the regulators in increasing capital leaves unresolved the social issue of the adequacy of capital. Not only are the private costs of loss of wealth by depositors at stake, and not only is the managerial integrity of the insuring fund in question, but an optimal rate of bankruptcy that would eliminate inefficient firms is also at issue. Identifying inefficiency is especially difficult when failure could be the result of the backfiring of calculated but sound risk taking. While there might be social benefits from a higher rate of failure, the social cost from cumulative failure and the quasi-private cost to the insurer has led to reluctance by the federal insuring agencies to accept any failure whatsoever.

Aside from the issues of the socially optimal rate of failure and hence a socially optimal capital ratio, the private question of capital adequacy revolves around the question: Can the financial firm meet its obligations? There is both a short-run and a long-run aspect to this question, and there are differences depending on whether losses stem from the current or the capital accounts. Obviously there are young firms that have negative current profits although they will ultimately become profitable. Alternatively, there are firms that have suffered losses in asset values but are otherwise currently profitable and, with the passage of time, will retain sufficient earnings to rebuild their capital base.

Today there are additional considerations rarely encountered before. In periods of high and rising interest rates, loans or securities might not go into default; nevertheless, their market values might diminish as compared to book values. The declining market value of the assets of the financial firm presents little danger if loans are ultimately paid at book value, but a major problem can result, even with positive current profits, if the high interest rates also result in disintermediation. That is, high interest rates not only reduce the market value of assets, but they also tend to cause deposit funds to flow out of financial institutions. If pressed to liquidate assets, the depository firm would be forced to realize capital losses. If disintermediation caused a sufficiently large deposit outflow, this might force the realization of capital losses in excess of the capital accounts. To complicate matters, at least for savings and loan associations, rising interest rates tend to escalate the deposit rate more rapidly than the asset earning rate, thus reducing profit margins from current operations. Therefore the issue of the adequacy of financial institution capital receives more attention when interest rates are rising, as current operating profit might be slim or negative and unrealized and realized asset losses might occur.

Some feel that no government standards need be set to arrive at a suitable level of capital adequacy. This position rests on the assumption that sufficient private incentives exist for the depository firm to maintain adequate capital. The private incentives for capital adequacy rest on the shareholders' concern for the market value of their equity shares. If the financial firm's assets are too risky relative to its earnings per share, then the value of equity shares on the market would be depressed. This in turn would cause the owners of a financial firm a loss in the value of their capital contribution and retained earnings if equity shares are sold in the marketplace. Such a reduction in market values relative to book values was experienced by savings and loan associations in the 1970s. These relationships are shown in Table 5.5. The discipline of the market would also prevent the firm from raising additional capital and debt on capital markets, except under unfavorable terms. The discipline of the market would include the deposit market, especially the noninsured negotiable certificates for which investor reluctance would force the firm to pay higher risk premiums.

Another aspect of the self-imposed desire to maintain capital arises from the cost of bankruptcy. In the following analyses, the change in the firm's net worth, which should include both current profit and changes in the value of assets less liabilities, is analyzed as a random variable. The random variable of changes in equity, denoted ΔE, has a probability density function the expected value of which is generally positive. There is, however, a finite probability that the change in the firm's net worth in each period could be negative, and possibly some of these negative values could exceed the current capital position, E^*. The probability density function

TABLE 5.5

Index of Savings and Loan Prices, Earnings, and Book Values[a]

Year-end	Return on book value	Price × trailing 12-mo. earnings	Price as % of book value
1972	15.3	11.4	160
1973	12.1	4.8	63
1974	7.9	3.9	37
1975	11.8	4.3	43
1976	16.1	4.9	66
1977	20.1	4.0	69
1978	20.6	3.7	68
1979	14.1	4.7	72

[a] In percentages. 1973 = 100. Source: A. G. Becker Incorporated, *Savings and Loan Index*. It is composed of 14 California companies and 10 nonCalifornia companies. Of the 24 companies, 14 are NYSE listed, 4 are ASE listed, and 6 are OTC listed.

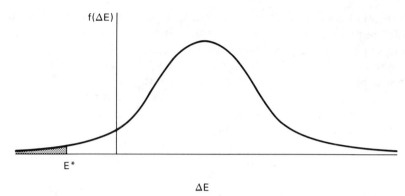

Figure 5.5   Probability density function of changes in net worth.

$f(\Delta E)$ is shown in Figure 5.5. If ΔE falls below E^*, losses are so great that they impair capital and surplus, and the financial firm is then forced into bankruptcy either by creditors or by the regulatory mechanism. It is thus in the firm's interest to set a value of E^* such that the present value of the marginal expected opportunity cost of foregone profits is equal to the marginal opportunity costs of supplying additional capital.

5.3   DIVIDENDS, THE CAPITAL CONSTRAINT, AND THE DEPOSIT RATE

Whatever a proper private or social policy regarding capital adequacy is, we can examine the effect of regulatory-imposed capital requirements on the deposit rate set by the depository institution. We shall assume that the regulatory-required equity position is a minimum fraction of the deposit level. This minimum capital requirement or capital constraint is

$$E = \bar{a}D, \qquad (5.7)$$

where $\bar{a}$ is now the regulatory-imposed minimum capital requirement. Given this imposed capital structure, we can examine the impact of capital adequacy requirements on the behavior of the depository firm.

The major change in the model is that the depository firm must preserve its equity–deposit ratio $\bar{a}$ so that any growth in the deposit level must be matched by proportionate additions to E. The required increase in capital reserves in a given annual period is equal to gE, where g is the annual growth rate of deposits. To meet this required increase in the capital account, the depository firm must set aside a portion of current profits as retained earnings. Current profit available for the payment of dividends is then reduced by an equal amount. Equation (5.8) presents a profit statement. The definition of profit P_d in this case is the profit available for dividend payments to the stockholders. It includes, as in Eq. (5.2), revenues generated by the investment of capital funds in earning assets $r_a bE$, and subtracts the required additions to the capital accounts necessitated by deposit growth. By the maximization of this profit measure, we imply that the depository firm might wish to maximize the profit available for dividend payments.

Making use of a Lagrangian multiplier to incorporate the capital constraint, the profit available for the payment of dividends is

$$P_d = r_a D - rD - C(D) - gE + r_a bE - \lambda(E - \bar{a}D). \qquad (5.8)$$

Profit available for dividend payments is then equal to the sum of the revenues yielded from invested deposits and capital funds, less the interest cost of deposits, the production costs, and the "cost" of making required additions to the capital account. The depository firm is assumed to pursue a policy of maximizing profit with respect to the deposit rate, and it selects a level of equity E, subject to the constraint that the required equity–deposit ratio is maintained. The first-order conditions for an optimum are then

$$\frac{\partial P_d}{\partial r} = r_a \frac{\partial D}{\partial r} - D - r\frac{\partial D}{\partial r} - \frac{\partial C}{\partial D}\frac{\partial D}{\partial r} + \bar{a}\lambda\frac{\partial D}{\partial r} = 0, \qquad (5.9)$$

$$\frac{\partial P_d}{\partial E} = r_a b - g - \lambda = 0, \qquad (5.10)$$

$$\frac{\partial P_d}{\partial \lambda} = E - \bar{a}D = 0. \qquad (5.11)$$

The first-order condition for λ indicates that the depository firm meets the minimum equity–deposit ratio $E/D = \bar{a}$. Though the stockholders must satisfy the minimum equity–deposit ratio, they are only willing to commit equity capital to the firm if it, at the margin, meets their minimum dividend rate criteria k. Setting $\partial P_d/\partial E$ equal to 0 would entail expanding the equity of the firm to the point where the last increment of equity capital earned a zero dividend rate.[13] The stockholder prevents this. Capital has an opportunity cost, and each dollar of equity capital must earn at least k. Therefore, the first-order condition (5.10) for additional equity is constrained to equal k.

$$r_a b - g - \lambda = k. \qquad (5.12)$$

By rearranging Eq. (5.12), we obtain a value for λ, which is substituted into Eq. (5.9) along with the assumed constant deposit elasticity ϵ. The constrained profit-maximizing deposit rate reduces to:

---

[13] The rate k is a marginal dividend rate on equity, whereas $\bar{q}$ from Section 5.1 is a minimum average return on equity capital.

$$r^* = \frac{\epsilon}{1 + \epsilon} \left(r_a(1 + \bar{a}b) - \frac{\partial C}{\partial D} - \bar{a}(g + k) \right).$$ (15.13)

This equation indicates that the deposit rate, as in Chapter 3, depends on net revenues and the proportion of revenues that the firm passes through to the depositor. As before, the depositor's proportion depends on the deposit elasticity. Net revenues per deposit dollar in this case are augmented by additional revenues earned from invested equity capital, where those additional revenues per deposit dollar are equal to $r_a ab$. The term a indicates the number of equity dollars for each deposit dollar, and b is the proportion of those dollars that are invested in earning assets. On the other hand, net revenues for distribution to depositors are reduced by the necessity to set funds aside for deposit growth and dividend payments. The amount of these funds per deposit dollar is $a(g + k)$. For capital requirements, this amount is ag or Eg/D, where the market growth rate times the equity base determines the required additions to retained earnings, and dividing by D places these required additions on a per deposit dollar basis. Similarly, ak is the dividend payout per deposit dollar. These rates $g + k$ represent the sum of the two costs of equity capital, with the payout rate determined by alternative market choices and the retention rate dictated by the growth rate of the deposit market.

When these two costs of capital are considered, they put downward pressure on net revenues and in turn on deposit rates. Hence, they tend to reduce firm size. As seen in Figure 5.1, a smaller deposit size, up to a point, tends to elevate profit margins. The firm adjusts to its capital costs by reducing deposit rates and deposit levels. Hence we obtain the interesting result that with a need to build capital imposed by a capital adequacy constraint, a fast-growing deposit market would cause the firm to pay lower deposit rates and actually restrain its deposit size at each point in time, since

$$\frac{\partial r^*}{\partial g} = -\frac{\epsilon}{1 + \epsilon} \bar{a} < 0.$$ (5.14)

Operating in a growth market would actually cause the firm to be less aggressive in seeking deposits in order to build up its capital accounts. This constraint would exist unless the firm was willing to sacrifice current dividend payments for deposit growth.

An examination of the optimal deposit rate reveals the impacts of regulatory capital requirements. The effect of a larger equity–deposit ratio or a higher value of $\bar{a}$ is given by Eq. (5.15):

$$\frac{\partial r^*}{\alpha \bar{a}} = \frac{\epsilon}{1 + \epsilon} (r_a b - (g + k)).$$ (5.15)

Higher capital ratios and the greater need to retain earnings would probably reduce deposit rates. This effect depends on the value of $r_a b$ compared to $g + k$. The first term is the revenue per equity dollar from invested capital, and the second term is the cost per equity dollar. Since b is
less than 1, and since it is unlikely that the asset earning rate would be
much greater than the target or minimum rate of return (since the asset
earning rate is a weighted average including cash reserves), it is likely that
the sum of the costs of capital ($g + k$) would exceed $r_a b$, the revenues
directly earned from invested capital. If there is negative growth, and g is
less than 0, the issue is somewhat unclear. In this case, with negative
growth in the deposit market, it is permissible not only to pay out all profit
in dividends, but it is quite possible to pay out previous retained earnings
in current dividends. In general, if the regulatory-imposed capital or
equity–deposit ratios exceeds private optimal capital ratios, increase in
the required capital ratio reduces deposit rates and deposit levels; if the
firm wishes to maintain its size, it can only do so at the cost of current dividends. In this way capital ratios affect deposit size and dividend rates.

5.4 TAXATION AND THE DEPOSIT RATE

In general, depository institutions are subject to the same tax rules as
any other profit-seeking corporation. However, Congress has allowed
special deductions for the depository firm, which has tended to reduce
their average and marginal tax rates. The major difference between the
tax treatment of the production firm and the depository firm is the opportunity to tax-shelter income by setting up tax-free loss reserve accounts.
These bad debt deductions, which are available to banks and thrift institutions, are in effect a device to reduce tax rates for qualifying institutions,
since these bad debt reserves have greatly exceeded any reasonable expectation of loss. The treatment of loss reserves differs between commercial banks and thrifts, and there are differences among thrifts.

In addition to this device that shelters earnings from taxation, large
commercial banks, owing to other tax advantages, generally pay a lower
average tax rate than do thrifts. The lower average rate for large banks results from other means of sheltering income, such as investments in
tax-exempt bonds, foreign operations that generate credits against United
States tax liabilities, and equipment leasing that generates high depreciation deductions and investment tax credits.

Apart from these specific tax advantages, we shall concentrate on the
effects of the bad debt allowance on the deposit rate setting activity of the
depository firm. The taxation of depository institutions rests on the com-

putation of taxable income and the loss reserve deductions therefrom, as outlined in Subchapter H of the Internal Revenue Code (hereafter referred to by section only).

For a commercial bank, the first requirement is that a banking organization meet the definition provided by the code. Section 581 defines a bank as any organization incorporated under the laws of the United States, the District of Columbia, any state, or any territory. The definition includes the following conditions: a substantial part of the organization's business consists of receiving deposits and making loans and discounts or exercising fiduciary powers similar to those permitted to national banks under the authority of the Comptroller of the Currency, and the organization is subject by law to supervision and examination by a state, territorial or federal authority that supervises banking institutions. Consequently, those organizations that enjoy the status of banks, in addition to deducting all ordinary and necessary expenses (similar to other corporate taxpayers), require special treatment with regard to reserves for bad debts, net operating losses, and sale of corporate or government bonds.

Commercial banks had been allowed favorable treatment in the computation of their bad debt reserves. However, these rules were substantially restricted as a result of the Tax Reform Act of 1969 and will be totally eliminated by 1988. Nevertheless, tax rules are still relatively more advantageous for commercial banks compared to other corporate taxpayers, at least until the end of 1987. Presently, Section 166 is the controlling authority for the deduction of bad debts by commercial banks (via Section 582(a)). Either of two methods are permitted: the specific charge-off method under Section 166(a), or the reserve method under Section 166(c). In general, there is a tax advantage from using the reserve method.

Under the reserve method, Section 585 governs the rules applicable for additions to the reserve. These additions are provided through the *experience* or *percentage* method. However, after 1987 only the experience method will be available.

In computing an addition to reserves under the experience method, a bank will compute a ratio of total bad debts for its six most recent taxable years, including the current year (adjusted for recoveries of bad debts), to the sum of loans outstanding at the close of each of the 6 years. This computed ratio will be applied to loans outstanding at the close of the current taxable year, and the results will constitute the permissible reserve balance. Thus, the additions to reserves in the current year will be the amount required to bring the reserves up to the permissible balance.

When computing additions to reserves under the percentage method, a bank must first determine the ratio of its actual reserve for bad debts at the close of a "base" year to its eligible loans outstanding at that time.

Every year thereafter, the bank may increase its reserves for losses to the allowable percentage, subject to certain limitations. As mentioned earlier, the allowable percentage is gradually being phased out, as illustrated below:

Taxable years	Base year	Maximum allowable percentage of eligible loans
1970–1975	1969	1.08
1976–1981	1975	1.2
1982–1987	1981	0.6

An overall limitation applies to the amount added to a bank's reserves under the percentage method in any single taxable year. The maximum addition to bad debt reserves is the greater of .6% of eligible loans outstanding or the amount necessary to bring the reserve up to .6% of eligible loans.

On the other hand, the specific charge-off method simply deducts bad debts as they are wholly or partially realized. This procedure, however, would seldom be used, since under the percentage method a bank is usually able to make additions to reserves that are greater than those justified under the bank's actual experience.

In addition to the special treatment already mentioned, financial institutions are subject to Section 582(c)(1), which requires that sales and exchanges of bonds, debentures, notes, and other forms of indebtedness not be considered a capital assets. Thus, banks and all financial institutions do not receive capital gain or loss treatment on these assets, but must instead recognize gains or losses as ordinary income or losses. Congress felt that banks often act as dealers in these securities, and without this restriction, would be allowed preferential capital gain treatment from the turnover of their inventory of assets. Still, this requirement should prove advantageous for banks more often. This is because banks are more likely to sell these items to obtain loanable funds when the demand for loanable funds is high and correspondingly interest rates are high. Consequently, the disposal of these assets will generally occur during periods of high loan rates, which will result in the realization of ordinary losses that can be used to offset ordinary income.

Mutual savings banks, cooperative banks, and domestic building and loan associations (all referred to as institutions) enjoyed exemption from taxation until 1951. At that time, the 1939 code was amended to make the treatment of these institutions more like that of commercial banks, but they were still allowed special treatment with respect to (1) bad debt reserves, (2) "dividends" paid to depositors, (3) repayment of United States loans, (4) life insurance departments, (5) acquisition of mortgages, (6) foreclosure on property securing loans, and (7) dividends receiving deductions. While these special tax attributes are all quite important for the tax treatment of the institutions, only the treatment of bad debt reserves will be addressed in this section.

The term *cooperative bank* is defined by the statute in Section 7701(a)(32) as an institution *without* capital stock that is organized and operated for mutual purposes but not for profit. The institution must meet requirements (A), (B), and (C) imposed on domestic building and loan associations. Presently, those requirements include

A. that the institution must be either an insured institution under the National Housing Act, or be subject by law to supervision and examination by state or federal authorities;
B. that its business consists principally of acquiring the savings of the public and investing in loans;
C. that at least 60% of its assets, at the end of the year consist of cash, government obligations, secured urban renewal or other residential real estate loans, loans secured by a deposit or share of a member, real estate acquired by default, loans secured by university or hospital property, college tuition loans, and property used by the institution in its business.

Credit unions, though mutual in form, do not qualify and are exempt from taxation.

Despite the 1954 amendment to the code that subjected these depository institutions to taxation, most institutions did not have to pay income tax however, because of the liberal reserve method allowed in accounting for bad debts. These provisions allowed the savings institutions to make tax-free additions to a bad debt reserve equal to the lesser of its taxable income before the bad debt deductions for that year, or the excess of 12% of total deposits at the end of the year over the sum of profits and reserves at the beginning of the year. Since this 12% limitation would only be operative with extraordinary high profit levels and low reserve levels, it was seldom applicable, and thus these institutions were allowed a bad debt deduction equal to their entire taxable income. As a result, a tax liability was rarely incurred.

The Revenue Acts of 1962 and 1969 served to curtail this liberal benefit by requiring that two deductible reserves for bad debts be established; the first for nonqualifying loans (simply loans that were not secured by improved real property), which required the institutions to make additions to reserves based on the experience method (identical to that used for banks). The second reserve was for "qualifying real property loans"; however, additions to these reserves could be based on any of three methods: the actual experience, percentage of real property loans, or the percentage of taxable income. The percentage of taxable income method has been used most often by financial institutions, since it provided the greatest deduction. However, the Revenue Act of 1969 has scheduled a gradual reduction in its benefits.

Computation of the addition to bad debt reserves under the percentage of income method is based on the institutions' adjusted taxable income. Presently 40% of income may be deducted in computing the tax-free additions to reserves. The savings and loans only qualify for the full 40% bad debt deduction if 82% or more of their investments are in qualifying assets, and a mutual savings bank can qualify for the 40% bad debt deduction only if 72% or more of its investments are in qualifying assets. These are not "all or nothing" tests. The percentage of deductible income declines by .75% for each percentage decline in qualifying assets below 82% for savings and loans. For mutual savings banks, the deduction declines by 1.5% for each percentage decline below 72%. When the investment in qualifying assets drops below 60% for savings and loans and 50% for mutual savings banks, the institutions do not qualify for the use of this method of tax sheltering.

Regardless of the method of calculating tax-free additions to the capital accounts, it is possible to analyze the effect of taxation on the depository firm as if there were two tax rates. The first tax rate τ is the tax subsidy applicable to retained earnings, while t is the average tax rate applicable to overall earnings. Although this is a simplification that does not exactly correspond to present tax treatment, it will serve as a useful approximation. As in the previous section, the firm is assumed to maximize profit available for dividend payouts, except that in this case, after tax profit P_d^t is relevant. This expression is

$$P_d^t = r_a D - rD - C(D) + r_a bE - t(r_a D - rD - C(D) + r_a bE)$$

$$- gE + \tau gE - \lambda(E - \bar{a}D). \tag{5.16}$$

The value of τ can range between 0 and infinity. If τ is equal to 1, the tax subsidy is exactly equal to additions to the capital account. From the brief review of the history of tax treatment of the depository firm, the value of τ has been defined in various ways and was sometimes large enough so that the tax shelter exceeded any tax liabilities. At other times there has been only partial coverage of the taxable income of the depository firm.

The after-tax profit available for dividends depends on current profits. The first term of Eq. (5.16) represents before-tax current profit from deposit activity and from invested equity funds. The second term represents the tax liability from current operations. From these after-tax profits, the required increase in the reserve accounts gE necessitated by the capital constraint is deducted, and the tax subsidy τgE is added. The tax subsidy, while not always defined as a multiple of retained earnings, can nonetheless be considered in this way, since the tax subsidy is justified by making additions to the reserve accounts. The effective value of τ depends on the current tax policy.

Maximizing after-tax profit available for dividend payments, subject to the Lagrangian constraint that the capital ratio $\bar{a}$ is satisfied, results in the following first-order conditions:

$$\frac{\partial P_d^t}{\partial r} = \left(r_a \frac{\partial D}{\partial r} - D - r \frac{\partial D}{\partial r} - \frac{\partial C}{\partial D}\frac{\partial D}{\partial r} \right)(1 - t) + \bar{a}\lambda \frac{\partial D}{\partial r} = 0 \quad (5.17)$$

$$\frac{\partial P_d^t}{\partial \lambda} = E - \bar{a}D = 0 \quad (5.18)$$

$$\frac{\partial P_d^t}{\partial E} = r_a b(1 - t) - g(1 - \tau) - \lambda = k. \quad (5.19)$$

Again, setting the marginal profitability of equity to the required rate of return k in Eq. (5.19) and substituting into Eq. (5.17) results in the following optimum deposit rate:

$$r^* = \frac{\epsilon}{1 + \epsilon}\left(r_a(1 + \bar{a}b) - \frac{\partial C}{\partial D} - \bar{a}\left(\frac{1 - \tau}{1 - t}g + \frac{1}{1 - t}k \right) \right). \quad (5.20)$$

From Eq. (5.20) it can be seen that if the depository firms sought to maximize after-tax profits available for dividend payouts, the tax liability would tend to reduce the deposit rate, and the tax subsidy would tend to increase the deposit rate. That is, the firm, in seeking to simultaneously meet capital requirements and target rates of return after paying its tax liability, will use its deposit rate as a means to adjust to these constraints. Lower deposit rates reduce the deposit level and tend to increase profit margins. With a lower deposit level, the higher profit margin is then sufficient to generate enough earnings per equity dollar to make required additions to the capital accounts and still meet the target after-tax dividend rate.

BIBLIOGRAPHY

Apilado, V. P., and Gies, T. G. "Capital Adequacy and Commercial Bank Failure," *The Bankers Magazine*, **13**, Summer 1972.

Baltensperger, E. "Cost of Bank Activities: Interaction Between Risk and Operating Cost," *Journal of Money, Credit and Banking*, **4**, August 1972.

Baumol, William. *Business Behavior, Value, and Growth*. New York: Harcourt, 1967.

Beighley, H. Prescott, Boyd, John H., and Jacobs, Donald P. "Bank Equities and Investor Risk Perceptions: Some Entailments for Capital Adequacy Regulation," *Journal of Bank Research*, **6**, Autumn 1975.

Bierman, H., Chopra, F., and Thomas, J. "Ruin Considerations: Optimal Working Capital and Capital Structure," *Journal of Financial and Quantitative Analysis*, **10**, May 1975.

Buser, Stephen A., Chen, Andrew H., and Kane, Edward J. "Implicit and Explicit Prices of Deposit Insurance and the Bank Capital Decision." In *Proceedings of a Conference on Bank Structure and Competition*, Federal Reserve Bank of Chicago, May 1980.

Edwards, Franklin R. "Managerial Objectives in Regulated Industries: Expense-Preference Behavior in Banking," *Journal of Political Economy*, **85**, February 1977.

Eisenbeis, R. A. "Financial Early Warning Systems: Status and Future Directions," *Issues in Bank Regulation*, **2**, Summer 1977.

Erikson, Walter E. "Capital Adequacy—Why?", *Federal Home Loan Bank Board Journal*, **10**, September 1977.

Gibson, W. E. "Deposit Insurance in the U.S.: Evaluation and Reform," *Journal of Financial and Quantitative Analysis*, **7**, March 1972.

Goodman, Laurie, and Sharpe, William F. "Perspective on Bank Capital Adequacy: A Time Series Analysis," National Bureau of Economic Research, Working Paper No. 247, May 1978.

Goodman, Laurie, and Sharpe, William F. "Comparative Measures of Bank Capital Adequacy," Salomon Brothers Center for the Study of Financial Institutions, Working Paper No. 174, July 1979.

Hadaway, Beverly L., and Hadaway, Samuel C. "An Investigation of the Impact of Savings and Loan Association Conversions from Mutual to Stock Form of Ownership," Federal Home Loan Bank Board, Research Working Paper No. 36, July 1980.

Hanweck, Gerald A. *Projected Bank Equity Capital Requirements Through 1979: A Simulation Model Approach*, Board of Governors, Federal Reserve System, November 1975.

Herzig-Marx, Chayim. "Financial Disclosure and Market Evaluations of Bank Debt Securities," Federal Reserve Bank of Chicago, Research Paper No. 76-4, 1976.

Hester, Donald D., "Ownership and Behavior in the Savings and Loan Industry." In *Conversion of Mutual Savings & Loan Associations to Stock Form: Legal and Economic Issues*, Federal Home Loan Bank Board, 1967.

Horovitz, Paul M. "Failures of Large Banks: Implications for Banking Supervision," *Journal of Financial and Quantitative Analysis*, **10**, November 1975.

Jahankhani, A. "Commercial Bank Financial Policies and Their Impact on Market-Determined Measures of Risk," *Journal of Bank Research*, **11**, Autumn 1980.

Kaplan, Donald M., and Smith, David L. *The Role of Short-Term Debt in Savings and Loan Management*. Federal Home Loan Bank of San Francisco, December 1979.

Malkiel, Burton G. *The Debt–Equity Combination of the Firm and the Cost of Capital: An Introductory Analysis*. New York: General Learning Press, 1971.

Mayer, T. "A Graduated Deposit Insurance Plan," *Review of Economics and Statistics*, **47**, February 1965.

Mayer, T. "Should Large Banks be Allowed to Fail?" *Journal of Financial and Quantitative Analysis*, **10**, November 1975.

Meyer, P. A., and Pifer, H. W. "Prediction of Bank Failures," *Journal of Finance*, **25**, September 1970.

Mingo, John. "Managerial Motives, Market Structures and the Performance of Holding Company Banks," *Economic Inquiry*, September 1976.

Mingo, John, and Wolkowitz, Benjamin. *The Cost of Capital and the Effects of Regulation on Bank Balance Sheet Decisions*. Board of Governors, Federal Reserve System, July 1974.

Morrison, Jay, "Interest-Rate Elasticity and Capital Adequacy in Commercial Banking: A Preliminary Investigation." Mimeographed. Berkeley, Calif.: University of California, Graduate School of Business, April 1976.

Peltzman, Sam. "Capital Investment in Commercial Banking," *Journal of Political Economy*, **78**, 1970.

Pringle, John J. "The Capital Decision in Commerical Banks," *Journal of Finance*, **29**, June 1974.

Rees, R. "A Reconsideration of the Expense Preference Theory of the Firm," *Economia*, **41**, August 1974.

Ryon, Sandra L. "History of Bank Capital Adequacy Analysis," Financial and Economic Research Section, Federal Insurance Corporation, Working Paper No. 69-4, 1969.

Santomero, Anthony M., and Watson, R. D. "Determining an Optimal Standard for the Banking Industry," *Journal of Finance*, **32**, September 1977.

Santomero, Anthony M. "Risk and Capital in Financial Institutions." Mimeographed. Federal Home Loan Bank of San Francisco, December 1979.

Sharpe, William F. "Bank Capital Adequacy, Deposit Insurance and Security Values," *Journal of Financial and Quantitative Analysis*, **13**, November 1978.

Shick, Richard A. "Bank Stock Prices as an Early Warning System for Changes in Condition," *Journal of Bank Research*, **11**, Autumn 1980.

Sinkey, Joseph F., Jr. *Problem and Failed Institutions in the Commercial Banking Industry*, Greenwich, Conn.: JAI Press, 1979.

Taggart, R. A., and Greenbaum, St. I. "Bank Capital and Public Regulation," *Journal of Money, Credit and Banking*, **10**, May 1978.

Tussing, A. D. "The Case for Bank Failures," *Journal of Law and Economics*, **10**, October 1967.

Verbrugge, James A., and Goldstein, Steven J. "Risk Return, and Managerial Objectives: Some Evidence from the Savings and Loan Industry," *Journal of Financial Research*, **4**, Spring 1981.

Vernon, J. "Ownership and Control Among Large Member Banks," *Journal of Finance*, **25**, June 1970.

Vernon, J. "Separation of Ownership and Control and Profit Rates: the Evidence from Banking: Comment," *Journal of Financial and Quantitative Analysis*, **6**, January 1971.

Weaver, Anne S., and Herzig-Marx, Chayim. "A Comparative Study of the Effect of Leverage on Risk Premiums for Debt Issues of Banks and Bank Holding Companies," Federal Reserve Bank of Chicago, Research Paper No. 78-1, 1978.

Witt, Robert C. "Pricing, Investment Income, and Underwriting Risk: A Stochastic View," *Journal of Risk and Insurance*, **41**, March 1974.

Williamson, O. "Managerial Discretion and Business Behavior," *American Economic Review*, **53**, December 1963.

Wolkowitz, Benjamin, "Bank Capital: The Regulator Versus the Market." In *The Deregulation of the Banking and Securities Industries*, eds. Lawerence G. Goldberg and Lawrence J. White. Lexington, Mass.: Lexington, 1979.

CHAPTER 6

The Costs of Disintermediation, Cash Reserves, and Short-Term Debt

6.1 THE COSTS OF DISINTERMEDIATION AND OPTIMAL CASH RESERVES

The depository firm, unlike the production firm, is faced with a unique problem arising from the continuing contractual claim of depositors. The financial claim issued by the depository firm in exchange for currency usually imposes upon the firm an obligation to return currency at a future time chosen by the claimant. The contractual obligation of returning currency, or the depository firm's raw material, creates an uncertain event and also imposes a cost on the depository firm—a cost that is not similarly borne by the production firm.

Because of the depositors' contractual liquidation rights, the depository firm could suffer net deposit losses or disintermediation. The prospect of disintermediation causes the firm to prepare for this contingency by holding some cash, obtaining lines of credit, and developing relationships with other financial institutions so that assets can be sold (perhaps with a repurchase agreement) to obtain liquidity on short notice. All of these options for attaining liquidity incur costs. There are the costs of managing the liquidity position, the costs of borrowing, the transaction costs from the sale of earning assets, and the opportunity costs from foregone revenue when noninterest or low-interest liquid assets are held in portfolios. The object is to find the minimum costs for any given appraisal of the prospective deposit outflows in the next market period. Since deposit outflows are an uncertain event, the deposit outflow is described by a probability density function that assigns a probability to each level of net deposit outflows or inflows in the following time period. In each economic situation, the depository firm has a subjective probability distribution of net inflows and outflows. In a growth environment, the expected value of random deposit fluctuations might reflect expected deposit inflows. However, even in a growth environment there is still a finite probability that net deposit outflows will occur, and though disintermediation is not likely, there is still a potential for it. In another environment—perhaps where the financial market is yielding high market rates relative to those the institutions can pay—the expected value of the change in deposits might be negative. In both cases, whether or not disintermediation is anticipated (as measured by the expected value of the probability distribution) or realized, there are costs incurred in preparing for this contingency, and it is the objective of the depository firm to keep these costs to a minimum. It does so by holding cash reserves and by borrowing reserves. The levels of reserves held in cash and anticipated borrowing, although strongly influenced by the firm's expectations of deposit outflows, are also affected by the opportunity costs of holding cash reserves, as well as the explicit costs of borrowing reserves.

As before, the depository firm operates in an imperfectly competitive deposit market and accepts all deposits at a rate it specifies. Thus the deposit demand equation, (3.1), still holds. The depository firm then purchases earning assets in a perfectly competitive asset market in which it is a rate taker and quantity setter. The firm also allocates some of its funds to cash reserves or money balances, M. The level of cash reserves or the proportion of reserves to deposits is an endogenous decision of the depository firm that is assumed to be free of regulatory minimums.

The timing of events is important. At the beginning of a period the firm sets a deposit rate r, attracts an initial level of deposits D, and purchases or makes a commitment to purchase a level $D - M$ of the earning asset which it holds for the entire period. This purchase of $D - M$ of the earning asset occurs before the depository firm knows the level of random withdrawals V by its depositors. It is assumed that the random net withdrawals, or disintermediation V, occur immediately after the financial firm makes this commitment. The implication of this assumption is that the firm incurs illiquidity costs for insufficient cash if $V > M$, since it must either borrow funds or liquidate assets. An additional implication of the assumptions made is that if borrowing is necessary because withdrawals exceed cash reserves, the reserves are borrowed and illiquidity costs are incurred for the entire period.

It is assumed that, given the firm's market environment, it postulates a continuous and differentiable conditional probability density function for $V, f(V|D)$. That is, positive values of V are net outflows or disintermediation that have an upper limit of total deposits D. Negative values of V are random net inflows where $|Z|$ is the maximum possible net deposit level the depository firm could attract. The lower limit depends on the size of financial markets from which the firm could draw deposits. The mean or the expected value of the distribution of V is defined to be L so that $E(V) = L$. If the firm anticipates disintermediation or a deposit loss, L is positive; conversely with deposit growth, deposit loss L is negative and the (positive) growth rate is $-L/D$. At this point it is useful to assume that the firm is in a static deposit environment and that L is 0.

If disintermediation levels exceed the money balances M set aside for this contingency, the firm is then assumed to meet these reserve needs by borrowing or selling assets[1] at a known penalty or borrowing rate r_p, where it is assumed that $r_p > r_a > 0$. The realized or ex post illiquidity cost[2] for insufficient reserves is $(r_p)(V - M)$ if $V \geq M$, but the ex ante or the expected penalty cost the firm uses in its planning is

$$r_p \int_M^D (V - M) f(V|D) \, dV. \tag{6.1}$$

In addition to the expected illiquidity cost for insufficient reserves, the depository firm incurs a production cost for factor inputs and an interest cost for deposits. It is assumed that the production cost depends only on initial deposits D. All transaction costs for administering the cash position are assumed to be included in r_p. Production cost is denoted by $C(D)$ and the deposit interest cost by rD. Note that the expected interest cost is rD, since interest is only paid for deposits made at the beginning of the period.

Now let us turn to the revenues of the depository firm. Revenues accrue as a return per period to those deposits that are invested in earning assets but are not committed to money balances, $D - M$. These period revenues are denoted $(r_a)(D - M)$, where r_a is the asset earning rate. (Notice that r_a, for the purposes of this chapter only, is the earning rate on invested assets, whereas it was previously defined to be the rate on all assets, including cash reserves.)

The objective function of the depository firm is assumed to be the maximization of the expected value $E(P)$ of the period profits. From the preceding assumptions, it follows that this is given by Eq. (6.2):

$$E(P) = r_a(D - M) - rD - C(D) - r_p \int_M^D (V - M) f(V|D) \, dV. \tag{6.2}$$

---

[1] If liquidity is obtained by sale of assets, r_p is the discount rate, including transaction costs.

[2] Note that it is possible to have disintermediation without incurring ex post borrowing costs if $0 < V < M$. However, liquidity costs would still be incurred if $M > 0$.

To obtain the optimal reserve level M^* for a given D, we maximize the objective function (6.2) with respect to M, which yields the following first-order condition (6.3):

$$-r_a + r_p \int_{M^*}^{D} f(V|D) \, dV = 0. \qquad (6.3)$$

Note that this is equivalent to minimizing the costs of deposit uncertainty CU with respect to M:

$$CU = r_a M - r_p \int_{M}^{D} (V - M) f(V|D) \, dV. \qquad (6.4)$$

From this expression it can be seen that the depository firm establishes cash reserve at an optimal level M^* by setting the marginal opportunity cost of holding cash reserves equal to the expected marginal penalty cost from being illiquid. At this point the total cost of deposit uncertainty is at a minimum. This is shown in Figure 6.1.

Rearranging Eq. (6.3) gives a particularly useful form of the first-order condition for optimal reserves M^*:

$$\int_{M^*}^{D} f(V|D) \, dV = \frac{r_a}{r_p}. \qquad (6.5)$$

That is, cash reserves M are adjusted until an M^* is found such that the cumulative probability of disintermediation at or above M^* is equal to the ratio of asset and borrowing rates r_a/r_p. This is shown in Figure 6.2. If the borrowing rates increase relative to the asset rate (hence reducing r_a/r_p),

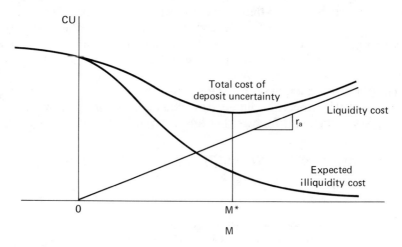

Figure 6.1   Liquidity Cost, illiquidity cost, and optimum cash reserves.

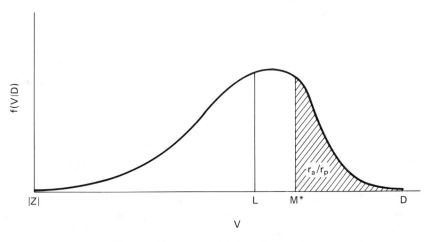

Figure 6.2 The probability of borrowing.

then M^* is increased to reduce the probability of incurring more expensive borrowing costs.

Note that M^* is contingent on D in Eq. (6.5) and that D is in turn contingent on the deposit rate r via Eq. (3.1). Since Eq. (6.5) must hold for any deposit rate, changes in r and hence changes in D will produce changes in M^*, which must continue to equal the unchanged ratio r_a/r_p. That is, M^* must be adjusted so that the cumulative probability of disintermediation at levels equal to or above M^* are the same for the new deposit level:

$$\frac{\partial}{\partial D}\left[\int_{M^*}^{D} f(V|D)\, dV\right] = f(D|D) + \int_{M^*}^{D} \frac{\partial f}{\partial D}\, dV - f(M^*|D)\frac{\partial M^*}{\partial D}$$

$$= 0. \tag{6.6}$$

Solving Eq. (6.6) for $\partial M^*/\partial D$ yields Eq. (6.7):

$$\frac{\partial M^*}{\partial D} = \left(f(D|D) + \int_{M^*}^{D}\frac{\partial f}{\partial D}\, dV\right)/(f(M^*|D)) \tag{6.7}$$

It can be seen that the response of optimal reserves to deposits depends on the value of the probability density function at both M^* and D, and depends also on the cumulative change in the density function between M^* and D. That is, when deposits increase, the probability density function for disintermediation can also change. The change in cash reserves for a higher deposit level could possibily become negative if, for example, the response to higher deposit rates is a reduction in the probability of disintermediation above the optimal reserve level. Optimal reserve ratios could also be constant. This, of course, occurs when the marginal reserve ratio $\partial M^*/\partial D$ is equal to the average reserve ratio M^*/D. The most plausible event is that higher deposit rates will tend to attract interest-sensitive or volatile deposits. In this case the "hot money" could alter the probability density function sufficiently to not only increase absolute levels of M^*, but also the M^*/D average reserve ratio.

6.2 DEPOSIT UNCERTAINTY AND SHORT-TERM DEBT

From the previous section, cash reserves M^* are adjusted so that an optimal cash reserve level is found such that the cumulative probability of disintermediation between M^* and D is equal to the fraction r_a/r_p.

The value of M^* is positive if the cumulative probability density from 0 to D is greater than the ratio of the asset rate relative to the penalty rate. That is, M^* is positive if

$$\int_0^D f(V|D) \, dV > \frac{r_a}{r_p}. \tag{6.8}$$

If the firm were in a stable deposit market, the expected value of random withdrawals would be 0. This implies that the cumulative probability function between 0 and D would be $\frac{1}{2}$ and that optimal reserves are positive only when the penalty rate is at least twice the asset earning rate.

At first glance, it is difficult to imagine penalty rates being twice asset earning rates, when depository institutions have access to short-term loan markets. Access to the discount window of the Federal Reserve is available to all depository institutions offering reservable transaction accounts and federal funds markets are available for all banks at rates which are generally below asset earning rates. However, it must be pointed out that it is assumed that the transactions cost and the administrative cost of the cash balance decision are incorporated into r_p. Furthermore, it has been pointed out by Shull that financial institutions are reluctant to borrow because of implicit costs associated with borrowing.[3] As for savings and loan associations, the assumption of penalty rates in excess of earning rates is somewhat more realistic, as rates on Federal Home Loan Bank advances generally exceed earning rates.

To more flexibly analyze the cash reserve level relative to the asset and

---

[3] Bernard Shull, "Report on Research Undertaken in Connection with a System Study," in *Reappraisal of the Federal Reserve Discount Mechanism* (Board of Governors, Federal Reserve System, August 1971).

borrowing rates, one must ask whether those lending to depository institutions would require increasing risk premiums as indebtedness increases. A more realistic assumption would seem to be that short-term borrowing rates increase with the amount of borrowing. In that case, r_p is functionally related to the amount of borrowing $V - M$:

$$r_p = r_p(V - M) \qquad \frac{\partial r_p}{\partial (V - M)} > 0. \qquad (6.9)$$

With this assumption, the cost of holding and possibly borrowing reserves is given by

$$CU = r_a M + \int_M^D r_p(V - M)(V - M) f(V|D) \, dV. \qquad (6.10)$$

The first-order condition for a minimization of cost with respect to the amount of reserves is

$$r_a = \int_{M^*}^D \left(\left(\frac{\partial r_p}{\partial (V - M)} \right) (V - M^*) + r_p \right) f(V|D) \, dV. \qquad (6.11)$$

It is also possible that in equilibrium, optimal cash reserves might be negative. Optimal negative reserves can be interpreted as ex ante or planned short-term debt as contrasted to the ex post borrowing that might take place if disintermediation exceeds M^*. That is, if the expected penalty cost from being illiquid is sufficiently small, firms will hold no cash and borrow in short-term money markets. If disintermediation were to occur, they would meet this contingency by adding to their short-term borrowings.

The level of planned cash holdings or planned indebtedness and its relationship to comparative asset and borrowing rates is more easily analyzed by evaluating the costs of deposit uncertainty on a per account basis. In this case, d, v, m, l, and z will denote their upper case counterparts on a per account basis, and n is the number of accounts. Let us further assume a homogeneous population of depositors each with deposit balances d. The random deposit withdrawal for the ith depositor is v_i, and the financial firm's probability density function for net deposit withdrawals for all depositors is $h(\bar{v}|n)$, where $\bar{v}$ is the firm's average deposit loss for its n deposit accounts. The depository firm experiences an average per account loss $\bar{v}$, and the probability density function of average losses from all depositors is normally distributed according to the central limit theorem. The probability density function $h(\bar{v}|n)$ is conditional on the number of accounts n with an expected value l or $E(\bar{v}|n) = \int_z^d h(\bar{v}|n) \, d\bar{v} = l$. If the depository firm has a homogeneous population of depositors who are independently distributed, then the expected value of the per account loss $\bar{\nu}$ is independent of n, or

$$\frac{dl}{dn} = 0. \tag{6.12}$$

But by the law of large numbers, the variance of the distribution Λ will decrease as n becomes larger

$$\frac{d\Lambda\,(\bar{\nu}|n)}{dn} < 0. \tag{6.13}$$

In the extreme case in which n becomes infinitely large, the variation of the firm's average deposit losses per account disappears, and the conditional probability density function $h(\bar{\nu}|n)$ collapses into a mass point probability density function with a value of 1 at the point $\bar{\nu} = l$ with value 0 elsewhere. That is, with a large number of independent depositors net withdrawals approach l, which is known with virtual certainty as the variance of the distribution of per account losses disappears.

Given these assumptions the optimal cash balance is obtained by minimizing the sum of the liquidity cost $r_a mn$ and the illiquidity cost $n \int_m^d r_p(\bar{\nu} - m)h(\bar{\nu}|d)\,d\bar{\nu}$, where now $r_p = r_p(\bar{\nu} - m)$.

Deposit uncertainty costs are $r_a mn + n \int_m^d r_p(\bar{\nu} - m)h(\bar{\nu}|d)\,d\bar{\nu}$, and the first-order condition for a minimum with respect to m is

$$r_a = \int_{m^*}^d \left(\frac{\partial r_p}{\partial(\bar{\nu} - m)}\,(\bar{\nu} - m^*) + r_p \right) h(\bar{\nu}|n)\,d\bar{\nu}. \tag{6.14}$$

As the number of depositors becomes large or as n approaches infinity, the probability density function collapses to a mass point at $\bar{\nu} = l$, and thus

$$r_a = \left(\frac{\partial r_p}{\partial(\bar{\nu} - m)} \right)(l - m^*) + r_p. \tag{6.15}$$

Solving for m^*, or optimal cash holdings per deposit account, yields

$$m^* = l + \left((r_p - r_a) \bigg/ \left(\frac{\partial r_p}{\partial(\bar{\nu} - m)} \right) \right). \tag{6.16}$$

Thus cash or money balances per account depends on l in such a way that as anticipated net deposit outflow per account increases, the result is higher cash balances per account. Conversely, if deposit growth is anticipated, l is negative, and it is possible that negative values of cash balances will be held. To reiterate, the interpretation of negative cash balances is planned or ex ante short-term borrowing in money markets where this short-term money market debt might be retired each period with the anticipated deposit inflows. In an alternative adjustment mechanism, depository firms could make loan commitments in excess of current free reserve levels, to be financed by expected future deposit inflows. If disintermediation were to occur (the probability of which is low), the depository firm would meet this contingency with additional short-term borrowing.

The economic incentives for short-term debt holdings for the depository firm are seen more clearly in this formulation. The interest rate–debt relationship is more transparent when the cash position is unaffected by either expected deposit growth or disintermediation. When the anticipated growth rate of deposits is 0, then money holding per account is

$$m^* = (r_p - r_a)\bigg/\left(\frac{\partial r_p}{\partial(\bar{\nu} - m)}\right). \tag{6.17}$$

With the rising cost of funds schedule, positive cash balances are held when the equilibrium borrowing rate exceeds the asset rate, but not by the necessary 2:1 ratio of Eq. (6.8). Also, as borrowing rates rise relative to the asset rate, more cash is held to avoid the need for more expensive borrowing if disintermediation were to occur. Furthermore, planned or ex ante borrowing occurs when the asset rate exceeds the borrowing rate if disintermediation is not anticipated.

6.3 DEPOSIT UNCERTAINTY AND THE DEPOSIT RATE STRUCTURE

Depository firms in the United States offer deposits with specified maturities from 30 days to almost a decade. A pressing cause for much of this innovation in financial instruments has been the net deposit withdrawals that have occurred intermittently since the summer of 1966. These periods of disintermediation or net deposit outflows, sometimes called "credit crunches," were especially severe at thrift institutions. The deposit certificate was a response to these pressures. It was designed to offer rates higher than passbook rates so that the depository firms could more successfully compete with open-market instruments. At the same time, the fixed maturity deposit contracts were designed to reduce illiquidity costs that were experienced during some of the earlier deposit runs. The lower anticipated illiquidity costs could be passed through to depositors to allow the payment of the higher rates on the certificates.

In Section 6.1 it was shown that the optimal level of reserves M^* is a function of the deposit level by Eq. (6.7). Once M^* is substituted for the reserve level M in the objective function (6.2), the optimal deposit rate r is obtained by differentiating the objective function with respect to r and then solving the resulting first-order condition:

$$\frac{\partial E(P)}{\partial r} = r_a \left(1 - \frac{\partial M^*}{\partial D}\right) \frac{\partial D}{\partial r} - D - r\frac{\partial D}{\partial r} - \frac{\partial C}{\partial D}\frac{\partial D}{\partial r}$$

$$- r_p(D - M^*)f(D|D)\frac{\partial D}{\partial r}$$

$$- r_p \int_{M^*}^{D} \left(-\frac{\partial M^*}{\partial D} f(V|D) + (V - M^*)\frac{\partial f}{\partial D}\right) \frac{\partial D}{\partial r} \, dV = 0.$$

$$(6.18)$$

Reorganizing the first-order condition by dividing through by $\partial D/\partial r$ and placing marginal revenue on the left-hand side and the sum of marginal costs on the right-hand side we obtain

$$r_a = D\frac{\partial r}{\partial D} + r + \frac{\partial C}{\partial D} + r_a\frac{\partial M^*}{\partial D} + r_p(D - M^*)f(D|D)$$

$$- r_p \int_{M^*}^{D} \frac{\partial M^*}{\partial D} f(V|D) \, dV + r_p \int_{M^*}^{D} (V - M^*)\frac{\partial f}{\partial D} \, dV. \quad (6.19)$$

Thus, with deposit uncertainty, the marginal revenue from the last deposit dollar in a profit-maximizing state is just balanced against the sum of the marginal interest costs, the marginal production costs, and the marginal liquidity and illiquidity costs. These relations are shown in Figure 6.3 where the sum of these costs is equal to the marginal revenues per deposit dollar r_a. The marginal deposit costs and marginal production costs have been analyzed in Chapters 3 and 4. The marginal liquidity cost is given by $r_a(\partial M^*/\partial D)$, and the marginal expected illiquidity costs henceforth denoted $\partial E(I|D)/\partial D$ are given by the terms

$$r_p(D - M^*)f(D|D) - r_p \int_{M^*}^{D} \frac{\partial M^*}{\partial D} f(V|D) \, dV + r_p \int_{M^*}^{D} (V - M^*)\frac{\partial f}{\partial D} \, dV.$$

These three terms account for the change in the probability distribution of random withdrawals and hence expected borrowing costs as the deposit level changes.

Solving the first-order condition for the profit-maximizing deposit rate (after assuming again that the elasticity of deposit demand with respect to the deposit rate is constant), the profit-maximizing deposit rate in the presence of deposit uncertainty is then given by

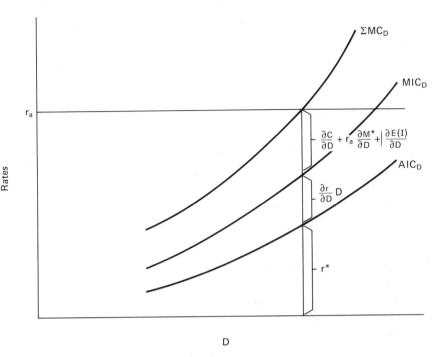

Figure 6.3 Deposit rates and the costs of deposit uncertainty.

$$r^* = \frac{\epsilon}{1 + \epsilon}\left(r_a - r_a \frac{\partial M^*}{\partial D} - \frac{\partial C}{\partial D} - \frac{\partial E(I|D)}{\partial D}\right). \quad (6.20)$$

In the presence of at least potential disintermediation with passbook savings accounts or transaction accounts, liquidity and illiquidity costs will be positive, thus reducing net revenues per deposit dollar and, in turn, the profit-maximizing deposit rate. Certificates of deposit or other fixed-maturity deposit accounts tend to reduce the mean and the variance of random deposit withdrawals and, in turn, liquidity and illiquidity costs. Thus the fixed maturity of the deposit certificate reduces the costs of deposit uncertainty, and this cost saving is passed through to depositors in the form of higher deposit rates. The proportion of the cost savings passed through depends on the deposit elasticity. Thus the deposit rate differential between passbook and the fixed-maturity accounts depends on the amount of these costs and the deposit elasticities for each type of account.[4]

6.4   HISTORICAL LIQUIDITY RATIOS

In this chapter, the level of cash reserves was analyzed as though the firm were free to choose that level that best suited its deposit market. In the earlier history of American depository institutions, this freedom did exist. It was not until the National Banking Act that the first minimum cash reserves were imposed on national banks. It was at this time that state banks also began to establish minimum cash standards. Even with regulatory-imposed minimum liquidity standards, the depository firm might elect, in its own best interest, to exceed the minimum level established by regulatory authorities.

Tables 6.1 and 6.2 together give some indication of the wide variation in liquidity needs among depository institutions and an indication of how these liquidity needs changed over time. Table 6.1 contains the reserves to total deposit ratios for Fed member banks as well as FDIC member banks. The exact cash accounts that are considered to fall within the definition of reserves have changed somewhat over time for Fed members and for state banks that are members of the FDIC system. The definition varies from state to state. Nevertheless, reserves in some cases include not only deposits at the Federal Reserve member banks, but cash and cash items in the process of collection.

It is interesting to find how great the variation in the perceived liquidity requirements of the commercial banking system has been through time. In the 1920s, when it was thought that a strong central bank could provide the liquidity when needed reserves were generally less than 10% of deposits. When the liquidity crunch of the early 1930s shocked the banking system, reserve ratios were only slowly built from 8% in 1930 to 11.5% in 1933. Reserves continued to build through the late 1930s and by 1940 had reached as much as 26.5% for Fed member banks and a high of 27.5% for FDIC members. During the war years, reserve accounts were reduced relative to deposits as highly liquid government bonds were added to bank portfolios. The decline in reserve ratios continued in the postwar era up until the late 1970s and, by 1976, had dropped below 5% for FDIC members.

Table 6.2 contains the cash items to total deposit ratios for commercial banks, mutual savings banks, and savings and loan associations. Cash

---

[4] This assumes production costs for each type of account are the same.

TABLE 6.1

Reserves to Total Deposit Ratios[a]

Year	Federal Reserve members	FDIC members	Year	Federal Reserve members	FDIC members
1919	9.9	—	1949	14.4	12.8
1920	10.0	—	1950	14.3	12.7
1921	9.6	—	1951	15.5	13.8
1922	9.1	—	1952	14.8	12.0
1923	8.6	—	1953	14.5	11.7
1924	8.7	—	1954	13.0	11.5
1925	8.2	—	1955	12.6	11.2
1926	7.9	—	1956	12.6	11.1
1927	8.2	—	1957	12.6	11.1
1928	7.6	—	1958	11.4	10.0
1929	7.7	—	1959	10.9	9.5
1930	8.2	—	1960	9.9	8.7
1931	8.1	—	1961	9.4	8.3
1932	10.2	—	1962	9.5	8.3
1933	11.5	—	1963	8.8	7.7
1934	13.8	12.4	1964	8.2	7.2
1935	16.2	14.5	1965	7.8	6.8
1936	16.9	15.1	1966	7.9	6.9
1937	18.5	16.5	1967	7.6	6.6
1938	21.7	19.3	1968	7.5	6.2
1939	25.2	27.5	1969	7.7	6.5
1940	26.5	23.9	1970	7.4	6.3
1941	21.8	19.8	1971	7.8	6.4
1942	18.0	16.3	1972	6.7	5.6
1943	15.1	13.7	1973	6.8	5.6
1944	14.0	12.6	1974	6.2	5.1
1945	13.3	11.9	1975	6.0	5.0
1946	14.8	13.1	1976	—	4.5
1947	15.8	14.0	1977	—	4.6
1948	18.0	15.8	1978	—	4.9

[a] Reserves include cash in vault, deposits with Federal Reserve Bank and, cash items in process of collection. Total deposits include those of individuals, partnerships, and corporations, as well as interbank deposits and federal and state government deposits. The ratios are expressed in percentages. Source: Tables A9.1–A9.7.

items is a broader category than reserves, as it includes not only the items previously mentioned but also interbank deposits. This notion of liquidity includes not only regulatory-imposed reserves, but also some accounts over which the depository institutions exercise some freedom of choice. This series shows similar trends to the reserve series for commercial

TABLE 6.2

Cash Items to Total Deposit Ratios[a]

Year	Commercial banks		Mutual savings banks	Savings and loan associations
	Federal Reserve members	FDIC members		
1919	28.1	—	—	—
1920	23.1	—	—	—
1921	21.7	—	—	—
1922	23.6	—	—	—
1923	23.8	—	—	—
1924	24.5	—	—	—
1925	23.7	—	—	—
1926	22.7	—	—	—
1927	21.1	—	—	—
1928	24.9	—	—	—
1929	23.6	—	—	—
1930	22.8	—	—	—
1931	20.3	—	—	—
1932	22.5	—	—	—
1933	23.2	—	—	—
1934	28.7	29.5	5.7	—
1935	31.9	31.3	6.9	—
1936	32.3	31.9	7.0	—
1937	32.4	31.6	7.1	—
1938	35.6	34.5	7.0	—
1939	40.0	39.0	9.4	—
1940	42.4	41.4	11.1	—
1941	37.4	37.1	8.4	—
1942	31.0	31.4	6.3	7.8
1943	25.7	26.1	7.4	8.2
1944	23.3	23.6	4.4	6.5
1945	22.9	23.2	4.1	6.0
1946	24.9	24.5	5.3	6.1
1947	26.7	26.0	5.5	5.7
1948	28.1	26.9	5.3	6.1
1949	25.2	24.8	5.0	7.2
1950	26.5	26.8	4.3	6.9
1951	27.8	27.9	4.5	6.7
1952	26.5	26.4	4.3	6.9
1953	26.1	25.6	4.3	6.6
1954	24.1	24.1	4.1	7.2
1955	25.2	24.8	3.6	6.5
1956	25.5	25.0	3.2	5.7
1957	25.0	24.2	2.8	5.1
1958	23.5	23.4	2.7	5.3
1959	23.4	22.6	2.4	4.0

TABLE 6.2 (*Continued*)

| Year | Commercial banks | | Mutual savings banks | Savings and loan associations |
	Federal Reserve members	FDIC members		
1960	23.6	23.1	2.4	4.2
1961	23.5	23.5	2.4	4.7
1962	21.5	21.1	2.1	4.9
1963	19.2	18.8	1.8	4.3
1964	20.5	20.6	2.0	3.9
1965	19.0	18.9	1.9	3.4
1966	20.7	20.0	1.7	2.9
1967	21.0	20.7	1.6	2.7
1968	20.6	19.5	1.5	2.2
1969	22.4	20.0	1.3	1.7
1970	21.0	20.2	1.7	2.1
1971	20.1	19.3	1.7	1.4
1972	19.8	19.3	1.7	1.3
1973	18.8	18.0	2.0	1.1
1974	18.3	17.6	2.1	1.1
1975	17.9	16.5	2.1	1.0
1976	—	15.6	1.8	1.1
1977	—	17.2	1.7	.8
1978	—	17.5	2.6	.6

[a] Cash items includes reserves, cash items in process of collection, cash in vault, and interbank deposits. Total deposits include those of individuals, partnerships, and corporations, as well as interbank deposits and federal and state government deposits. The ratios are expressed as percentages. Source: Tables A9.1–A9.13.

banks, although with less variability than in the reserve to deposit ratios. In the 1920s Fed member banks had liquidity ratios above 20%, which grew to 40% by the late 1930s. From that period, cash items to total deposit ratios began to decline and reached a low of 15% in 1976 for FDIC members. These liquidity ratios are shown in Figure 6.4.

For the thrift institutions, the data series is somewhat shorter and begins in the 1930s. The liquidity levels of the thrift institutions are strikingly lower than those of commercial banks, with a high of 11% in 1940 for mutual savings banks and declining gradually for savings and loan associations to less than 1% in 1977. Throughout these time series the liquidity levels for the thrifts are strikingly low as compared to commercial banks, with an obvious downtrend. For savings and loan associations experiencing strong growth in the first two decades after World War II, one

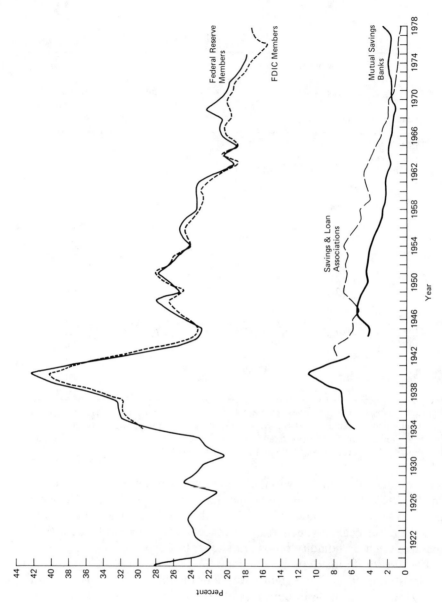

Figure 6.4 Historical liquidity. Cash items–deposit ratios.

would anticipate low levels of cash reserves. What is surprising, however, it that even with the episodes of disintermediation that began in the summer of 1966, cash reserves have not increased appreciably. This may be indicative of the improved liquidity mechanism available to the savings and loan associations.

BIBLIOGRAPHY

Baltensperger, E. "Economies of Scale, Firm Size and Concentration in Banking," *Journal of Money, Credit and Banking,* **4,** August 1972.

Baltensperger, E. "The Precautionary Demand for Reserves," *American Economic Review,* **64,** March 1974.

Baltensperger, E., and Milde, H. "Predictability of Reserve Demand, Information Costs, and Portfolio Behavior of Commerical Banks," *Journal of Finance,* **31,** June 1976.

Baumol, William. *Portfolio Theory: The Selection of Asset Combinations.* New York: General Learning Press, 1972.

Cootner, P. H. "The Liquidity of the Savings and Loan Industry." In *Study of the Savings and Loan Industry,* Federal Home Loan Bank Board, Washington, D.C., 1969.

Frost, Peter A. "Banks' Demand for Excess Reserves," *Journal of Political Economy,* **79,** July–August 1971.

Goldfeld, Stephen, and Kane, Edward. "The Determinants of Member Borrowing," *Journal of Finance,* **21,** September 1966.

Knobel, A. "The Demand for Reserves by Commercial Banks," *Journal of Money, Credit and Banking,* **9,** February 1977.

Orr, D., and Mellon, W. G. "Stochastic Reserve Losses and Expansion of Bank Credit," *American Economic Review,* **51,** September 1961.

Poole, William. "Commercial Bank Reserve Management in a Stochastic Model: Implications for Monetary Policy," *Journal of Finance,* **23,** December 1968.

Rentz, William F., and Spellman, Lewis J. "Optimal Reserves and Deposit Rates of Financial Intermediaries: Some Theorems," Bureau of Business Research, University of Texas at Austin, Working Paper No. 74-6, 1973.

Rochester, David P. "Savings and Loan Review Requirements," *Federal Home Loan Bank Board Journal,* **12,** October 1979.

Sealey, C. W., Jr. "A Further Reconsideration of Optimal Reserve Management at Commercial Banks," *Southern Economic Journal,* **44,** July 1977.

Spellman, Lewis J., Witt, Robert C., and Rentz, William F. "Investment Income and Non-Life Insurance Pricing," *Journal of Risk and Insurance,* **42,** December 1975.

Weinrobe, Maurice, "Liquidity Behavior of Savings and Loan Associations: 1974-1978," Federal Home Loan Bank Board, Working Paper No. 34, March 1980.

CHAPTER 7

Deposit Ceilings

7.1 HISTORICAL PERSPECTIVE OF INTEREST RATE CEILINGS

Restrictions on interest payments date back to biblical times. Usury restrictions arose out of a sense that interest payments exploited poor debtors to the enrichment of creditors. This was seen as unjust income redistribution, as loans were generally made for the purpose of smoothing consumption patterns over time. Another justification for interest rate ceilings was the belief that lenders were engaged in monopolistic practices that exploited borrowers with limited access to and information about competitive borrowing alternatives. Given the precedent of usury ceilings, many states in the twentieth century set ceilings on the interest rate that banks could pay for deposits. Maximum interest rates for state-chartered banks were in some states set at a lower level than those paid by national banks. To remedy this competitive imbalance, the Federal Reserve Act was amended in 1927 to limit the deposit rates paid by national banks on time, savings, and other deposits to the maximum permitted state banks in the same state. It was not until the depression that deposit ceilings become generally applicable to commercial bank deposits.

Deposit ceilings have been imposed on United States commercial bank deposits since 1933 and on the deposits of thrift institutions since 1966. The 33 years between the introduction of deposit ceilings to banks and to thrifts arose out of different economic pressures and circumstances affecting both the economy and the financial institutions. What was similar, however, was that the motivation for installing deposit ceilings stemmed from a desire to protect the solvency of the financial institutions. None of the original motivations for the limitation of interest payments were present in either case. In the 1920s it was common for demand deposits to

138

earn interest, and it was common practice to allow interest-bearing savings deposits to be checkable, much like demand deposits. The competitive environment forced the banks to be flexible. The sequence of events causing the abandonment of this flexible depository environment and the adoption of deposit ceilings was lengthy.

A competitively induced consolidation of the industry was under way despite the economic boom of the 1920s—even when business conditions were strong.[1] The onset of the business adversities of the depression accelerated that contraction of the banking industry. Not only were there adverse business conditions affecting banks, but financial shocks outside the industry had major impacts on the banks. Of these financial shocks, the most celebrated was the stock market contraction of 1929. This adversity affected commercial banks because of the numerous loans made to leverage common stock purchases. Falling prices on the stock market reduced the value of the banks' collateral and called into question the solvency of the banks themselves.

Another event of great importance was the British departure from the gold standard in September 1931. This set in motion a demand for liquidity by the public, which desired currency that still had gold backing. The shift in desired portfolio composition by the public from deposits to currency in turn forced commercial banks to liquidate assets to meet deposit withdrawals. The Federal Reserve moved to meet the liquidity needs of commercial banks, and a sharp rise in discounts occurred despite higher discount rates. As the depression intensified and business and bank failures cumulated, the Fed was less accommodating after mid-1932. Federal Reserve bond purchases ceased in August, 1932, and discounts and bills bought from commercial banks fell from July on. After much soul searching, the Federal Reserve decided it was undesirable to assist troubled banks with short-term loans to meet liquidity needs.[2] The banks were then on their own in the scramble for liquidity. This reluctance by the Federal Reserve to assist in the extreme liquidity demands of the banks arose out of an attitude that regarded bank failures as, at best, a regrettable consequence of bad management or bad banking practices. Alternatively, the banks' demand for liquidity was viewed as an inevitable consequence of prior speculative excesses. When the Federal Reserve did not provide the needed bank liquidity, the commercial banks' only recourse

---

[1] The forces causing the contraction of the banking industry in the 1920s are discussed in Chapter 10.

[2] For an excellent discussion of the Federal Reserve's actions during this difficult period of time, see Milton Friedman and Anna Schwartz, *A Monetary History of the United States, 1867–1960* (Princeton, N.J.: Princeton Univ. Press, 1963) pp. 345–359.

was to sell loans or investments on the open market. But as the business climate deteriorated in the 1930s, the loans and investments declined in market value. As commercial banks added to the selling pressure, asset prices were further depressed.

In these circumstances, a run on any bank, for whatever reason, became self-fulfilling, as the failure of one bank led in turn to the failure of what were otherwise solvent banks. This was true whatever the ex ante quality of bank assets, since market prices generally fell sharply. The impairment in the market value of bank assets denied them the ability to meet their fixed dollar deposit obligations. This loss in market value of bank assets due to heavy selling and higher perceived business risk affected the value of commercial bank assets more than it directly caused actual defaults. That is, the loss of market value caused technical insolvency, which only turned into actual insolvency when a bank was forced to liquidate assets at prices below book value to meet deposit withdrawals. In the scramble for liquidity, the price of government bonds fell 10% between 1929 and 1933, the price of high-grade corporate bonds fell 20%, and for assets with greater risk, prices fell even more sharply. The chain of events was finally arrested with the Emergency Banking Act of March 9, 1933. This act authorized the bank holiday, but by that time the contraction of commercial bank deposits that began in 1929 amounted to 42% of total deposits.

There then followed many measures to re-establish the viability of commercial banking; deposit ceilings were just one of those measures. By the Banking Acts of 1933 and 1935, banks were prohibited by law from paying interest on demand deposits and restrained by Regulation Q from paying interest on time deposits above levels specified by the Board of Governors of the Federal Reserve System for member banks and by the Federal Deposit Insurance Corporation for insured nonmember banks.

The immediate needs of the commercial banking industry were less competition, greater liquidity, and lower insolvency risk. Deposit ceilings were seen to contribute to all of these ends. In the common view of the 1930s, the payment of interest on deposits led to or caused "excessive" competition among banks. It was felt that the country banks especially were unable to pay competitive deposit rates. This "forced" banks to make riskier loans in order to earn high asset returns to pay high deposits. Not only would banks be forced to hold high-yielding but riskier assets, but in addition they would be induced to increase the proportion of earning assets in their portfolios, reducing their liquidity position and thus making them more vulnerable to runs.

This rationale for the introduction of deposit ceilings in the 1930s presents a firm adjustment process which is contrary to the models presented in Chapters 3 through 6. In these models, the financial firm passes through to depositors earnings net of bad debt losses in proportion to the intensity of competition in the deposit markets, and liquidity levels are a self-imposed protection from disintermediation.[3] That is, deposit rates competitively adjusted to net earnings—whereas in the 1930s view, earnings were adjusted to deposit rates (by reaching for higher-yielding, riskier assets and by reducing cash reserves). It is of interest that part of the rationale for deposit ceilings was their ability to influence ex ante cash reserves and thus control deposit runs. However, during a financial panic, the ability to marshal additional liquidity or ex post liquidity was more relevant than ex ante liquidity.

While this chain of events was to affect commercial banking in the 1930s, it was not until 1966 that a different but analogous sequence of events was experienced by the thrift institutions. These events similarly resulted in deposit ceilings. In Chapter 9 (Tables 9.2 and 9.5), it will be shown that competitive forces in the thrift institutions grew after 1950 and resulted in rising deposit rates and gradual reductions in current profit margins. Some competitive pressures for the savings deposits of thrifts emanated from the commercial banking industry when Regulation Q ceilings were increased in the 1960s to offset the increasing market share of savings deposits flowing to thrift institutions. In addition to this interindustry financial competition, additional competitive pressure for savings deposits emanated from open-market instruments.

In early 1966, as Vietnam War expenditures were added to a full employment economy, the first signs of an inflationary surge became evident. While capital markets were rather sluggish in placing inflation premiums on open-market instruments, upward pressure on interest rates resulted from strong loan demand from the private sector and a Federal Reserve resolve to lean against the inflationary winds. To this tight demand–supply imbalance in financial markets, the federal government added further pressure. The borrowing needs to finance new war expenditures were strong, especially since additional taxation was initially ruled out as a means of financing the war. Not only were federal demands on credit markets strong, but in addition the federal government attempted to place the burden of financing the war on the private sector by accelerating corporate tax payments. This resulted in additional corporate borrowing for the payment of accrued taxes, which further added to demand pressures on financial markets. The result of these cumulative forces was the "credit crunch" of the summer of 1966. The credit crunch pushed

---

[3] The asset earning rate r_a was defined in Chapter 3, Footnote 3, as earnings net of bad debt losses.

short-term market rates above Regulation Q limits on commercial bank deposits, and these market interest rates were also beyond the income-generating capacity of the portfolios of the thrift institutions. The first postwar inversion of the yield curve in which short-term rates exceeded long-term rates caused what is now known as disintermediation, as net deposit withdrawals from thrift institutions occurred.

While commercial banks in the 1930s were faced with financial runs inflamed by a general financial panic, the thrifts in 1966 also faced a run, although of smaller proportions. Though the withdrawals were relatively small, for some institutions they exceeded the cash reserves set aside to meet this contingency. After two postwar decades of continuous deposit growth, the thrift institutions were in relatively low cash reserve positions, and furthermore, the mechanism for borrowing from federal sources was limited. In addition, the organized secondary market, particularly for savings and loan association mortgages, was in its infancy. Thus, the combination of competitive pressures for rising deposit rates and consequently dwindling profit margins, deposit outflows, insufficient cash reserves, limited federal borrowing sources, and no organized secondary asset market, along with declining market values of prime assets put the thrift institutions in a squeeze analogous to that which befell the commercial banks in the 1930s. The legislative response was similar. Deposit ceilings were extended to thrift institutions through the Interest Rate Control Act of 1966. The stated purpose of the bill was to restrain competition between banks and thrift institutions for savings dollars. This was to be accomplished by setting ceilings on deposit rates for these institutions such that a fixed differential was maintained between similar commercial bank and savings association deposits.

The bill directed the Federal Reserve Board, the secretary of the Treasury, the Federal Home Loan Bank Board, and the Federal Deposit Insurance Corporation to take actions to reduce deposit rates to the extent feasible under prevailing money market and economic conditions. The Federal Reserve Board was given the power to set ceiling rates for different classes of bank deposits, the FDIC set maximum rates allowable for mutual savings banks, and the Home Loan Bank Board applied dividend restrictions to the savings and loan associations.

The differential in deposit ceilings initially allowed the thrifts a 50 basis point advantage over commercial banks for the same deposit class, which was felt to be necessary in order to maintain the existing market shares of banks and thrifts. To further inhibit deposit rate competition by blocking open-market instruments as competitors for savings deposits, minimum Treasury offerings were set at $10,000, well above the average account size of thrift depositors.

The difficulties experienced in 1933 and 1966 of deposit outflows, loss in the market value of assets, and illiquidity led to deposit ceilings. This regulatory device, whatever its dubious ability to maintain liquidity and thwart competition, is a price-fixing device that tends to increase rate spreads and profit margins. When these rate spreads become more favorable, it becomes profitable to expand deposit levels. In the case of a private price-fixing cartel, the device would likely result in cheating and a policing problem for the members of the cartel. When the price-fixing arrangement is imposed by government, other, legal avenues of evasion are attempted. The financial institutions, particularly in 1966, initially responded to ceilings by adding new deposit classes and other short-term instruments that were not subject to deposit ceilings. However, the regulatory authorities moved quickly to place ceilings on these new instruments. With the blocking of this approach, the imposition of deposit rate ceilings created incentives for financial institutions to attempt to attract profitable deposits by inducements to depositors that did not involve the payment of explicit deposit rates. In a deposit-rate-constrained deposit market, competition took the form of providing additional financial services and goods at below cost or no cost to the depositor. This was an attempt to differentiate an otherwise perfectly homogeneous product — insured deposits, all with the same deposit rates. Such inducements as free checking services or giveaways are obvious. There are also many subtle techniques of attracting deposits that involve outlays by the financial firm, such as parking, branching and/or drive-in facilities, or merely additional tellers, which provides a service to consumers, who are rewarded with greater leisure or a reduced cost of transacting financial services. These nonrate competitive techniques to attract deposits are the financial analog to nonprice competition. These side payments can be considered an implicit deposit rate, and they become the equilibrating adjustment mechanism whenever there is a rate controlled deposit market.

Thus, while deposit ceilings reduce interest costs and in the first instance increase profit margins, they subsequently tend to cause the firms to incur costs to compete for these more profitable deposits. The result is that some of the regulatory-induced profit will be lost. The extent of the dissipation of profit from these competitive costs is analytically explored in Section 7.3 and empirically estimated in Chapter 8.

In addition to these induced costs, deposit ceilings also tend to induce higher levels of disintermediation costs as the mean and variance of the distribution of anticipated deposit outflows increase. Hence, as ceilings are effective in reducing interest costs, they stimulate offsetting levels of nonrate competitive costs, deposit uncertainty costs, and slower deposit growth. These combined offsetting effects have caused the depository firms to acquiesce to the gradual elimination of ceilings. Whether the schedules set in the 1980 Deregulation Act are met or whatever happens to deposit ceilings in the future, the behavior of the depository firm as it strives to maximize profit subject to this regulatory constraint is next developed.

7.2   DEPOSITORY FIRM BEHAVIOR UNDER DEPOSIT CEILINGS

It is assumed that because of regulatory-imposed limitation to entry, the depository intermediary still operates in an imperfectly competitive deposit market. In this market, the firm has two competitive methods of attracting deposits D. The intermediary pays an explicit deposit rate per dollar of deposits r, as well as what will be considered an implicit deposit rate per dollar of deposits in the form of financial services or goods, i. Thus, the deposit demand function is stated as

$$D = D(r, i) \quad \frac{\partial D}{\partial r} > 0, \qquad \frac{\partial D}{\partial i} > 0. \qquad (7.1)$$

Given the deposit level, the depository firm places these funds in additions to a risk-diversified portfolio. The financial intermediary is capable of participating in national markets for securities, and it is assumed that effective markets exist to purchase loans outside local loan markets. As a result, for any firm, the average earning rate on assets r_a does not decline with the quantity of earning assets, as the intermediary is able to place increasing quantities of funds at national market rates. The revenues accruing each period are thus equal to $r_a D$.

As in Chapter 3, the depository firm incurs a cost for factor inputs and intermediate products in order to process both deposits and earning assets. These financial production costs are again assumed to depend on the level of deposits. The total production cost function is thus denoted $C(D)$. The depository firm still incurs an interest cost on deposits, but now dividends or interests accrue to the deposits at the ceiling rate $\bar{r}$, and thus total deposit cost per period is $\bar{r}D$. In addition, the intermediary incurs costs to induce larger deposit levels. Deposit-increasing costs can be stated as iD, where i is the annual cost of financial services or goods per deposit dollar; or viewed alternatively, i is the implicit rate at which goods and services are paid to depositors. The goods and services are considered a monetary payment to the depositor and are valued at the firm's cost. To evaluate the relative size of this payment, they are measured as a rate, just as the explicit deposit rate is measured.

The overall objective function of the firm is still assumed to be the maximization of profit P. From the preceding assumptions it follows that this is given by Eq. (7.2):

$$P = r_a D(\bar{r}, i) - C(D(\bar{r}, i)) - \bar{r}D(\bar{r}, i) - iD(\bar{r}, i). \tag{7.2}$$

In periods when the market deposit rate is above the regulatory-controlled limit, the firm maximizes profit with respect to i, as it is the only variable at its discretion. The derivative of the profit function, with respect to i, is set equal to 0, and the first-order condition is:

$$r_a \frac{\partial D}{\partial i} = \frac{\partial C}{\partial D}\frac{\partial D}{\partial i} + \bar{r}\frac{\partial D}{\partial i} + i\frac{\partial D}{\partial i} + D. \tag{7.3}$$

With a constant implicit deposit elasticity ϵ_i, Eq. (7.3) can be rewritten and solved for the profit-maximizing level of the implicit deposit rate i^*:

$$i^* = \frac{\epsilon_i}{1 + \epsilon_i}\left(r_a - \bar{r} - \frac{\partial C}{\partial D}\right). \tag{7.4}$$

From this it can be seen that the level of the implicit deposit rate depends essentially upon two terms. The term $(r_a - \bar{r} - \partial C/\partial D)$ represents the net rate spread per deposit dollar. That is, the firm earns r_a from a deposit dollar, from which it pays a ceiling deposit rate $\bar{r}$ and also its marginal cost of production, $\partial C/\partial D$.

The net rate spread per deposit dollar constitutes the available funds to be passed through to the depositor in the form of an implicit deposit rate. This contrasts to net revenues $r_a - \partial C/\partial D$ of Chapter 3 that are paid as an explicit deposit rate. Since the net rate spread is less than net revenues, the potential for implicit deposit rates is more limited than for explicit deposit rates. As before, the proportion of net revenues that are passed through to depositors depends on the strength of the depositors' response to the goods and services provided by the implicit deposit rate. When the market response is low, or when ϵ_i approaches 0, the term $\epsilon_i/(1 + \epsilon_i)$ approaches 0, and, from Eq. (7.4), the implicit deposit rate approaches 0. Conversely, a very large deposit response to implicit deposit rates results in a very high value of ϵ_i and the pass-through proportion $\epsilon_i/(1 + \epsilon_i)$ approaches unity. In this event, it is in the firm's interest to set i^* such that it approaches the net rate spread. Thus, the greater the deposit sensitivity to i, the larger will be the proportion of the net rate spread paid in implicit deposit rates. In the limit, as ϵ_i approaches infinity, the implicit deposit rate approaches the net rate spread.

7.3 PROFIT MARGINS, COSTS, AND RATE SPREADS
UNDER DEPOSIT CEILINGS

The profit margin can be obtained by substituting the value of the implicit deposit rate i^* of Eq. (7.4) into the profit equation, (7.2). With the simplifying assumption that marginal and average production costs are constant and equal, profit per deposit dollar then reduces to

$$p = \frac{1}{1 + \epsilon_i}\left(r_a - \bar{r} - \frac{\partial C}{\partial D}\right). \tag{7.5}$$

Hence, the profit margin per deposit dollar is determined much in the same way as the implicit deposit rate. The net rate spread is distributed to the depositor through an implicit deposit rate, and the residual share accrues to the stockholder as a profit margin. The share of the net rate spread accruing to the depositor is $\epsilon_i/(1 + \epsilon_i)$, and the share accruing to the equity position is $1/(1 + \epsilon_i)$ so that these shares completely exhaust the net rate spread. This distribution of the net rate spread, of course, depends on the intensity of competition. With low competitive levels and low levels of ϵ_i, the equity position receives a higher proportion of the net rate spread. In a highly competitive market with large values of ϵ_i, the depositor receives the larger share, and, asymptotically as ϵ_i approaches infinity or perfect competition, the profit margin dwindles to 0, leaving no economic profit at all. The decline in the profit margin in highly competitive markets results from the fact that the depository firm pays higher implicit deposit rates to the depositor. Since the form taken by implicit deposit rates is additional services or goods, they are subsumed in the firm's expense records as additional labor expense, additional occupancy expense, advertising, or other miscellaneous expenditures. Thus, the competitive technique of nonrate competition results in higher recorded expenses or higher observed costs for the financial firm. The firm's expenses, which consist of outlays for both production purposes and for competitive purposes, would tend to increase with greater competitive pressures in deposit markets.

Given the profit-maximizing level of the implicit deposit rate, average observed costs oc can then be expressed as the sum of average production costs C/D, denoted c plus the implicit deposit rate i^*

$$oc = c + i^*, \tag{7.6}$$

which, from Eq. (7.4) can be written

$$oc = c + \frac{\epsilon_i}{1 + \epsilon_i}\left(r_a - \bar{r} - \frac{\partial C}{\partial D}\right). \tag{7.7}$$

This expression contains terms for both average and marginal production costs. If these costs are equal, the equation can be further simplified to

$$oc = (\epsilon_i/(1 + \epsilon_i))(r_a - \bar{r}) + (1/(1 + \epsilon_i))c. \qquad (7.8)$$

In the extreme case of ϵ_i approaching 0, all observed costs are production costs, and in the perfectly competitive extreme, observed costs fill the gap in asset and deposit rates.

Deposit ceilings, by restraining explicit deposit rates from reaching competitive levels, obviously tend to increase rate spreads. This is shown in Figure 7.1 where r^* is the competitive deposit rate, $\bar{r}$ is the regulatory ceiling rate, s_f is the gross rate spread in a free market, and s is the gross spread in a deposit-rate-constrained market. The rate spread, however, might be increased by more than the difference between the profit-maximizing deposit rate and the deposit ceiling. This would occur if there were any asset rate elasticity. That is, as shown in Figure 7.2, with a depressed deposit rate $\bar{r}$ and deposit level $\bar{D}$, the gross rate spreads would increase by an amount greater than the merely suppressed deposit rate. That is because with a downward sloping average revenue curve with a smaller deposit level, the average earning rate is higher, since there are fewer funds to be placed in loan markets. The rate spread increases by more than the suppression of the deposit rate. If this were the case, deposit ceilings would result in higher loan rates. This response to deposit ceilings would, of course, cause consternation among those committed to

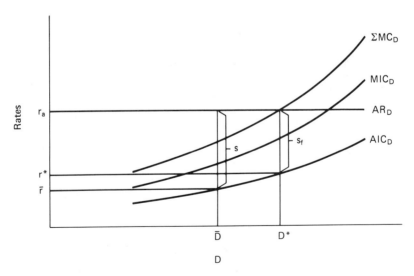

Figure 7.1 Rate spreads with deposit ceilings.

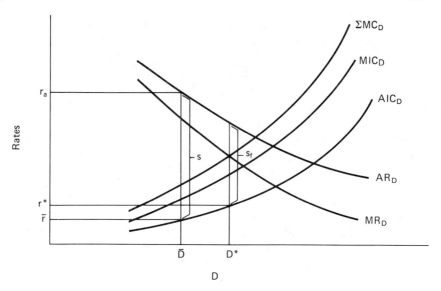

Figure 7.2   Rate spreads with asset rate elasticity.

a low interest rate policy because the suppressed deposit rates, rather than reducing loan rates, tend to increase them.[4]

7.4   REGULATORY RENT AND INCOME DISTRIBUTION UNDER DEPOSIT CEILINGS

While deposit ceilings were originally intended to increase liquidity and reduce the risk of insolvency, their first impact is to control deposit costs. Deposit ceilings are a price-fixing arrangement under government auspices that tend to reduce explicit deposit costs and bestow benefits on the financial firm. These potential benefits might be termed regulatory rent in the sense that the depressed deposit costs represent an unearned windfall income for the firm as the result of a regulatory restriction. We have seen that when explicit deposit rates are held down by regulation, the financial firm then competes strenuously for relatively inexpensive deposits by paying implicit deposit rates in order to attract deposit holdings. The resulting impact on the profit margin and on income distribution then de-

---

[4] While the individual firm might not face a declining asset rate as it increases its loan portfolio, for the overall aggregate economy deposit ceilings would tend to reduce the level of savings and drive a wedge between the economywide loan rate and deposit rate. This is because the marginal productivity of capital and hence loan rates decline with the amount of capital. This phenomenon is specifically addressed in Chapter 14.

pends on the amount of regulatory rent bestowed on the financial firm and the extent to which this regulatory rent is lost through nonrate competition.

Regulatory rent per deposit dollar rr depends on the amount by which the regulated deposit rate $\bar{r}$ is suppressed below what would be the competitive market rate r^*:

$$rr = r^* - \bar{r}. \tag{7.9}$$

Regulatory rent only exists if $\bar{r}$ is below r^*, and this is an issue that in turn depends on the explicit deposit elasticity ϵ. From Eq. (3.5), the value of regulatory rent is

$$rr = \frac{\epsilon}{1 + \epsilon}\left(r_a - \frac{\partial C}{\partial D}\right) - \bar{r}. \tag{7.10}$$

Regulatory rent exists only if deposit ceilings are binding. The condition for binding deposit ceilings and positive levels of regulatory rent is that the competitive deposit rate exceeds the ceiling deposit rate. That is, if

$$\frac{\epsilon}{1 + \epsilon}\left(r_a - \frac{\partial C}{\partial D}\right) > \bar{r} \tag{7.11}$$

or if

$$\epsilon/(1 + \epsilon) > \bar{r}\Big/\left(r_a - \frac{\partial C}{\partial D}\right). \tag{7.12}$$

Thus, the test of binding deposit ceilings rests not on the relationships of deposit ceilings to rates on alternative open-market instruments, but rather on the explicit deposit elasticity and the relationship of the ceiling rate $\bar{r}$ to net revenues.

The proportion of regulatory rent lost by the financial firm in deposit competition is the ratio of the implicit deposit rate to regulatory rent rr. Obtaining the value i^* from Eq. (7.4), where ϵ_i is the implicit deposit elasticity, we obtain an expression for the proportion of regulatory rent lost in implicit deposit rate competition:

$$\frac{i^*}{r^* - \bar{r}} = \left(\frac{\epsilon_i}{1 + \epsilon_i}\left(r_a - \bar{r} - \frac{\partial C}{\partial D}\right)\right)\Big/\left(\frac{\epsilon}{1 + \epsilon}\left(r_a - \frac{\partial C}{\partial D}\right) - \bar{r}\right). \tag{7.13}$$

The proportion of dissipated rent depends on both the implicit and explicit deposit elasticity. The distribution of regulatory rent can be seen most clearly when the ceiling is established to protect the firm in a highly competitive deposit market in which ϵ approaches infinity. The dissipation of

regulatory rent to the depositor then depends solely on the market
response to implicit deposit rates as Eq. (7.13) reduces to

$$i^*/(r^* - \bar{r}) = \epsilon_i/(1 + \epsilon_i). \tag{7.14}$$

Thus, for the depository firm in a highly explicit-rate-sensitive market, the
ability to protect profits through deposit ceilings rests completely on the
value of the implicit deposit elasticity. Furthermore, if the deposit
response to the goods and services offered in lieu of an explicit deposit
payment is also quite high, the depositors' share of regulatory rent would
approach unity. With a highly sensitive deposit response to both explicit
and implicit deposit rates, the device of a deposit ceiling is rendered
useless as a means to protect profit. If the implicit deposit elasticity is
high, it serves to reduce the profit margin, just as a high explicit deposit
elasticity in an unregulated market does. With highly sensitive deposit
markets with respect to both explicit and implicit deposit rates, all economic profit is sacrifed to attract deposits, and the depositor has the same
total payment, which accrues in a combination of explicit and implicit
rates.

The profit margin under deposit ceilings $p_{\bar{r}}$ can be compared to the
free-market profit margin. In Eq. (7.15) the ceiling rate profit margin is
stated as a ratio of the freely competitive profit margin given by Eq.
(3.11):

$$\frac{p_{\bar{r}}}{p} = \left(\frac{1}{1 + \epsilon_i}\left(r_a - \bar{r} - \frac{\partial C}{\partial D}\right)\right) \Big/ \left(\frac{1}{1 + \epsilon}\left(r_a - \frac{\partial C}{\partial D}\right)\right). \tag{7.15}$$

This expression reduces to

$$p_{\bar{r}}/p = \left(\frac{(1 + \epsilon)}{(1 + \epsilon_i)}\right)\left\{1 - \left(\bar{r}\Big/\left(r_a - \frac{\partial C}{\partial D}\right)\right)\right\}. \tag{7.16}$$

Thus, for any given ceiling $\bar{r}$, the proportionate increase in the profit
margin depends on the relative size of the explicit and implicit deposit
elasticities. The smaller the implicit deposit elasticity, the larger will be
the proportionate increase in profit margins, under deposit ceilings. The
ratio of profit margins under the two regimes also depends on the relationship of the ceiling rate to net revenues. The lower the ceiling rate relative
to net revenues, the higher will be the profit margin in the deposit-rate-
regulated market. When ceilings are set at 0, as is the case with demand
deposits, the proportionate gain in the profit margin then depends only on
the relative size of the deposit elasticities.

Again, the distribution of income to the depositor accrues in the form of
both an explicit and an implicit rate. The utility gain to the depositor from
nonrate competitive expenditures, however, has been questioned. The

argument is similar to that made in analyzing the utility gain from a redistribution of income as compared to the utility gain from the redistribution of goods. That is, if consumers are awarded additional income, they are able to purchase a market basket that maximizes their utility, whereas a distribution of goods of the same dollar amount is not likely to promote the same gain in utility. Thus, it is possible that deposit ceilings could be a device that would not only fail to protect the financial firm, but at the same time might result in expenditures that yield lower utility levels to the depositor than those that would have existed in a free market. This has been the basis of allegations that deposit ceilings tend to promote inefficiency in resource allocations.

Nevertheless, it is still possible to state the depositors' share of revenues net of average production costs. The depositors' total return as the sum of the explicit and implicit rates is

$$\bar{r} + i^* = \bar{r} + \frac{\epsilon_i}{1 + \epsilon_i}\left(r_a - \bar{r} - \frac{\partial C}{\partial D}\right)$$
$$= \frac{1}{1 + \epsilon_i}\bar{r} + \frac{\epsilon_i}{1 + \epsilon_i}\left(r_a - \frac{\partial C}{\partial D}\right). \qquad (7.17)$$

With binding deposit rates, the depositors' share of average net revenues is determined completely by the implicit deposit elasticity ϵ_i. If ϵ_i approaches infinity, and if, in addition, marginal and average production costs are constant and equal, then the depositors' share of average net revenues is unity. In this event the depositors capture the entire net revenues:

$$(\bar{r} + i^*)\left/\left(r_a - \frac{\partial C}{\partial D}\right)\right. = 1. \qquad (7.18)$$

Thus, it can be seen that the ability to generate regulatory rent or alter income distribution rests solely on the market response to implicit deposit rates. This is an empirical matter that will be explored in Chapter 8.

BIBLIOGRAPHY

Avio, Kenneth L. "On the Effects of Statutory Interest Rate Ceilings," *Journal of Finance*, **29**, December 1974.
Douglas, George W., and Miller, James C. III. "Quality Competition, Industry Equilibrium, and Efficiency in the Price-Constrained Airline Market," *American Economic Review*, **64**, September 1974.
Federal Home Loan Bank Board, *Annual Report of the Federal Home Loan Bank Board*, Washington, D.C., 1967.
Friedman, Milton, and Schwartz, Anna J. *A Monetary History of the United States, 1867–1960*. Princeton, N.J.: Princeton Univ. Press, 1963.

Gambs, C. M. "Bank Failures: An Historical Perspective," *Federal Reserve Bank of Kansas City. Monthly Review,* June 1977.

Greer, Douglas F. "Rate Ceilings, Market Structure, and the Supply of Finance Company Personal Loans," *Journal of Finance,* **29,** December 1974.

Havrilesky, Thomas, and Schweitzer, Robert. "Non-Price Competition Among Banking Firms," *Journal of Bank Research,* **6,** Summer 1975.

Kane, Edward J. "Short-Changing the Small Saver: Federal Government Discrimination Against Small Savers During the Vietnam War, A Comment," *Journal of Money, Credit and Banking,* **2,** November 1970.

Kareken, J. H. "Commercial Banks and the Supply of Money: A Market-Determined Demand Deposit Rate," Federal Reserve Bulletin 53, October 1967.

Klein, Benjamin. "Competitive Interest Payments on Bank Deposits and the Long-Run Demand for Money," *American Economic Review,* **64,** December 1974.

Klein, Michael B., and Murphy, Neil B. "The Pricing of Bank Deposits: A Theoretical and Empirical Analysis," *Journal of Financial and Quantitative Analysis,* **6,** March 1971.

Lindsay, R. "The Economics of Interest Rate Ceilings," *New York University. Institute of Finance Bulletin,* December 1970.

Lloyd-Davies, Peter R. *The Macroeconomic Effects of Allowing Interest Payment on Demand Deposits.* Board of Governors, Federal Reserve System, June 1977.

Mitchell, Douglas W. "Explicit and Implicit Demand Deposit Interest: Substitutes or Complements from the Bank's Point of View?", *Journal of Money, Credit and Banking,* **11,** May 1979.

Osborne, Dale K., and Spellman, Lewis J. "Non-Rate Competition in Rate Constrained Financial Markets." Paper presented to the Western Finance Association, June 1978, Anaheim, Calif.

Rosse, Jim. "On Estimating Cost Parameters Without Using Cost Data: Illustrated Methodology," *Econometrica,* **38,** April 1970.

Stigler, George. "Price and Non-Price Competition," *Journal of Political Economy,* **76,** January 1968.

Stuhr, David P. "Competition and Commercial Bank Behavior." In *Proceedings of a Conference on Bank Structure and Competition,* Federal Reserve Bank of Chicago, October 1972.

Taggart, Robert A., Jr. "Effects of Deposit Rate Ceilings," *Journal of Money, Credit and Banking,* **10,** May 1978.

U.S., Congress, Senate, Committee on Banking, Housing and Urban Affairs, Subcommitte on Financial Institutions. *Extensions of Regulation Q and NOW accounts.* Hearing, 93rd Cong., 1st sess., March 1973.

White, Lawrence J. "Price Regulation and Quality Rivalry in a Profit-Maximizing Model: The Case of Bank Branching," *Journal of Money, Credit and Banking,* **8,** February 1976.

White, Lawrence J. "Quality Variation When Prices are Regulated," *The Bell Journal of Economics and Management Science,* **3,** Autumn 1972.

CHAPTER 8

Empirical Measurement of Implicit Deposit Rates, Average Production Costs, and Income Distribution

8.1 THE ADJUSTMENTS TO DEPOSIT CEILINGS

The direct and immediate effect of deposit ceilings is to depress deposit rates below competitively set rates. With depressed deposit rates, one would expect the spread between the asset and the effective deposit rate to increase for depository institutions. Such an increase in the rate spread did occur after 1966, when deposit ceilings were imposed on thrift institutions. These results are reported in Tables 9.1, 9.2, and 9.3.

For savings and loan associations, the rate spread in the early 1950s was at a high of 2.11%, it dwindled to 1.24% in 1967. After ceilings came into effect and asset rates continued to climb, savings and loan associations began to offer certificates of deposit with rates that increased with the length of maturity. The result was increased average deposit costs. Despite this shifting of funds into the special accounts at higher average deposit rates, rate spreads continued to increase as asset earning rates rose more rapidly than effective deposit rates. By 1978 the rate spread had increased to 2.05%, or just slightly below the 1950 level. This increase in rate spreads amounted to 81 basis points and continued to increase, despite the introduction of new certificate accounts, including the money market certificate in the summer of 1978. Mutual savings bank spreads followed a similar pattern as rate spreads declined from a high of 2.10% in 1940 to 64 basis points in 1966. From the 1967 low of 51, rate spreads increased to 1.42% by 1978.

For commercial banks that were members of the Federal Reserve System, the pattern before and after the imposition of deposit ceilings in 1933 showed a somewhat different pattern. In 1933, a deposit rate prohibition was placed on demand deposits, and a nonbinding deposit rate constant on savings accounts was initiated. The weighted average deposit rate thereafter declined from 1.80% in 1930 to .78% in 1934. The average asset earning rate after 1933 declined primarily because of the growing proportion of cash reserves in the portfolios of commercial banks; nevertheless, rate spreads decreased as asset rates declined more than deposit rates. It was not until the postwar period that one could see the clear effects of deposit ceilings on rate spreads for banks. From an immediate postwar rate spread of less than 1%, the spread climbed gradually, until in the 1970s it had reached 4% in some years. This level of 4% is more than double the less than 2% in the free-market era of the 1920s.

Larger rate spreads tend to translate into higher profit margins, if not totally offset by costs. The profit margins for the deposit activity of savings and loan deposits was .62% or 62 basis points in 1950; from this level it declined to .9 basis point in 1967. After the imposition of deposit ceilings, profit margins rose erratically to 42 basis points in 1973 and to a level of 50 basis points in 1978. As shown in Section 7.4, the proportionate increase in the profit margin as a result of deposit ceilings depends on both the relationship of implicit and explicit elasticities to each other and the relationship of the ceiling deposit rate to net revenues. After this initial adjustment, movements in profit margins over time depend significantly on movements in deposit elasticities, production costs, and the level of the ceiling deposit rate.

The adjustment by the firm that dissipates the improved rate spread is the offsetting increases in implicit deposit rates. These implicit deposit rates are first seen as changes in observed costs. Since observed cost is the sum of production costs as well as nonrate competitive costs, it is not possible to say a priori how these separate components of costs change because we only observe the sum of the two components. It is possible that implicit deposit rates could have increased in a more competitive deposit environment, and it is also possible that technical change could have occurred to affect average production costs. That is, from an examination of average operating costs alone, it is difficult to draw a conclusion regarding the magnitude of implicit deposit rates, even though the cost data do suggest some movement in nonrate competitive costs, as average observed costs increased after deposit ceilings were put into effect.[1]

For savings and loan associations, observed average costs were at a level of 1.52% in 1946. From this postwar high, average costs declined to 1.23% by 1967. This drop of approximately 27 basis points was then very quickly reversed, after the imposition of deposit ceilings. By 1978 average

---

[1] Cost accounting techniques estimate implicit deposit rates by assigning arbitrary weights to various cost categories. This method has been used to derive implicit deposit rate estimates from the Federal Reserve System's *Functional Cost Analysis. 1979 Average Banks* (Washington, D.C.: 1980).

costs stood at 1.55%, or a level higher than 1946, and represented a 31 basis point increase that took place after the introduction of deposit ceilings. This would suggest either a deterioration in productive efficiency or an increase in implicit deposit rates.

Though a technique will be developed subsequently to separate nonrate competitive costs from production costs, it is still possible to draw some inferences regarding the type of nonrate competitive costs from the components of costs. For example, in Table 8.1 (for savings and loan associations), the labor component of cost stood at a postwar high in 1946 of .72% per deposit dollar, and then declined to .57% in 1967. From this low the labor component or wages per deposit dollar increased to .77% per deposit dollar after ceilings went into effect. This was an increase of 20 basis points. The office occupancy expense as a percentage of deposits was a bit more erratic, rising from .10% in the early postwar period to .16% in 1960. In 1967 it had declined to .10%, but since the imposition of deposit ceilings it has risen again to .16%. While the percentage increase in office occupancy expense since 1967 was greater than for labor costs, the absolute magnitude of the increase in cost, however, was considerably smaller, as office occupancy expenses rose only 5 basis points.[2] Thus, to the extent that nonrate competition manifests itself in capital equipment such as branches, drive-in facilities, or excess building, this increase in capital equipment accounted for only a small part of the increase in overall operating expenses.

Another expense category often associated with nonrate competition is advertising. Advertising per deposit dollar fluctuated in a narrow range of 9 to 17 basis points in the entire postwar period. Its pattern of change was rather interesting. From a low in 1946 of 9 basis points, advertising per deposit dollar rose to 15 basis points when deposit ceilings were enacted. Thereafter there was some small increase to 17 basis points by 1970, but then advertising per deposit dollar began to decline and stood at only 10 basis points in 1977 and 12 basis points in 1978. These levels were equal to those experienced in the late 1940s and early 1950s.

A hypothesis to account for this historical trend of advertising expenses is the possibility that savings and loans experimented to find the most cost-effective techniques of nonrate competition. Advertising has its merits—it is an expense that can be easily adjusted at the margin and does not involve a long-term commitment, as plant and equipment or labor might. In any event, advertising never exceeded more than 10% of total cost, and it is of interest that office occupancy was also a relatively

---

[2] Although deposit ceilings were established in late-1966, it is likely that they were not binding until 1968. Hence, 1967 was the last year of explicit deposit rate competition.

TABLE 8.1

Selected Expense Categories per Deposit Dollar,
Savings and Loan Associations[a]

Year	Wages	Office occupancy	Advertising
1942	.59	.08	.08
1943	.62	.09	.07
1944	.64	.09	.08
1945	.69	.10	.09
1946	.72	.10	.09
1947	.72	.10	.12
1948	.72	.11	.12
1949	.71	.12	.12
1950	.72	.13	.12
1951	.73	.14	.10
1952	.71	.14	.14
1953	.69	.14	.13
1954	.68	.14	.13
1955	.67	.14	.13
1956	.65	.15	.13
1957	.64	.15	.13
1958	.62	.15	.13
1959	.63	.15	.13
1960	.61	.16	.13
1961	.61	.15	.13
1962	.59	.15	.13
1963	.60	.15	.14
1964	.62	.12	.15
1965	.60	.12	.15
1966	.58	.12	.15
1967	.57	.10	.15
1968	.57	.11	.15
1969	.60	.12	.16
1970	.63	.14	.17
1971	.63	.12	.15
1972	.62	.12	.13
1973	.65	.14	.13
1974	.69	.15	.15
1975	.70	.16	.13
1976	.70	.16	.11
1977	.71	.16	.10
1978	.73	.16	.12
1979	.77	.16	.13

[a] Expressed in percentages. Source: *Combined Financial Statements, FSLIC-Insured Savings and Loan Associations, 1942–1979*. Washington, D.C., U.S. Govt. Printing Office, 1942–1980.

minor expense, never exceeding 13% of total expenditures, while labor was generally about 50% of total operating expenses.

8.2   MEASUREMENT OF THE IMPLICIT DEPOSIT RATE

While it is possible to examine these data for hints as to the adjustment process to deposit ceilings, there are several structural parameters that need to be measured to calculate the level of the implicit deposit rate and average production costs. Essentially, one must have an estimate of the structural parameter ϵ_i and an estimate of $\partial C / \partial D$ from the parameters of the production cost curve in order to calculate the implicit deposit rate via Eq. (7.4). The rate spread $r_a - \bar{r}$ can be calculated from the balance sheet and income statements:

$$i^* = \frac{\epsilon_i}{1 + \epsilon_i} \left(r_a - \bar{r} - \frac{\partial C}{\partial D} \right). \tag{7.4}$$

With these structural parameters, it is possible to calculate i^* and examine its effect on profit margins.

To begin, it is necessary to make an assumption regarding the functional form of the cost curve. For example, assume as in Section 4.1 that the production cost curve has a constant elasticity with respect to the deposit level. This functional form is quite tractable and has lent itself to empirical verification. With the constant elasticity cost curve

$$C = \gamma_0 D^{\gamma_1}, \tag{8.1}$$

cost is multiplicatively related to a scale parameter γ_0, and the exponent γ_1 determines the shape of the cost curve. If γ_1 exceeds unity, costs rise more than in proportion to the deposit level, so that γ_1 values greater than 1 result in diseconomies of scale. Similarly, with a value of γ_1 ranging between 0 and 1, costs rise less than in proportion to the deposit level, producing economies of scale. A value of γ_1 equal to 1, of course, results in proportionate production cost increases as deposit levels increase. The marginal and average costs from this cost function are then

$$\frac{\partial C}{\partial D} = \gamma_0 \gamma_1 D^{\gamma_1 - 1} \tag{8.2}$$

and

$$C/D \equiv c = \gamma_0 D^{\gamma_1 - 1}. \tag{8.3}$$

Marginal costs with this cost function are then a constant proportion of average costs

$$\frac{\partial C}{\partial D} = \gamma_1 c, \tag{8.4}$$

where the constant proportion is γ_1. If γ_1 is greater than 1, marginal costs exceed average costs. Furthermore, the shape of the average curve depends solely on γ_1, with values greater than 1 causing average costs to increase.

An alternative assumption regarding production costs is that the cost curve is linear. This cost curve is also both tractable and easily measured empirically. The linear cost curve of Eq. (8.5),

$$C = \alpha_0 + \alpha_1 D, \tag{8.5}$$

also has two parameters, and the marginal and average costs for this cost function are given by Eq. (8.6) and (8.7):

$$\partial C/\partial D = \alpha_1 \tag{8.6}$$

$$C/D \equiv c = (\alpha_0/D) + \alpha_1. \tag{8.7}$$

With this functional form, the parameter α_1 completely expresses marginal costs, whereas both parameters describe average costs. It should be pointed out, however, that the shape of the cost curve depends completely on the value α_0. If α_0 is positive, average costs decline with the deposit level, whereas if α_0 is negative, average costs increase with the deposit level. In either case, average costs asymptotically approach the constant α_1 as D increases. An empirically determined value of α_0 equal to 0 indicates constant average and marginal costs both equal to α_1.

It is possible to substitute either cost specification into Eq. (7.4) for the optimum implicit deposit rate. Marginal and average costs are then stated in terms of the structural parameters of the assumed cost curve.

Regardless of the assumed specification of the cost function (and a number of alternatives, including a U-shaped cost curve are possible), the same empirical problem presents itself. The problem is that the dependent variable i^* is only observed as a component of total cost and thus cannot be directly employed in a regression estimation. To empirically measure implicit deposit rates, we must resort to indirect least squares. Basically, we must identify structural parameters as a function of observed variables. There are several possibilities.

One could substitute the assumed cost parameters into the behavioral equation (7.4) for i^* and in turn substitute Eq. (7.4) into the profit equation (7.2):

$$P = r_a D - rD - C(D) - iD. \tag{7.2}$$

With these substitutions, profit can be expressed in terms of the parameters of the production cost function, the implicit deposit rate elasticity as measured by ϵ_1, the scale of deposit activity D, and the prevailing asset and deposit rates:

$$P = -\alpha_0 - (\alpha_1/(1 + \epsilon_i))D + (1/(1 + \epsilon_i))(r_a - \bar{r})D. \qquad (8.8)$$

Dividing through by D results in a profit margin equation

$$p = -\frac{\alpha_0}{D} - (\alpha_1/(1 + \epsilon_i)) + (1/(1 + \epsilon_i))(r_a - \bar{r}). \qquad (8.9)$$

Profit and profit margins are reduced by larger values of α_0 and α_1, which determine average and marginal production costs. Profit and profit margins are also reduced with greater competitive pressures as measured by ϵ_1. Larger rate spreads increase profit and profit margins, and higher deposit levels increase profit as fixed production costs α_0 are spread over a larger dollar volume of deposits.

In order to indirectly obtain estimates of the unobserved parameters ϵ_1, α_0, and α_1, we can directly estimate the following equation:

$$P = b_0 + b_1D + b_2(r_a - r)D + u. \qquad (8.10)$$

In this equation, total profit is stated as a linear function of D and $(r_a - r)D$, where u is a disturbance term.

When the regression coefficients b_0, b_1, and b_2 are estimated from a sample, they are an estimate of some combination of the structural coefficients. That is,

$$\hat{b}_0 = -\alpha_0, \qquad \hat{b}_1 = -\alpha_1/(1 + \epsilon_i), \qquad \hat{b}_2 = 1/(1 + \epsilon_i). \qquad (8.11)$$

It is possible to form a three-equation system in the unknown parameters α_0, α_1, and ϵ_1 so that these parameters can be solved in terms of the regression coefficients

$$\hat{\alpha}_0 = -\hat{b}_0, \qquad \hat{\alpha}_1 = -\hat{b}_1/\hat{b}_2, \qquad \hat{\epsilon}_i = (1 - \hat{b}_2)/\hat{b}_2. \qquad (8.12)$$

Given the regression coefficients, the structural parameters can be estimated, and it is then possible to solve for average and marginal production costs and implicit deposit rates, along with many other auxiliary calculations such as the distribution of income, net revenues, and regulatory rent. That is, the vector of regression coefficients leads us to the vector of structural coefficients by Eq. (8.12), and the vector of structural parameters leads us to marginal and average costs and the implicit deposit rate by Eqs. (8.6), (8.7), and (7.4).

In addition to regression equation (8.10), which estimates the parameters relating observed variables to each other via Eq. (8.8), it is also possible to estimate a regression equation corresponding to Eq. (8.9):

$$p = b_0 + b_1(1/D) + b_2(r_a - \bar{r}). \tag{8.13}$$

In this case the regression coefficients become estimates of the following structural parameters:

$$\hat{b}_0 = -\alpha_1/(1 + \epsilon_i), \qquad \hat{b}_1 = -\alpha_0, \qquad \hat{b}_2 = 1/(1 + \epsilon_i). \tag{8.14}$$

Once these regression coefficients are obtained using this specification, it is possible to solve for the structural parameters in terms of the regression coefficients as before.

In addition to substitutions into the profit statement, another possible avenue of approach exists to indirectly obtain estimates of the structural variables. It is useful to note that observed cost per deposit dollar oc is composed of the sum of both average production costs and the implicit deposit rate:

$$oc = c + i^*. \tag{8.15}$$

That is, the level of expenses we observe in accounting data is composed of the sum of production costs plus nonrate competitive costs. Having made this construction, it is possible to substitute the value of the profit-maximizing implicit deposit rate into Eq. (8.15):

$$oc = c + (\epsilon_i/(1 + \epsilon_1))\left(r_a - \bar{r} - \frac{\partial C}{\partial D}\right). \tag{8.16}$$

In turn one could substitute the parameters of any appropriate cost function for average and marginal costs. A great simplification is achieved when it is appropriate to use the constant elasticity cost curve (8.1), since from Eq. (8.4) marginal cost is multiplicatively related to average costs. That is,

$$\frac{\partial C}{\partial D} = \gamma_1 c. \tag{8.4}$$

Making this substitution for marginal costs and simplifying, we obtain the following expression:

$$oc = ((1 + \epsilon_i - \gamma_1\epsilon_i)/(1 + \epsilon_i))c + (\epsilon_i/(1 + \epsilon_i))(r_a - \bar{r}). \tag{8.17}$$

In this functional form we have now obtained an equation where the observed operating cost per deposit dollar oc is stated as a simple linear function of another observed variable, the rate spread. This functional form is particularly tractable for measuring savings and loan implicit deposit rates, since in past studies, the constant cost elasticity γ_1 has been estimated to be very close to .92.[3] Using this exogenous information for the value of γ_1, a simple linear regression equation

$$oc = b_0 + b_1(r_a - r) + u \qquad (8.18)$$

yields regression coefficients that are related to the structural coefficients in the following way:

$$\hat{b}_0 = ((1 + \epsilon_i - \gamma_1\epsilon_i)/(1 + \epsilon_i))c \qquad \text{and} \qquad \hat{b}_1 = \epsilon_i/(1 + \epsilon_i). \quad (8.19)$$

Thus, by indirect least squares, it is again possible to solve for the unobserved structural variables ϵ_i, c, and $\partial C/\partial D$:

$$\hat{\epsilon}_i = \hat{b}_1/(1 - \hat{b}_1) \qquad \text{and} \qquad \hat{c} = \hat{b}_0/(1 - \gamma_1\hat{b}_1). \quad (8.20)$$

Equation (8.20) yields an estimate for average cost, but it is possible to go beyond this and solve for the cost curve parameter γ_0 from Eq. (8.3). Furthermore, the implicit deposit rate i^* is then solved via Eq. (7.4) from the estimated parameters as well as the observed rate spread.

In an alternative specification, one could substitute the values of marginal and average costs from Eq. (8.2) and (8.3) into Eq. (8.16). In that case we obtain the following equation:

$$oc = \gamma_0((1 + \epsilon_i - \gamma_1\epsilon_i)/(1 + \epsilon_i))D^{\gamma_1-1} + (\epsilon_i/(1 + \epsilon_i))(r_a - \bar{r}). \quad (8.21)$$

In this case the multiple regression equation of the form

$$oc = b_0D^{\gamma_1-1} + b_1(r_a - \bar{r}) \qquad (8.22)$$

could be fitted to the data to obtain estimates of b_0 and b_1, which in turn are related to the structural variables in the following way:

$$\hat{b}_0 = \gamma_0((1 + \epsilon_i - \gamma_1\epsilon_i)/(1 + \epsilon_i)) \qquad \text{and} \qquad \hat{b}_1 = \epsilon_i/(1 + \epsilon_i). \quad (8.23)$$

Again, employing exogenous information regarding the value of the cost elasticity γ_1, we can directly obtain an estimate of γ_0 and hence the production cost structure and the implicit deposit rate:

$$\hat{\gamma}_0 = \hat{b}_0/(1 - \gamma_1\hat{b}_1). \qquad (8.24)$$

---

[3] The estimate of the constant cost elasticity is contained in George J. Benston, "Economies of Scale in Financial Institutions," *Journal of Money, Credit and Banking* **4** (May 1972).

8.3 EMPIRICAL ESTIMATES OF IMPLICIT
DEPOSIT RATES AND PRODUCTION COSTS IN
COMMERCIAL BANKING

Table 8.2 presents the estimated regression coefficients corresponding
to Eq. (8.8) for commercial banks. These regression coefficients were obtained in seven separate cross-sectional estimates corresponding to the
years 1969 to 1975. The sample was large; the observations included most
of the FDIC-insured commercial banks for each year.

An examination of the t statistics and summary statistics from the regression equations reveals that the model performs well. The t statistics
are large and statistically significant at high levels of confidence. The adjusted coefficients of determination range between .43 and .73.

The derived structural coefficients of the linear production cost curve
are presented in Table 8.3. Marginal production costs per deposit dollar
were at a level of 220 basis points in 1969. After an increase to 228 basis

TABLE 8.2

Regression Coefficients, All FDIC-Insured Commercial Banks, 1969–1975[a]

Year	b_0	b_1	b_2	R^2 (Adjusted)	F	n
1969	34.70 (3.34)	−.009286 (−62.51)	.4216 (81.74)	.45	5562	13,463
1970	70.34 (4.78)	−.007264 (−25.39)	.3193 (.4138)	.43	5082	13,498
1971	4.684 (0.48)	−.006850 (−32.74)	.3278 (48.70)	.48	6149	13,601
1972	−22.40 (−2.18)	−.006782 (−29.69)	.3593 (44.55)	.55	8391	13,720
1973	−63.37 (−4.77)	−.008031 (−36.26)	.4478 (62.03)	.71	17,168	13,964
1974	−135.6 (−8.05)	−.008694 (−32.01)	.4862 (56.69)	.73	19,527	14,214
1975	−101.8 (−6.65)	−.003839 (−16.83)	.2304 (30.41)	.41	5036	14,366

[a] The t values are reported in parentheses below regression coefficients. The observed
variables used in the regression equations are defined as follows: r_a is the weighted average
earning rate net of loan losses of a typically invested deposit dollar of the bank's portfolio. It is a weighted average of the yields of the assets of the portfolio, including the
cash reserves of the commercial bank. r is the effective weighted average deposit rate
of the commercial bank. It is the ratio of the interest expense of deposits to total deposits,
including demand deposits. The gross rate spread $r_a - r$ is thus the difference between the
average return of an invested dollar and the average rate paid for that deposit.

TABLE 8.3

Derived Structural Variables, Commercial Banks, 1969–1975[a]

Year	$\hat{\alpha}_0$ (thousands)	Marginal cost $\hat{\alpha}_1$	Average production cost $\hat{c}$	Implicit deposit elasticity $\hat{\epsilon}_i$	Net rate spread $r_a - \bar{r} - \dfrac{\partial \hat{C}}{\partial D}$	Implicit deposit rate $\hat{i}*$	Proportion of nonrate expenses $\hat{i}*/(oc)$
1969	−34.70	2.20	2.09	1.37	1.12	.65	23
	(10.40)	(.03)		(.03)			
1970	−70.34	2.28	2.08	2.13	1.14	.78	27
	(14.71)	(.08)		(.08)			
1971	−4.68	2.09	2.08	2.05	1.10	.74	23
	(10.72)	(.06)		(.06)			
1972	22.40	1.89	1.94	1.78	1.15	.74	24
	(10.28)	(.06)		(.06)			
1973	63.37	1.79	1.92	1.23	1.51	.83	25
	(13.30)	(.04)		(.04)			
1974	135.6	1.79	2.05	1.06	1.73	.89	25
	(16.84)	(.05)		(.04)			
1975	101.8	1.67	1.86	3.34	1.57	1.22	38
	(15.32)	(.08)		(.14)			

[a] Expressed in percentages. Standard errors are reported in parentheses below derived structural variables.

points in 1970, marginal costs declined to 167 basis points in 1975. The cost curve coefficients reveal an interesting trend. It appears that there was an underlying shift in the production cost curve for United States commercial banking over the observed time period. The coefficient α_0 exhibits an upward trend, and α_1 exhibits a downward trend. Since α_1 by itself measures marginal production costs by Eq. (8.6), its reduction translates into reductions in these costs.

The level of average costs in any year depends not only on the parameters of the cost curve, but also on the level of deposits, by Eq. (8.7). Average costs measured at the mean deposit level have been calculated for each year. In Table 8.3, average production costs per deposit dollar were at approximately 208 basis points between 1969 and 1971. Thereafter, some decline was experienced, with the low of 186 basis points reached in 1975. While reductions in average cost appear to be the result of gains in technical efficiency, it is also possible that some of these cost reductions were due to a change in deposit composition. Over the 1969–1975 period, time and savings accounts, with lower average costs, grew from 40 to 50% of total bank deposits.

While the values of the cost curve parameters affect the level of average and marginal costs, interestingly, the slope of the average cost curve depends solely on the sign of α_0. As previously noted, the sign of α_0 from Eq. (8.7) determines whether average costs rise or fall with a higher deposit level. For 1969 and 1970, negative values of this parameter imply increasing average costs and hence diseconomies of scale. In 1971 the value of α_0 was insignificantly different from 0 and hence implied constant average costs. Positive values of α_0 in more recent years imply declining average costs and economies of scale. Thus, not only was there a downward trend in average and marginal cost over time, but changes in the shape of the production cost curve suggest a tendency for the emergence of economies of scale on an average deposit dollar basis. Figure 8.1 indicates the effect of the changes in the cost parameters on the shape of the average production cost curve.

The implicit deposit rates reported in Table 8.3 show a noticeable upward trend from 1969 to 1975, increasing from 65 to 122 basis points, with a large increase occurring in 1975. The implicit deposit rate can increase either because the net rate spread increases and/or because the deposi-

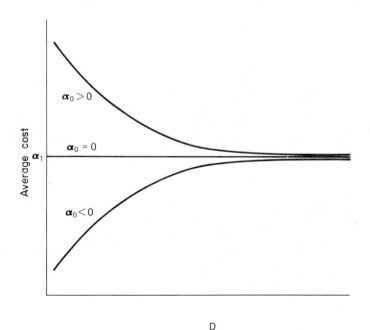

Figure 8.1   Average cost c and the linear cost function.

tor's share of the net rate spread might increase. Both events occurred as the net rate spread increased from 112 basis points in 1969 to a high of 173 basis points in 1974. The depositors' share of the implicit deposit rate depends on the competitiveness of the deposit market, as measured by the implicit deposit elasticity ϵ_i. The implicit deposit elasticity ranged between 1.06 in 1974 and 3.34 in 1975. The large implicit deposit rate of 1975 was the result of both a large net rate spread as well as a large implicit deposit elasticity.

There is some relationship between changes in production costs and changes in the implicit deposit rate. Since the implicit deposit rate depends on the net rate spread, reductions in marginal production costs tend to raise the net rate spread and result in higher implicit deposit rates. In fact, the increasing implicit deposit rate between 1969 and 1974 was largely offset by lower production costs. That is, the reduction in production costs allowed the shifting of expenditures to nonrate competitive uses, so that between 1969 and 1973 the production cost savings were largely passed through to depositors in the form of implicit deposit rates with little effect on overall operating costs. After 1973, the gains in productive efficiency were not sufficient to offset growing competitive costs, as average operating costs rose 33 basis points, from 281 in 1973 to 314 in 1975.[4] As a result of these trends, the proportion of total expenditures used in deposit-seeking activities increased from 23 to 38% of total expenditures over the 7-year period. Conversely, the proportion of expenditures for production purposes declined from 77 to 62%.

8.4   EMPIRICAL ESTIMATES OF IMPLICIT DEPOSIT RATES AND PRODUCTION COSTS IN THE SAVINGS AND LOAN INDUSTRY

Regression equations corresponding to the functional form of Eq. (8.17) were calculated on a cross section of state data points for FSLIC-insured savings and loan associations for the years 1965 through 1977. These results are reported in Table 8.4.

After the enactment of deposit ceilings for savings and loan deposits, there was an almost immediate market interest rate decline, and open-market rates were generally below deposit ceilings throughout 1967. It was not until the summer of 1968 that interest rates in the open market began to climb, and they rose again in late 1969 and early 1970 so that

---

[4] Average operating costs can be derived by dividing the implicit deposit rate by the proportion of nonrate expenses.

TABLE 8.4

Regression Coefficients, FSLIC-Insured Savings
and Loan Associations, 1965–1977[a]

Year	b_0	b_1	R^2 (Adjusted)	F [b]
1965	1.237	.028	.00	.09
	(9.06)	(.29)		
1966	1.306	−.044	.01	.41
	(15.53)	(−.64)		
1967	1.236	−.016	.00	.08
	(18.65)	(−.29)		
1968	1.184	.055	.02	.94
	(16.08)	(.97)		
1969	1.247	.071	.03	1.37
	(16.62)	(1.17)		
1970	1.302	.062	.02	1.09
	(19.19)	(1.04)		
1971	1.098	.155	.09	4.77
	(12.63)	(2.18)		
1972	.550	.490	.39	31.65
	(4.28)	(5.63)		
1973	.503	.545	.29	18.40
	(2.47)	(4.29)		
1974	.664	.534	.21	12.06
	(2.82)	(3.47)		
1975	.668	.506	.39	29.32
	(4.69)	(5.41)		
1976	.557	.535	.42	33.37
	(3.60)	(5.78)		
1977	.554	.530	.42	32.96
	(3.50)	(5.74)		

[a] The t values are reported in parentheses below regression coefficients.

[b] The data points are state aggregates, so there are 52 observations for each year.

competition for funds by open-market instruments became more intense. The nonrate competitive response by savings and loans to attract deposits first began to emerge in 1971.

Although the adjusted coefficient of determination for 1971 was .09 for the implicit deposit rate model, the t statistics for the regression coefficients were significant at the .95 level. In 1972 the implicit rate model begins to behave very well—the coefficient of determination jumps to .39, and in all years thereafter all t statistics and F values were significant at the .95 level. From these regression coefficients, the values for the implicit deposit elasticity and average production costs were calculated via Eq. (8.20). The implicit deposit rate was calculated from Eq. (7.4). These data appear in Table 8.5.

It would appear from the data that deposit ceilings did not seriously affect behavior of the savings and loan industry until 1972. There was one exception, however. The imposition of deposit ceilings tended to cause the net rate spreads to rise immediately after ceilings became binding in 1968. However, in the first few years of deposit ceilings the relatively low implicit deposit elasticities resulted in negligible implicit deposit rates. Most of the increase accrued to the profit margin. It was not until 1972, when net rate spreads were above 50 basis points and the implicit deposit elasticity had increased to unity, that the payment of implicit deposit rates begin to alter the cost and profit structure of the savings and loan industry.

Commencing in 1972 the implicit deposit rate fluctuated between 27 and 49 basis points. To offset this increase in cost, it would appear that average production costs declined somewhat during this time period from those that existed prior to the imposition of deposit ceilings. For the savings and loan industry, production cost savings did not fully offset the

TABLE 8.5

Derived Structural Variables, Savings and Loan Associations, 1965–1977[a]

Year	Average cost $\hat{c}$	Marginal cost $\dfrac{\partial \hat{C}}{\partial D}$	Implicit deposit elasticity $\hat{\epsilon}_i$	Net rate spread $r_a - \bar{r} - \dfrac{\partial \hat{C}}{\partial D}$	Implicit deposit rate $\hat{i}*$	Proportion of nonrate expenses $\hat{i}*/(oc)$
1965	1.27	1.14	—[b]	.42	—[b]	—[b]
1966	1.26	1.13	—[b]	.26	—[b]	—[b]
1967	1.22	1.10	—[b]	.15	—[b]	—[b]
1968	1.25	1.13	.06	.30	.02	1.6
1969	1.33	1.20	.08	.39	.03	2.2
1970	1.38	1.24	.07	.32	.02	1.4
1971	1.28	1.15	.18	.42	.06	4.4
1972	.98	.88	.97	.75	.37	27.9
1973	1.00	.90	1.16	.90	.49	25.0
1974	1.28	1.15	1.09	.53	.28	18.7
1975	1.23	1.11	1.02	.54	.27	17.5
1976	1.07	.96	1.15	.75	.40	26.3
1977	1.06	.95	1.13	.91	.48	31.7

[a] Expressed in percentages.
[b] Values are not significantly different from 0.

increase in nonrate competitive costs, which resulted in higher observed costs per deposit dollar. The shift in the cost structure commencing in 1972 can be seen clearly by examining the proportion of nonrate competitive costs to all operating costs. In 1972 implicit deposit costs had risen to nearly 28% of operating costs, and they remained close to that level thereafter.

It is of interest to make some comparisons between commercial banks and savings and loan associations. When average production costs for the two types of depository institutions are examined independent of nonrate competitive costs, we find that average production costs of the commercial banking industry were estimated to be approximately 80% higher per deposit dollar than those of the savings and loan industry. Implicit deposit rates for commercial banks were more than twice those paid by the savings associations. The banks' higher implicit deposit rates and higher production costs, however, were made possible by higher gross as well as net rate spreads. The banks' larger implicit rates were the result of not only greater net revenues, but also a larger pass-through proportion. At the margin, any increase in the net rate spread, either because asset earning rates increase relative to deposit ceilings or any *ceteris parabis* reduction in deposit ceilings, would be allocated to implicit deposit rates according to the pass-through ratio $\epsilon_i/(1 + \epsilon_i)$. Since the implicit elasticity was consistently close to unity for savings associations, half of any change in the spread, at the margin, would be passed through to depositors in the form of implicit deposit rates. For commercial banks the pass-through proportion ranged between 51 and 77%.

8.5   THE DISTRIBUTION OF INCOME AND REGULATORY RENT

The distribution of income is explicitly addressed in Table 8.6. The depositors' share of average net revenues $r_a - \hat{c}$ is composed of some combination of explicit deposit rates $\bar{r}$ and the implicit deposit rate i. In the commercial banking industry, the explicit deposit rates represented a smaller proportion of average net revenues. For commercial banks, the distribution of average net revenues through explicit deposit rates was between 63.1 and 70.3% between 1969 and 1975; whereas in the savings and loan industry, the explicit deposit rate fell from 99.4% under the free-market conditions of 1967 to 88.6% in the rate-controlled market of 1977.

It would appear that competitive forces in a flexible deposit rate market caused savings and loan associations to pay out virtually all of average net revenues in explicit deposit rates in 1967. Thus, from this measure alone it would certainly appear that the industry approached a perfectly competi-

TABLE 8.6

Measures of Income Distribution: Depositors' Share of the Net Rate Spread and Average Net Revenues[a]

Year	Commercial banks				Savings and loan associations			
	Implicit share of net revenues $\dfrac{i}{r_a - \bar{r} - \frac{\partial C}{\partial D}}$	Share of average net revenues			Implicit share of net revenues $\dfrac{i}{r_a - \bar{r} - \frac{\partial C}{\partial D}}$	Share of average net revenues		
		Explicit share $\dfrac{\bar{r}}{r_a - \hat{c}}$	Implicit share $\dfrac{\hat{i}}{r_a - \hat{c}}$	Total share $\dfrac{\bar{r} + \hat{i}}{r_a - \hat{c}}$		Explicit share $\dfrac{\bar{r}}{r_a - \hat{c}}$	Implicit share $\dfrac{\hat{i}}{r_a - \hat{c}}$	Total share $\dfrac{\bar{r} + \hat{i}}{r_a - \hat{c}}$
1967	—	—	—	—	0	99.4	0	99.4
1968	—	—	—	—	6.6	96.3	.4	96.7
1969	58.0	63.1	19.5	82.6	7.6	94.8	.6	95.4
1970	68.4	62.9	21.6	84.5	6.3	96.6	.4	97.0
1971	67.3	68.4	21.1	89.5	14.4	94.8	1.1	95.9
1972	64.3	68.8	20.9	89.8	48.9	88.9	6.0	94.9
1973	54.9	65.9	20.5	86.4	54.4	87.1	7.7	94.8
1974	51.4	68.6	19.0	87.6	53.4	94.0	4.4	98.4
1975	77.7	70.3	26.2	96.6	50.6	93.3	4.1	97.4
1976	—	—	—	—	53.4	90.4	5.8	96.2
1977	—	—	—	—	53.0	88.6	6.6	95.2

[a] Expressed in percentages. Source: Tables 8.3 and 8.5.

tive situation in which virtually all revenues after production costs were directed to depositors and no economic rent accrued to the equity position. The ability of deposit ceilings to create regulatory rent can be seen to have had a gradual effect on the savings and loan industry as the explicit rates were pushed down relative to average net revenues. However, as nonrate competitive pressures increased, part of the regulatory rent accrued to depositors. In the 1970s the savings and loan depositors' total distribution seems to have reached equilibrium at 95% of average net revenues. Regulatory rent can be seen more obviously for commercial banks, as their explicit deposit rate shares of average net revenues are well below those of savings associations. The obvious reason is that the prohibition of interest payments on demand deposits by commercial banks caused a greater amount of regulatory rent to accrue to banks. They, however, pass through a greater proportion of the regulatory rent.

The year 1972 was an apparent turning point for savings associations. An examination of the depositors' share of explicit and implicit deposit rates makes it evident that deposit ceilings became effective at that time. After 1972 there was a change in the composition of payments to depositors, with relatively little change in their overall share of average net revenues.

The time patterns of the total share accruing to depositors are somewhat different when the industries are compared. The depositors' share in commercial banking grew over time, indicating growing competitive pressures, whereas with the savings and loan industry, the effectiveness of deposit ceilings in maintaining some regulatory rent resulted in a declining depositors' share. What is of interest, however, is that in 1975 both industries seemed to converge to a depositors' total share of 97%. This total share was, of course, composed quite differently, with banks paying a considerably high proportion of their total payments in implicit deposit rates.

BIBLIOGRAPHY

Barro, Robert J., and Santomero, Anthony J. "Household Money Holdings and the Demand Deposit Rate," *Journal of Money, Credit and Banking,* **4,** May 1972.
Bradford, William, Osborne, Alfred, and Spellman, Lewis J. "The Efficiency and Profitability of Minority Controlled Savings and Loan Associations," *Journal of Money, Credit and Banking,* **10,** February 1978.
Federal Reserve System. *Functional Cost Analysis, 1979 Average Banks,* Washington, D.C.: 1980.
Flannery, Mark J. "A Method for Empirically Assessing the Impact of Market Interest Rates on Intermediary Profitability." In *Proceedings of a Conference on Bank Structure and Competition,* Federal Reserve Bank of Chicago, May 1980.

Heggestad, Arnold A., and Mingo, John J. "Prices, Nonprices, and Concentration in Selected Banking Markets." In *Conference on Bank Structure and Competition*, Federal Reserve Bank of Chicago, March 1974.

Longbrake, William A. "Commercial Bank Capacity to Pay Interest on Demand Deposits," *Journal of Bank Research*, **7**, Spring 1976.

Pyle, David H. "The Losses on Savings Deposits from Interest Rate Regulation," *The Bell Journal of Economics and Management Science*, **5**, Autumn 1974.

Schweitzer, Robert, and Spellman, Lewis J. "Profit Margins in U.S. Commercial Banking: 1969–1975," unpublished paper presented to the Western Finance Association, Honolulu, Hawaii, June 1978.

Spellman, Lewis J. "Non-Rate Competition for Savings Deposits," *Journal of Bank Research*, **8**, Autumn 1977.

Spellman, Lewis J. "Deposit Ceilings and the Efficiency of Financial Intermediation," *Journal of Finance*, **35**, March 1980.

Spellman, Lewis J., Osborne, Alfred, and Bradford, William. "Comparative Operating Efficiency of Black Savings and Loan Associations," *Journal of Finance*, **32**, May 1977.

Startz, Richard. "Implicit Interest on Demand Deposits," *Journal of Monetary Economics*, **5**, October 1979.

CHAPTER 9

The Historical Record

9.1 REVENUES, COSTS, AND PROFIT MARGINS PER DEPOSIT DOLLAR FOR THE DEPOSITORY INSTITUTIONS

It is possible to compare the performance of all depository institutions with each other and over time by expressing revenues, costs, and profit margins on a per deposit dollar basis. Expressed as rates, these data will afford us the opportunity to examine long-term movements in market and regulatory forces using standardized measures.

Revenues per deposit dollar, referred to as the asset earning rate r_a, is calculated to reflect the average earnings of a deposit dollar. This takes account of the depository institutions' portfolio selection that is subject to regulatory-imposed requirements to hold cash reserves and all other quantity and quality regulatory restrictions on asset selection, as well as asset rate or usury restrictions. In general, average revenues per deposit dollar are calculated as the gross operating incomes of the depository institutions' portfolios less any capital gains, capital losses, or other revenues not associated with the portfolio activity. These revenues are divided by average annual levels of total monetary and financial assets. The later figure is total assets less the physical plant of the depository institution. The specific accounts used to calculate the asset earning rate for each of the depository institutions are noted in the footnotes of the tables in Apendix A.

The asset earning rates for the depository institutions from Table 9.1 are depicted in Figure 9.1. What stands out most is the dominance in the earnings record of the federal credit unions compared to the relatively lower earning levels for commercial banks. For the most part, between these two extremes are the savings and loan associations and mutual savings banks with the former tending to have realized higher yields through time. The relative position of banks improved however, and their asset earning rates caught up to the mutuals in the 1960s and the savings and loans in the mid-1970s. Any differences in asset earning rates reflect port-

TABLE 9.1

Asset Earning Rates r_a and Market Interest Rates[a]

| | Commercial banks | | | | | |
Year	Federal Reserve members	FDIC members	Mutual savings banks	Savings and loan associations	Federal credit unions	Moody's AAA rates
1919	4.37	—	—	—	—	5.49
1920	5.14	—	—	—	—	6.12
1921	5.23	—	—	—	—	5.97
1922	4.97	—	—	—	—	5.10
1923	4.80	—	—	—	—	5.12
1924	4.68	—	—	—	—	5.00
1925	4.65	—	—	—	—	4.88
1926	4.74	—	—	—	—	4.73
1927	4.52	—	—	—	—	4.57
1928	4.55	—	—	—	—	4.55
1929	4.86	—	—	—	—	4.73
1930	4.44	—	—	—	—	4.55
1931	4.21	—	—	—	—	4.58
1932	4.05	—	—	—	—	5.01
1933	3.47	—	—	—	—	4.49
1934	3.28	—	—	—	—	4.00
1935	2.77	3.13	3.78	—	—	3.60
1936	2.71	2.89	3.73	—	—	3.24
1937	2.75	3.02	3.73	—	—	3.26
1938	2.63	2.91	3.94	—	—	3.19
1939	2.45	2.72	4.26	—	—	3.01
1940	2.21	2.47	4.04	—	8.87	2.84
1941	2.14	2.37	3.57	—	8.25	2.77
1942	1.96	2.10	3.66	4.10	5.90	2.83
1943	1.80	1.90	5.20	4.21	4.20	2.73
1944	1.73	1.80	3.27	4.13	3.91	2.72
1945	1.64	1.74	3.05	4.26	3.80	2.62
1946	1.82	1.92	2.93	4.32	4.16	2.53
1947	2.00	2.04	2.89	4.24	5.14	2.61
1948	2.16	2.24	2.93	4.43	6.12	2.82
1949	2.26	2.36	3.00	4.50	6.53	2.66
1950	2.35	2.45	3.10	4.63	7.23	2.62
1951	2.47	2.57	3.12	4.63	7.02	2.86
1952	2.64	2.72	3.19	4.66	7.01	2.96
1953	2.84	2.92	3.34	4.77	7.49	3.20
1954	2.89	2.97	3.42	4.85	7.42	2.90
1955	3.06	3.13	3.55	4.96	7.42	3.06
1956	3.36	3.43	3.70	4.99	7.48	3.36
1957	3.65	3.71	3.90	5.14	7.69	3.89
1958	3.68	3.74	3.99	5.23	7.58	3.79

(Continued)

TABLE 9.1 (*Continued*)

Year	Commercial banks		Mutual savings banks	Savings and loan associations	Federal credit unions	Moody's AAA rates
	Federal Reserve members	FDIC members				
1959	4.00	4.06	4.16	5.42	7.66	4.38
1960	4.27	4.33	4.40	5.58	7.86	4.41
1961	4.12	4.19	4.45	5.66	8.03	4.35
1962	4.23	4.31	4.59	5.84	8.09	4.33
1963	4.42	4.50	4.72	5.77	8.12	4.26
1964	4.55	4.63	4.84	5.80	8.08	4.40
1965	4.65	4.73	4.94	5.79	8.04	4.49
1966	5.02	5.08	5.07	5.84	8.16	5.13
1967	5.09	5.17	5.24	5.91	8.22	5.51
1968	5.35	5.43	5.43	6.10	8.33	6.18
1969	5.98	6.06	5.69	6.39	8.85	7.03
1970	6.30	6.37	5.43	6.61	9.08	8.04
1971	5.95	6.07	5.40	6.86	8.91	7.39
1972	5.80	5.93	5.60	7.03	8.83	7.21
1973	6.82	6.86	5.89	7.36	9.04	7.44
1974	8.18	7.93	6.04	7.63	9.46	8.57
1975	7.20	7.33	6.27	7.90	9.35	8.83
1976	—	8.01	6.53	8.05	9.42	8.43
1977	—	8.15	6.71	8.28	9.43	8.02
1978	—	9.15	7.04	8.58	—	8.73

[a] Expressed in percentages. Source: Tables 9.6–9.10.

folio composition and earning rate differentials of the assets of the different institutions. Commercial banks, of course, with relatively smaller proportions of risk assets and higher proportions of cash and liquid assets in their portfolios, generated less revenues than did the other institutions. The savings and loan associations held very high proportions of assets in long-term residential mortgages and, with substantial deposit growth through the mid-1960s, held relatively little cash and thus enjoyed relatively higher portfolio yields.

From these earning yields, the depository institutions covered their costs. Deposit costs, or the effective deposit rate, was calculated as the ratio of dividends or interest on deposits to average total deposit levels. These are shown in Table 9.2 and Figure 9.2. It can be seen that through most of the period a pattern existed with credit union deposit rates dominating those of savings and loan associations, the savings and loan association deposit rates dominating mutual savings banks, and the mutual savings banks dominating the banks.

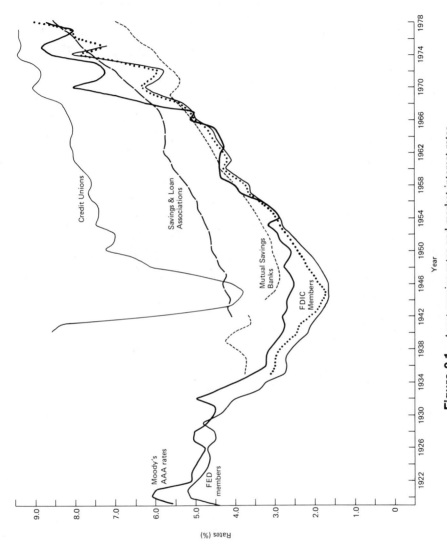

Figure 9.1 Asset earning rates and market interest rates.

TABLE 9.2

Effective Deposit Rates r^a

Year	Commercial banks		Mutual savings banks	Savings and loan associations	Federal credit unions
	Federal Reserve members	FDIC members			
1919	1.77	—	—	—	—
1920	1.86	—	—	—	—
1921	1.97	—	—	—	—
1922	2.01	—	—	—	—
1923	1.96	—	—	—	—
1924	1.95	—	—	—	—
1925	1.93	—	—	—	—
1926	1.95	—	—	—	—
1927	1.77	—	—	—	—
1928	1.78	—	—	—	—
1929	1.79	—	—	—	—
1930	1.80	—	—	—	—
1931	1.55	—	—	—	—
1932	1.34	—	—	—	—
1933	.98	—	—	—	—
1934	.78	—	—	—	—
1935	.56	.63	2.18	—	—
1936	.44	.50	1.98	—	—
1937	.42	.48	1.92	—	—
1938	.40	.47	1.91	—	—
1939	.34	.40	2.19	—	—
1940	.27	.33	1.94	—	3.95
1941	.23	.28	1.64	—	3.33
1942	.18	.22	1.73	2.19	2.16
1943	.14	.17	2.46	2.26	1.51
1944	.14	.16	1.61	2.28	1.40
1945	.15	.17	1.48	2.32	1.54
1946	.17	.18	1.46	2.41	1.76
1947	.19	.21	1.53	2.37	2.21
1948	.20	.22	1.57	2.44	2.62
1949	.21	.23	1.78	2.51	2.98
1950	.21	.23	1.84	2.52	3.26
1951	.22	.24	1.90	2.59	3.23
1952	.25	.27	2.27	2.69	3.32
1953	.28	.30	2.36	2.81	3.50
1954	.32	.34	2.43	2.87	3.56
1955	.33	.36	2.60	2.94	3.65
1956	.39	.41	2.76	3.03	3.84
1957	.54	.57	2.99	3.26	3.92

TABLE 9.2 (*Continued*)

| Year | Commercial banks | | Mutual savings banks | Savings and loan associations | Federal credit unions |
	Federal Reserve members	FDIC members			
1958	.63	.66	3.10	3.38	4.00
1959	.69	.72	3.21	3.53	4.07
1960	.75	.79	3.57	3.85	4.29
1961	.85	.88	3.53	3.85	4.41
1962	1.09	1.11	3.83	4.13	4.51
1963	1.27	1.29	3.96	4.11	4.58
1964	1.39	1.40	4.06	4.19	4.62
1965	1.58	1.59	4.08	4.23	4.62
1966	1.83	1.82	4.43	4.45	4.76
1967	1.96	1.97	4.73	4.67	4.84
1968	2.08	2.04	4.76	4.67	4.94
1969	1.99	2.19	4.85	4.80	5.13
1970	2.21	2.28	4.58	5.05	5.32
1971	2.32	2.39	4.46	5.30	5.37
1972	2.31	2.39	4.55	5.38	5.44
1973	3.04	3.05	4.76	5.54	5.69
1974	3.95	3.90	5.03	5.97	5.93
1975	3.39	3.43	5.27	6.23	6.05
1976	—	3.25	5.40	6.31	6.06
1977	—	3.24	5.47	6.40	6.11
1978	—	3.66	5.61	6.52	—

[a] Expressed in percentages. Source: Tables 9.6–9.10.

The effective deposit rates cover free-market eras for commercial banks prior to 1933 and for the thrifts prior to 1967. After those dates, the deposit rates were a reflection of the deposit ceilings then applicable. In the free-market eras, the deposit rate depended on the net earnings of the portfolio less the marginal cost of production. From net revenues per deposit dollar, competitive pressures determined how much of these revenues passed through to depositors. These forces are outlined in Chapter 3. Thus, in the pre-rate-controlled eras, the competitive environment in the deposit markets, the earning capacity of the portfolios, and the industry's productive efficiency determined deposit rates. Specific liability authority and the existence of ceilings affected weighted average deposit rates during the regulated eras. In the 1920s, commercial banks offered demand deposits, but without an interest prohibition on these accounts. The weighted average deposit costs were significantly higher in the 1920s than in the 1930s, after interest rate prohibitions were introduced.

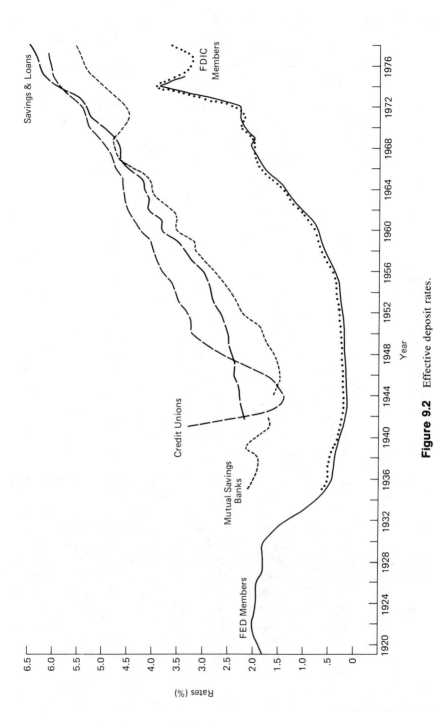

Figure 9.2 Effective deposit rates.

As for the thrift institutions, their effective deposit rates were all quite similar in both the free and regulated eras. In the first era, it was market forces that tended to produce similarity in deposit rates, since they all offered an essentially homogeneous product. In the regulated era, it was the actions of the regulatory authorities, acting in concert to set small differentials, that caused similarities in the average cost of funds.

These differing earning and deposit rate patterns affected the gross rate spreads. When the different depository institutions are compared, they show in Table 9.3 and Figure 9.3 a somewhat mixed pattern for this im-

TABLE 9.3

Rate Spreads s^a

	Commercial banks				
Year	Federal Reserve members	FDIC members	Mutual savings banks	Savings and loan associations	Federal credit unions
1919	2.59	—	—	—	—
1920	3.28	—	—	—	—
1921	3.25	—	—	—	—
1922	2.96	—	—	—	—
1923	2.84	—	—	—	—
1924	2.73	—	—	—	—
1925	2.72	—	—	—	—
1926	2.78	—	—	—	—
1927	2.75	—	—	—	—
1928	2.76	—	—	—	—
1929	3.06	—	—	—	—
1930	2.63	—	—	—	—
1931	2.65	—	—	—	—
1932	2.71	—	—	—	—
1933	2.48	—	—	—	—
1934	2.50	—	—	—	—
1935	2.21	2.49	1.59	—	—
1936	2.26	2.48	1.75	—	—
1937	2.32	2.53	1.80	—	—
1938	2.22	2.44	2.03	—	—
1939	2.11	2.32	2.06	—	—
1940	1.93	2.14	2.10	—	4.92
1941	1.91	2.09	1.92	—	4.92
1942	1.78	1.88	1.93	1.91	3.74
1943	1.66	1.73	2.73	1.94	2.69
1944	1.59	1.64	1.66	1.84	2.51
1945	1.49	1.56	1.57	1.94	2.26

(Continued)

TABLE 9.3 (*Continued*)

Year	Commercial banks		Mutual savings banks	Savings and loan associations	Federal credit unions
	Federal Reserve members	FDIC members			
1946	1.64	1.73	1.46	1.90	2.40
1947	1.80	1.83	1.35	1.87	2.93
1948	1.95	2.02	1.36	1.99	3.50
1949	2.04	2.13	1.21	1.98	3.55
1950	2.14	2.22	1.26	2.11	3.97
1951	2.25	2.32	1.22	2.04	3.79
1952	2.38	2.45	.92	1.96	3.69
1953	2.56	2.61	.98	1.96	3.99
1954	2.57	2.62	.99	1.97	3.86
1955	2.72	2.77	.94	2.02	3.77
1956	2.97	3.01	.94	1.96	3.64
1957	3.10	3.13	.90	1.88	3.77
1958	3.04	3.07	.89	1.85	3.58
1959	3.36	3.33	.94	1.89	3.59
1960	3.51	3.54	.82	1.73	3.57
1961	3.27	3.31	.91	1.81	3.62
1962	3.13	3.19	.75	1.71	3.58
1963	3.15	3.20	.76	1.60	3.54
1964	3.16	3.22	.77	1.61	3.46
1965	3.07	3.14	.85	1.55	3.42
1966	3.18	3.25	.63	1.39	3.40
1967	3.13	3.20	.50	1.24	3.38
1968	3.27	3.39	.67	1.42	3.39
1969	3.99	3.86	.84	1.59	3.71
1970	4.09	4.09	.85	1.55	3.76
1971	3.63	3.68	.94	1.56	3.54
1972	3.49	3.54	1.04	1.64	3.38
1973	3.77	3.80	1.12	1.82	3.34
1974	4.22	4.02	1.00	1.70	3.53
1975	3.81	3.89	1.00	1.66	3.29
1976	—	4.75	1.12	1.74	3.35
1977	—	4.90	1.23	1.80	3.29
1978	—	5.49	1.42	2.05	—

[a] Expressed in percentages. Source: Tables 9.6–9.10.

portant variable. Federal credit unions have always enjoyed high rate spreads, with a peak of almost 500 basis points in 1940. Thereafter federal credit union rate spreads tended to be between 300 and 400 basis points, with some decline in the late 1970s when usury ceilings adversely affected their portfolio yields. In the 1920s, when there are unfortunately no com-

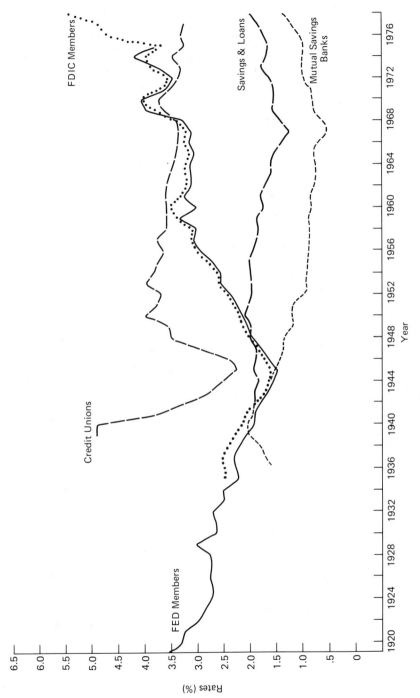

Figure 9.3 Rate spreads.

parable data available for thrifts, commercial rate spreads at times reached an order of magnitude of 300 basis points. This rate spread then declined through the depression and war years, at which point it began to build. By the late-1970s, rate spreads again at times exceeded 400 basis points and for FDIC-member commercial banks stood at a historical high of 549 basis points in 1978. It should be noted that this growth rate spread does not include the implicit deposit rate, which took up some part of this gap. For the mutual savings banks and the savings and loan associations, competitive forces resulted in rate spreads that tended to be somewhat lower. The rate spreads for the savings and loan associations were the most stable; they varied between 124 and just over 200 basis points per year. The year 1978 produced rate spreads of over 200 basis points for the first time since the mid-1950s. Mutual savings banks also had a buildup in rate spreads in the late-1970s, and these spreads reached 142 basis points in 1978, which was the highest since the early postwar period. Again, as with banks, these large spreads in the 1970s are partly a reflection of deposit ceilings, whereas the earlier large spreads reflected less vigorous explicit deposit rate competition. In the period of intense explicit rate competition of the 1950s and the 1960s, rate spreads for mutual savings banks were less than 100 basis points and even dropped as low as 50 basis points in 1967.

Out of these sharply differing rate spreads, the depository institutions must cover their operating costs per deposit dollar. That which is left over is profit per deposit dollar. Disparities between rate spreads among the different depository institutions in some years amounted to almost 400 basis points, leaving room for vastly different patterns of cost and profit.

Average annual operating costs per deposit dollar, defined as the ratio of total operating cost to average total deposits, includes both production costs as well as the nonrate competitive costs that have been expressed as an implicit deposit rate. Table 9.4 and Figure 9.4 indicate very substantial differences in total operating costs per deposit dollar both over time as well as across depository institutions. These operating costs per deposit dollar are the sum of production and nonrate competition costs. The sum of these costs varied between a low of 70 basis points per deposit dollar per year to a high of 444 basis points. Production costs depend on the maturity and turnover rates of both assets and liabilities as costs are incurred from cash management and asset management. In these cost records, throughout virtually the entire data series, federal credit unions had higher costs per deposit dollar per year, despite the fact that they were often the recipients of donations of both labor services and buildings and equipment. This relatively higher cost pattern, however, is partly understandable given the short-term maturities of their assets and their

TABLE 9.4

Total Operating Costs Per Deposit Dollar, oc^a

Year	Commercial banks		Mutual savings banks	Savings and loan associations	Federal credit unions
	Federal Reserve members	FDIC members			
1919	1.55	—	—	—	—
1920	1.91	—	—	—	—
1921	2.08	—	—	—	—
1922	1.98	—	—	—	—
1923	1.93	—	—	—	—
1924	1.85	—	—	—	—
1925	1.78	—	—	—	—
1926	1.83	—	—	—	—
1927	1.87	—	—	—	—
1928	1.85	—	—	—	—
1929	1.94	—	—	—	—
1930	1.91	—	—	—	—
1931	1.91	—	—	—	—
1932	2.03	—	—	—	—
1933	1.71	—	—	—	—
1934	1.68	—	—	—	—
1935	1.44	1.87	1.27	—	—
1936	1.39	1.78	1.44	—	—
1937	1.40	1.82	1.57	—	—
1938	1.39	1.79	1.61	—	—
1939	1.28	1.68	1.62	—	—
1940	1.16	1.55	1.39	—	3.46
1941	1.10	1.54	1.29	—	3.37
1942	1.15	1.33	1.27	1.22	3.19
1943	.98	1.13	1.83	1.26	2.69
1944	.88	1.01	1.05	1.31	2.42
1945	.82	.94	.80	1.43	2.20
1946	.93	1.04	.78	1.51	2.24
1947	1.07	1.18	.79	1.48	2.45
1948	1.14	1.30	.80	1.50	2.68
1949	1.19	1.37	.79	1.48	2.76
1950	1.22	1.41	.82	1.48	2.89
1951	1.26	1.45	.71	1.49	3.01
1952	1.33	1.52	.72	1.48	2.98
1953	1.42	1.62	.72	1.44	3.05
1954	1.46	1.68	.73	1.42	3.06
1955	1.51	1.74	.71	1.40	3.02
1956	1.61	1.86	.71	1.39	3.08
1957	1.70	1.97	.73	1.38	3.14

(*Continued*)

TABLE 9.4 (*Continued*)

Year	Commercial banks		Mutual savings banks	Savings and loan associations	Federal credit unions
	Federal Reserve members	FDIC members			
1958	1.74	2.02	.71	1.37	3.15
1959	1.83	2.11	.72	1.40	3.19
1960	1.94	2.25	.74	1.39	3.32
1961	1.89	2.22	.74	1.38	3.31
1962	1.90	2.23	.72	1.35	3.28
1963	1.96	2.29	.73	1.42	3.28
1964	1.97	2.30	.71	1.34	3.22
1965	1.94	2.26	.70	1.29	3.16
1966	2.01	2.33	.71	1.26	3.18
1967	2.06	2.38	.70	1.23	3.25
1968	2.14	2.38	.70	1.25	3.31
1969	2.66	2.81	.74	1.32	3.45
1970	2.86	3.29	.76	1.39	3.51
1971	2.71	3.16	.75	1.35	3.48
1972	2.59	3.00	.76	1.32	3.34
1973	2.63	3.05	.83	1.39	3.35
1974	2.77	3.33	.89	1.49	3.48
1975	2.87	3.58	.98	1.53	3.53
1976	—	3.96	1.08	1.51	3.54
1977	—	4.06	1.10	1.51	3.56
1978	—	4.44	1.19	1.54	—

[a] Calculated as the ratio of total operating expenses to average deposits and expressed in percentages. Includes production costs and nonrate competitive costs (implicit deposit rate). Source: Tables 9.6–9.10.

naturally higher labor costs per loan compared with those of savings and loan associations, mutual savings banks, or commercial banks. Savings and loan association costs in a free deposit rate era, when presumably all costs were production costs, were remarkably stable, varying between 120 and 150 basis points. The mutual savings banks' costs, which were typically less than 100 basis points, were considerably lower, perhaps because more of their portfolios are directed to open-market instruments. Cost reductions were experienced by all the depository institutions during the war years, when the purchase of government bonds tended to dominate asset selection. Of all the institutions, the commercial banks showed the greatest variability in cost levels over time. In the free-market era prior to 1933, commercial banks averaged a little under 200 basis points per year in cost. From this level, operating costs declined substantially

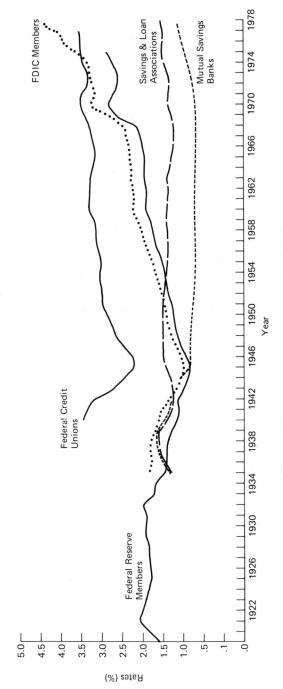

Figure 9.4 Total operating costs per deposit dollar.

through the depression and the war years as these institutions placed higher proportions of their assets in cash and open-market securities, particularly government bonds.

There are several trends worthy of note. It is not a coincidence that average costs per deposit dollar declined to a low point for both mutual savings banks and savings and loan associations in 1967, when competitive pressures were extreme. Although deposit ceilings were instituted in late-1966, in all likelihood they were not binding in 1967, as market interest rates declined immediately. The increasing competitive pressure from the early-1950s until 1967 caused these institutions to adjust to growing competitive pressures by the use of cost-cutting production methods. The effect of nonrate competition on costs after 1967 can be clearly seen in the time series for these two institutions as operating costs began to increase and nonrate competitive costs became a growing share of total costs. The costs of savings and loan associations increased from 123 basis points to 154 basis points, and mutual savings bank costs increased from 70 to 119 basis points by the end of 1978. Though deposit ceilings were also established for credit unions, the rate differential was favorable to them and allowed them enough flexibility to compete for deposits on a rate, rather than a nonrate, basis. As a result, their costs increased relatively less over time. For commercial banks, the establishment of deposit ceilings in 1933 did not result immediately in the payment of implicit deposit rates and nonrate competition. In fact, there was a downtrend in operating costs from the late-1920 and early-1930 levels all the way through the end of the war period. At that time, more expensive portfolio operations apparently added to costs and the competition for deposits that lead to the payment of implicit deposit rates apparently commenced at that time, as operating costs grew continuously from the entire wartime period through the late-1970s. This increase in cost was large. For FDIC members, costs more than quadrupled from 94 basis points in 1945 to 444 in 1978.

There is, then, an interesting relationship between competition and costs. In a free deposit rate market, greater competitive pressures and their commensurately slimmer profit margins forced the depository institutions to be more cost-efficient in order to maintain profit margins. This is consistent with the X-efficiency phenomenon previously noted for production firms, in which greater competition not only squeezes profit margins, but causes a downshift in the average cost curve.[1] In a deposit ceiling era, on the other hand, competition for deposits manifests itself by

---

[1] See William S. Comanor and Harvey Leibenstein, "Allocative Efficiency, X-Efficiency, and the Measurement of Welfare Losses," *Economica* **36** (August 1969).

the payment of implicit deposit rates and tends to increase total operating costs per deposit dollar.

Profit margins per deposit dollar are a residual. They are the difference between the rate spread and operating costs and are shown in Table 9.5 and Figure 9.5. Despite substantial dissimilarities in earning rates, rate

TABLE 9.5

Profit Margin Per Deposit Dollar from the Deposit Activity p^a

	Commercial banks		Mutual savings banks	Savings and loan associations	Federal credit unions
Year	Federal Reserve members	FDIC members			
1919	1.04	—	—	—	—
1920	1.36	—	—	—	—
1921	1.17	—	—	—	—
1922	.98	—	—	—	—
1923	.86	—	—	—	—
1924	.87	—	—	—	—
1925	.93	—	—	—	—
1926	.95	—	—	—	—
1927	.87	—	—	—	—
1928	.91	—	—	—	—
1929	1.12	—	—	—	—
1930	.71	—	—	—	—
1931	.73	—	—	—	—
1932	.67	—	—	—	—
1933	.77	—	—	—	—
1934	.82	—	—	—	—
1935	.76	.62	.32	—	—
1936	.87	.69	.30	—	—
1937	.91	.71	.22	—	—
1938	.83	.64	.41	—	—
1939	.82	.63	.43	—	—
1940	.77	.58	.70	—	1.46
1941	.80	.55	.63	—	1.55
1942	.63	.55	.65	.68	.55
1943	.68	.59	.90	.67	.00
1944	.70	.54	.61	.52	.09
1945	.66	.62	.76	.50	.06
1946	.71	.68	.68	.38	.15
1947	.73	.64	.56	.39	.48
1948	.80	.71	.55	.48	.81
1949	.85	.75	.42	.50	.79
1950	.92	.81	.43	.62	1.08

(Continued)

TABLE 9.5 (*Continued*)

Year	Commercial banks		Mutual savings banks	Savings and loan associations	Federal credit unions
	Federal Reserve members	FDIC members			
1951	.99	.87	.50	.54	.77
1952	1.05	.92	.19	.48	.70
1953	1.14	.98	.25	.52	.93
1954	1.11	.94	.26	.55	.79
1955	1.21	1.03	.22	.61	.74
1956	1.35	1.15	.22	.56	.55
1957	1.40	1.15	.17	.49	.63
1958	1.30	1.05	.17	.47	.43
1959	1.53	1.22	.22	.49	.40
1960	1.56	1.28	.08	.34	.25
1961	1.37	1.09	.16	.43	.30
1962	1.23	.96	.02	.35	.29
1963	1.19	.91	.02	.18	.26
1964	1.19	.92	.06	.27	.23
1965	1.13	.87	.15	.26	.25
1966	1.16	.91	−.07	.12	.21
1967	1.06	.82	−.19	.00	.12
1968	1.13	1.00	−.02	.17	.07
1969	1.32	1.05	.09	.26	.26
1970	1.22	.79	.08	.16	.24
1971	.91	.52	.19	.21	.06
1972	.89	.53	.28	.32	.03
1973	1.15	.75	.29	.42	−.01
1974	1.45	.69	.11	.21	.05
1975	.94	.31	.02	.13	−.23
1976	—	.79	.03	.22	−.18
1977	—	.83	.13	.36	−.26
1978	—	1.04	.23	.50	—

[a] Calculated as the average asset earning rate less the effective deposit rate less total operating expenses per deposit dollar. Expressed in percentages. Source: Tables 9.6–9.10.

spreads, and operating costs, profit margins per deposit dollar for all the depository institutions tended to move within a relatively small range. Profit margins from deposit activity fluctuated between a high of 156 basis points for commercial banks in 1960 and a low of −26 basis points for federal credit unions in 1977. In all, there were only seven instances of negative profit margins for any of the depository industries. The mid- and late-1970s were particularly hard on federal credit unions, laboring under usury constraints, and in the mid-1960s mutual savings banks experienced

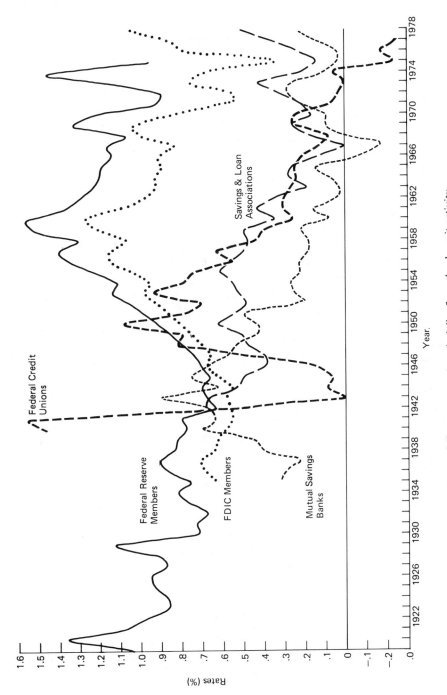

Figure 9.5 Profit per deposit dollar from the deposit activity.

extreme competitive pressures. Comparing the four depository industries, commercial banks' profit margins tended to dominate thrifts, with
Fed members tending to dominate all FDIC members.[2]

Among the thrifts, the savings and loan associations exhibited a greater
stability of profit over time, without a single recorded year of losses
between 1942 and 1979. The mutual savings banks fared well during the
war years and immediate postwar period, but subsequently encountered
difficulties in the mid-1960s and again in the mid-1970s. The federal credit
unions perhaps vacillated most in their fortunes, with very good profit
records entering the World War II period and in the highly profitable
postwar era—but with growing competitive pressures and usury ceiling
adversities affecting them in the 1970s.

These profit margins in both a free deposit rate market and a rate-
regulated market depend on a great number of variables. It is interesting
to examine the effect of competitive pressures on profit margins in the
free-market deposit rate era for commercial banks prior to 1933 and for
the thrifts prior to 1967. Table 11.1 contains the explicit deposit elasticities calculated from Eq. (3.15). Deposit elasticity, technically, is a measure of deposit level sensitivity to deposit rate changes. From Eq. (3.11) it
can be seen that the profit margin in a rate-competitive environment depends on this deposit elasticity. This derives from the commonsense notion that the depository firm is forced to pay increasing proportions of net
revenues in deposit rates, which whittles away at profit as the competitive
forces of the market build. The estimates of these deposit elasticities in
the deposit rate free-market era for the thrift institutions give evidence
that competitive pressures were easing from the mid-1930s through the
war years.

Data available from 1935 onward for mutual savings banks indicate that
deposit elasticities of between 6 and 8 in the mid- to late-1930s declined to
less than 3 during most of the war years. It might be recalled that the proportion of net revenues preserved in profit margins is equal to $1/(1 + \epsilon)$.
With relatively low deposit elasticities of approximately 3, this means that
25% of net revenues were retained as profit. Deposit elasticity, calculated
similarly for savings and loan associations and credit unions shows that
competitive forces declined until a low was reached for credit unions and

---

[2] It should be carefully noted that calculating of the profit margin per deposit dollar was
designed to capture both the revenues and costs associated with the deposit activity alone.
In doing so, both the revenues and costs associated with borrowed funds were omitted from
consideration. This probably had the strongest impact on the calculated profit margins for
commercial banks. Commercial banks are more capable of borrowing short for purposes of
exploiting short-run differences between asset and borrowing rates. On the other hand, this
procedure also excluded borrowing costs due to deposit withdrawals.

savings and loan associations in 1950. From the early-1950s, when the pace of entry began to quicken (see Chapter 11), the competitive environment for all depository institutions intensified. For mutual savings banks, deposit elasticities rose especially sharply, from a low of 1.94 in 1945 to over 100 in 1962, which indicates an approach to perfect competition in which elasticities are infinite. The increase in deposit elasticities for savings and loan associations was a bit slower through the 1950s as elasticity rose from 4 to 7 by the end of the decade. This was followed by sharp increases in the 1960s; by 1967 for those institutions too deposit elasticities were in the hundreds and, for all practical purposes, approached perfect competition. The climb of deposit elasticity for federal credit unions was a bit slower and never reached the same extreme competitive heights experienced by the other thrift institutions. This is not to say that the federal credit unions were left alone in a highly insulated protected market, because by 1967 deposit elasticities reached 37, or a profit retention rate of $\frac{1}{38}$. It is little wonder, with these extreme competitive levels in the deposit rate free-markets, that the protective device of deposit ceilings was the forthcoming response.

It is interesting to note the recovery of profit margins that took place for the thrift institutions after the initiation of deposit ceilings. The mutual savings banks recovered from 3 years of negative profit margins to achieve almost 30 basis points of profit in 1973, as shown in Table 9.5. Similarly, the savings and loan association profit margins increased from a low of less than one basis point to 42 basis points in that single year. The high interest rate tight-money period of 1974 and 1975 caused profit margins for these institutions to decline, and, in fact, mutual savings bank profit margins became negligible in 1975 at 2 basis points, and savings and loan profit margins declined to 13 basis points. From there recovery began, again, as a result of three factors. The mutual savings banks in the New England states were granted NOW account authority in 1976, which reduced the pressure on weighted average deposit rates. In addition, during this rising interest rate period many certificates of deposit were withdrawn, with penalties absorbed by depositors, for the purchase of new certificates with yet higher yields as interest rates increased. These penalties from certificate of deposit turnover were a windfall for the thrift institutions that helped their short-run profit position, but over time, the higher cost of funds produced adverse effects. Another factor affecting the savings and loan associations in the late-1970s was the increasing revenues from fees and discount points earned by associations, particularly in states with usury ceilings. In order to lend funds at competitive rates when there is a binding usury ceiling, these associations must charge fees and points that generate enough revenue at the origination of the mortgage loan so that over the life of the mortgage they will earn competitive rates. This time pattern of income from a mortgage loan tends to elevate revenues in the initial year of a loan, which again accounts for the very high earning rates of savings and loan associations in 1978.

Rising interest rates can yield short-term benefits to thrifts if deposit cost adjusts sluggishly at first. However, over time, increasing interest rates tend to have adverse effects on a depository institution, especially if the maturity of the assets well exceeds the maturity of the liabilities. The relatively shorter the maturity of the liabilities, the more rapidly depositors are in a position to earn higher deposit rates, either because ceilings increase or because they shift from passbook or other lower yielding accounts to higher yielding certificates. The introduction of the money market certificate in June 1978 with a deposit ceiling that floated a half point above market rates provided a stimulus for such account switching. Though the longer term implications for thrifts were not sanguine, they did result in a short-run windfall gain as early withdrawal penalties were incurred. Thus, rising interest rates in the late-1970s, rather than having immediate adverse effects on savings and loan associations, actually benefited them in the short run, so that profit margins rose to levels not experienced since the mid-1950s.

Another important determinant of how well thrift institutions will fare when interest rates increase depends on their net deposit inflows. Thrift institutions must have net deposit inflows in order to place funds in higher-yielding assets. Short of net deposit inflows, their only opportunity to obtain and lock in current higher interest rates would be from asset turnover when mortgages are refinanced or from principal repayments as loans are amortized. When inflation rates increased in the 1970s, there was a sluggish adjustment of both earning and deposit rates. Although the initial impact of rising inflation was not adverse to profit margins, since effective deposit rates adjusted less quickly, the relatively shorter deposit maturity and relatively insignificant deposit inflows would be expected to have adverse future implications. This longer term adjustment to rising inflation and interest rates had begun to be felt at the end of the 1970s as savings and loan association profit margins dipped to 21 basis points in 1979.

These recent movements in revenues, costs, and profit can be summarized for each of the depository institutions. For mutual savings banks the relatively more rapid adjustment of asset earning rates than effective deposit rates began as early as 1967. The imposition of deposit ceilings tended to hold down rates, and the introduction of the NOW account authority resulted in the switching of savings deposit to lower interest-bearing transaction accounts. This growing rate spread was offset to some extent by rising operating costs per deposit dollar, which rose almost 50 basis points in the same time period. This increasing level of operating costs was no doubt partly caused by the need to administer transaction accounts, as well from a burst of branching activity that occurred in the 1970s.[3]

The longer term trends are clearest with savings and loan associations, as they were relatively free of unique regulatory factors that affected the mutual savings banks and credit unions. The free-market era, with its competitive ebb in 1950, produced large profit margins. The growing free-market pressures over the next decade and a half caused profit margins to then dwindle. At first, the rate ceiling era witnessed growing profit margins as rate spreads increased from 124 to 182 basis points from 1967 to 1973. During the 1970s, this rate spread increase was partly offset by a 32% increase in cost due to the payment of implicit deposit rates. The inflation burst in the late 1970s had at first the short-run effect of moderating increases in deposit rates as early withdrawal penalties were absorbed by depositors in 1978. For savings and loan associations, the longer term adverse inflationary effects became evident beginning in 1979.

While mutual savings banks and savings and loan associations fared relatively well from 1975 to 1978, federal credit unions did not. The reason for the asymmetry in these inflationary impacts on thrift institutions was the rigid 1% per month usury ceiling imposed on the loans of credit unions at this time. With the credit unions unable to increase asset earning rates after 1974, but still having to compete for deposits in a rising interest rate market, the rate spreads declined after that year. The decline in the rate spread was not great but, it began from a base of an essentially break-even profit margin. In fact, in 1973 the deposit activity incurred a 1 basis point loss and in 1974 a negligible 5 basis point profit. In 1977 federal credit unions were running a 26 basis point deficit on their deposit activity, but have since recovered. These and other time trends for the thrift institutions and the commercial banks are shown in Tables 9.6–9.10 and the corresponding Figures 9.6–9.10. The basic balance sheet and income and expense data for the commercial banks and thrifts are found in Appendix Tables A9.1–A9.12.

9.2   ERAS OF COMMERCIAL BANK PERFORMANCE

There are several discernible eras when both market and regulatory forces affected the performance of the commercial banking industry.

---

[3] Robert A. Taggart in "Effects of Deposit Rate Ceilings" (*Journal of Money Credit and Banking* 10 [May 1978]) concluded that for mutual savings banks, a sizable fraction of excess expenditures incurred under rate regulation appeared to be attributable to branching.

Since data exist for Federal Reserve member banks dating from 1919 and
for FDIC members from 1934, these two series will be examined to see
the impact of the different forces on commercial banks.

9.2.1   The Post-World War I Expansion: 1919–1923

In this era of laissez faire, free enterprise in commercial banking, legal
barriers to entry and regulatory restrictions placed on commercial banks

TABLE 9.6

Savings and Loan Associations: Revenues, Spreads, Costs,
and Profit Per Deposit Dollar[a]

Year	r_a Asset earning rate[b]	r Effective deposit rate[c]	$r_a - r$ Rate spread	oc Total operating cost rate[d]	p Profit margin[e]	$p/(r_a - r)$ Profit margin divided by rate spread
1942	4.10	2.19	1.91	1.22	.68	35.81
1943	4.21	2.26	1.94	1.26	.67	34.91
1944	4.13	2.28	1.84	1.31	.52	28.56
1945	4.26	2.32	1.94	1.43	.50	26.09
1946	4.32	2.41	1.90	1.51	.35	20.40
1947	4.24	2.37	1.87	1.48	.39	20.98
1948	4.43	2.44	1.99	1.50	.48	24.37
1949	4.50	2.51	1.98	1.48	.50	25.44
1950	4.63	2.52	2.11	1.48	.62	29.68
1951	4.63	2.59	2.04	1.49	.54	26.57
1952	4.66	2.69	1.96	1.48	.48	24.80
1953	4.77	2.81	1.96	1.44	.52	26.70
1954	4.85	2.87	1.97	1.42	.55	28.02
1955	4.96	2.94	2.02	1.40	.61	30.54
1956	4.99	3.03	1.96	1.39	.56	28.96
1957	5.14	3.26	1.88	1.38	.49	26.39
1958	5.23	3.38	1.85	1.37	.47	25.75
1959	5.42	3.53	1.89	1.40	.49	25.86
1960	5.58	3.85	1.73	1.39	.34	19.63
1961	5.66	3.85	1.81	1.38	.43	23.90
1962	5.84	4.13	1.71	1.35	.35	20.81
1963	5.77	4.11	1.60	1.42	.18	11.39
1964	5.80	4.19	1.61	1.34	.27	16.81
1965	5.79	4.23	1.55	1.29	.26	17.26
1966	5.84	4.45	1.39	1.26	.12	9.14
1967	5.91	4.67	1.24	1.23	.00	.73
1968	6.10	4.67	1.42	1.25	.17	12.25
1969	6.39	4.80	1.59	1.32	.26	16.81
1970	6.61	5.05	1.55	1.39	.16	10.41

TABLE 9.6 (*Continued*)

Year	r_a Asset earning rate[b]	r Effective deposit rate[c]	$r_a - r$ Rate spread	oc Total operating cost rate[d]	p Profit margin[e]	$p/(r_a - r)$ Profit margin divided by rate spread
1971	6.86	5.30	1.56	1.35	.21	13.70
1972	7.03	5.38	1.64	1.32	.32	19.54
1973	7.36	5.54	1.82	1.39	.42	23.24
1974	7.63	5.97	1.70	1.49	.21	12.44
1975	7.90	6.23	1.66	1.53	.13	7.79
1976	8.05	6.31	1.74	1.51	.22	12.94
1977	8.28	6.40	1.88	1.51	.36	19.46
1978	8.58	6.52	2.05	1.54	.50	24.62

[a] Expressed in percentages. Source: Tables A9.11–A9.13.

[b] The asset earning rate is an estimate of the weighted average of the individual asset rates in the portfolio including cash. It is calculated as the ratio of earnings to average annual financial assets. The rate is net of taxes other than income taxes, bad debts, and other asset losses.

[c] The effective deposit rate is an estimate of the weighted average of rates paid on all deposit accounts. It is calculated as the ratio of interest cost to average deposits.

[d] The total operating cost rate is the ratio of all operating expenses to average deposits. It nets out all nonoperating expenses.

[e] The profit margin is profit per deposit dollar. It is calculated as $r_a - r - oc$.

were relatively insignificant. The national banking system was intact, and all national banks were members of the Federal Reserve. The Federal Reserve System of 12 regional banks was in place to provide an elastic currency and cash reserves to the banking system when the need for liquidity arose. None of these Fed operations had a significant effect on the competitive structure of the depository industry.

The essence of the 1919 to 1923 era derived not only from the general tone of laissez faire, but also from the environment of an expanding economy despite a short-lived contraction in 1921. The combination of regulatory freedom, good economic times, and a greater degree of security because of the newly formed central bank no doubt generated a feeling of optimism in the industry. In this environment, asset and deposit rates were determined by the market, and with no barriers to entry, market forces also determined the number of competitors. As will be more thoroughly discussed in Chapter 11, the number of competitors in the depository markets increased and, in fact, reached peaks in the early 1920s, both in absolute terms and relative to the population. From the Federal Reserve member banks data in Table 9.9, we are provided with a

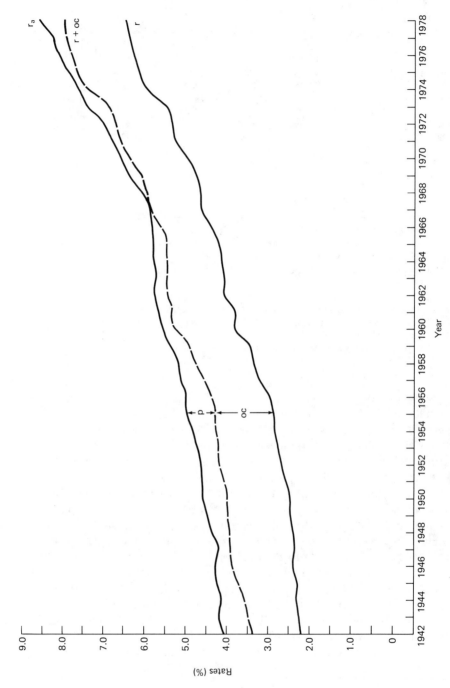

Figure 9.6 Savings and loan associations time trends.

TABLE 9.7

Mutual Savings Banks: Revenues, Spreads, Costs, and Profit Per Deposit Dollar[a]

Year	r_a Asset earning rate[b]	r Effective deposit rate[c]	$r_a - r$ Rate spread	oc Total operating cost rate[d]	p Profit margin[e]	$p/(r_a - r)$ Profit margin divided by rate spread
1934	—	—	—	—	—	—
1935	3.78	2.18	1.59	1.27	.32	20.26
1936	3.73	1.98	1.75	1.44	.30	17.72
1937	3.73	1.92	1.80	1.57	.22	12.52
1938	3.94	1.91	2.03	1.61	.41	20.34
1939	4.26	2.19	2.06	1.62	.43	21.20
1940	4.04	1.94	2.10	1.39	.70	33.66
1941	3.57	1.64	1.92	1.29	.63	32.84
1942	3.66	1.73	1.93	1.27	.65	34.03
1943	5.20	2.46	2.73	1.83	.90	33.05
1944	3.27	1.61	1.66	1.05	.61	36.84
1945	3.05	1.48	1.57	.80	.76	48.69
1946	2.93	1.46	1.46	.78	.68	46.48
1947	2.89	1.53	1.35	.79	.56	41.67
1948	2.93	1.57	1.36	.80	.55	40.83
1949	3.00	1.78	1.21	.79	.42	35.19
1950	3.10	1.84	1.26	.82	.43	34.39
1951	3.12	1.90	1.22	.71	.50	41.40
1952	3.19	2.27	.92	.72	.19	21.40
1953	3.34	2.36	.98	.72	.25	26.27
1954	3.42	2.43	.99	.73	.26	26.28
1955	3.55	2.60	.94	.71	.22	23.77
1956	3.70	2.76	.94	.71	.22	24.18
1957	3.90	2.99	.90	.73	.17	19.69
1958	3.99	3.10	.89	.71	.17	19.50
1959	4.16	3.21	.94	.72	.22	23.86
1960	4.40	3.57	.82	.74	.08	9.66
1961	4.45	3.53	.91	.74	.16	18.49
1962	4.59	3.83	.75	.72	.02	3.06
1963	4.72	3.96	.76	.73	.02	3.54
1964	4.84	4.06	.77	.71	.06	8.10
1965	4.94	4.08	.85	.70	.15	17.94
1966	5.07	4.43	.63	.71	−.07	−11.44
1967	5.24	4.73	.50	.70	−.19	−38.34
1968	5.43	4.76	.67	.70	−.02	−3.82
1969	5.69	4.85	.84	.74	.09	11.04
1970	5.43	4.58	.85	.76	.08	10.29
1971	5.40	4.46	.94	.75	.19	20.29
1972	5.60	4.55	1.04	.76	.28	26.69
1973	5.89	4.76	1.12	.83	.29	26.30
1974	6.04	5.03	1.00	.89	.11	11.04

(*Continued*)

TABLE 9.7 (*Continued*)

Year	r_a Asset earning rate[b]	r Effective deposit rate[c]	$r_a - r$ Rate spread	oc Total operating cost rate[d]	p Profit margin[e]	$p/(r_a - r)$ Profit margin divided by rate spread
1975	6.27	5.27	1.00	.98	.02	1.98
1976	6.53	5.40	1.12	1.08	.03	3.46
1977	6.71	5.47	1.23	1.10	.13	10.49
1978	7.04	5.61	1.42	1.19	.23	16.16

[a] Expressed in percentages. Source: Tables A9.8–A9.10.

[b] The asset earning rate is an estimate of the weighted average of the individual asset rates in the portfolio including cash. It is calculated as the ratio of earnings to average annual financial assets. The rate is net of taxes other than income taxes, bad debts, and other asset losses.

[c] The effective deposit rate is an estimate of the weighted average of rates paid on all deposit accounts. It is calculated as the ratio of interest cost to average deposits.

[d] The total operating cost rate is the ratio of all operating expenses to average deposits. It nets out all nonoperating expenses.

[e] The profit margin is profit per deposit dollar. It is calculated as $r_a - r - oc$.

limited snapshot of the market forces at work. In 1919 and 1920 profit margins were high and rising, reaching a peak of 136 basis points in 1920. The deposit elasticities in those years were quite low, indicating that even though there were a great number of depository institutions, they were apparently distributed in such a way that competitive forces were not very strong. The reason for this is that a large number of these institutions were comparatively small and were spread out in many small towns across the country. This early period of market freedom was responsible for many interesting records. The average asset earning rate reached a peak of 5.23% in 1921, a level that would not be reached again until 1968, and the effective deposit rate reached a peak of 2.01% in 1922, a peak which also was not reached again until 1968. Rate spreads were also quite high, with a 1920 peak of 3.28% not equaled again until 1959. Finally, profit margins per deposit dollar had reached a peak of 136 basis points in 1920, a level which would not be surpassed until 1957.

9.2.2   A Period of Consolidation: 1923–1929

In 1922 the number of banking offices reached a high of 31,259, and thereafter some consolidation of the industry began. The number of commercial banks declined from 29,458 to 24,026 in 1929. This decline was

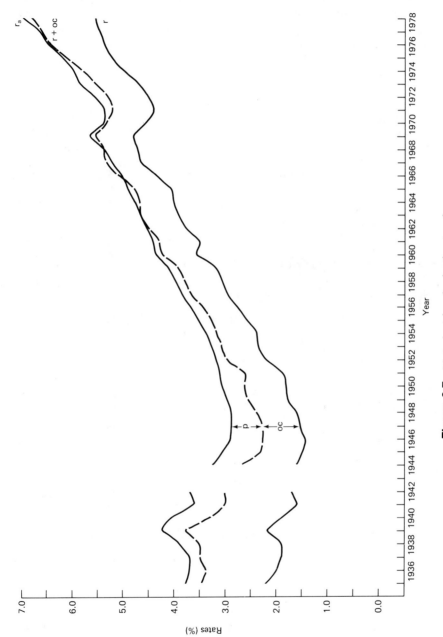

Figure 9.7 Mutual savings banks time trends.

due to merger, voluntary withdrawal from the market, and some suspensions. It was partially offset by larger numbers of branches as branch offices rose from 1801 to 3353. This consolidation period had its most obvious effect on total operating costs per deposit dollar. In 1921, average production costs stood at 208 basis points, and during this period of consoli-

TABLE 9.8

Federal Credit Unions: Revenues, Spreads, Costs, and Profit Per Deposit Dollar[a]

Year	r_a Asset earning rate[b]	r Effective deposit rate[c]	$r_a - r$ Rate spread	oc Total operating cost rate[d]	p Profit margin[e]	$p/(r_a - r)$ Profit margin divided by rate spread
1940	8.87	3.95	4.92	3.46	1.46	29.76
1941	8.25	3.33	4.92	3.37	1.55	31.48
1942	5.90	2.16	3.74	3.19	.55	14.85
1943	4.20	1.51	2.69	2.69	−.00	−.14
1944	3.91	1.40	2.51	2.42	.09	3.77
1945	3.80	1.54	2.26	2.20	.06	2.91
1946	4.16	1.76	2.40	2.24	.15	6.41
1947	5.14	2.21	2.93	2.45	.48	16.37
1948	6.12	2.62	3.50	2.68	.81	23.27
1949	6.53	2.98	3.55	2.76	.79	22.30
1950	7.23	3.26	3.97	2.89	1.08	27.21
1951	7.02	3.23	3.79	3.01	.77	20.47
1952	7.01	3.32	3.69	2.98	.70	19.05
1953	7.49	3.50	3.99	3.05	.93	23.42
1954	7.42	3.56	3.86	3.06	.79	20.62
1955	7.42	3.65	3.77	3.02	.74	19.74
1956	7.48	3.84	3.64	3.08	.55	15.30
1957	7.69	3.92	3.77	3.14	.63	16.78
1958	7.58	4.00	3.58	3.15	.43	12.15
1959	7.66	4.07	3.59	3.19	.40	11.20
1960	7.86	4.29	3.57	3.32	.25	7.18
1961	8.03	4.41	3.62	3.31	.30	8.45
1962	8.09	4.51	3.58	3.28	.29	8.18
1963	8.12	4.58	3.54	3.28	.26	7.37
1964	8.08	4.62	3.46	3.22	.23	6.84
1965	8.04	4.62	3.42	3.16	.25	7.51
1966	8.16	4.76	3.40	3.18	.21	6.26
1967	8.22	4.84	3.38	3.25	.12	3.81
1968	8.33	4.94	3.39	3.31	.07	2.24
1969	8.85	5.13	3.71	3.45	.26	7.04
1970	9.08	5.32	3.76	3.51	.24	6.59
1971	8.91	5.37	3.54	3.48	.06	1.69

TABLE 9.8 (*Continued*)

Year	r_a Asset earning rate[b]	r Effective deposit rate[c]	$r_a - r$ Rate spread	oc Total operating cost rate[d]	p Profit margin[e]	$p/(r_a - r)$ Profit margin divided by rate spread
1972	8.83	5.44	3.38	3.34	.03	1.15
1973	9.04	5.69	3.34	3.35	−.01	−.35
1974	9.46	5.93	3.53	3.48	.05	1.47
1975	9.35	6.05	3.29	3.53	−.23	−7.21
1976	9.42	6.06	3.35	3.54	−.18	−5.57
1977	9.43	6.13	3.29	3.56	−.26	−8.07

[a] Expressed in percentages. Source: For the years 1940 to 1966, adapted from Table 1, Selected Data for Federal Credit Unions, Joseph M. Burns, "An Examination of the Operating Efficiency of Three Financial Intermediaries," *Journal of Financial and Quantitative Analysis*, **4**, September 1969. The source of Table 1 was U.S. Department of Health, Education and Welfare, Bureau of Federal Credit Unions, *Federal Credit Unions, Report of Operations*, various years. For 1967 to 1977, National Credit Union Administration, *Annual Report*, various years.

[b] Total gross income minus interest refund/average financial assets. Average financial assets have been estimated to be 99% of total assets.

[c] Total dividends on shares minus life savings insurance/average deposits.

[d] Total expenses minus interest on borrowed money minus life savings insurance/average deposits.

[e] The profit margin per deposit dollar is $r_a - r - c$.

dation, they declined to 178 in 1925 and then experienced a small increase by 1929. The essential change of this era was the growing concentration of deposit funds, both through the growth of branch systems and from the chain and group banking systems that were becoming fairly common. Market conduct in the mid-1920s was openly collusive. It was generally felt that banks operated outside the orbit of the Sherman Act because of their quasi regulation by the central bank. In many cities, clearing house associations acted as the focal point to prescribe such things as interest rates on loans and deposits, banking hours, and service charges. The data lend credence to the existence of collusion in depository markets, since deposit elasticities at that time were extremely low (close to 2), despite the large number of depository institutions in both absolute and relative terms. (See Table 11.1.) Certainly these deposit elasticities of the 1920s were considerably lower than those faced by the thrift institutions in the early postwar era. With deposit elasticities hovering near 2, the profit retention rate was one-third of net revenues.

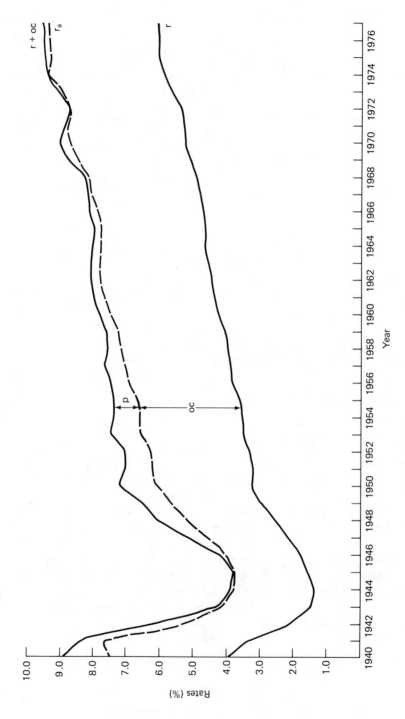

Figure 9.8 Federal credit unions time trends.

TABLE 9.9

Federal Reserve Member Banks: Revenues, Spreads, Costs,
and Profit Per Deposit Dollar[a]

Year	r_a Asset earning rate[b]	r Effective deposit rate[c]	$r_a - r$ Rate spread	oc Total operating cost rate[d]	p Profit margin[e]	$p/(r_a - r)$ Profit margin divided by rate spread
1919	4.37	1.77	2.59	1.55	1.04	0.40
1920	5.14	1.86	3.28	1.91	1.36	0.41
1921	5.23	1.97	3.25	2.08	1.17	0.36
1922	4.97	2.01	2.96	1.98	.98	0.33
1923	4.80	1.96	2.84	1.93	.86	0.30
1924	4.68	1.95	2.73	1.85	.87	0.32
1925	4.65	1.93	2.72	1.78	.93	0.34
1926	4.74	1.95	2.78	1.83	.95	0.34
1927	4.52	1.77	2.75	1.87	.87	0.32
1928	4.55	1.78	2.76	1.85	.91	0.33
1929	4.86	1.79	3.06	1.94	1.12	0.37
1930	4.44	1.80	2.63	1.91	.71	0.27
1931	4.21	1.55	2.65	1.91	.73	0.28
1932	4.05	1.34	2.71	2.03	.67	0.25
1933	3.47	.98	2.48	1.71	.77	0.31
1934	3.28	.78	2.50	1.68	.82	0.33
1935	2.77	.56	2.21	1.44	.76	0.34
1936	2.71	.44	2.26	1.39	.87	0.38
1937	2.75	.42	2.32	1.40	.91	0.39
1938	2.63	.40	2.22	1.39	.83	0.37
1939	2.45	.34	2.11	1.28	.82	0.39
1940	2.21	.27	1.93	1.16	.77	0.40
1941	2.14	.23	1.91	1.10	.80	0.42
1942	1.96	.18	1.78	1.15	.63	0.35
1943	1.80	.14	1.66	.98	.68	0.41
1944	1.73	.14	1.59	.88	.70	0.44
1945	1.64	.15	1.49	.82	.66	0.44
1946	1.82	.17	1.64	.93	.71	0.43
1947	2.00	.19	1.80	1.07	.73	0.41
1948	2.16	.20	1.95	1.14	.80	0.41
1949	2.26	.21	2.04	1.19	.85	0.42
1950	2.35	.21	2.14	1.22	.92	0.43
1951	2.47	.22	2.25	1.26	.99	0.44
1952	2.64	.25	2.38	1.33	1.05	0.44
1953	2.84	.28	2.56	1.42	1.14	0.44
1954	2.89	.32	2.57	1.46	1.11	0.43
1955	3.06	.33	2.72	1.51	1.21	0.44
1956	3.36	.39	2.97	1.61	1.35	0.45
1957	3.65	.54	3.10	1.70	1.40	0.45

(Continued)

TABLE 9.9 (*Continued*)

Year	r_a Asset earning rate[b]	r Effective deposit rate[c]	$r_a - r$ Rate spread	oc Total operating cost rate[d]	p Profit margin[e]	$p/(r_a - r)$ Profit margin divided by rate spread
1958	3.68	.63	3.04	1.74	1.30	.43
1959	4.00	.69	3.36	1.83	1.53	.44
1960	4.27	.75	3.51	1.94	1.56	.44
1961	4.12	.85	3.27	1.89	1.37	.42
1962	4.23	1.09	3.13	1.90	1.23	.39
1963	4.42	1.27	3.15	1.96	1.19	.38
1964	4.55	1.39	3.16	1.97	1.19	.38
1965	4.65	1.58	3.07	1.94	1.13	.37
1966	5.02	1.83	3.18	2.01	1.16	.36
1967	5.09	1.96	3.13	2.06	1.06	.34
1968	5.35	2.08	3.27	2.14	1.13	.34
1969	5.98	1.99	3.99	2.66	1.32	.33
1970	6.30	2.21	4.09	2.86	1.22	.30
1971	5.95	2.32	3.63	2.71	.91	.25
1972	5.80	2.31	3.49	2.59	.89	.25
1973	6.82	3.04	3.77	2.63	1.15	.30
1974	8.18	3.95	4.22	2.77	1.45	.34
1975	7.20	3.39	3.81	2.87	.94	.25
1976	—	—	—	—	—	—
1977	—	—	—	—	—	—
1978	—	—	—	—	—	—

[a] Expressed in percentages. Source: Tables A9.1–A9.3.

[b] The asset earning rate is an estimate of the weighted average of the individual asset rates in the portfolio including cash. It is calculated as the ratio of earnings to average annual financial assets. The rate is net of taxes other than income taxes, bad debts, and other asset losses.

[c] The effective deposit rate is an estimate of the weighted average of rates paid on all deposit accounts. It is calculated as the ratio of interest cost to average deposits.

[d] The total operating cost rate is the ratio of all operating expenses to average deposits. It nets out all nonoperating expenses. Service charges are also netted out so that these revenues reduce net operating costs.

[e] The profit margin is profit per deposit dollar. It is calculated as $r_a - r - oc$.

9.2.3   The Depression Years: 1930–1933

While the mid-1920s was a period of consolidation, the depression years, when over 11,000 banks were either absorbed, suspended or liquidated voluntarily, resulted in a compression of the banking industry. It is of interest to note, in examining the condition of the banking system in 1929, that this massive shakeout of firms was not the direct result of competitive pressures. In 1929, profit margins were at the substantial level of 112 basis points per deposit dollar.

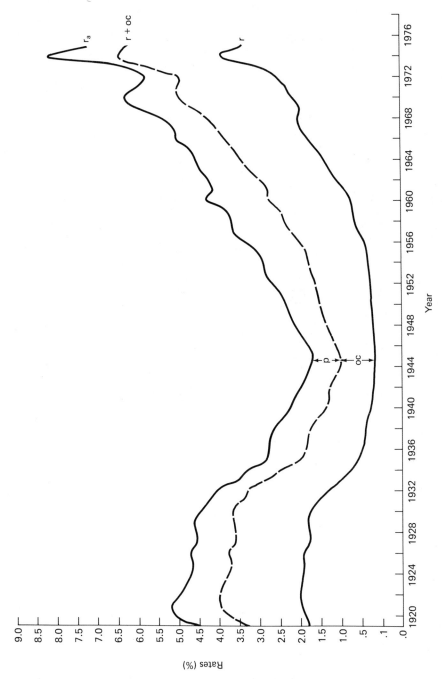

Figure 9.9 Federal Reserve member banks time trends.

TABLE 9.10

FDIC Commercial Banks: Revenues, Spreads, Costs,
and Profit Per Deposit Dollar[a]

Year	r_a Asset earning rate[b]	r Effective deposit rate[c]	$r_a - r$ Rate spread	oc Total operating cost rate[d]	p Profit margin[e]	$p/(r_a - r)$ Profit margin divided by rate spread
1934	—	—	—	—	—	—
1935	3.13	.63	2.49	1.87	.62	25.09
1936	2.99	.50	2.48	1.78	.69	28.03
1937	3.02	.48	2.53	1.82	.71	28.16
1938	2.91	.47	2.44	1.79	.64	26.34
1939	2.72	.40	2.32	1.68	.63	27.50
1940	2.47	.33	2.14	1.55	.58	27.32
1941	2.37	.28	2.09	1.54	.55	26.27
1942	2.10	.22	1.88	1.33	.55	29.26
1943	1.90	.17	1.73	1.13	.59	34.46
1944	1.80	.16	1.64	1.01	.54	33.05
1945	1.74	.17	1.56	.94	.62	40.02
1946	1.92	.18	1.73	1.04	.68	39.51
1947	2.04	.21	1.83	1.18	.64	35.24
1948	2.24	.22	2.02	1.30	.71	35.49
1949	2.36	.23	2.13	1.37	.75	35.47
1950	2.45	.23	2.22	1.41	.81	36.47
1951	2.57	.24	2.32	1.45	.87	37.41
1952	2.72	.27	2.45	1.52	.92	37.87
1953	2.92	.30	2.61	1.62	.98	37.82
1954	2.97	.34	2.62	1.68	.94	36.02
1955	3.13	.36	2.77	1.74	1.03	37.28
1956	3.43	.41	3.01	1.86	1.15	38.25
1957	3.71	.57	3.13	1.97	1.15	36.93
1958	3.74	.66	3.07	2.02	1.05	34.16
1959	4.06	.72	3.33	2.11	1.22	36.64
1960	4.33	.79	3.54	2.25	1.28	36.22
1961	4.19	.88	3.31	2.22	1.09	32.94
1962	4.31	1.11	3.19	2.23	.96	30.18
1963	4.50	1.29	3.20	2.29	.91	28.55
1964	4.63	1.40	3.22	2.30	.92	28.71
1965	4.73	1.59	3.14	2.26	.87	27.90
1966	5.08	1.82	3.25	2.33	.91	28.15
1967	5.17	1.97	3.20	2.38	.82	25.69
1968	5.43	2.04	3.39	2.38	1.00	29.68
1969	6.06	2.19	3.86	2.81	1.05	27.26
1970	6.37	2.28	4.09	3.29	.79	19.53
1971	6.07	2.39	3.68	3.16	.52	14.22
1972	5.93	2.39	3.54	3.00	.53	15.04
1973	6.86	3.05	3.80	3.05	.75	19.79

TABLE 9.10 (*Continued*)

Year	r_a Asset earning rate[b]	r Effective deposit rate[c]	$r_a - r$ Rate spread	oc Total operating cost rate[d]	p Profit margin[e]	$p/(r_a - r)$ Profit margin divided by rate spread
1974	7.93	3.90	4.02	3.33	.69	17.13
1975	7.33	3.43	3.89	3.58	.31	8.01
1976	8.01	3.25	4.75	3.96	.79	16.69
1977	8.15	3.24	4.90	4.06	.83	17.07
1978	9.15	3.66	5.49	4.44	1.04	18.97

[a] Expressed in percentages. Source: Tables A9.1–A9.3.

[b] The asset earning rate is an estimate of the weighted average of the individual asset rates in the portfolio including cash. It is calculated as the ratio of earnings to average annual financial assets. The rate is net of taxes other than income taxes, bad debts, and other asset losses.

[c] The effective deposit rate is an estimate of the weighted average of rates paid on all deposit accounts. It is calculated as the ratio of interest cost to average deposits.

[d] The total operating cost rate is the ratio of all operating expenses to average deposits. It nets out all nonoperating expenses. Service charges are also netted out so that these revenues reduce net operating costs.

[e] The profit margin is profit per deposit dollar. It is calculated as $r_a - r - oc$.

Not only was there a shakeout in the number of firms, but total assets of Fed members fell almost \$15 billion, or 30%, from year-end 1929 to year-end 1933, and total deposits fell almost 28% in the same period. Banks were forced to reduce the amount of loans outstanding, and these declined dramatically by \$13 billion, or a staggering 51%, as banks strove to increase the liquidity of their ever-smaller portfolios. Treasury items, for example, increased by \$3.4 billion, or 88%. (See Table A9.1.) The impact of these violent portfolio shifts on the earning rates of the portfolio was substantial. Asset earning rates declined 140 basis points from the end of 1929 to the end of 1933, when they reached a level of 3.47%. Not only did asset rates decline, but effective deposit rates also declined just slightly less than earning rate, so that rate spreads tended to remain just below the level of the late-1920s. This decline in deposit rates could well have been the result of declining competition as banks fell by the wayside with deposit elasticities decreasing from 2.51 in 1930 to 1.27 in 1933. With these lower deposit elasticities, commercial banks were able to retain a larger share of the net rate spread in profit. Another possible reason for a decline in deposit elasticities and deposit rates is that during a deflationary period, the real return to monetary assets increases. Thus, without receiving an explicit deposit yield on demand deposits, depositors were still rewarded with an enhanced purchasing power of their deposits.

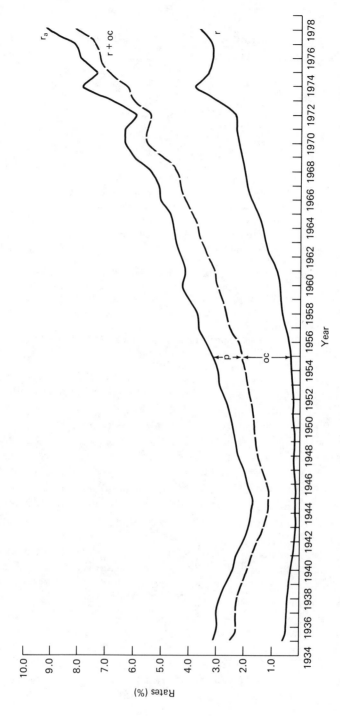

Figure 9.10 FDIC member banks time trends.

Furthermore, the introduction of federal deposit insurance might have reduced deposit sensitivity to open-market rates.

With rate spreads essentially maintained, profit margins were only dented by rising operating costs per deposit dollar. Operating costs in 1932 rose to 203 basis points, a level which would not be reached again until 1967. These higher production costs were probably the result of costs incurred from the turnover of both deposits and assets. Despite these higher costs, profit margins from the deposit activity never fell below 68 basis points per deposit dollar. The reader should carefully note, however, the narrow definition of profit margins used here. These profit margins exclude capital gains and losses of the portfolio, as well as both the revenues and the costs of borrowed funds. Certainly, in a period of net deposit withdrawals these costs were no doubt significant. A reconciliation of the effect of these costs on the overall profit position is introduced in Chapter 11. For banks able to absorb those costs and survive until 1933, the major intervention of the federal government into the structure and conduct of the financial industry resulted in a considerably less competitive environment.

9.2.4   The Post-Depression Reorganization: 1934–1941

The reorganization of the banking structure forced by the Depression was largely completed by the end of 1934. At that time there were 15,220 commercial banks and 3,017 branch offices, so that a total of 18,237 banking offices was left in operation. The next 7 years were characterized by relative stability in the structure of banking. Principally as a result of mergers, the number of banks declined slowly to 14,219 by the end of 1941. The number of branch offices increased by approximately 600, so that the net number of commercial banking offices declined slightly from 1934 to 1941. This was a period of moderate consolidation. With the introduction of anticompetitive regulatory devices (discussed in Chapter 2) and with a very sluggish economy during this time, there was very little feedback from economic pressures to market structure, conduct, or regulation.

During this period, asset earning rates of Federal Reserve members were falling continuously, with the exception of 1937. A decline in earning rates of 114 basis points from 1934 to 1941, amounting to 35%, occurred, since short-term prime rates fell to 1.5% and high-quality bonds fell to 3% in 1941. Banks, still wary of the avalanche of bank failures of the preceding years, continued to demonstrate a high liquidity preference. Banks held highly liquid, low-risk, and low-yielding Treasury items in greater proportion than ever before. While loans increased from \$12.028 billion in

1934 to $18.021 billion in 1941, or a 50% gain, Treasury items rose from $11 billion to $19 billion or, a 79% increase, and cash rose 78%. These greater proportions of noninterest and low-interest assets all served to pull down the asset earning rate. Part of the cause of this portfolio reorganization was the increase in cash reserve requirements by the Fed in 1937. The increase in reserves or in cash items, however, was not confined to that year alone. From Table 6.2 we find that cash items to total deposits ratios increased from 23% in 1929 to a high of 42% in 1940, and from Table 6.1, reserves to deposits ratios (a more narrow definition than cash items) for Fed member banks increased from 7.7% in 1929 to 26.5% in 1940.

Not only were asset earning rates declining, but effective deposit rates also declined between 1934 and 1941—although only by 55 basis points—so that rate spreads declined to 191 basis points in 1941. To offset this reduced rate spread, average operating cost per deposit dollar also declined each year during this period of contraction, with a total reduction of 57 basis points. The net effect then, for these two components of cost, deposit cost and operating cost, was that they virtually offset each other so that profit margins were maintained at approximately 80 basis points. The adjustments of the late-1930s could all have been considerably more profitable to the commercial banks had there not been such an extreme liquidity preference on the part of the banks, as well as the bank regulators. With the weighted average cost of deposit funds down to between .5% and .25%, deposit funds could scarcely have been less costly. Despite this, rate spreads declined as commercial banks, not unlike their depositors, exhibited a very strong liquidity preference.

During the same 1934–1941 period, FDIC member banks were experiencing much the same trends as Federal Reserve members. However, the latter had lower operating costs and higher profit margins per deposit dollar than the FDIC members. Some interesting contrasts could be made between the two banking series. The FDIC members included the relatively smaller banks outside money market centers. It appears, as one would expect, that competition was somewhat less intense, as average deposit costs are lower. In contrast, asset earning rates for FDIC members are more nearly in line with those of Federal Reserve members. This speaks strongly for the notion that these small banks do have access to the broader national and international asset markets, just as the larger banks that are characteristically Federal Reserve members. They therefore enjoy very similar asset earning rates, which gives a strong indication of smooth resource allocations across loan markets. This gives substance to the assumption of Chapter 3 of a perfectly elastic asset earning rate. This combination of less competitive local deposit markets and access to national capital markets resulted in higher rate spreads for FDIC members. This did not, however, translate into higher profit margins, since these larger rate spreads are generally offset by higher operating costs.

9.2.5 The War Years: 1942–1945

Wartime finance and a wartime economy were to have major effects on the depository institutions. Savings rates from income were quite high, and the rate of monetary creation was rapid. Since the Federal Reserve took the position that it would peg the government bond rate at very low levels, it imposed upon itself the necessity of entering the government bond market to purchase bonds whenever bond prices softened as the result of new Treasury offerings. This residual position taken by the Federal Reserve in the government bond market put ceilings on interest rates. It, however, committed the Fed to purchase large quantities of bonds, which in turn became reserves to the banking system. These added reserves then allowed for a multiple expansion of the deposits and assets of commercial banks.

Part of that asset expansion consisted of government bonds, and since they were pegged at low interest rates, the average asset earning rates of both Fed members and FDIC members dropped continuously each and every year during the war. During this period member banks increased their holdings of Treasury items from $19.5 billion at the beginning of 1942 to $78.3 billion in 1945, an incredible increase of nearly 400% in 4 years. This increase was in addition to the banks' already liquid asset position. At the same time the FDIC member banks behaved similarly, with Treasury items increasing 323%. This, of course, caused the average asset earning rate to fall from 2.14% to an all-time low of 1.64% for Federal Reserve members and from 2.37% to an all-time low of 1.74% for FDIC members. These declines of 50 and 64 basis points, respectively, represent decreases of 20 and 27% in earning rates.

Meanwhile, the effective deposit rates were also dropping, but since they were already at such low levels at the beginning of the war period, the decline in the deposit rate amounted to only 13 basis points as the Fed member banks' average deposit cost shrank from 27 basis points to an incredible low of 14 basis points in 1944. The same, of course, was true with FDIC member banks.

Since there was so little competition from open-market instruments and such a high savings rate, depositors were willing to hold deposits, particularly in demand accounts, and earn relatively low returns, despite the first signs of inflation. With virtually no downward movement possible in deposit rates, rate spreads were suffering because the drop in asset earning rates could not be matched by similar drops in effective deposit rates. Rate spreads declined from 1.91 to 1.49% for Fed members during this period. These were, of course, the all-time lows over 60 years of observed data. To offset these small rate spreads, banks became more cost-efficient than they had ever been, and were able to offset this drop in rate spreads and actually increase profit margins per deposit dollar during each year except 1945. This reduction in average costs was, of course, made somewhat easier, since open-market investments dominated portfolio decisions, cash management problems were minimal, and with this influx of deposits, there was no need to resort to nonrate competition. Operating costs per deposit dollar decreased continuously from 1.15% in 1942 to only 82 basis points in 1945 for Fed members, or a reduction of 27%. The combined effect of these forces was a slight increase in profit margins per deposit dollar through 1944, with a slight drop occurring in 1945. Fed members experienced a slight increase from 63 basis points in 1942 to a high during this period of 70 basis points in 1944, only to slide back again to 66 basis points in 1945. Despite these modest profit margins, total profit was more robust, since deposits increased 110% during the war years. The gains to net total profit, however, were somewhat offset by the imposition of taxes for the first time.

9.2.6 The Post-World War II Depository Boom: 1946–1960

The most striking feature of the banking structure in 1946 was the fact that fewer commercial banking offices were in operation than in 1935, the year that marked the end of the drastic reorganization of the depository industries. Yet, in the interim, wartime demands had generated a high level of economic activity and population had increased substantially. After an initial fear of a postwar depression passed, it became clear that the war years had created both a backlog of demand for consumer goods and as a backlog of financial resources to create a postwar economic boom. During the 1946–1960 period, economic growth was rapid, with the real gross national product 56% higher in 1960 than in 1946. Within this economic boom, the need for additional banking facilities gradually became clear. This was especially true in the new suburban areas of the major cities.

To meet these potential banking needs partially, in the 15 years from the end of 1945 to the end of 1960, the number of commercial banking offices increased from 18,208 to 24,103, an increase of 5,895 offices or 32%. The number of banks actually declined from 14,183 to 13,484, a decrease of 5% primarily as the result of merger and absorptions. This was offset by a large increase in de novo branches. Branch offices, including those from mergers, increased from 4,025 at the end of 1945 to 10,619 at the end of 1960, an increase of 164%.

When the overall increase of 32% in commercial banking offices over the long period from 1946 to 1960 failed to keep pace with economic and population growth, this, coupled with a relatively static industrial structure in the thrift industry, led to a less competitive depository environment. Evidence of low competitive pressures, as reflected in the thrifts' low explicit deposit elasticities, was clear in the early postwar period. Mutual savings bank elasticities were lowest in 1945, and savings and loan associations and credit union elasticities reached low points in 1950. Furthermore, although deposit ceilings were applicable to commercial banks' time and savings accounts, they were not binding through most of the postwar period. In this environment, with solid economic growth only interrupted by four minor recessions, one would anticipate profit margins to grow.

The increase in profit margins derived, first, from an increase experienced in average asset earning rates. These rates increased because the Federal Reserve gradually moved away from its pegging operation and finally ceased its support of Treasury bond prices in 1951. As the excess liquidity built up during the wartime finance effort became gradually absorbed, asset earning rates experienced an upward trend, with only some small variations during recessions. Earning rates increased because of rising market interest rates and because of the shift in the composition of commercial bank portfolios from Treasury items to higher yielding loans. Average asset earning rates for Fed banks increased continuously from a level of 1.82% in 1946 to 4.27% in 1960, a long, unhalted gain of 245 basis points.

In the meantime, effective deposit rates increased from their all-time low of .17% in 1946 to .75% in 1960, or an increase of 58 basis points. The deposit rate increase experienced by FDIC banks was an almost identical 61 basis points. These increases in effective deposit rates were due to a depositors' shift from demand deposits to time and savings deposits. Time and savings deposits increased 116% in the period for Federal Reserve members, compared to a 48% increase in demand accounts.

The net result of these comparative rate increases was a dramatic change in the rate spreads. Rate spreads rose continuously from 1946 to 1960 for Fed members from a level of 1.64% to a level of 3.51%, an increase of 187 basis points. FDIC member banks also experienced an increase in rate spreads in every year except the recession year of 1958. Rate spreads in excess of 300 basis points had not been experienced in the commercial banking industry since the early 1920s.

Of course, as portfolios shifted from Treasury items to loans, average operating costs per deposit dollar began to increase. Furthermore, as commercial banks became more profitable with higher net rate spreads, the inducement to attract savings deposits was sufficient to bid up deposit rates, even when the market was not highly competitive. That is, as net revenues per deposit dollar increased, deposit rates would follow. By the middle 1950s Regulation Q ceilings started to become binding, and it is quite possible that the commercial banks responded with some nonrate competition that tended to increase their operating costs. Operating costs per deposit dollar rose continuously during this period also, perhaps because an increase in branching occurred. The increase in operating costs of 101 basis points from .93 to 1.94% in 1960, of course, offset some of the gain in the rate spread. The net effect of these forces still allowed profit margins per deposit dollar to grow every year with only two exceptions: the recession years of 1954 and 1958. The net increase in profit margins per deposit dollar was 85 basis points, from .71 to 1.56%. For FDIC members, profit margins rose every year with three exceptions: 1947, 1954, and 1958.

9.2.7 The Period of Economic Expansion: 1961–1967

Between 1961 and 1967 the nation enjoyed its longest uninterrupted expansion since the 1920s. Real gross national product was 19% higher in 1967 than at the beginning of the decade. In 1961, Comptroller of the Currency James Saxon began to encourage bank entry because of the benefits derived from competition. Certainly, the banking industry was at a point where greater competitive levels were called for, since profit margins had reached all-time highs of 1.56% for Fed members in 1960.

During this period of expansion, there was continued emphasis on the growth of branch systems, but in addition, de novo entry of unit banks increased for the first time in decades. Despite this crack in the door with both new federal and state charters, there really was not a significant change in the number of commercial banks. However, the combined impact of not only larger numbers of commercial bank branches, but also savings and loan branches and additional new federal credit unions, had a combined impact resulting in increasing pressures in deposit markets. These increased competitive pressures were to manifest themselves in somewhat lower profit margins between 1960 and 1967. For Fed members profit margins declined from 1.56% in 1960 to 1.06% in 1967. These declining profit margins were not the result of a decline in average asset earning rates, but rather due to more rapidly increasing effective deposit rates, as well as moderate growth in operating costs per deposit dollar.

Average asset earning rates actually increased in the early- to mid-1960s, not so much because of rising market rates, but rather because of a continued portfolio shift away from open-market securities, particularly Treasury items, to higher-yielding bank loans. Fed member loans increased from $106 billion in 1961 to $197 billion in 1967, an increase of 86%. In the meantime, Treasury items fell in absolute amount.

During the period of expansion, effective deposit rates for Fed member banks increased continuously, from .85% in 1961 to 1.96% in 1967, an increase of 111 basis points, so that at these levels the effective deposit cost of funds reached levels typically found in the early 1920s. Again, with interest prohibition on demand deposit accounts, these increasing effective deposit rates reflected a shift in the liability structure of commercial banks. The net effect of these movements in asset rates and deposit rates was a small decrease in the rate spreads after much fluctuation. However, increasing operating costs per deposit dollar, due both to branching and added implicit deposit rates, caused operating costs to increase from 1.89 to 2.06% in 1967, an increase of 17 basis points.

9.2.8 The Inflation Era: 1968-1980

The 1968-1980 era was characterized by two major movements. After the imposition of deposit ceilings on the thrift institutions, their profit margins began to recover. Once again, entry by branching was sanctioned, and increased competitive pressures in deposit markets derived from a vast increase in the number of thrift offices. In addition, between 1968 and 1978 the total number of banking offices increased a dramatic 50%, from 32,920 in 1968 to 49,461 in 1978. There was also some small increase in the number of banks, amounting to 8%. The second major thrust of this period was the rising inflation rate associated at first with the Viet Nam war and later with natural resource shortages, a chronic federal budget imbalance, and poor productivity performance. Given the rising inflation rates of this era, inflation premiums caused interest rates to rise, with sharp cyclical peaks occurring at the end of 1969 and in early 1970, mid-1974, and early 1980. While the thrift institutions tended to suffer adverse effects from rising and variable inflation rates, inflation impacts on the commercial banks were somewhat different.

Profit margins for commercial banks tended to decline from competitive effects, but tended to show great procyclical variability, as they were able to capture the high yields available on the market better than any other depository institution. In the period of rising interest rates, rate spreads increased, indicating that despite all the new high-yielding liability instruments, asset rates still increased more rapidly than average deposit costs. For Fed member banks the rise in the rate spread was 54 basis points between 1968 and 1975 (comparable data were not available for later years), and for FDIC banks the rate spread rose even more, with a 210 basis point increase. In this period of rising market interest rates, with the exception of two short lulls, one in the easy-money period of 1971–1972 and the other in 1975, average asset earning rates increased. The effective deposit rates continued to rise and fall with asset rates and had minor declines in 1969, 1972, and 1975 for Fed member banks and 1975–1977 for FDIC banks.

Because of the shift from demand deposits to certificates of deposit and other higher-yielding time and savings accounts, by the end of the decade less than 30% of total deposits were in demand accounts. This, however, had less adverse effect on profitability than the increase in operating costs. Operating costs per deposit dollar rose from 2.38% in 1968 to 4.44% in 1978 for FDIC members, with most of the increase occurring after 1973, probably as the result of both higher production costs through branching and higher implicit deposit rates. These operating costs were generally higher than those of Fed members; for example, in the last year of comparable data, 1975, FDIC members had operating costs 75 basis points above Fed members. For Fed members, for which the longest continuous data series exists, operating costs per deposit dollar of 2.87% in 1975 exceeded any other year on record. This increase in operating costs in excess of rate spread increases resulted in a general downtrend in profit margins. Within this downtrend in profit, there were extreme cyclical variations, with profit margins tending to rise during tight money periods and decline during easy money periods. This was certainly the case for commercial banks in 1969 and 1974, and for FDIC members, the strongest profit performance was shown in 1969 and 1978, although in 1974 their profit margins were dissipated by a large increase in operating costs. In general, even with a downtrend in profit margins, the commercial banks weathered the inflation shock of the 1970s far better than the thrifts.

BIBLIOGRAPHY

Board of Directors of the F.D.I.C. *Annual Report of the F.D.I.C.,* Washington, D.C.: U.S. Govt. Printing Office, 1934–1978.
Board of Governors of the Federal Reserve System. *Annual Statistical Digest, 1971–1975,* Washington, D.C.: U.S. Govt. Printing Office, 1976.
Board of Governors of the Federal Reserve System. *Banking and Monetary Statistics, 1914–1941* and *Annual Supplements,* various years, Washington, D.C.
Board of Governors of the Federal Reserve System. *Banking and Monetary Statistics, 1941–1970* and *Annual Supplements,* various years, Washington, D.C.
Board of Governors of the Federal Reserve System. *Flow of Funds Accounts, 1945–1972,* Washington, D.C., 1973.

Bradford, William D. "Mortgage-Backed Bonds for Savings and Loan Associations: Management and Public Policy Issues," paper prepared for Federal Home Loan Bank of San Francisco, December 1979.

Burger, Albert E. "A Historical Analysis of the Credit Crunch of 1966," *Federal Reserve Board of St. Louis. Review,* September 1969.

Comanor, William S., and Leibenstein, Harvey. "Allocative Efficiency, X-Efficiency, and the Measurement of Welfare Losses," *Economica,* **36,** August 1969.

Council of Economic Advisers. Economic Report of the President Together with the *Annual Report of the Council of Economic Advisers,* Washington, D.C.: U.S. Govt. Printing Office, various years.

Craine, Roger N., and Pierce, James L. "Interest Rate Risk," *Journal of Financial and Quantitative Analysis,* **13,** November 1978.

Federal Home Loan Bank Board, *Combined Financial Statements, FSLIC-Insured Savings and Loan Associations,* Washington, D.C.: U.S. Govt. Printing Office, 1942–1980.

Fortune, Peter. "The Effectiveness of Recent Policies to Maintain Thrift-Deposit Flows," *Journal of Money, Credit and Banking,* **7,** August 1975.

Frederickson, E. Bruce. "The Geographic Structure of Residential Mortgage Yields." In *Essays on Interest Rates,* vol. 2, ed. Jack Guttentag. New York: Columbia Univ. Press, 1971.

Friedman, Benjamin M. "Regulation Q and the Commercial Loan Market in the 1960s." *Journal of Money, Credit and Banking,* **7,** August 1975.

Gambs, Carl M. "Variable Rate Mortgages—Their Potential in the United States," *Journal of Money, Credit and Banking,* **7,** May 1975.

Gambs, Carl M. "Bank Failures: An Historical Perspective," *Federal Reserve Bank of Kansas City. Monthly Review,* June 1977.

Gibson, William E. "Deposit Demand, Hot Money, and the Viability of Thrift Institutions." In *Brookings Papers on Economic Activity 3,* eds. Arthur M. Okum and George L. Perry, Washington, D.C.: Brookings Institution, 1974.

Greenbaum, Stuart I. "A Profits Model of the Banking Industry," In *Proceedings of a Conference on Bank Structure and Competition,* Federal Reserve Bank of Chicago, 1971.

Greenbaum, Stuart I., Ali, M. M., and Merris, Randall C. "Monetary Policy and Banking Profits," *Journal of Finance,* **32,** March 1976.

Jaffee, Dwight M. "The Asset–Liability Maturity Mix of S&Ls: Problems and Solutions," In *Change in the Savings and Loan Industry,* Federal Home Loan Bank Board of San Francisco, December 1976.

Kane, Edward J. "Short-Changing the Small Saver: Federal Government Discrimination Against Small Savers During the Vietnam War, A Comment," *Journal of Money, Credit and Banking,* **2,** November 1970.

Kaufman, George G. "The Thrift Institution Problem Reconsidered," In *Proceedings of a Conference on Bank Structure and Competition,* Federal Reserve Bank of Chicago, 1971.

Maisel, Sherman J., and Jacobson, Robert. "Interest Rate Changes and Commercial Bank Revenues and Costs," paper presented to the Western Finance Association, June 1978 Honolulu, Hawaii.

National Credit Union Administration, *Annual Report,* Washington, D.C., various years.

Peterson, Richard L. "Consumer Lending by Savings and Loan Associations," paper prepared for Federal Home Loan Bank of San Francisco, December 1980.

Rosenblum, Harvey. "Interest Rate Volatility, Regulation Q and the Problems of Thrift Institutions," In *Proceedings of a Conference on Bank Structure and Competition,* Federal Reserve Bank of Chicago, May 1980.

U.S. Department of Commerce, Social and Economic Statistics Administration, Bureau of the Census, *Historical Statistics of the United States.* parts 1 and 2, Washington, D.C.: U.S. Govt. Printing Office, 1973.

U.S. Department of Commerce, Social and Economic Statistics Administration, Bureau of the Census, *Statistical Abstract of the United States* Washington, D.C.: U.S. Govt. Printing Office, 1950–1978.

U.S. Department of Health, Education and Welfare, Bureau of Federal Credit Unions, *Annual Reports of the National Credit Union Administration,* Washington, D.C.: U.S. Govt. Printing Office, 1940–1978.

U.S. League of Savings Associations. *Savings and Loan Fact Book,* Chicago, Ill., 1979 and various other years.

Volio, Jose E. "Analysis of Performance and Competition in The Regulated Depository Industries of the United States," professional report for MBA degree, University of Texas at Austin, August 1980.

Watro, Paul R. "Competition between Thrift Institutions and Banks in Ohio," *Federal Reserve Bank of Cleveland Research Department. Economic Commentary,* July 1980.

CHAPTER 10

Industrial Structure in the Depository Industries

10.1 THE MARKET AND REGULATORY PROCESS AND THE NUMBER OF DEPOSITORY INSTITUTIONS

The workings of the invisible hand causes capital resources to flow to an industry in which the rate of return compares favorably with alternative investments of similar risk. The economic incentive of differential rates of return causes capital to flow, but the specific form of expansion depends on a number of factors. For example, in the depository industry, if economies in production exist in the gathering or handling of deposits this capital might take the form of additional physical facilities for existing depository institutions. These additional facilities could be either branches or other physical forms of deposit-gathering equipment such as an electronic transfer system—especially if the deposit market is geographically dispersed. Alternative vehicles that exist to increase the scale of deposit-gathering activity include merger or consolidation through holding company acquisition. Often regulatory constraints determine the vehicle for consolidation. If no such production economies exist, it is possible that the additional infusion of capital might take the form of separate new firms entering the market.

In addition to issues of production economies in deposit gathering, another factor determining the form of expansion might be economies in the asset selection process. There also might be a relationship of loan size to the loan rate. If loan economies exist or if the highest rates of return were earned on very large loans, this would create incentives for accumulations of large blocks of loanable funds and consolidation in the form of a large branch system, merger, or holding company. On the other hand, if the highest returns were earned on smaller loans, this would more likely result in a depository system with numerous small entities. Additional incentives for the concentration of deposits would occur if the diversification of a large loan portfolio reduced risk. Such risk reduction might result from the dispersion of loans by industry and by location. Another consideration instrumental in determining the form of expansion and industrial structure is illiquidity costs. If reductions in illiquidity costs were realized by balancing the net deposit inflows of different geographic areas, of firms with differing seasonal or cyclical patterns, or of merely greater numbers of independent accounts, these cost factors would influence the shape of the response to expansion.

There is simultaneity in the relationship between the number of firms and the rate of return. Not only do comparatively high rates of return tend to attract additional firms, but the additional number of firms tends to reduce rates of return. The dynamic process ebbs and flows, moving toward an equilibrium. Additional numbers of firms, of course, set off competitive forces, raising deposit rates and tending to reduce asset rates. Not only are rate spreads reduced but the higher deposit rate elasticities tend to suppress profit margins when depositors receive a larger share of net revenues.

Entry requires a commitment of capital to the depository firm, not only for the bricks and mortar that have amounted to a relatively small proportion of equity capital (see Table 5.1), but to purchase financial assets or cash reserves to be held as a buffer against asset losses and current deficits. This equity buffer reduces the risk of insolvency and hence attracts deposits. The incentives for entry and the continuation of the commitment of equity capital in the depository industries rest on an adequate risk-adjusted rate of return. This rate of return, in turn, depends upon the profit margins of the deposit activity and the number of deposit dollars each dollar of equity supports. These deposit–equity ratios and rates of return to the depository firms will be examined in Section 10.2.

Of equal importance to rates of return is the investor's perception of risk from engaging in depository activities. The element of risk, one assumes, loomed larger in the free-market banking era when there was no government commitment to maintain the liquidity and solvency of the banking and thrift institutions. Without central bank resources to offset financial shocks, there were many episodes when liquidity was insufficient to withstand deposit runs. When the cumulative forces of deposit withdrawal rippled through the financial community, a shakeout of firms would result, but the surviving depository firms would likely find themselves in a less competitive environment and hence earning higher rates of return. The episodic financial crises of the nineteenth century must have demonstrated very clearly the risks involved in committing equity capital in the depository industries. One could only speculate, in the absence of data, that relative rates of return in the depository industries increased after a financial panic, not only because of the fewer firms remaining in the industry but because of the higher risk premiums that must exist before attracting additional capital and additional firms.

If promoting safety and soundness is indeed a goal of regulation, government intervention in the depository process would be expected to reduce risk premiums necessary for the commitment of equity capital to the industry. Certainly the very low incidence of depository firm failure in the post-Depression era gives strong evidence of that commitment. The introduction of the Federal Reserve as a central bank or bankers' bank was perceived as a means for providing an elastic currency, which from the banking firms' point of view was a commitment to provide liquidity to member banks by rediscounting commercial paper. This was a major step toward solving the liquidity problems of the depository system, since liquidity was no longer constrained by the finite amount of available gold in the private banking system. The printing of legal tender tied only nominally to gold supplies could be accomplished rapidly and without practical limit, if need be. Furthermore, this liquidity mechanism could be used to stand behind not only member bank liquidity runs, but through correspondent, interbank, and interdepository lending could be used ultimately to support nonmember banks as well as thrifts. In addition to providing for liquidity, requiring legal cash reserves against deposits probably reduced the perceived risk of an equity investment in banking. In the 1920s a major expansion in the number of depository firms took place not only in banking, but in the savings and loan and mutual savings bank industries. Although much has been made of other inducements to attract this number of firms, one could speculate that a perceived reduction in liquidity and solvency risk played a part in that expansion.

In the 1930s the opposite undoubtedly occurred. The massive failure rate among depository institutions very likely generated skepticism and doubts that probably translated into the requirement of higher risk premiums before additional capital would be committed to depository activities. As a potential offset to these higher perceived risks, the general commitment by the federal government to intervene in the affairs of the depository industries to prevent failure emerged. While this commitment to safety and soundness was viewed as a condition necessary for overall aggregate economic stability and growth, it reduced risk premiums for the surviving firms in the industry. Since that time, the federal backing of the depository institutions has become even stronger, if for no other reason than that the federal insuring agencies operate with relatively small reserves and hence find themselves to also be vulnerable to high rates of depository failure.

The strengthening of defenses against depository failure after the debacle of the Great Depression included not only federal deposit insurance, but also a reorganization of the Federal Reserve when the Glass–Steagall Act of 1932 authorized each Federal Reserve bank to make advances to member banks on the basis of promissory notes that were sufficiently secured in the opinion of the Federal Reserve bank. This act substantially increased the flexibility of the Federal Reserve banks to meet commercial bank liquidity needs. The mechanism for providing liquidity to the savings and loan industry came through the Federal Home Loan Bank Act of 1932. This act was the enabling legislation to establish the Federal Home Loan Bank System and to grant authority to its board to create a body of rules under which advances could be made to associations. In fact, an important enticement to obtain a federal savings and loan charter was access to Federal Home Loan Bank (FHLB) advances, which could be secured for up to a 10-year period.

For credit unions, the National Credit Union Central Liquidity Facility was established in the early-1970s to meet the liquidity needs of credit unions. Loans are available on a short-term basis to meet temporary requirements for funds, seasonal credit requirements, and even protracted adjustment credit in the event of unusual or emergency circumstances of a longer term nature resulting from national, regional, or local difficulties.

Aside from the provision of insurance and liquidity, failure has been prevented in unusual circumstances when the existing regulatory agencies or newly created authorities have stepped into the market either to support asset prices or even to make direct subsidized asset purchases from depository institutions. An example of this in an emergency environment was the Reconstruction Finance Corporation (RFC). The RFC, chartered in February 1932, was provided with an initial capital of $500 million and was also given extensive borrowing powers. The RFC was to extend emergency assistance to financial institutions by making loans against assets. In addition, the Homeowners Loan Corporation, also established at that time, was created to purchase mortgages directly from savings and loan associations between 1933 and 1936.

There have been other examples of direct market intervention as well. Some of the federal activities in credit markets have been designed with as much intention of helping the depository institutions as of helping such special sectors as housing and agriculture. The savings and loan associations and, in fact, all depository institutions benefit from the liquidity pumped into capital markets, even if in the first instance credit activities of mortgage-related agencies are directed at a particular sector. The Federal National Mortgage Association, Federal Home Loan Mortgage Corporation, Federal Housing Administration, Veterans Administration, and Government National Mortgage Association all deal in this market. Federal credit agencies involved in agriculture are the Federal Land Banks, Federal Intermediate Credit Banks, and Banks for Cooperatives.

In addition to these liquidity facilities, there have been various times when the Federal Reserve was authorized to make loans or support asset prices on an emergency basis. One such example was the summer of 1966, when the thrift institutions experienced the first credit crunch of the post-war era. In 1975, when the municipal bond market experienced a large sell-off because of the problems faced by the city of New York, the central bank would likely have interceded in that market if prices continued to fall, because of the technical insolvency facing many banks that held large quantities of municipals in their portfolios. Though the Fed's direct or implied authority to make loans to thrifts or support the municipal bond market was never utilized in these crunches, the proclivity of the government to intercede on behalf of the depository institutions in a vulnerable position has surely reduced the perception of risk to potential investors in depository firms.

Not only have risk premiums been altered by government intervention in the depository environment, but the government has demonstrated a willingness to alter both legislation and regulation in order to change the depository firms' rate of return. The reduction of capital requirements during the war years, the recent establishment of interest payments on reserve accounts at the Federal Reserve, changes in tax rates, and changes in both borrowing rates and dividend payout rates to member banks and federal associations are but a few examples. An additional and more obvious effort to maintain profit margins was the Interest Rate Control Act of 1966, which established deposit ceilings for thrift institutions. Furthermore, the 1980 Deregulatory Act provides for a study of options available to federal agencies to assist thrifts in times of economic difficulties.[1]

The regulatory agencies and federal government have displayed a commitment to preserving the depository institutions not only because of their own insurance risk exposure, but because of the perception that the social cost of failure exceeds the private cost. Given that commitment to low failure rates, the most important element of any such policy is strict controls on entry and industrial structure.

Controlling competitive forces is the most fundamental method of preserving the existing competitors. In examining criteria for entry and branching in the commercial bank and savings and loan industries, the general standards are quite similar. Furthermore, standards are similar for both state- and federally chartered institutions, since virtually all deposi-

---

[1] See U.S., Congress, House, Committee on Banking, Finance and Urban Affairs, *Report of the Interagency Task Force on Thrift Institutions,* 96th Cong., 2nd sess., 1980.

tory institutions obtain insurance from federal agencies and must therefore submit to their review. The general criteria by which an application is
evaluated are the financial history and condition of the firm, the adequacy
of its capital structure, the probability of its becoming profitable in a reasonable length of time, the general character of its management, the convenience and needs of the community to be served, and the assurance that
there will be no undue harm or injury to existing financial institutions.

These standards are so judgmental and loosely defined that they constitute in effect a delegation by the legislative branch to the administrative
agency to develop policy regarding entry. To the extent that objective criteria are proposed to meet these tests, such variables as population
growth, income growth, and savings in a "service area" have often been
cited. Furthermore, the service area is subjectively defined to the firm's
advantage as a city, county, Standard Metropolitan Statistical Area
(SMSA) or some other gerrymandered territory. Thus not only are the
legal requirements for entry rather fuzzy, but where conscientiously implemented, the tests are often based on variables that have little to do with
the measurement of competition.

Not only are entry decisions made with little relevance to objective
measures of competitive forces, but bank failure is usually explained by
examiners as being the result of an internal deficiency or external shock,
rather than competitive factors. Factors commonly cited are a large
number of doubtful, slow, or past due loans, large loans to officers or
directors, defalcation or embezzlement, excessive loans to businesses
with which officers or directors are affiliated, and overall poor management. External causes are also cited, such as heavy deposit withdrawals,
unexpectedly large depreciation of securities and investments, the failure
of a bank correspondent, and the failure of a substantial borrower. This
myopic view of failure tends to rationalize the cumulative effects of competition. Competitive forces lower profit margins, reducing the firms' ability to absorb external shocks and internal mismanagement.

In highly competitive environments, a common reaction by depository
institutions, often aided by the deposit insurance agency, is merger.
Merger presents the possibility of taking advantage of economies of scale
in production, risk reduction associated with portfolio diversification, and
reduced vulnerability to deposit withdrawals. In the case of merger, the
question always arises as to whether the benefits to the depository institutions would outweigh the loss of responsiveness to local needs that is
characteristic of highly competitive environments.

Merger, branching, and integration through a holding company, however, evoke a concern over the potential concentration of power in a few
large institutions. In response to these concerns in the 1950s, many indi-

vidual states adopted laws that varied widely in the handling of branching and consolidation of banks. In order to standardize some of these laws, the Bank Holding Company Act was enacted in 1956, giving the Federal Reserve power to regulate multibank holding companies. In 1960, the Bank Merger Act was passed, splitting the responsibility for approving bank mergers between the three federal banking agencies. In 1970, one-bank holding companies were also added to the Federal Reserve's jurisdiction. As with branching and chartering, federal approval of bank mergers by the appropriate federal agency as well as the Justice Department became necessary with the Merger Act of 1970.

Prior to that, bank mergers were subject to control almost exclusively through state agencies, and their positions regarding competitive criteria were numerous. This set the stage for the landmark decision of the Supreme Court in the Philadelphia–Girard decision of June 17, 1963. The court held that the proposed merger of the second and third largest commercial banks in Philadelphia would be in violation of Section 7 of the Clayton Act. There followed a debate as to whether Section 7 of the Clayton Act or the Bank Merger Act was the governing legislation. To clarify this, the Bank Merger Act of 1966 attempted to provide a criterion for merging banks: The merger would be approved if the expected benefits to the community outweighed the anticompetitive effect. These standards are clearly difficult to measure, and tests used by the courts, such as the deposit concentration ratio in the market, were blunt and unsatisfying measures of competitiveness. The community was defined arbitrarily, and it could alternatively be argued that either greater or less deposit concentration was more beneficial to the community. Given the inherent difficulty of the economist to provide conclusive and consistent measures of competition, both the regulatory authorities and the courts tended to decide issues in a rather ad hoc or judgmental way, which was probably consistent with the intent of the act.

In the postwar era, these decisions regarding industrial structure have tended to favor both merger and branching as a means to control the competitive environment. Mergers have typically occurred in highly competitive and slow deposit growth areas. Branching has been used as a tool to extend services with relatively less competitive shock than one would expect from a new institution. Expansion by branching and holding company expansion also allows industrial expansion with low risk of insolvency for either a new institution or for the existing institutions. The branching movement of the 1960s and 1970s was favored by the regulatory agencies because it minimized competitive shock and risk, but it was also favored by the existing firms, which wished to attract additional deposits as regulatory rent existed under the constraint of deposit ceilings. With deposit ceilings restraining the ability of depository institutions to differentiate their deposit contracts from those other institutions, the location of a branch in a new geographic area was in effect the alternative to paying higher deposit rates to attract additional deposits. A further cause of an explosion in the branching movement has been a reduction in restrictions regarding branching. The laws concerning branching authority have varied widely from state to state, but they generally deal with the number of branches, distance, location, population, and capital requirements. There have been numerous recent changes in the 1970s that have made entry through de novo branching more liberal. For example, New York and New Jersey authorized statewide branching in the banking industry, and other states, such as Arkansas and Florida, moved from unit banking to limited branch banking. A further development that might tend to inhibit both new-unit depository institutions and brick and mortar branches was the approval in 1980 of auxiliary teller windows and remote service units as low-cost alternatives to a new office.

A regulatory commitment to avoid failure has led to a policy of restricting de novo entry and the facilitation of the ability of depository firms to absorb financial shocks. This, by itself, tends to elevate rates of return and lower risks for existing institutions. These elevated returns to equity capital in turn raise the pressure for entry in an industry when the value of a new charter exceeds the costs of obtaining one. The problem of keeping risk-adjusted rates of return somewhat in line with alternative investments has been dealt with in the main by a substantial increase in the number of branches in expanding markets and merger in contracting markets. The holding company movement has tended to occur where state laws limit branching.

10.2 RATES OF RETURN AND THE NUMBER OF DEPOSITORY INSTITUTIONS

This section explores the historical record of the relationship between the number of depository institutions and branches and rates of return from the early-1920s through the 1970s. This six-decade period, for which at least partial data were available, reflects eras of free-market expansion and contraction as well as differing eras of regulatory policy. While the changes in number of depository institutions and their branches do not bear a one-to-one relationship to the incentives for further capital commitment in the depository industries, they are nonetheless a historical record that yields some insights.

The number of depository institutions has ebbed and flowed throughout our history. The number of commercial banks increased irregularly in the nineteenth century, with occasional contractions as the result of panics and deposit runs that resulted in bank failure. Probably the most note-worthy of these was the panic of 1873. In the free-market era of the first two decades of the twentieth century, there was substantial growth in the number of all depository institutions in the United States. This growth in-cluded not only commercial banks, but savings and loan associations, mutual savings banks, and credit unions, with all thrift institutions being state-chartered. The increase was due almost entirely to new-unit deposi-tory institutions, each with relatively few branch offices. The sole excep-tion was commercial banking. The growth of depository institutions in those years was a market-induced phenomenon, and in the early 1920s, the number of depository institutions stood at approximately 40,000, which exceeded the levels of the late-1970s by approximately one-third.

As has been previously discussed in Chapter 2, the impetus for this ex-pansion was the industrialization and agricultural advances that took place at that time. The 1920s produced an environment of rapid economic growth, with relatively stable prices and interest rates. The phenomenon of financial stability and economic growth was reinforced by an unprece-dented degree of confidence that stemmed from the newly formed central bank. Furthermore, economic growth at that time was not only intensive but was also extensive, as many of the new depository institutions were concentrated in the Midwest, the Great Plains, and the Far West.

From Table 10.1 it can be seen that the crest in the total number of depository institutions was in 1925, at levels well above those that existed in the 1970s. Since the population in the 1920s stood at a little over 100 million, the total number of institutions per 1000 inhabitants stood at a peak of .37 in 1921 as compared to .15 in 1978. This translates into as few as 2700 persons per institution in 1921. These numbers, of course, reflect the fact that in the 1920s many depository institutions were located in relatively small towns and served relatively few customers. The data also fail to reflect the influence of chain banking, which in effect tied many banks together in a system of ownership, if not operations. Table 10.2 breaks down the totals by type of institution. Within these totals, the peak in the number of commercial banks was in 1921, at just under 30,000, and savings and loan associations were most numerous in 1927. Mutual savings banks, operating in a much smaller geographic region, were far fewer in number and exhibited a rather slow decline, which began even prior to the 1920s.

The data regarding the total number of depository offices, including branches, on a per capita basis, tells a somewhat different story. While institutions per capita declined by more than 50% between the 1920 peaks

TABLE 10.1

United States Population and Number of Depository Institutions, All Types[a]

Year	Depository institutions	Offices	Population[b]	Depository institutions per 1000 inhabitants	Offices per 1000 inhabitants
1914	32,766	—	99,118	.33058	—
1915	33,317	—	100,549	.33135	—
1916	33,922	—	101,966	.33268	—
1917	34,732	—	103,266	.33634	—
1918	35,575	—	103,203	.34471	—
1919	36,277	—	104,512	.34711	—
1920	38,348	—	106,466	.36019	—
1921	39,674	—	108,541	.36552	—
1922	40,095	—	110,055	.36432	—
1923	40,249	—	111,950	.35953	—
1924	40,650	—	114,113	.35623	—
1925	40,660	—	115,832	.35103	—
1926	39,993	—	117,399	.34066	—
1927	39,220	—	119,038	.32947	—
1928	38,245	—	120,501	.31738	—
1929	36,975	—	121,770	.30365	—
1930	34,550	—	123,077	.28072	—
1931	31,412	—	124,040	.25324	—
1932	29,309	—	124,840	.23477	—
1933	25,611	—	125,579	.20394	—
1934	26,680	—	126,374	.21111	—
1935	26,980	—	127,250	.21202	—
1936	27,508	—	128,053	.21481	—
1937	26,872	—	128,825	.20859	—
1938	26,780	—	129,825	.20627	—
1939	26,273	—	130,880	.20074	—
1940	26,227	—	132,594	.19779	—
1941	26,316	—	133,894	.19654	—
1942	26,939	31,247	135,361	.19800	.23084
1943	25,187	29,544	137,250	.18357	.21525
1944	24,804	29,302	138,916	.17855	.21093
1945	24,631	29,156	140,468	.17534	.20756
1946	24,622	29,356	141,936	.17347	.20682
1947	24,657	29,512	144,698	.17040	.20395
1948	24,822	29,792	147,208	.16861	.20238
1949	25,317	31,165	149,767	.16904	.20803
1950	25,825	31,926	152,271	.16959	.20966
1951	26,054	31,905	154,878	.16822	.20600
1952	26,546	32,736	157,553	.16848	.20777
1953	27,142	33,726	106,184	.16944	.21054
1954	27,673	34,933	163,026	.16974	.21427

TABLE 10.1 (*Continued*)

Year	Depository institutions	Offices	Population[b]	Depository institutions per 1000 inhabitants	Offices per 1000 inhabitants
1955	28,161	36,153	165,931	.16971	.21787
1956	28,694	37,554	168,903	.16988	.22234
1957	29,034	38,757	171,984	.16881	.22535
1958	29,297	39,910	174,882	.16752	.22821
1959	29,674	41,253	177,830	.16686	.23197
1960	30,224	42,941	180,671	.16703	.23767
1961	30,476	44,370	183,691	.16590	.24154
1962	30,872	46,129	186,538	.16549	.24729
1963	31,295	48,041	189,242	.16537	.25386
1964	31,781	49,996	191,889	.16562	.26054
1965	32,052	51,680	194,202	.16495	.26597
1966	32,344	53,385	196,560	.16455	.27159
1967	32,490	54,797	198,792	.16343	.27564
1968	32,730	56,528	200,706	.16307	.28164
1969	32,934	58,276	202,677	.16249	.28753
1970	32,845	60,130	204,875	.16031	.29349
1971	32,485	62,012	207,045	.15689	.29951
1972	32,442	64,519	208,842	.15534	.30893
1973	31,534	67,780	201,396	.15657	.33655
1974	32,732	71,854	211,782	.15455	.33928
1975	32,798	75,424	213,559	.15357	.35317
1976	32,748	78,140	215,152	.15220	.36313
1977	32,707	81,025	216,880	.15080	.37359
1978	32,690	84,162	218,717	.14946	.38479

[a] Source: F.D.I.C., *Annual Report*, various years; U.S. Savings and Loan League, *Savings and Loan Fact Book*, various years; National Credit Union Administration, *Annual Report*, various years; U.S. Bureau of the Census, *Statistical Abstract of the United States*, various years.
[b] In thousands.

and the late 1970s, it would appear that by the late 1970s, the total depository offices per capita had risen to the previous peaks of the early 1920s. Though the number of mutual savings bank branches and savings and loan branches was unavailable for the 1920s (but assuming their number to be quite small), the ratio of offices per 1000 inhabitants was probably as high in the early-1920s as in the late-1970s. These ratios stood at approximately .38 per thousand inhabitants.

From these early peaks, an attrition in the number of financial institutions began. The contraction of the commercial banking system occurred not because of deteriorating profit margins as the result of over-banking, as

TABLE 10.2

Number of Depository Institutions, Branches, and Offices by Type of Institution[a]

Year	Com-mercial banks	Com-mercial bank branches	Com-mercial bank offices	Mutual savings banks	Mutual savings bank branches	Mutual savings bank offices	Savings and loan associ-ations	Savings and loan associ-ations branches	Savings and loan associ-ation offices	Federal credit unions
1914	25,510	—	—	640	—	—	6,616	—	—	—
1915	25,875	785	26,660	636	—	—	6,806	—	—	—
1916	26,217	—	—	633	—	—	7,072	—	—	—
1917	26,831	—	—	632	—	—	7,269	—	—	—
1918	27,457	—	—	634	—	—	7,484	—	—	—
1919	27,859	1,192	29,051	630	—	—	7,788	—	—	—
1920	29,087	1,281	30,368	628	—	—	8,633	—	—	—
1921	29,788	1,455	31,243	631	—	—	9,255	—	—	—
1922	29,458	1,801	31,259	628	—	—	10,009	—	—	—
1923	28,877	2,054	30,931	628	—	—	10,744	—	—	—
1924	28,185	2,297	30,482	621	—	—	11,844	—	—	—
1925	27,638	2,525	30,163	619	—	—	12,403	—	—	—
1926	27,651	2,703	29,454	616	—	—	12,626	—	—	—
1927	25,800	2,914	28,714	616	—	—	12,804	—	—	—
1928	24,968	3,138	28,106	611	—	—	12,666	—	—	—
1929	24,026	3,353	27,379	607	—	—	12,342	—	—	—
1930	22,172	3,522	25,694	601	—	—	11,777	—	—	—
1931	19,375	3,467	22,842	595	—	—	11,442	—	—	—
1932	17,802	3,195	20,997	592	—	—	10,915	—	—	—
1933	14,440	2,784	17,224	575	—	—	10,596	—	—	—
1934	15,320	3,017	18,337	577	122	699	10,744	—	—	39
1935	15,374	3,248	18,622	568	129	697	10,266	—	—	772
1936	15,151	3,365	18,516	564	124	687	10,042	—	—	1,751

Year										
1937	14,882	3,482	18,364	562	124	686	9,225	—	—	2,313
1938	14,703	3,517	18,220	555	131	686	8,762	—	—	2,760
1939	14,534	3,561	18,095	551	132	683	8,006	—	—	3,182
1940	14,399	3,593	17,992	551	135	686	7,521	—	—	3,756
1941	14,329	3,632	17,961	548	135	683	7,211	—	—	4,228
1942	14,307	3,813	18,120	546	138	684	6,941	357	7,298	5,145
1943	14,206	3,864	18,070	545	136	681	6,498	357	6,855	3,938
1944	14,167	4,001	18,168	543	140	683	6,279	357	6,636	3,815
1945	14,183	4,025	18,208	542	143	685	6,149	357	6,506	3,757
1946	14,227	4,220	18,447	541	157	698	6,093	357	6,450	3,761
1947	14,234	4,237	18,471	533	171	704	6,045	357	6,492	3,845
1948	14,221	4,431	18,652	532	182	714	6,011	357	6,368	4,058
1949	14,308	4,864	19,600	531	199	730	5,983	357	6,340	4,495
1950	14,320	5,158	19,851	529	213	742	5,992	357	6,349	4,984
1951	14,132	5,264	19,396	529	230	759	5,995	360	6,352	5,398
1952	14,088	5,587	19,675	529	246	775	6,004	357	6,361	5,925
1953	14,024	5,957	19,981	528	270	798	6,012	357	6,369	6,578
1954	13,881	6,443	20,324	528	308	836	6,037	509	6,546	7,227
1955	13,756	7,062	20,818	528	329	857	6,071	601	6,672	7,806
1956	13,680	7,740	21,420	528	366	894	6,136	754	6,890	8,350
1957	13,607	8,372	21,979	523	405	928	6,169	946	7,115	8,735
1958	13,540	9,068	22,608	520	425	945	6,207	1,120	7,327	9,030
1959	13,486	9,790	23,276	518	448	966	6,223	1,341	7,564	9,447
1960	13,484	10,619	24,103	515	487	1,002	6,320	1,611	7,931	9,905
1961	13,444	11,499	24,943	515	544	1,059	6,246	1,851	8,097	10,271
1962	13,439	12,491	25,930	512	587	1,099	6,289	2,179	8,468	10,632
1963	13,582	13,652	27,234	510	625	1,135	6,248	2,469	8,717	10,955
1964	13,775	14,771	28,546	506	675	1,181	6,222	2,769	8,991	11,278
1965	13,818	15,918	29,736	506	716	1,222	6,185	2,994	9,179	11,543
1966	13,785	17,087	30,872	506	758	1,264	6,112	3,206	9,318	11,941
1967	13,741	18,119	31,860	503	831	1,334	6,036	3,357	9,393	12,210

(Continued)

TABLE 10.2 (Continued)

Year	Commercial banks	Commercial bank branches	Commercial bank offices	Mutual savings banks	Mutual savings bank branches	Mutual savings bank offices	Savings and loan associations	Savings and loan associations branches	Savings and loan association offices	Federal credit unions
1968	13,698	19,222	32,920	501	909	1,410	5,947	3,667	9,614	12,584
1969	13,681	20,418	34,099	497	986	1,483	5,835	3,938	9,773	12,921
1970	13,705	21,880	35,585	494	1,087	1,581	5,669	4,318	9,987	12,977
1971	13,804	23,370	37,174	490	1,196	1,686	6,474	4,961	10,435	12,717
1972	13,950	24,872	38,822	486	1,354	1,840	5,298	5,851	11,149	12,708
1973	13,194	26,718	40,912	482	1,492	1,974	5,170	7,036	12,206	12,688
1974	14,481	28,705	43,186	480	1,642	2,122	5,023	8,775	13,798	12,748
1975	14,654	30,262	44,916	476	1,846	2,322	4,931	10,518	15,449	12,737
1976	14,697	31,404	46,101	473	2,080	2,553	4,821	11,908	16,729	12,757
1977	14,724	32,915	47,639	472	2,316	2,788	4,761	13,087	17,848	12,750
1978	14,740	34,721	49,461	470	2,589	3,059	4,723	14,162	18,885	12,757

[a] Source: See Table 10.1.

has sometimes been charged. Rather, as transportation systems improved and the population became more concentrated in the cities, banks in the very small communities were less viable because they could not attain the scale economies of the city banks. In the savings and loan industry, this attrition in numbers was due mainly to merger activities in the late-1920s. The combination of restricted deposit inflows and the cessation of home building through the 1930s caused suspensions and further consolidation. The immediate cause of the contraction of the commercial banking system in the 1930s was again not insufficient profit resulting from extreme competitive forces, since in 1929 profit margins were quite high (see Section 9.2.2 and Table 9.5). The banks suffered the consequences of both an insufficient liquidity mechanism and a depressed asset market that did not allow the commercial banks to raise sufficient cash to withstand a general deposit run.

Until 1933, the views of regulators regarding entry and failure were symmetric. They found no need to restrain entry, nor did they find the need to intercede to prevent failure. The Federal Reserve at that time apparently felt that the insolvency of commercial banks was born of excessive risk taking, a condition for which they felt the proper remedy was bank failure. Between 1929 and 1935 more than 9000 banks failed.

For the decade and a half following the bottom of the depression, there was some continued consolidation of depository institutions. In 1934 there were 15,000 commercial banks and less than 3000 branch offices in operation. Primarily as a result of merger, the number of banks declined over the next 12 years, which included World War II, to 14,000, and the number of branches increased by 1000, partly because some merged banks continued to operate as branch offices. The net effect was a small decline in the number of commercial banking offices during this period of relative stability in industrial composition. Mergers were more prevalent in the savings and loan industry; the number of these institutions contracted from under 11,000 in 1934 to approximately 6000 in 1945. During this time, both the state and the newly formed federal regulatory agencies symmetrically deterred entry—if indeed there were any economic incentives for entry; and in addition, these agencies and the insuring agencies especially, actively sought to deter failure.

By 1946 the depository industries were consolidated to the point that there were even fewer firms operating than at the end of the drastic reorganization of the mid-1930s. Yet, in the interim years, the war economy had generated high levels of income, and population had increased substantially. Gross national product between 1934 and 1946 in constant dollars increased approximately 100%, whereas the population during this time increased by 11%.

Not only was the economy strong in the mid-1940s, but at this time there were shifts in the concentration of population from major cities to suburban areas. It was becoming clear that there was an expanding deposit and asset market, and the spreads between asset and deposit rates afforded large profit margins and high rates of return. Despite the very high profit margins and rates of return that existed, the thrust of expansion that occurred in the immediate postwar period largely took the form of branching by existing institutions. In the 14 years from the end of 1946 to the end of 1960, the number of commercial banking offices increased from over 18,000 to over 24,000, despite the fact that there was a small decline from 14,227 to 13,484 in the number of commercial banks. Branch offices, including those resulting from mergers, increased from 4,220 at the end of 1946 to 10,619 at the end of 1960. It should be noted, however, that there were significant variations among the states in branching activity, since some states permitted no branching (unit banking), some states had limited branching, and others allowed statewide branching. Of the increases in the number of offices, including both new institutions and branches, 67% occurred in statewide branching states, 35% in limited branching states, and 10% in unit banking states. Of the changes in banking between 1947 and 1960, there were approximately 1300 newly organized commercial banks and only 41 bank failures that required disbursements by the FDIC.

The prosperity of the postwar era also began to stimulate entry by savings and loan associations. In this case, the number of new entrants to the market approximately equaled the number of mergers, so that the number of associations did not change; but branch activity, which was dormant through the 1940s, began to recover in 1950, when savings and loan profit margins reached their peak. Between 1950 and 1960 the number of savings and loan branches increased from 357 to 1611. Mutual savings banks were still confined to their traditional northeastern markets and showed very little movement, but the federal credit unions in the postwar era started increasing in 1945 from a base of 3757 institutions to 11,941 institutions in 1966.

The early 1960s saw a significant change in the pace of entry in the commercial banking industry. In 1961, the philosophy of the comptroller's office regarding de novo entry had changed dramatically. The position was that not only were additional banking offices needed to meet population shifts and growth, but the comptroller believed that the depositor would benefit from the stimulus provided by additional competition. With this change in regulatory posture, in the years between 1962 and 1965, 512 new national banks were chartered, and, in addition, 502 state banks gained approval. When a few of these new banks teetered on the brink of failure, the pace of entry was halted as a moratorium on new national bank charters was put into effect in most areas. This curtailment was also put into effect by most state bank chartering agencies. By the middle 1960s increases in numbers of banks had slowed to a trickle as the competitive forces that gripped the depository industries began to deter private desires for entry and to elicit a growing reluctance by the depository insuring agencies to allow greater competition and risk of failure.

In 1966, as previously discussed, the Interest Rate Control Act extended deposit ceilings to the thrift institutions. This deposit ceiling action had significant impacts on the industrial structure of the depository industries, since additional branches became one of the few deposit-attracting competitive techniques available to commercial banks, savings and loan associations, and mutual savings banks. For those thrift institutions, after a brief period of approximately 5 years in which profit margins recovered under deposit ceilings, there followed a burst of branching activity. The branches of mutual savings banks between 1970 and 1978 increased from slightly over 1000 to over 2500, savings and loan branches over the same period increased from 4300 to over 14,000. Commercial bank branches also increased from just under 22,000 to just under 35,000. This phenomenal burst of branching activity, the great majority of which represented de novo branch offices, brought the number of depository offices per capita to levels similar to those existing in the early-1920s.

It is, of course, of interest to explain the incentives for the commitment of equity capital in the depository industries. To do this in a rough way, we can examine rates of return to the depository firms. There are three rates of return measures shown in Tables 10.3, 10.4, and 10.5. The first is the rate of return on the deposit activity, the second is the before-tax rate of return, and the last is the after-tax rate of return. The rate of return on the deposit activity reflects the profit levels on the deposit activity alone as developed in Chapter 9.[2]

It should be recalled that the profit margin as calculated in Chapter 9 omitted the revenues and costs of such activities as trust management and capital gains or losses from the purchase or sale of assets, and did not consider other extraordinary or nonrecurring activities. Another major exclusion from this calculation of the deposit activity's profit margin was the revenues and costs associated with nondeposit borrowed funds. The reader should be reminded that great care was taken in constructing the profit margin series to focus on the profit from the deposit activity alone. It would have been preferable to include as a cost of the deposit activity

---

[2] The profit margin of the deposit activity is equal to $r_a - r - c$. See the footnotes to the Chapter 9 tables and Appendix A for the accounts used to construct these variables for each of the depository institutions.

TABLE 10.3

Rates of Return on the Deposit Activity[a]

| | Commercial banks | | | | Moody's AAA |
| | Federal Reserve members | FDIC members | Mutual savings banks | Savings and loan associations | long-term interest |
Year					rates
1919	7.01	—	—	—	5.4
1920	8.36	—	—	—	6.1
1921	6.83	—	—	—	5.9
1922	5.70	—	—	—	5.1
1923	5.49	—	—	—	5.1
1924	5.90	—	—	—	5.0
1925	6.63	—	—	—	4.8
1926	6.62	—	—	—	4.7
1927	5.81	—	—	—	4.5
1928	5.87	—	—	—	4.5
1929	6.46	—	—	—	4.7
1930	4.09	—	—	—	4.5
1931	4.15	—	—	—	4.5
1932	3.72	—	—	—	5.0
1933	4.37	—	—	—	4.4
1934	4.95	—	—	—	4.0
1935	5.35	4.19	2.51	—	3.6
1936	6.70	5.13	2.29	—	3.2
1937	7.13	5.38	1.70	—	3.2
1938	6.48	4.84	3.42	—	3.1
1939	6.92	5.17	4.03	—	3.0
1940	7.22	5.24	7.99	—	2.8
1941	8.05	5.34	6.89	—	2.7
1942	7.26	6.13	6.71	7.94	2.8
1943	8.95	7.69	8.43	9.64	2.7
1944	10.32	7.82	6.14	5.69	2.7
1945	10.57	9.90	7.66	5.67	2.6
1946	10.97	10.48	6.64	4.48	2.5
1947	10.39	9.47	5.51	4.53	2.6
1948	11.18	10.01	5.33	5.55	2.8
1949	11.38	10.13	4.10	5.75	2.6
1950	12.19	10.65	4.10	6.92	2.6
1951	13.30	11.55	4.65	5.97	2.8
1952	14.17	12.36	1.92	5.63	2.9
1953	14.99	12.92	2.60	6.32	3.2
1954	13.98	11.92	2.70	6.90	2.9
1955	15.21	12.84	2.37	7.75	3.0
1956	16.50	13.90	2.46	7.16	3.3
1957	16.28	13.47	1.94	6.20	3.8
1958	14.89	11.99	1.91	5.95	3.7

TABLE 10.3 (*Continued*)

| Year | Commercial banks | | Mutual savings banks | Savings and loan associations | Moody's AAA long-term interest rates |
	Federal Reserve members	FDIC members			
1959	17.35	13.65	2.43	6.05	4.38
1960	17.03	13.87	.84	4.23	4.41
1961	13.92	11.74	1.76	5.37	4.35
1962	13.32	10.29	.24	4.36	4.33
1963	12.68	9.73	.29	2.31	4.26
1964	12.63	9.84	.72	3.43	4.40
1965	11.43	9.38	1.78	3.36	4.49
1966	12.60	9.93	−.85	1.54	5.13
1967	11.70	9.02	−2.42	.11	5.51
1968	12.84	11.72	−.33	2.18	6.18
1969	14.65	11.82	1.16	3.15	7.03
1970	13.24	8.64	1.29	1.92	8.04
1971	9.98	5.66	2.87	2.76	7.39
1972	9.87	9.08	4.34	4.40	7.21
1973	12.97	8.41	4.47	5.66	7.44
1974	16.60	7.78	1.64	2.80	8.57
1975	10.55	3.69	.30	1.89	8.83
1976	—	9.13	.60	3.47	8.43
1977	—	9.81	1.96	5.65	8.02
1978	—	12.11	3.36	7.56	8.73

[a] Source: Tables A9.1–A9.13. Calculated as the ratio of estimated profit on deposit activity to capital account and expressed in percentages. Estimated profit on deposit activity is calculated as the product of profit margin per deposit dollar and total deposits. Profit margin per deposit dollar is calculated as average asset earning rate minus effective deposit rate minus total operating expenses per deposit dollar.

the actual illiquidity costs of borrowing funds necessitated by unexpected deposit withdrawals, but since it was not possible to determine the extent to which borrowing costs were forced illiquidity as opposed to profit oriented, planned short-term borrowing costs, both the imputed revenues and explicit costs of borrowing were excluded from the profit margin estimates. This exclusion of the cost and imputed revenues from borrowing probably had a larger quantitative impact on commercial banks' profit margin estimates than those of thrift institutions since the former engage more heavily in borrowing to satisfy deposit drains.

The profit from the deposit activity depends on the profit margin or profit per deposit dollar p and the number of deposit dollars D. The rate of return on the deposit activity is pD/E or $p(D/E)$, where E is the level of equity. This measure of the rate of return depends on the profit margin

TABLE 10.4

Before-Tax Rates of Return[a]

	Commercial banks				Moody's AAA long-term interest rates
Year	Federal Reserve members	FDIC members	Mutual savings banks	Savings and loan associations	
1919	9.92	—	—	—	5.49
1920	9.62	—	—	—	6.12
1921	7.16	—	—	—	5.97
1922	8.00	—	—	—	5.10
1923	7.70	—	—	—	5.12
1924	7.97	—	—	—	5.00
1925	8.97	—	—	—	4.88
1926	8.72	—	—	—	4.73
1927	8.36	—	—	—	4.57
1928	8.54	—	—	—	4.55
1929	8.29	—	—	—	4.73
1930	4.64	—	—	—	4.55
1931	.20	—	—	—	4.58
1932	−4.71	—	—	—	5.01
1933	−7.17	—	—	—	4.49
1934	−4.44	−5.52	2.88	—	4.00
1935	4.11	3.34	4.68	—	3.60
1936	8.82	8.32	5.37	—	3.24
1937	6.26	6.02	1.35	—	3.26
1938	4.89	4.73	−9.42	—	3.19
1939	6.11	6.02	−1.17	—	3.01
1940	6.12	6.09	−11.80	—	2.84
1941	6.62	7.37	2.86	—	2.77
1942	7.38	7.37	2.09	—	2.83
1943	10.38	10.27	3.46	—	2.73
1944	11.95	11.94	7.23	—	2.72
1945	13.94	13.89	14.31	—	2.62
1946	12.88	13.19	12.74	—	2.53
1947	10.74	11.13	7.05	3.89	2.61
1948	9.70	10.04	6.70	3.90	2.82
1949	10.47	10.86	6.09	3.97	2.66
1950	11.86	12.09	6.37	4.06	2.62
1951	12.19	12.30	7.44	3.95	2.86
1952	13.35	13.38	4.98	4.09	2.96
1953	13.76	13.66	5.76	4.41	3.20
1954	15.56	15.51	6.00	4.67	2.90
1955	13.11	12.99	5.86	4.87	3.06
1956	12.77	12.68	6.14	4.94	3.36
1967	14.17	13.88	5.85	5.10	3.89
1958	16.85	16.34	6.04	5.23	3.79

TABLE 10.4 (*Continued*)

Year	Commercial banks		Mutual savings banks	Savings and loan associations	Moody's AAA long-term interest rates
	Federal Reserve members	FDIC members			
1959	12.49	12.33	6.83	5.39	4.38
1960	16.83	16.39	5.45	5.66	4.41
1961	15.89	15.37	6.44	5.78	4.35
1962	14.12	13.72	5.04	6.04	4.33
1963	13.82	13.34	5.33	6.05	4.26
1964	12.75	12.50	5.89	6.19	4.40
1965	11.96	11.85	6.83	6.19	4.49
1966	11.73	11.71	4.45	6.15	5.13
1967	12.87	12.70	3.18	6.42	5.51
1968	12.83	12.81	5.41	6.66	6.18
1969	17.05	14.75	5.76	6.69	7.03
1970	16.77	15.74	5.05	6.77	8.04
1971	14.28	14.68	8.70	7.67	7.39
1972	13.81	13.71	11.27	8.36	7.21
1973	14.93	14.34	10.62	8.91	7.44
1974	14.55	13.98	7.20	8.86	8.57
1975	13.36	13.61	7.51	10.90	8.83
1976	—	13.72	9.20	15.12	8.43
1977	—	14.58	10.91	18.87	8.02
1978	—	17.27	11.60	20.31	8.73

[a] Source: Tables A9.1–A9.13. Calculated as the ratio of net income before tax to capital account and expressed in percentages.

and the deposit–equity ratio. The equity–deposit ratios are contained in Table 5.2, and their inverses represent the number of deposit dollars each equity dollar supports. Over time, variations in deposit–equity ratios or in leverage influenced rates of return for the depository industries.

The before-tax rates of return calculations of Table 10.4 include the previously omitted cost and revenue items, and the after-tax rate of return figures of Table 10.5 take account of local, state, and federal taxes. The rates of return are calculated relative to the book value of the capital account for the depository institution.

The information content of these rates of return is unfortunately somewhat weak. We can only surmise that when rates of return on book value exceed alternative market rates on investments of similar risks, an excess demand for charters existed. An alternative and more desirable comparison would have been between market value and book value. That is, if an

TABLE 10.5

After-Tax Rates of Return[a]

| | Commercial banks | | | | Moody's AAA |
Year	Federal Reserve members	FDIC members	Mutual savings banks	Savings and loan associations	long-term interest rates
1919	9.92	—	—	—	5.49
1920	9.62	—	—	—	6.12
1921	7.16	—	—	—	5.97
1922	8.00	—	—	—	5.10
1923	7.70	—	—	—	5.12
1924	7.97	—	—	—	5.00
1925	8.97	—	—	—	4.88
1926	8.72	—	—	—	4.73
1927	8.36	—	—	—	4.57
1928	8.54	—	—	—	4.55
1929	8.29	—	—	—	4.73
1930	4.64	—	—	—	4.55
1931	.20	—	—	—	4.58
1932	−4.71	—	—	—	5.01
1933	−7.17	—	—	—	4.49
1934	−4.44	−5.52	1.60	—	4.00
1935	4.11	3.34	4.68	—	3.60
1936	8.82	8.28	5.37	—	3.24
1937	6.26	5.94	1.35	—	3.26
1938	4.89	4.66	−9.42	—	3.19
1939	6.11	5.95	−1.17	—	3.01
1940	6.12	6.01	−11.73	—	2.84
1941	6.62	6.64	2.56	—	2.77
1942	6.27	6.24	1.89	—	2.83
1943	8.60	8.55	3.37	—	2.73
1944	9.31	9.40	7.16	—	2.72
1945	10.38	10.44	14.08	—	2.62
1946	9.36	9.71	12.23	—	2.53
1947	7.71	8.02	6.57	3.89	2.61
1948	7.05	7.33	6.34	3.90	2.82
1949	7.48	7.80	5.77	3.95	2.66
1950	8.05	8.30	6.02	4.04	2.62
1951	7.39	7.61	7.08	3.95	2.86
1952	7.70	7.86	4.45	4.07	2.96
1953	7.64	7.73	5.28	4.38	3.20
1954	8.97	9.15	5.44	4.64	2.90
1955	7.70	7.70	5.41	4.85	3.06
1956	7.51	7.59	5.71	4.93	3.36
1957	8.03	8.04	5.46	5.09	3.89
1958	9.42	9.35	5.63	5.21	3.79

TABLE 10.5 (*Continued*)

| Year | Commercial banks | | Mutual savings banks | Savings and loan associations | Moody's AAA long-term interest rates |
	Federal Reserve members	FDIC members			
1959	7.72	7.73	6.39	5.38	4.38
1960	9.70	9.69	4.99	5.65	4.41
1961	8.18	9.02	5.94	5.77	4.35
1962	8.53	8.43	4.50	6.03	4.33
1963	8.69	8.50	4.69	5.92	4.26
1964	8.39	8.32	5.19	6.03	4.40
1965	8.43	8.40	6.09	6.01	4.49
1966	8.40	8.47	3.55	6.03	5.13
1967	9.28	9.23	2.29	6.31	5.51
1968	9.33	9.35	4.34	6.50	6.18
1969	10.76	10.95	4.44	6.49	7.03
1970	11.21	11.36	3.43	6.57	8.04
1971	11.04	11.16	6.35	7.33	7.39
1972	10.67	10.54	8.11	7.93	7.21
1973	11.20	11.37	7.47	8.25	7.44
1974	11.12	11.20	4.77	8.49	8.57
1975	10.64	10.89	5.11	7.58	8.83
1976	—	10.55	6.35	10.57	8.43
1977	—	11.01	7.73	13.09	8.02
1978	—	11.59	8.37	11.36	8.73

[a] Source: Tables A9.1–A9.13. Calculated as the ratio of net income after tax to capital account and expressed in percentages.

excess demand for entry into the depository industries existed, one means of entry would be to purchase the shares, where available on the open market, of existing depository institutions. This would, of course, cause market prices to exceed book values. The difficulty with this approach, however, is that some of our depository institutions are mutual in form, and no such share pricing exists. Furthermore, even in the case of commercial banks, a great majority of the shares are not traded in public markets. Even with these shortcomings, some inferences can be made by comparisons with rates of return on the book values of manufacturing corporations. These data were available after 1947.

From an examination of the rates of return to the deposit activity, several interesting observations can be made. In the 1920s, despite relatively high profit margins, the Fed member banks had relatively low rates of return that were not much higher than Moody's long-term AAA bond rates. The high profit margins, it seems, were more than offset by the low deposit to equity ratios that existed at the time. That is, in a comparatively free-market era when the depository institutions had a more severe and more recent history of failure, the degree of leverage was considerably less than in the postwar period. Deposit–equity ratios in the 1920s for member banks were in the range of 6 or 7 to 1. With this relatively smaller degree of leverage, the higher profit margins tended to yield rates of return that were reasonably close to the long-term AAA rate. When account is taken of all revenue and cost items, including capital gains, the rates of return to the Fed member banks increase, and the before-tax and after-tax rates of return are then in the neighborhood of 300 to 400 basis points above the long-term AAA rate. The before- and after-tax rates were the same, as there was no taxation driving a wedge between these rates at that time. Examination of this era is, of course, of great interest since it was still within the era of free-market banking when it was comparatively easy to enter and retreat from the depository industries.

The effect of the onset of the Great Depression can also be seen in the Fed member bank series. In 1929 the rate of return on the deposit activity stood at 6.5% and declined only to 3.7% in 1932. Of course, this measure does not take account of the extreme liquidity costs and capital losses of this time period. When account is taken of these items, both the before- and after-tax rates of return decline from 8.3% in 1929 to become negative between 1932 and 1934, with a low of −7% reached in 1933.

The Great Depression is evident not only in the Fed members series, but in an FDIC series for all insured commercial banks. The latter part of the 1930s saw some recovery in the rates of return for all insured commercial banks and Fed members. This, in turn, reflected a gradual increase in profit margins back to the levels of the early 1920s and a slight increase in the degree of leverage, so that before- and after-tax rates of return rose and exceeded the corporate AAA series by about 300 basis points. Even with this larger differential, it is questionable whether the perceived risk premiums were sufficient to attract capital to the industry.

As for the mutual savings banks, their profit margins and rates of return to the deposit activity were below those of commercial banks, but they nevertheless held up and were positive from 1935 forward. However, when capital losses were taken into account, savings banks, which wrote off mortgage losses between 1938 and 1940, showed negative before- and after-tax rates. These losses amounted to as much as −11.8% in 1940.

During the war years, despite extremely low interest rates and despite the reduction in the proportion of risk assets in their portfolios, commercial banks still generated positive profit margins. Furthermore, since leverage was allowed to increase as the regulatory authorities relaxed capital requirements, rates of return from the deposit activity rose from approximately 7 to 10% for Fed members and from about 5 to 10% for FDIC members. During the war years, taxation for the first time reduced after-tax rates of return. While before-tax rates of return in 1945 rose to almost 14% for commercial banks, after tax these rates of return dropped below 11%. When the before-tax rate of return is compared to the open-market rate, the divergence becomes extraordinarily high; in 1945 banks enjoyed a more than 1000 basis point spread over AAA bonds. In fact, the mutual savings banks began to do well and not only reached peaks in profit margins in the late war years, but their rates of return both before and after taxes exceeded those of commercial banks at the conclusion of the wartime period.

Several generalizations can be made about the postwar era. First, the rates of return to Federal Reserve member banks tended to be insignificantly different from those of all FDIC member banks (of which they are a subset). However, commercial banks did enjoy significantly higher rates of return than either mutual savings banks or savings and loan associations on both a before- and after-tax basis. Even with taxation, rates of return in commercial banking were well above AAA bond rates in all postwar years, although the differential narrowed in the late-1970s.

Rates of return for the thrifts were considerably more modest than those for commercial banking. After-tax rates of return to savings and loan associations grew persistently during the postwar era, exhibiting a smoothing process not evidenced by the current profit margin series. From the early-postwar period to the late-1960s, rates of return for savings and loans exceeded the AAA series. The mutual savings banks' rates of return, on the other hand, did tend to reflect more sensitively the difficulties experienced in the mid-1960s, when profit margins were negative. However, even with negative current profit margins from the deposit activity at that time, they still showed positive rates of return both before and after tax. In general, the mutual savings banks have lost considerable ground to open-market rates since 1946.

The factor most affecting the trend in rates of return has been the change in leverage. Commercial banks came out of World War II with low capital to deposit ratios of under 7%, which were then built up to over 9% in the early 1960s. On the other hand, the trend for mutual savings banks has been just the opposite; they came out of the war years a capital to deposit ratio of just under 11%, which has gradually slipped to between $6\frac{1}{2}$ and 7% in the 1970s. This increase in leverage has tended to elevate their rates of return. In the postwar era, savings and loan associations also experienced slight trend reductions in their capital accounts: from 9% of deposits down to 7% in 1978, which substantially increased returns. By the late 1970s, however, there was a tendency for convergence in the capital to deposit ratios for all depository institutions, so that differences in earning rates by the late 1970s reflect differences in profit margins rather than leverage.

Despite the recoveries made by the depository institutions in the post-war era, the rates of return after tax with few exceptions were lower than ratios of after-tax earnings to equity book values for manufacturing corporations. (See Table 10.6.) There were a few exceptions when manufacturing after-tax rates of return slipped below those of commercial banks. They occurred in the postwar recession years, which affected manufacturing more adversely than the depository industries. It is difficult to conclude that incentives for entry did not exist, since the depository industries enjoy a considerably lower risk of insolvency when firms are aided by legislative and regulatory actions in times of economic adversity.

While it is not possible to conclude definitively from these aggregated rates of return that a situation of excess risk-adjusted profits existed in the depository industries, the case appears to be most clearly made for commercial banking in the early postwar record. For thrifts, however, the reverse appears to be more clearly the case in most of the postwar period. Certainly, the low rates of return to the mutual savings banks would lead

TABLE 10.6

Relation of Profits After Taxes to Stockholders' Equity,
All Manufacturing Corporations[a]

Year	Ratio	Year	Ratio
1947	15.6	1963	10.3
1948	16.0	1964	11.6
1949	11.6	1965	13.0
1950	15.4	1966	13.4
1951	12.1	1967	11.7
1952	10.3	1968	12.1
1953	10.5	1969	11.5
1954	9.9	1970	9.3
1955	12.6	1971	9.7
1956	12.3	1972	10.6
1957	10.9	1973	12.8
1958	8.6	1974	14.9
1959	10.4	1975	11.6
1960	9.2	1976	13.9
1961	8.9	1977	14.2
1962	9.8	1978	15.0

[a] Source: Federal Trade Commission. Annual ratios based on average equity for the year as calculated from the quarter-end figures. Expressed in percentages.

to a prediction of low entry rates, and in fact, net mergers, which did occur. The same can also be said to some degree for savings and loan associations, in which mergers did outnumber new entrants to the market. However, these aggregated data probably overwhelm any regional differences that might exist, so that incentives for entry might still have been strong in certain geographic areas.

10.3 DEPOSITORY INSTITUTION MARKET SHARE TRENDS: 1942–1978

The purpose of this section is to present deposit market share information and to identify general trends in these shares from 1942–1978. Figure 10.1 shows the percentage of savings and time deposits held by each institution. The corresponding data are contained in Appendix Table B10.1.

The commercial banks' share of the savings deposit market has hovered near the 50% level for most of the period. However, there have been large changes in the thrifts' shares. Mutual savings banks held the second largest market share at 32.1% in 1942, but this share has declined steadily ever since. While mutual savings bank continued to grow within their limited geographic market, they did so at a slower rate than the other depository institutions. Over the 36-year period, mutual savings banks grew at a compound annual rate of 5.8%, while total savings and time deposits grew at a 6.16% rate. Commercial banks grew slightly faster than the total growth in savings deposits at a 6.3% rate, but savings and loans and credit unions enjoyed the highest average annual growth rates of 7.7 and 9.3%, respectively. Savings and loans and credit unions, then, increased market shares at the expense of the savings banks.

Just as the savings banks' share fell steadily, the market share of credit unions increased. These institutions grew at a rate almost twice that of the total savings deposit market, and they have experienced a drop in market share on only one occasion since 1945. The trend in credit union market shares shown in Figure 10.1 appears relatively flat compared to the market share trends of the other institutions because of the credit unions' small percentage of the total. However, with the fastest growth rate among the intermediaries, credit unions became a factor in the competition with a savings deposit market share of nearly 5% by the late-1970s.

Unlike the steady movement in credit union and mutual savings bank market shares, commercial bank and savings and loan market shares fluctuated over time. For the most part, these depository institutions moved in opposite directions; apparently one's gain was the other's loss. From the years after World War II until 1960, commercial bank market shares

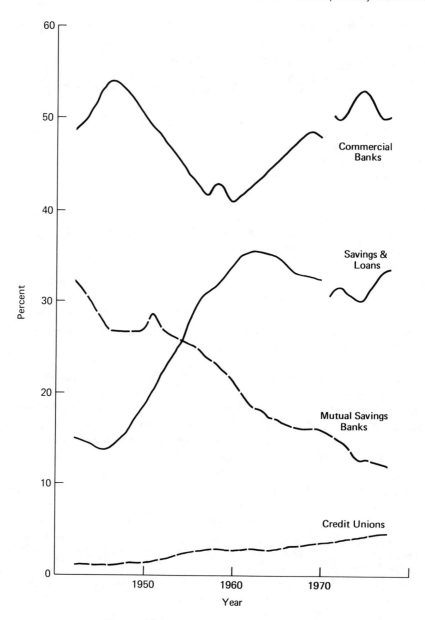

Figure 10.1   Savings deposit market shares.

fell, and the market share gap between savings and loan associations and commercial banks fell from 40.8% in 1946 to 5.4% in 1960. This trend was reversed in the 1960s, as commercial banks made a strong comeback in competing for savings deposits in the late-1960s and early-1970s.

Figure 10.2 shows total deposit market shares for each institution. Insured commercial bank demand deposits added to commercial bank savings and time deposits account for the market share differences between Figures 10.1 and 10.2. The data for Figure 10.2 are contained in Appendix Table B10.2.

While commercial banks' savings deposit market share registered a net increase of 2.0 percentage points over the 36-year period, their total deposit market share fell by 18.4 percentage points, since there was a large shift from demand to time and savings deposits.

Between 1946 and 1960, savings and loans offered a return that averaged 1.45% higher than that offered to savers at commercial banks. Before 1966, thrifts not subject to Regulation Q ceilings consistently paid higher average rates than the maximum ceiling rate for commercial banks from 1950 through 1964. Since a favorable term structure of interest rates existed throughout this period, savings and loans investing in long-term markets were able to generate earnings that were passed through to savers who responded in turn to the deposit rate differentials.

Because of the common bond requirement for credit unions and the isolation of the mutual savings banks, savers were left with the choice between commercial banks and savings associations. This choice depended largely on relative deposit rates. To offset some loss of household time and savings accounts, the commercial banks began to compete more actively for funds that would ordinarily go to open-market instruments. In attempting to maintain or even gain corporate funds, banks turned to the certificate of deposit market at the beginning of the 1960s. These jumbo CDs were quite interest rate-sensitive and, they gave the banks a vehicle with which to compete for open-market funds. The commercial bank liability structure has been changing continuously since the end of World War II, with time and savings deposits moving from a minority to a majority portion. Figure 10.3 indicates that at the end of the war savings deposits were less than one-third the level of demand deposits, and by the mid-1960s they became the majority source of funds, which continued through the 1970s.

The willingness of commercial banks to compete after 1960 in the highly rate-sensitive markets obviously allowed them to recapture their share of the savings deposit market. However, since depositors in general were (and are still) becoming more rate sensitive, the shift toward interest-bearing deposit accounts continued, and the commercial banks' overall

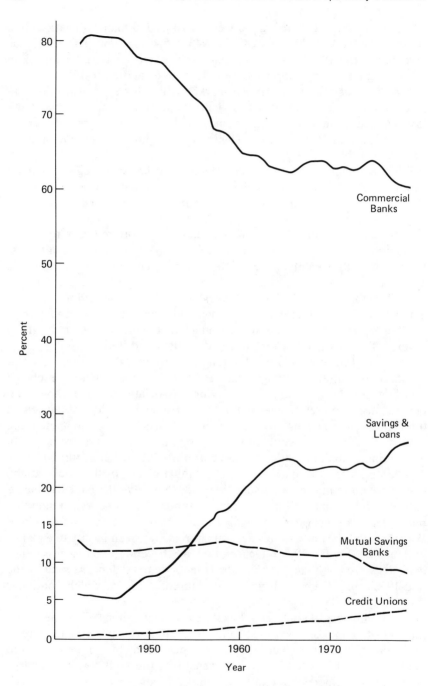

Figure 10.2   Total deposit market shares.

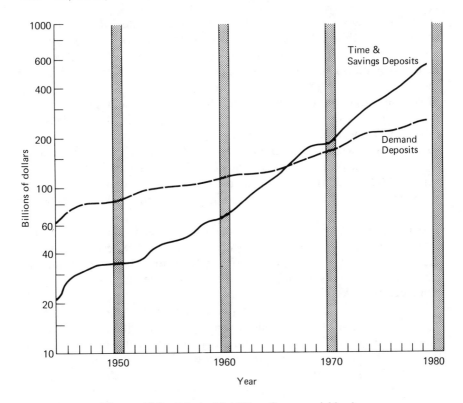

Figure 10.3 Principal liabilities of commercial banks.

share of the total deposit market continued to decline in the early 1960s, as can be seen in Figure 10.2.

By 1966 the Interest Rate Control Act placed ceilings on the deposit accounts of all depository institutions. From then on, the ability to adjust deposit ceiling differentials to affect relative market shares was singularly within the hands of the regulatory authorities. There emerged a number of new deposit accounts, each with its own applicable rate ceiling that depended on both maturity and deposit size.

When deposit ceilings were set, not only were relative market shares between the depository institutions at issue, but in addition, since open-market rates were rising more rapidly than depository institution deposit rates, these institutions were losing their share of total savings. There were three major revisions of Regulation Q ceilings in 1970, 1973, and 1978 that were intended to counter the declining deposit growth that resulted from stiff rate competition from the open market.

The first major revisions of Regulation Q occurred in January and June

1970, following a sharp increase in market rates in late-1969. In January, regulators established three separate maturity categories of small time deposits, with the intent of lengthening the average maturity of deposits at commercial banks and thrifts. The regulatory authorities at this time were more concerned with protecting institutions from large-scale withdrawals of rate-sensitive, short-term deposits. In June 1970, ceilings were eliminated on large CDs of $100,000 or more maturing in 90 days or less.

The 1973 revisions were similar to, but more extensive than, those of 1970. Ceilings were raised, and two new maturity categories replaced the "greater than 2-year" category. The new "$2\frac{1}{2}$- to 4-year" category had a ceiling of 6.5%, and the "greater than 4-year" division had no rate ceiling. Also, deposit ceilings were eliminated on all remaining CDs of $100,000 or more.

Because they had no rate ceiling, the 4-year deposits became known as "wild card" deposits. Wild cards were a short-lived experiment; authorities placed ceilings on these deposits in November 1973, since the wild cards were rightfully blamed for large shifts of deposits from thrifts to commercial banks.

The third major ceiling revision during the 1970s came in June 1978. The authorization of the 6-month money market certificate, with ceiling rates tied to the average return from the weekly Treasury bill (T-bill) auction, was the first meaningful concession to the depository institutions in their battle against disintermediation. The minimum denomination of these certificates was set at $1000, the same as for Treasury bills. Banks could offer the average T-bill rate, and the thrifts received a 25 point differential. In the past, as market rates rose above Q ceilings, Treasury securities had been the most common alternative for rate-sensitive depositors holding funds at banks and at thrifts. Money market certificates provided an alternative to Treasury securities for such depositors. This differential of 25 basis points was the result of a gradual trend to reduce the size of the differential. The differential on savings deposits, set at 75 points in 1966, dropped to 50 points in 1970 and to 25 points in 1973.

As the empirical analysis of Chapter 8 indicates, there are differences in the implicit deposit rates paid by savings and loan associations and commercial banks in addition to differentials in explicit rates. While implicit deposit rates have been higher for commercial banks than savings and loan associations, it is difficult to quantify their effect on market share. The explicit and implicit rate differentials were not the only tools in the tug-of-war for market share. After commercial banks began their aggressive drive to attract household savings deposits from thrifts, the thrifts countered in the 1970s by challenging commercial banks' historic dominance of the transaction services market. The clear distinction between demand and savings deposit eroded, interest-bearing transaction accounts evolved, and vigorous competition for deposits between banks and thrifts was stimulated. By competing for transaction-type deposits, thrifts hoped to further stabilize their source of funds and to reduce the convenience advantage of one-stop banking for the commercial banks. The first of the new powers for thrifts came in 1970 when savings and loan associations received permission to make prearranged, nonnegotiable transfers from household savings accounts in order to pay household expenses. Other alternatives to checking accounts soon followed, and as with NOW accounts, offered interest on funds held essentially for transaction purposes. Consumers could telephone their thrifts and order payments on accounts as desired, and remote service units, or point of sale funds transfer systems, were allowed by the Federal Home Loan Bank Board on an experimental basis in January 1974. Customers were able to use on line computer terminals and offline automated teller machines to conduct financial transactions. Banks, too, received more flexibility regarding transaction services. In 1978 banks were permitted to arrange automatic transfer of funds for nonbusiness customers when checking account balances fell below an agreed-upon level. In effect, these automatic fund transfer services provided interest on transaction funds.

The most sweeping legislative changes that could have profound effects on market shares stem from the Depository Institutions Deregulation Act of 1980. By this act, federally insured commercial banks, savings and loan associations, and mutual savings banks were allowed to offer NOW accounts effective December 31, 1980. In addition, commercial banks are permitted to offer automatic transfer accounts, authority for remote service units for federal savings and loans is now permanent, and federally and state-chartered federally insured credit unions can offer share draft accounts. Since the act also calls for the phasing out of interest rate ceilings over a 6-year period, explicit deposit rate competition could also have an effect on the distribution of deposits as well as the relative share of the depository institutions in total personal savings.

The relationship between the savings and loan–commercial bank rate spread and the percentage of household savings held in banks is shown in Figure 10.4 for the years 1945 to 1976. (The data for this Figure are presented in Appendix Table B10.3.) Since savings and loans were not permitted to hold business deposits, it is in the struggle for household savings that bank and savings and loan competition is the strongest. The least squares regression line plotted for the values of the spread in deposit rates and the percentage change in household savings deposited at commercial banks indicates that as savings and loan deposit rates become relatively more favorable, the commercial banks' share of household savings

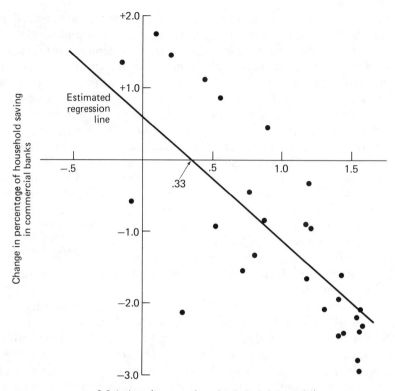

Figure 10.4   The relationship between rate spread and changing commercial bank share of savings.

declines. The least squares regression line indicates that with a rate differential of 33 basis points in favor of savings and loan associations, the commercial banks' share of household savings would stabilize. That is, if the differential became more than 33 basis points, the commercial banking industry would tend to lose its share of household savings to the savings and loans and possibly other thrift institutions.

BIBLIOGRAPHY

Abramson, Victor. "Private Competition and Public Regulation," *The National Banking Review*, **3,** January 1966.

Beighley, H. Prescott, Boyd, John H., and Jacobs, Donald P. "Bank Equities and Investor Risk Perceptions: Some Entailments for Capital Adequacy Regulation," *Journal of Bank Research*, **6,** Autumn 1975.

Benson, Bruce, "Spatial Microeconomics: Implications for the Relationship Between Concentration of Ownership and Bank Performance," In *Proceedings of a Conference on Bank Structure and Competition*, Federal Reserve Bank of Chicago, May 1980.

Benston, George J. "Savings Banking and the Public Interest," *Journal of Money, Credit andl Banking*, **4**, February 1972.

Benston, George J. "The Optimal Banking Structure," *Journal of Bank Research*, **4**, March 1973.

Boorman, John T. "The Prospects for Minority-Owned Commercial Banks: A Comparative Performance Analysis," *Journal of Bank Research*, **5**, Winter 1974.

Broadus, J. Alfred, Jr. "Banking Market Structure and Bank Performance," In *Proceedings of a Conference on Bank Structure and Competition*, Federal Reserve Bank of Chicago, October 1972.

Edwards, Franklin R. "The Banking Competition Controversy," *The National Banking Review*, **2**, September 1965.

Fellows, James A. "Some Welfare Implications of Legal Restrictions on Commercial Bank Entry," *Journal of Bank Research*, **11**, Autumn 1980.

Fischer, Gerald C. *American Banking Structure*. New York: Columbia Univ. Press, 1968.

Flechig, T. *Banking Market Structure and Performance*. Washington, D.C.: Board of Governors of the Federal Reserve System, 1965.

Fraser, D. R., and Rose, Peter S. "Static and Dynamic Measures of Market Structure and the Performance of Commercial Banks," *Journal of Economics and Business*, **28**, Winter 1976.

Gilbert, Gary G. "The Potential Competition Doctrine in Commercial Banking: Theory and Policy." In *Proceedings of a Conference on Bank Structure and Competition*, Federal Reserve Bank of Chicago, March 1974.

Goodman, Oscar. "A Review of Recent Legislative and Judicial Trends Affecting Banking Structure," In *Proceedings of a Conference on Bank Structure and Competition*, Federal Reserve Bank of Chicago, March 1967.

Goodman, Oscar. "A Survey of Judicial and Regulatory Opinions Affecting Banking Competition Under the Bank Merger Acts of 1960 and 1966," In *Proceedings of a Conference on Bank Structure and Competition*, Federal Reserve Bank of Chicago, May 1969.

Greenbaum, Stuart I. "Competition and Efficiency in the Banking System—Empirical Research and Its Policy Implications," *Journal of Political Economy Supplement*, **75**, August 1967.

Hanweck, G. A. "Predicting Bank Failures," Washington, D.C. Board of Governors of The Federal Reserve System, November 1977.

Harth, Jean G. "Additional Offices and Facilities of Savings Associations," *National Savings and Loan League. Legal Bulletin*, May 1974.

Heggestad, Arnold A. "Market Structure, Risk and Profitability in Commercial Banking," *Journal of Finance*, **32**, September 1977.

Hultquist, Timothy A. "Concentration and Stability of Market Shares in Banking," In *Proceedings of a Conference on Bank Structure and Competition*, Federal Reserve Bank of Chicago, March 1974.

Jacobs, Donald P. *Business Loan Costs and Bank Market Structure: An Empirical Estimate of Their Relations*. National Bureau of Economic Research, Paper No. 115, New York, 1971.

Kallas, Raid J. *Deregulation and Bank Profit*. Graduate School of Business Professional Report. Austin: University of Texas, May 1980.

Peltzman, Samuel. "Bank Entry Regulation: Its Impact and Purpose," The National Banking Review, **3**, January 1966.

Peltzman, Samuel. "Capital Investment in Commercial Banking and its Relationship to Portfolio Regulation," *Journal of Political Economy*, **78**, January/February 1970.

Phillips, Almarin. "A Critique of Empirical Studies of Relations Between Market Structure and Profitability," *Journal of Industrial Economics,* **24** June 1976.

Phillips, Almarin. "Competitive Policy for Depository Financial Institutions." In *Promoting Competition in Regulated Markets,* ed. Almarin Phillips. Washington, D.C.: Brookings Institution, 1975.

Rhoades, Stephen A. "Diversification, Competition, and Aggregate Concentration," In *Proceedings of a Conference on Bank Structure and Competition,* Federal Reserve Bank of Chicago, March 1974.

Rhoades, Stephen A. "Structure—Performance Studies in Banking: A Summary and Evaluation," Washington, D.C. Board of Governors of the Federal Reserve System, Staff Economic Studies 92, 1977.

Scott, Kenneth E. "In Quest of Reason: The Licensing Decisions of the Federal Banking Agencies," *The University of Chicago Law Review,* **42,** Winter 1975.

Spector, Louis E. "Entry, Branching, and Merging: How the State and Federal Bank Regulatory Systems Operate." In *State and Federal Regulation of Commercial Banks,* vol. 1, Washington, D.C.: Federal Deposit Insurance Corporation, 1980.

Spellman, Lewis J. "Competition for Savings Deposits in the U.S.: 1940–1966," Stanford University, Center for Research in Economic Growth, Memorandum No. 183, Stanford: December 1974.

Spellman, Lewis J. "Entry: The Prologue to Deposit Ceilings," In *Proceedings of a Conference on Bank Structure and Competition,* Federal Reserve Bank of Chicago, May 1975.

Spellman, Lewis J. "Entry and Profitability in a Rate Free Savings and Loan Market," *Quarterly Review of Economics and Business,* **18,** Summer 1978.

Stigler, George J. *The Organization of Industry.* Homewood, Ill., Richard D. Irwin, Inc., 1968.

Throop, Adrian, W., "Capital Investment and Entry in Commercial Banking: A Competitive Model," *Journal of Money, Credit and Banking,* **7,** May 1975.

CHAPTER 11

Competition and Its Measurement

11.1 INDUSTRIAL STRUCTURE AND COMPETITION

The strength of competitive forces facing an industry is not directly measurable. Furthermore, it is difficult to gauge the competitive level with an industrial structure containing different combinations of unit, branch, and holding company systems for both commercial banks and thrifts. An approach to the problem of measuring the level of competition was suggested as early as the 1930s by Abba Lerner[1]. Though Lerner was addressing the problem of measuring the intensity of competition in goods markets, the same principle applies to deposit markets. He suggested the elasticity of demand as a barometer of competition. When applied to deposit markets, the logic is that the more rate sensitive the deposits, the more elastic is the demand curve facing the individual firm and the smaller is the profit margin. Indeed, the profit retention rate in the explicit and implicit deposit rate models, Eqs. (3.11) and (7.5), depends only on the deposit elasticity. Perfect competition is said to prevail where demand elasticities approach infinity and profit margins are 0. In general, the larger the number of firms in the market, the larger are deposit elasticities; an increase in deposit rates tends to cause a large deposit flow, since any one firm can attract deposits from a large number of other firms.

Since the values of the deposit elasticities serve as a useful guide to evaluate the competitive level, some insights are gained from examining these elasticities. In Table 11.1 the explicit deposit elasticities during the deposit rate free-market eras for commercial banks and thrifts have been calculated as specified by Eq. (3.15). The conditions of the model developed in Chapter 3 are reasonably approximated by the commercial banking industry prior to 1933 and by thrift institutions in the United States prior to 1968. Until those dates banks and thrifts, respectively,

[1] Abba Lerner, "The Concept of Monopoly and the Measurement of Monopoly Power," *Review of Economic Studies*, **2**, June 1934.

TABLE 11.1

Explicit Deposit Elasticities[a]

| | Commercial banks | | | | |
| | Federal Reserve members | FDIC members | Mutual savings banks | Savings and loan associations | Federal credit unions |
Year					
1915	—	—	—	—	—
1916	—	—	—	—	—
1917	—	—	—	—	—
1918	—	—	—	—	—
1919	1.70	—	—	—	—
1920	1.36	—	—	—	—
1921	1.00	—	—	—	—
1922	2.04	—	—	—	—
1923	2.28	—	—	—	—
1924	2.22	—	—	—	—
1925	2.07	—	—	—	—
1926	2.05	—	—	—	—
1927	2.03	—	—	—	—
1928	1.96	—	—	—	—
1929	1.59	—	—	—	—
1930	2.51	—	—	—	—
1931	2.12	—	—	—	—
1932	1.98	—	—	—	—
1933	1.27	—	—	—	—
1934	—	—	—	—	—
1935	—	—	6.74	—	—
1936	—	—	6.53	—	—
1937	—	—	8.53	—	—
1938	—	—	4.64	—	—
1939	—	—	5.02	—	—
1940	—	—	2.75	—	2.69
1941	—	—	2.61	—	2.15
1942	—	—	2.63	3.21	3.88
1943	—	—	2.72	3.34	[b]
1944	—	—	2.62	4.34	14.74
1945	—	—	1.95	4.57	23.33
1946	—	—	2.15	6.21	11.43
1947	—	—	2.71	6.04	4.60
1948	—	—	2.82	5.03	3.21
1949	—	—	4.17	4.97	3.76
1950	—	—	4.26	4.02	3.02
1951	—	—	3.74	4.78	4.16
1952	—	—	11.48	5.53	4.72
1953	—	—	9.15	5.34	3.74
1954	—	—	9.33	5.19	4.47

TABLE 11.1 (*Continued*)

Year	Commercial banks		Mutual savings banks	Savings and loan associations	Federal credit unions
	Federal Reserve members	FDIC members			
1955	—	—	11.64	4.77	4.90
1956	—	—	12.06	5.34	6.88
1957	—	—	16.71	6.57	6.18
1958	—	—	17.85	7.07	9.17
1959	—	—	14.22	7.21	10.10
1960	—	—	44.68	11.34	16.69
1961	—	—	20.93	8.88	14.41
1962	—	—	166.91	11.57	15.39
1963	—	—	146.81	22.49	17.55
1964	—	—	64.49	15.46	19.49
1965	—	—	26.51	15.74	17.98
1966	—	—	$\rightarrow \infty$	35.05	22.35
1967	—	—	$\rightarrow \infty$	519.00	37.52

[a] Calculated from Eq. (3.15) from data contained in Tables 9.6–9.10.
[b] Not available.

were free to set competitive deposit rates on local deposit markets. The funds raised in local deposit markets were predominantly placed in local loan markets, and since securities purchased on national security markets were a portfolio alternative to the local loan market, there was a floor below which earning rates would not fall as deposits increased. While slight economies of scale have at times been found for some depository institutions, the deviations from a constant cost industry were not large. With the conditions of the models met to a reasonable extent, the explicit deposit elasticities were derived from the calculated asset and deposit rates and the average production costs of Tables 9.1, 9.2, and 9.4.

The calculated explicit deposit elasticities show a wide variation. It is of interest that the explicit deposit elasticities for Fed member banks in the 1920s were quite low and never exceeded 2.28, despite the very large numbers of depository institutions that were operating at that particular time. Corresponding to the low elasticities were the high profit retention rates shown in Table 11.2 and Figure 11.1. There are several explanations that are plausible. First, though there were a great number of commercial banks in both absolute numbers and relative to the population, a great majority of those banks operated in geographically isolated one- and two-bank towns, so that these institutions were either monopolists or

TABLE 11.2

Profit Retention Rate[a]

Year	Commercial banks	Mutual savings banks	Savings and loan associations	Federal credit unions
1919	37	—	—	—
1920	42	—	—	—
1921	50	—	—	—
1922	33	—	—	—
1923	30	—	—	—
1924	31	—	—	—
1925	33	—	—	—
1926	33	—	—	—
1927	33	—	—	—
1928	34	—	—	—
1929	39	—	—	—
1930	28	—	—	—
1931	32	—	—	—
1932	34	—	—	—
1933	44	—	—	—
1934	—	—	—	—
1935	—	13	—	—
1936	—	13	—	—
1937	—	10	—	—
1938	—	18	—	—
1939	—	17	—	—
1940	—	27	—	27
1941	—	28	—	32
1942	—	28	24	b
1943	—	27	24	b
1944	—	27	19	b
1945	—	34	18	b
1946	—	32	14	b
1947	—	27	14	18
1948	—	26	17	24
1949	—	19	17	21
1950	—	19	20	24
1951	—	21	17	19
1952	—	8	15	17
1953	—	10	16	21
1954	—	10	16	18
1955	—	8	17	17
1956	—	8	16	13
1957	—	6	13	14
1958	—	5	12	10
1959	—	7	12	9
1960	—	2	8	6

TABLE 11.2 (*Continued*)

Year	Commercial banks	Mutual savings banks	Savings and loan associations	Federal credit unions
1961	—	4	10	6
1962	—	1	8	6
1963	—	1	4	5
1964	—	2	6	5
1965	—	4	6	5
1966	—	< 0	3	4
1967	—	< 0	0	3

a Expressed in percentages. The profit retention rate is $1/(1 + \epsilon)$. Source: Table 11.1.
b The war years are omitted for federal credit unions because of their extreme effects on the durable goods and consumer credit markets.

oligopolists. The influence of the collusive banking arrangements found in the larger cities and the existence of chain banking could also have moderated the competitive level. Not only were deposit elasticities for Fed member banks relatively low, but there was an evident down-drift in competitive forces after the mid-1920s with profit retention rates of about one-third. At first this could have reflected the merger movement, and later the great reduction in the number of commercial banks between 1929 and 1933.

For the thrift institutions, the data series begins in 1935 for mutual savings banks, with initial deposit elasticities between 6 and 8, which is higher than those for commercial banks in the 1920s. The mutual savings bank series indicates some reduction in competitive forces after 1935 through the war years, with a low of 1.95 in 1945 and a corresponding robust profit retention rate of 34%. For savings and loan associations and federal credit unions, competitive pressures continued to be reduced through the immediate postwar period and reached a low point for both institutions in 1950. At that time all three thrift institutions had very similar deposit elasticities of between 3 and 4, which were consistent with profit retention rates of between 20 and 24%. From this low, obvious increases in competitive pressures began. These competitive pressures were most noticeable for mutual savings banks as deposit elasticities in the 1950s reached a level of 18 in 1958. The elevation of the elasticities for the savings associations was more gradual, and comparably competitive heights were not reached until 1963. The credit unions, in a more insulated deposit market, tended to have slightly lower deposit elasticities, though their levels also rose steadily until 1966, when deposit ceilings

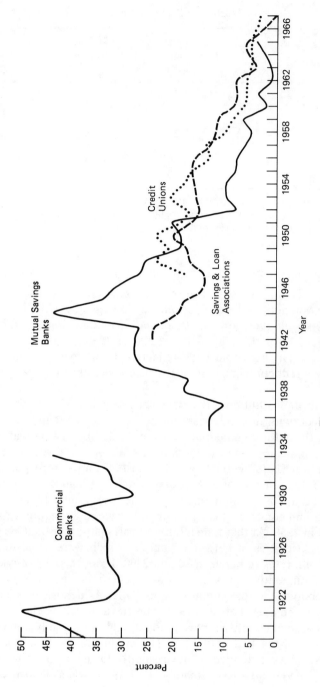

Figure 11.1 Profit retention rates.

were enacted. It has been pointed out previously that in 1967, although deposit ceilings existed, it is likely that they were set at rates above market rates; and for mutual savings banks and savings and loan associations, deposit elasticities, for all practical purposes, reached levels that could be characterized as perfect competition as profit retention rates hovered near 0. Credit unions were not immune from these competitive pressures, and in 1967 their deposit elasticities reached 37, for which the corresponding profit retention ratio is $\frac{1}{38}$ or 2.6% of net revenues.

In the deposit ceiling era it is also possible to characterize competition by the elasticity level, although in this case the relevant elasticity is the elasticity of the implicit deposit rate. It has been noted in Chapter 8 that the implicit deposit elasticity for savings and loan associations in the mid-1970s rose to slightly more than unity, whereas commercial bank implicit deposit elasticites ranged between 1 and 3.34 in 1975. With implicit deposit elasticities relatively low compared with explicit deposit elasticities, regulatory rent exists, since the deposit ceiling device is an effective tool to reduce competitive elasticities and preserve profit retention rates and hence profit margins.

11.2 THE EMPIRICAL RELATIONSHIP OF NUMBERS OF COMPETITORS AND COMPETITIVE PRESSURES IN DEPOSIT MARKETS

It is fundamental to microeconomics that individual firm elasticities depend on the number of independent competitors in a market. Stigler presents a proof that under certain stringent conditions in goods markets, individual firm elasticities are proportional to the number of competitors in the market.[2]

In order to obtain rough estimates of the relationship of the number of competitors to deposit elasticities in a deposit rate free market, we shall assume that the deposit elasticity is a function of n such that higher levels of n produce higher elasticities

$$\epsilon = f(n) \qquad \partial\epsilon/\partial n > 0. \qquad (11.1)$$

Substituting this functional relationship for the deposit elasticity into the profit equation (3.11), we can test the proposition that the number of firms

---

[2] George J. Stigler, *The Theory of Price*, (New York: Macmillan Co., 1966) p. 90. The conditions are that the firms in a market equally divide the number of units of output sold in that market and that a new entrant to the market gains not from existing competitors, but rather from an expansion of the total market.

affect elasticities and hence affect profit margins

$$p = [1/(1 + f(n))](r_a - c). \tag{11.2}$$

The model of Chapter 3 is set in the environment of the deposit rate free market, so that the empirical tests will be applied to the savings and loan industry between 1942 and 1966, when deposit rates were competitively set. As a variation on the profit margin equation (11.1), we might multiply through both sides of the equation by D in order to obtain the relationship of the number of competitors to total profit:

$$p = [1/(1 + f(n))]((r_a - c)D) \tag{11.3}$$

In addition we might also test the sensitivity of the profit retention rate to the number of firms by dividing Eq. (11.2) by $(r_a - c)D$:

$$p/(r_a - c) = [1/(1 + f(n))]. \tag{11.4}$$

The ratio $p/(r_a - c)$ is the profit retention rate of net revenues per deposit dollar or conversely, the proportion of net revenues that have not been bid away in deposit rate competition. Accepting the proposition (11.1), the profit retention rate depends only on the number of competitors in the market. The absolute profit margin per deposit dollar depends on n and on net revenues, while total profits depend on these variables as well as the deposit level. From an inspection of Eqs. (11.2), (11.3), and (11.4), it is obvious that all three profit measures are inversely related to the number of competitors in the deposit market.

These relationships will be empirically estimated for the savings and loan industry over the 25-year period prior to the imposition of deposit ceilings. The number of savings and loan offices will be used as a proxy for n, with the premise that branches constitute some degree of market penetration. Over the two and one-half decades, net revenues first declined from the 1942 level of 2.88% until 1946, then increased from 2.80 to 4.58% in 1966. Despite the substantial increase in net revenues, absolute profit margins began to decline after 1950, concurrently with the turnabout in the number of savings and loan offices. The profit proportion of net revenues, or the profit retention rate, which by Eq. (11.4) depends on n, closely followed movements in the number of competitors. These trends in numbers of offices and the profit retention rate are shown in Figure 11.2.

To relate these trends in the savings deposit market to the number of competitors, regression equations corresponding to Eqs. (11.2), (11.3), and (11.4) were estimated in both linear and log linear form. The results are reported in Table 11.3. With the log linear equations, the regression coef-

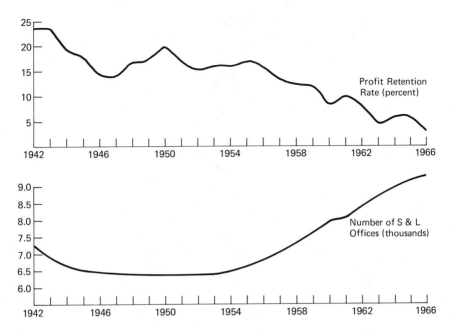

Figure 11.2 Number of savings and loan offices and the profit retention rate.

ficients are a constant elasticity estimate, while elasticities about the mean of the independent variables were calculated for the linear estimates. In all cases the two estimates of the elasticities were similar.

In the regression equations on total profits corresponding to Eq. (11.3), the independent variables are net revenues and n, represented by the total number of savings and loan offices defined as savings and loan associations plus branches. The linear regression coefficient on the deposit level indicates that on the average over the period, with net revenues held constant, each deposit dollar would have yielded 52 basis points of profit. The elasticity of total profit with respect to the deposit level was approximately unity under either estimate. Thus, doubling the deposit level while holding net revenues and entry constant has resulted in a doubling of profits.

The effect of additional numbers of savings and loan offices was significantly related to profits. The elasticity of total profits with respect to the number of competitors was -4.8 for the linear estimate and -3.2 for the constant elasticity estimate. Increases in net revenues with the number of competitors held constant increased total profits with alternative elasticity estimates of 3.41 and 1.86. The profit margin regression equation also

TABLE 11.3

Profit and Number of Offices[a]

Equation	Statistic[b]	Constant	Savings and loan offices	$r_a - c$	D	R^2 (adj.)	$D - W$
			Total savings and loan profits				
(11.2)							
Linear	b	34.17	−.0154	20.70	.52		
	t	1.84	−4.86	4.34	6.06	.93	1.57
	e		−4.76	3.41	.90		
Log linear	b	11.15	−3.20	1.86	.95	.98	2.00
	t	8.03	−7.78	4.17	24.36		
			Savings and loan profit margins				
(11.3)							
Linear	b	1.56	−.000249	.24			
	t	19.66	−7.75	4.26		.85	1.96
	e		−2.67	1.36			
Log linear	b	11.14	−3.16	1.53		.83	1.93
	t	7.91	−7.60	4.16			
			Savings and loan profit as a proportion of net revenue				
(11.4)							
Linear	b	.56	−.0000519				
	t	26.64	−18.11			.93	1.75
	e		−2.06				
Log linear	b	9.29	−2.61			.92	1.87
	t	15.60	−16.89				

[a] Source: *Combined Financial Statements, 1942–1966*, Federal Home Loan Bank Board; *Savings and Loan Fact Book*, U.S. Savings and Loan League.

[b] e is the elasticity about the mean.

performed according to a priori expectations. And the profit retention rate equation relating profit proportions to the number of offices, was also impressive, with an R^2 of .93 and .92 and elasticity estimates of −2.06 and −2.61.

Thus in a deposit rate free market, the competitive force of greater numbers of firms tended to increase deposit rates relative to net revenues, which tended to reduce total profit, profit margins, and the profit retention rate. The effect was significant in all three equations, where the elasticities ranged from −4.8 to −3.2 on total profit, −2.7 to −3.2 on profit margins, and −2.1 to −2.6 on profit retention rates.

It should be pointed out that a time series analysis is vulnerable to the cumulative effects of variables not held constant in the regression analysis. Despite the fact that there might have been other causes for increases in explicit deposit rate elasticities, total profit, profit margins, and the profit proportion were highly sensitive to the number of savings and loan offices. Furthermore, this relationship held over three distinctly separate subperiods between 1942 and 1966. From 1942 to 1946 net revenues declined. This decline in net revenues was moderated by sluggish competitive pressures. As a result, the profit margin failed to decline in proportion to net revenues. From 1946 to 1950, net revenues increased and competitive pressures eased slightly, with both forces producing increases in the profit margin. Over the longer 1950 to 1966 period, net revenues increased 136 basis points as a result of increases in average earning rates and reductions in average costs. This increase in net revenues was more than offset by competitive pressure, and profit margins declined 50 basis points despite the large gain in net revenues.

This analysis provides strong evidence that there is a close relationship between the number of offices and profit margins, as the number of offices affects deposit elasticities, which in turn affect the distribution of net revenues. As a rough rule of thumb, in the deposit rate free-market era of 1942 to 1966, an additional 200 savings and loan offices would increase the deposit elasticity by 1.[3]

After 1966, with the imposition of deposit ceilings and the reestablishment of healthy profit margins, entry by additional savings and loan offices accelerated. By the late 1970s savings and loan offices doubled from 9,000 to more than 18,000. This increase of almost 9,000 offices could be expected to have drastic effects on explicit deposit rate elasticities if the phaseouts of deposit ceilings called for in the 1980 deregulation act are accomplished. The magnitude of these effects is substantial. If the rough estimate of 200 offices for each unit increase in the deposit elasticity were to continue to hold in the 1980s, explicit deposit elasticities would be raised by a large order of magnitude. If perfect competition in the savings and loan industry was approached in 1966 with a level of 9,000 offices, it would certainly be expected to prevail again if the number of offices were doubled. From this, it is quite clear that the return of explicit deposit rate competition, with its very high elasticities replacing the low implicit deposit elasticities typical of nonrate competition, would dramatically reduce profit margins. One could then anticipate a retrenchment within the industry through mergers and the voluntary closing of branches.

[3] This result was obtained by Riad J. Kallas (*Deregulation and Bank Profit*, Graduate School of Business Professional Report, Austin: University of Texas, May 1980) from a least squares regression between deposit elasticities and the number of savings and loan offices between 1942 and 1966.

11.3 INTERINDUSTRY COMPETITION AND THE
EFFECT OF MERGER

While these results attest to the growing pressures that result from the addition of new savings and loan offices over time, one could also study the effect of the numbers of competitors (both unit associations and branches) as well as the effect of commercial banks and their branches at a given point in time. This section addresses not only the issue of interindustry competition between banks and savings and loan associations, but also the effect of the unit–branch structure of those banking and savings and loan offices. Given estimates of the effect of the number of unit entities and their branches, the effect of merger can be inferred as the cumulative result of a reduced number of independent entities and a corresponding increase in the number of branches.

In the following study conducted on a cross section of 106 SMSAs in 1972 during the era of deposit ceilings, the profit level of the depository firm from Eq. (7.5) is given by Eq. (11.5)

$$P = [1/(1 + \epsilon_i(n))]((r_a - \bar{r} - c)D). \qquad (11.5)$$

The total profit level P depends on net revenues, the deposit level and the implicit deposit elasticity. In the empirical analysis, the profit level is the total profit for all savings and loan associations in the 106 SMSAs. The effect of the industrial structure on the savings and loans' aggregate market profit was analyzed by separately introducing the number of savings and loan associations, their branches, the number of banks, and bank branches.

All regression equations in Table 11.4 contain the independent variable D for the deposit level, as well as net revenues. The asset earning rate was calculated as the effective rate earned on the financial assets of the associations in the SMSA, and r was the effective weighted average deposit rate. The unobserved average production cost c was estimated to be 1.27%, which was the level of observed average cost prior to the imposition of deposit ceilings and thus prior to the need to resort to implicit rate competition. These independent variables, as well as the number of savings and loan associations, commercial banks, and their branches, were tested in various combinations. In most equations, the coefficients were significantly different from 0 at the .01 level or above. The adjusted coefficient of determination was quite high in all cases, .83 or above.

The regression coefficient for the deposit level D indicates that the addition of a deposit dollar, with rate spreads and number of competitors held constant, contributed between 46 and 56 basis points of profit per deposit dollar. Increases in net revenues per deposit dollar, with the deposit level

TABLE 11.4

Savings and Loan Market Profit, 106 SMSAs, 1972[a]

Equation	Statistic[b]	Deposits D	Net revenues $r_a - \bar{F} - c$	Banks — Banks	Banks — Bank branches	Savings and loan associations — Associations	Savings and loan associations — Branches	Savings and loan associations — Total offices	Savings and loan associations — Associations/total offices	R^2 (adj.)
1	b	.0055	156.6	−.093		−.146				.88
	t	27.67	4.41	−7.12		−8.52				
	e	2.41	.72	−1.07		−1.03				
2	b	.0046	89.9	−.079		−.155	.058			.89
	t	16.42	2.38	−6.13		−9.51	3.76			
	e	2.06	.41	−.91		−1.10	.56			
3	b	.0048	100.17	−.091	−.008	−.144				.90
	t	16.99	2.70	−6.75	−2.47	−8.66				
	e	2.12	.46	−1.05	−.28	−1.02				
4	b	.0056	191.57	−.102	−.002			−.043	−5.11	.83
	t	15.86	4.98	−8.86	−.493			−2.63	−2.76	
	e	2.47	.89	−1.12	−.07			−.71	−.85	
Mean		$1,342.5 (billions)	.0013	35.0	45.6	21.5	29.5			

[a] Source: *Combined Financial Statements, 1973; Summary of Savings Accounts; Member Savings and Loan Associations, 1972* (Washington D.C.: Federal Home Loan Bank Board. *Summary of Accounts and Deposits of All Commercial Banks* (Washington D.C.: Federal Deposit Insurance Corporation).

[b] e is the elasticity about the mean. The mean value for the dependent variable profit was $3.054 (billion).

and the number of competitors held constant, increased profit levels, with elasticity estimates between .41 and .89. This elasticity of less than unity would be expected because part of net revenues is dissipated in the form of implicit deposit rates according to Eq. (7.4). Furthermore, the regression coefficient measures the *ceteris paribus* impact on changes in deposit ceilings. Reductions in deposit ceilings or the failure to increase ceilings when earning rates increase will increase net revenues and contribute to profits.

The profit effect from the number of unit savings and loan associations and commercial banks was highly stable. Greater numbers of either type of competitor adversely influenced savings and loan market profits, with a virtually identical elasticity of close to -1 in all equations. If the effects of entry could be inferred as a *ceteris parabis* change in the number of competitors, savings and loan market profits are as adversely influenced by the chartering of a unit bank as by a unit savings and loan association. The influence of bank branches on savings and loan profits was statistically significant and negative in regression equation (3), although with a smaller elasticity of $-.28$. Thus, a commercial bank branch, as would be expected, was not as damaging as a unit commercial bank to savings and loan market profits.

The influence of the number of savings and loan branches on SMSA market profits was positive when estimated as an independent variable in regression equation (2). The influence of a greater number of savings and loan branches on savings and loan market profits works through the cost structure. It has been fairly well documented that expansion of the financial intermediary industry through branching tends to raise average production costs.[4] On the other hand, when a given market is serviced with relatively more branches, there might be a reduction in implicit deposit rates. It would appear from this result that the reduction in competitive costs outweighs whatever production cost increases that might have occurred.

To examine branching effects further, regression equation (4) seeks to

[4] In the depository cost literature there are several studies that indicate the slightly higher cost of the expansion of the depository system through branching. For example, Benston ("Economies of Scale on Marginal Costs in Banking Operations," *National Banking Review*, **2**, May 1972) found that consolidation of unit banks into a branch bank system raises costs slightly. Frederick W. Bell and Neil B. Murphy ("Economies of Scale and the Division of Labor in Commercial Banking," *Southern Economic Journal*, **35**, October 1968) also concluded there were higher costs associated with branching operations. Similarly, Eugene F. Brigham and R. Richardson Pettit ("Effects of Structure on Performance in the Savings and Loan Industry," in *A Study of the Savings and Loan Industry*, Federal Home Loan Bank Board, Washington D.C., 1969) found the average cost curve for an association shifts upward as the number of branches of an association increases.

measure the influence of the relative proportion of branches to associations in a market. It yielded statistically significant results. In this regression equation, the total number of savings and loan offices (the sum of branches and unit associations) is entered as an independent variable, as is the ratio of unit associations to total offices. The effects of the number of offices can then be separated from the effects of changes in the proportion of branches to unit associations. In this regression equation, the effect of the number of offices had a statistically significant negative elasticity of $-.71$ on profit, while the ratio of unit associations to total offices had a significant negative effect with an elasticity of $-.85$.

The result indicates that entry by a unit association reduces profits through the effects of both numbers and changes in the composition of offices. On the other hand, entry by a branch has a mixed impact because it reduces profit through the number effect, but increases profit through the composition effect. The net impact of branching, inferred from the size of the coefficients of this equation as well as from regression equation (2), would seem to increase profits.

Regression equation (4) also provides a quantitative estimate of the profit impact of savings and loan mergers. When one assumes that merged institutions continue to operate as branches, the number of offices servicing a market is held constant, but this reduces the proportion of unit associations to total associations. When this occurs, the impact on profits is positive. A 10% reduction in the number of associations, with the number of offices held constant, increases market profits by 8.5%. Thus, merger can provide relief from deteriorating profit margins.

Regulatory authorities can strongly influence financial institution profit levels and profit margins and the distribution of profit not only through deposit rate ceilings, but also by governing the rates of entry and merger, the number of branches, and the branch per institution ratio. Since savings deposit accounts insured by a federal insurance agency are homogeneous products denominated in dollars, with explicitly stated rates of return, they can only be differentiated by nonprice competition. In this environment, one would expect interindustry competition to exist so that additional savings and loan associations are likely to affect banks just as banks and their branches affected the profits of savings and loan associations. It is of interest to note that with this homogeneous product, the independent effect of larger numbers of commercial banks had impacts on savings and loan profit equal to those of greater numbers of savings associations. Branches of commercial banks also tended to reduce savings and loan profit, although to a smaller extent than an additional commercial bank. Increases in savings and loan branches had an effect on profit when branching seemed to be a substitute for additional unit associations. That is, when additional savings and loan branches increased the proportion of branches to unit associations, profit margins increased. When the proportion of branches to associations was held constant, the effect of larger numbers of savings and loan offices tended to reduce profit margins, as one would expect, since there would be greater overlap in market areas within an SMSA.

These results point to the need for coordination among the various state and federal agencies charged with entry and merger for both thrifts and banks because the numbers of these institutions and their industrial structure affect competitive levels and hence their viability. This is true whether or not deposit ceilings are in effect.

BIBLIOGRAPHY

Alhadeff, D. C. *Monopoly and Competition in Banking*. Berkeley: Univ. of California Press, 1954.

Bradford, William D., Osborne, Alfred E., and Spellman, Lewis J. "The Efficiency and Profitability of Minority Controlled Savings and Loan Associations," *Journal of Money, Credit and Banking*, **10**, February 1978.

Burns, Joseph M. "The Relative Decline of Commercial Banks: A Note," *Journal of Political Economy*, **77**, January–February 1969.

Carson, Deane, and Horvitz, Paul M. "Concentration Ratios and Competition," *The National Banking Review*, **1**, September 1963.

Fraser, Donald R., and Rose, Peter S. "Bank Competition and Performance in a Unit Banking Environment," *Proceedings of a Conference on Bank Structure and Competition*, Federal Reserve Bank of Chicago, May 1971.

Fraser, Donald R., and Rose, Peter S. "Bank Entry and Bank Performance, *Journal of Finance*, **27**, March 1972.

Gilbert, Gary G., and Longbrake, William A. "The Effects of Branching by Financial Institutions on Competition, Productive Efficiency, and Stability: An Examination of the Evidence, Part 1," *Journal of Bank Research*, **4**, Autumn 1973.

Gilbert, Gary G., and Longbrake, William A. "The Effects of Branching by Financial Institutions on Competition, Productive Efficiency and Stability: An Examination of the Evidence, Part 2," *Journal of Bank Research*, **5**, Winter 1974.

Gilbert, R. Alton. "Measures of Potential for De Novo Entry in Bank Acquisition Cases: An Evaluation," *Proceedings of a Conference on Bank Structure and Competition*, Federal Reserve Bank of Chicago, March 1974.

Hall, George. "Measures of Banking Competition and Convenience: Problems Real and Unreal," *Proceedings of a Conference on Bank Structure and Competition*, Federal Reserve Bank of Chicago, March 1967.

Hanweck, Gerald. "Bank Entry into Local Markets: An Empirical Assessment of the Degree of Potential Competition via New Bank Formation," *Proceedings of a Conference on Bank Structure and Competition*, Federal Reserve Bank of Chicago, May 1971.

Heggestad, Arnold A., and Mingo, John J. "The Competitive Condition of U.S. Banking Markets and the Impact of Structural Reform," *Journal of Finance*, **32**, June 1977.

Horvitz, Paul M., and Shull, Bernard. "The Impact of Branch Banking on Bank Performances," *The National Banking Review*, **1** December 1964.

Lerner, A. "The Concept of Monopoly and the Measurement of Monopoly Power," *Review of Economic Studies*, **2**, June 1934.

Mote, Larry. "Bank Structure and Competition: The Weight of Evidence and Implications for Future Research," *Proceedings of a Conference on Bank Structure and Competition*, Federal Reserve Bank of Chicago, March 1967.

Mote, Larry. "A Conceptual Optimal Banking Structure for the United States," *Proceedings of a Conference on Bank Structure and Competition*, Federal Reserve Bank of Chicago, May 1969.

Osborne, Dale K. "Bank Structure and Performance—Survey of Empirical Findings on the Cost of Checking Accounts," *Federal Reserve Bank of Dallas. Review*, **57**, May 1977.

Osborne, Dale K., and Wendel, Jeanne. "The Main Fault with Traditional Research on Banking Competition," Federal Reserve Bank of Dallas Research Paper No. 7805, September 1978.

Osborne, Dale K., and Wendel, Jeanne. "On Banking Structure and Checking Account Prices," Federal Reserve Bank of Dallas Research Paper No. 7806, October 1978.

Peltzman, Samuel. "Entry in Commercial Banking," *Journal of Law and Economics*, **8**, October 1965.

Phillips, Almarin. "Competition, Confusion, and Commercial Banking," *Journal of Finance*, **19**, March 1964.

Phillips, Almarin. "Competitive Policy for Depository Financial Institutions." In *Promoting Competition in Regulated Markets*, ed Almarin Phillips. Washington, D.C., Brookings Institutions, 1975.

Rhoades, Stephen A., and Yeats, A. J. "Growth Consolidation and Mergers in Banking," *Journal of Finance*, **29**, December 1974.

Shull, Bernard, and Horvitz, Paul. "Branch Banking and the Structure of Competition," *The National Banking Review*, **1**, March 1964.

Spellman, Lewis J. "Competition for Savings Deposits: 1936–1966," *Journal of Financial and Quantitative Analysis*, **10**, November 1975.

Spellman, Lewis J. "Commercial Banks and the Profits of Savings," *Journal of Bank Research*, **12**, Spring 1981.

Stigler, George J. *The Theory of Price*. New York: Macmillan Co., 1966.

Yeats, Alexander, J. "An Analysis of the Effect of Mergers on Banking Market Structures," *Journal of Money, Credit and Banking*, **5**, May 1973.

PART III

The Depository System's Influence on the Aggregate Economy

CHAPTER 12

The Financial System and Capital Accumulation[1]

12.1 FOREIGN, FISCAL, AND MONETARY TECHNIQUES FOR CAPITAL ACCUMULATION

In response to a world of vast differences in wealth and per capita consumption, the field of development economics evolved in the immediate postwar period to understand, explain, and find means to accelerate the economic advances of the less-developed nations. Initially, attention was focused on the problems of the "labor-surplus" economy; with time, however, it became understood that the labor-surplus economy was the equivalent of a capital-scarce economy. More recently, attention has shifted to means to increase capital accumulation. These attempts to accelerate capital accumulation in the less-developed world have provided us with an array of extremes in economic circumstances and economic policies. It also provides us with deeper insights into the relationship of the financial system, capital accumulation, and economic output. The relationships between finance and capital accumulation, seen most transparently in the experiences of the less-developed countries (LDCs), have led to generalizations that are equally applicable to developed nations, even though they have not recently been subject to the same extremes of economic experience.

In the early postwar period, attention was given to the need to obtain capital from foreign sources when it was thought that countries with low income levels would not be able to generate domestic savings. The international transfer of capital from the wealthy to the less wealthy has taken a number of forms. Direct aid, outright grants, and soft loans have been among the many channels of government-to-government foreign economic assistance. These means of capital transfer, however, have proved to be temporal and limited in scope, as they have often become used as in-

---

[1] The calculus notation used in this chapter and throughout Part III is common to the growth theory literature. For example, the notation for a partial derivative for the marginal productivity of capital is Y_K, rather than $\partial Y / \partial K$.

struments of foreign policy. In an effort to place aid on an economic basis, free of political constraints, aid funds became allocated by international lending agencies such as the International Bank for Reconstruction and Development, which is but one of several agencies funneling aid on a multinational basis to individual governments for either capital formation or trade credits. Additionally there have been efforts on the part of development agencies or development banks in the LDCs to obtain capital on foreign capital markets, from foreign depository institutions, or from international agencies.

In addition to these government or quasi-government transfers, the private sector has at times served as a conduit to channel capital from developed to less-developed countries. Sometimes financial institutions are at the heart of these private channels, and at other times the transfer of capital is effected by the multinational corporations when the transfer shifts production facilities and funds from country to country.

The flow of international capital from developed to developing countries has many attractions. Not only do physical capital inflows increase capital–labor ratios and, it is hoped, output and productivity; when financial capital inflows occur, they tend, in the short run, to supply developing countries with foreign exchange. In addition to capital resources and foreign exchange, the influx of foreign capital often brings with it technological advances, as new technologies are often embedded in imported capital equipment.

Despite these advantages, the international movement of capital has brought with it political as well as economic problems for the LDCs. The infusion of foreign capital, when accompanied by foreign management and control, has often led to waves of economic xenophobia. Furthermore, the eventual need for the repatriation of earnings can trigger sentiments of outrage. Charges of mercantilism or capitalistic exploitation tend to polarize public opinion, lending to expropriation and nationalization of the assets or the nationalization of the earnings through exploitative tax rates. Not only does foreign capital become the symbolic target of a population with a skewed income distribution, but pressures build when the repatriation of earnings results in a drain of accumulated foreign exchange reserves. This is often at odds with efforts to hoard these scarce supplies of foreign exchange for a variety of purposes, often military.

It is thus not surprising that the few successes among today's developed or developing countries occurred when the capability to export was gained during the development process. As a result, these countries generate supplies of foreign exchange that could be used to repatriate the earnings accruing to imported capital. Furthermore, when exports earn the foreign exchange necessary for dividend and interest payments, the flow of foreign capital continues unabated. Most notably, this has been the experience of West Germany and Japan in the early postwar era, and it is important in the more recent successes of Taiwan and Korea, for example.

Not only are there political and economic difficulties surrounding the use of foreign capital, but in many instances this capital is underutilized when its allocation is controlled either by government fiat or through a regulated price system. When a regulated price and wage system creates incentives to allocate capital to certain earmarked industries, the misallocations common in the dual economy can result. When capital is loaned at rates that do not reflect its scarcity, it is not being put to its highest and best use. Furthermore, in the dual economy, an industrialized sector, often centered in the higher income urban areas, exists in sharp contrast to a poor rural countryside. This, of course, sows the seeds of political and social discontent.

The conflicts arising from foreign capital often come to a head when the earnings of hard currencies are captured by the government to be allocated for other uses. Attempts have been made to alleviate the foreign exchange shortage by developing a major agricultural crop or by extracting a natural resource for the foreign market. To be competitive on world markets, this generally requires subsidies of capital and/or labor for that industry. Though this use of resources is often an inefficient means of generating foreign exchange, it still might have been successful. However, dependence on the single crop or commodity has too often caused great instability when the crop is subject to the vagaries of the weather and fluctuations of world prices. Furthermore, the exportation of natural resources tends to be viewed as an exploitative transfer to the capitalist world. Despite occasional successes, the subsidies of capital and labor to develop an export industry should be measured against other possible uses of resources that could generate domestic savings. Tourism has been used also as an alternative for generating foreign exchange. But this possibility must also be judged for its efficiency. Whatever the foreign exchange payoff, tourism also generates political discontent because the foreign enclaves, with living standards in sharp contrast to those available to nationals, breed resentment.

With such problems surrounding the importation of foreign capital, developing countries have more recently turned to the domestic alternatives available from the use of the fiscal and monetary system. These alternatives, however, have also proved to be less than a panacea. The fiscal techniques are various. Revenues from the tax system could be used to finance social overhead capital, that is, dams, roads, harbors, etc. A more usual fiscal technique to accumulate capital is differential tax rates designed to increase individual savings and business-retained earnings, especially if those earnings are reinvested in additional capital. Occasionally fiscal revenues are allocated to development banks for reallocation to favored industries. Alternatively, in a rarely used incentive program, government revenues could be used as matching funds for private individual savings. This acts as an important incentive to generate higher levels of private savings, as the return to savings is increased.

The monetary techniques take some form of seigniorage. Seigniorage, the income from the production of money, often accrues to the central bank from the purchasing power it generates through its right to print money. The printing of money provides the central bank with purchasing power that could conceivably be spent on capital goods or financial assets. Even if the seigniorage revenues are directed at capital accumulation, the printing of currency, however, has an important side effect— inflation. Because of this, the capture of real resources from what has been called the "inflation tax" has shown itself to be quite limited.[2]

Often seigniorage does not take the overt form of monetary creation by the central bank. Seigniorage revenues can also accrue to the private banking system when monetary expansion, particularly at low deposit rates, generates net revenues for commercial banks. If bank income is reinvested in new loans, capital expansion can thus result. In another form of seigniorage, incentives for capital formation are enhanced when banks are instructed to allocate loans to favored industries at subsidized loan rates. In this case, the seigniorage revenues accrue to the firm receiving the loan rather than to the banking industry. As another variation on the use of seigniorage revenues, the central bank can purchase foreign exchange from exporting industries at rates of exchange above market rates. In this case, the windfall revenues from monetary creation accrue to the earmarked exporting industries.

The difficulties with these techniques are clear. Any rate of monetary creation in excess of the rate of growth of real output tends to cause inflation. Furthermore, the leakages from the real creation of money to capital formation are numerous when monetary creation subsidizes either banks, domestic loans, or exporting industries.

In addition to these disadvantages of using either fiscal or monetary techniques to stimulate capital accumulation, their use has led to a curious interaction resulting in extremely high rates of inflation. The use of the monetary techniques alone tends to accelerate inflation when the expansion of the money supply exceeds the growth rate of money income.

[2] For an estimate of the present value of government revenue relative to the inflation rate see Charles D. Cathcart, "Monetary Dynamics, Growth, and The Efficiency of Inflationary Finance," Journal of Money, Credit and Banking **6** (May 1974).

An increase in the inflation rate, in turn, often tends to generate fiscal deficits, as the revenue-generating capacity of the tax system generally lags behind expenditures in an inflationary environment. This has particularly been the case in instances when strategic industries have been nationalized. Very often the nationalized industries are run as an instrument of social welfare. With rising inflation rates, the government workers in the nationalized industries receive wage increases that reflect the increase in the inflation rate, but the prices charged for the goods or services produced by those industries often lag behind. The implication is rising deficits for the nationalized industries, which must in turn be covered by government tax revenues. The nationalized industry deficit increases the overall fiscal deficit, which is inevitably covered through additional monetary creation. Thus, with this monetary–fiscal interaction, a burst of inflation from any cause often tends to give rise to larger deficits, necessitating additional monetary creation and hence rising inflation rates. This self-reinforcing inflationary spiral can often generate triple-digit inflation rates that are sometimes contained just short of hyperinflation.

This inflationary acceleration, in turn, has had other extremely unsettling effects on private capital formation. For one, the rising inflation rates, particularly when coupled with attempts to maintain exchange rates (in order to prevent the rise in price of imported consumables), tend to give savers the expectation of an imminent devaluation of the home currency. This, in turn, leads to a flight of domestic savings to safer foreign currencies, in order to preserve or gain purchasing power. Furthermore, capital inflows are held back by investors who anticipate the devaluation of the home currency. To further exacerbate the problems of capital formation in an inflationary environment, financial institutions are generally faced with ceiling deposit rates defined in nominal terms. With high inflation rates, the real rate of return to savings or the real deposit rate becomes distinctly negative, and domestic savings flow out of the financial system. If savings are trapped domestically through currency controls or other means to restrict the flight of domestic capital, what domestic capital remains is generally directed to land, gold, or other forms of wealth that are inflation hedges but do not enhance the productive capacity of the economy.

12.2   THE DOMESTIC FINANCIAL SYSTEM AND CAPITAL ACCUMULATION

Since monetary and fiscal techniques tend to be ineffective or even perverse tools to stimulate the rate of capital accumulation, attention has increasingly focused on the potential presented by the financial industry.

In recent years, exponents of the role of finance in economic development have commanded increasing attention. This emphasis, principally stemming from the work of Shaw and McKinnon, has been heavily reinforced by empiricists, such as Goldsmith, who have found that as a country develops, the financial system tends to play a more strategic role in the process of capital accumulation.[3]

Given these inferences regarding finance and economic development, it seems appropriate to identify more precisely the ties between the financial system and the real economy. To understand the unique role of finance in economic development, one should note the differences in the time patterns of labor and capital in the production of goods. Labor is often employed with no more than an oral agreement between employer and employee, and when specific contracts for labor services do exist they are generally short-term and nontransferable to third parties. In contrast, the use of capital in production generally requires financial contracts which are explicit, long-term, and often transferable through financial markets to third parties. The reason for this asymmetry between the contractual arrangements for labor and capital derives from the fact that capital as an input to production is supplied prior to the time of production—and before the input has generated output and revenue to repay those who supplied the capital. These conditions are less likely to obtain for the use of labor.

For example, funds borrowed on financial markets could be used to purchase resources for the building of a dam, roadway, or irrigation system. This type of project requires substantial blocks of capital inputs; many years may pass before the project is completed, and many subsequent years may elapse before sufficient revenues are generated through taxation or user fees to reimburse those who supplied the funds. In a more typical situation, borrowed funds utilized for the purchase of machinery and equipment only gradually generate revenues to repay the lenders. In the consumer sector, expenditures on consumer durables and housing are similar; these goods produce services through time, yet often their high cost makes it necessary for the user to repay those who financed the purchases only as the services accrue. The commitment of capital and the lagged revenue generation also exist at the short-term end of the financial spectrum. The working capital of business firms embodied in inventory is different only in that it has a shorter gestation period between the borrowing of funds and the revenue generation resulting from these funds.

[3] Edward S. Shaw, *Financial Deepening in Economic Development* (London/New York: Oxford Univ. Press, 1973); Ronald McKinnon, *Money and Capital in Economic Development* (Washington, D.C.: Brookings Institution, 1973); Raymond Goldsmith, *Financial Structure and Development* (New Haven, Conn.: Yale Univ. Press, 1969).

Thus, characteristically, the amount of funds required for the purchase of capital goods far exceeds the income these investments will yield in the year in which the borrowing takes place. From the point of view of the producer, the investment in real physical capital will only gradually generate sufficient funds to repay financial obligations of principal and interest or dividends. Since funds flow to projects such as plant and equipment, dams, or consumer durables, with varying gestation periods and varying risk, the economic unit employing the capital can only offer terms on the obligations securing the capital that in some way fits the pattern of expected revenue generation from the real investment. As a result, there exists an array of financial instruments as diverse as the productive activity for which the funds are loaned. Some contracts, such as mortgages, require fixed periodic payments over a lengthy period of time because of the steady flow of income from the real housing investment. The underlying investment in housing results in a flow of either explicit or implicit rents that facilitates the continuous, steady payment of interest as well as the gradual repayment of principal. On the other hand, some financial instruments, such as equity shares of corporations, do not provide for any principal repayment but do present the potential for income streams in the future, as well as a claim on the net worth of the enterprise. At the other extreme, short-term bonds and corporate commercial paper sold at discount provide only for principal repayment and offer no explicit income stream. Thus, financial instruments differ not only with respect to maturity, but with respect to the conditions and timing of the returns.

The fact that primary securities are designed to fit the productive activity can be troublesome, however, as these primary securities might not also fit the needs or desires of the wealth-owners who ultimately supply the funds. In order for producers to be able to borrow funds from wealth-owners, these differences must somehow be reconciled. The most common methods are the financial intermediary and the secondary financial market.

The financial intermediary that most directly serves to bridge this gap is the depository institution. The depository institutions offer financial instruments to wealth-owners that have many of the characteristics they desire. The savings instruments are highly liquid, risk-diversified, and offer specific payments of principal and interest in at least nominal terms and sometimes in real terms if the interest payment is indexed. The funds secured through the sale of these savings instruments are used in turn for the purchase of the financial instruments of end users, the terms of which are more directly related to the idiosyncrasies of the productive activity.

Financial resales on secondary markets play a critical role in the process of eliciting savings and financial investments. They provide liquidity for

wealth-owners or financial institutions that have purchased long-term obligations. Since wealth-owners desire liquidity as well as safety, long-term
bonds or equities would not be viable, were it not for secondary markets
in which these bonds could quickly be liquidated with low transaction
costs. The securities are liquidated from the resources of other wealth-
owners or financial institutions without the need to liquidate the assets of
the firm and interfere with the production activity.

Another important role of financial institutions is the reduction in the
variability of the return to wealth-owners. This can be accomplished by
such financial institutions as mutual funds. Since these institutions hold
portfolios containing many diverse financial instruments, the pooling of
independent risk has the desired effect of reducing the risk of the total
portfolio and its shares. This device permits heterogeneity of productive
activity and heterogeneity of financial instruments and at the same time
provides the wealth-owner with a more liquid and steady income.

The creation of financial institutions and markets that are adequate to
facilitate the transfer of funds from wealth-owners to producers is, of
course, of great importance to economic development. For this to occur,
there must be sufficient economic incentives to cause financial entrepreneurs to perform this middleman role in the capital accumulation process.
The existence of financial intermediaries depends first of all on the
freedom of entry of financial institutions into the market—a freedom
often constrained by governments. But were barriers to entry are absent,
the likelihood of entrepreneurial activity in the financial sector will depend on the economic viability of the financial intermediary.

The financial intermediary will have real costs of labor and capital invested in its own physical plant. These must be offset by revenues sufficient to provide equity holders with a rate of return comparable to those
in other activities in order to make it worthwhile to provide financial intermediation services. The financial intermediary, like the production firm,
must meet the market test. It must carry out the intermediary function efficiently, so that it can offer deposit rates high enough to attract funds and
still cover its cost of operations; and the more competitive the financial
service markets, the higher the deposit rate it must pay.

Similarly, the existence of secondary financial markets depends on the
test of economic viability. The spread between bid and asked prices in
secondary markets, along with the volume of transactions, provides
financial dealers with the revenues to cover their costs and still provide a
return commensurate with risk. Often secondary markets do not emerge
when the financial system is shallow, as the volume of trade is not sufficient to justify their existence. Similarly, financial intermediaries are
often unable to operate where finance is shallow, as the small volume of

transactions does not permit economies of scale that would make specialization in the provision of intermediation services profitable.

In addition to bridging the gap between producers' and wealth-owners' needs, financial intermediaries influence economic development through their ability to raise large blocks of capital and to allocate this capital efficiently. The knowledge required to efficiently allocate funds has tended to produce specialization in the asset purchases of financial intermediaries. Some institutions tend to specialize in housing loans, some in short-term business loans, and others in long-term business loans. It is of interest that this specialization on the asset side has tended to produce specialization on the liability side as well. For example, if savings banks place their funds in long-term illiquid assets, they need to reduce the volatility of deposit outflows. They attempt to do this by offering incentive deposit rates for funds placed on deposit for stated periods of time. This movement has clearly been observed in the development of the certificate of deposit market.

Thus, it can be seen that the basic structure of financial instruments and financial institutions will vary from economy to economy, depending upon the comparative advantages of the underlying productive activities. For example, in an economy with an abundance of natural resources that require capital-intensive processing techniques, long-term, large-scale capital commitments may be vital. Such an economy would require large blocks of long-term finance, whereas an economy characterized by commerce and light manufacturing would require funds for shorter time periods and in smaller blocks. In the first economy, one would anticipate a greater concentration of wealth administered by financial intermediaries, and in the second, one would anticipate a diffusion of wealth and more specialized intermediaries. Each economy would benefit from finance, although it is not likely that the basic structure of financial instruments, financial institutions, and financial markets in these economies would be similar.

Dissimilarities in financial structure might also exist because of market and nonmarket obstacles to the development of finance. If financial instruments are taxed either directly or indirectly through inflation, there would logically follow a reduction in the demand for these assets. Similarly, if the deposit rates paid by financial intermediaries are subject to deposit ceilings, this would tend to reduce the relative size of intermediaries in the financial system. In an analogous fashion, undervalued foreign exchange would tend to reduce the attractiveness of domestic financial instruments and deter the flow of capital to domestic productive activity. Thus, a host of governmental policies imposed upon the basic structure of productive opportunities and upon the corresponding financial system can influence financial institutions, financial instruments, financial markets, and the prices and structure of flows in these markets.

The financial system plays the crucial role of providing for the flow of funds to be spent on physical capital for the production of goods. Given the long-term commitment of capital required to undertake production, the financial system must address itself to the delicate problem of securing funds from wealth-owners for extended periods of time on terms acceptable to both borrower and lender. Confidence in the financial institutions and financial instruments must exist, such that investors believe that the funds loaned will be repaid in real terms at some future time with a suitable return to capital. If this is not the expectation, wealth-owners will seek alternative outlets such as foreign currency, foreign securities, land, precious metals, and other stores of wealth. The use of resources for this purpose might result in a reduction in the productive capacity of the economy. Thus, the failure to provide a suitable environment for the issuance, holding, and exchange of financial instruments can result in a distortion of production and a restraint on growth.

Where there are no significant barriers to financial intermediation, the financial structure of an economy at any time is a reflection of underlying production activities and the distribution of wealth-ownership. The financial structure of instruments and institutions depends on the technologies of each industry and the financial channels that most efficiently serve the capital accumulation of each industry. Preferences of wealth-owners for different types of financial assets will also affect the distribution of capital between sectors. Competitive pressures for capital inputs will cause the institutions and instruments of efficient intermediary channels to emerge.

12.3   A FINANCIAL SYSTEM, FINANCIAL STRUCTURE, AND ECONOMIC OUTPUT

It is commonly thought that a developed financial system and a complex structure of financial instruments are beneficial to an economy. Given these suppositions concerning finance and development, it is of interest to establish the ties between a financial system and economic output. A second related but independent puzzle is the relationship between a complex structure of financial instruments and economic output. That is, what are the real impacts of a financial system and are these real impacts enhanced by the existence of a complex structure of financial instruments?

These issues have been raised in many places, but with little common analytical framework. It is the purpose of this section to suggest a framework by relating finance to the production possibility frontier of an economy. The real costs and benefits of finance are then analyzed through shifts in the economy's production possibility frontier, either because of changes in total resources or because of changes in the efficiency with which they are utilized. In this regard three notations of efficiency are delineated: financial efficiency, allocative efficiency, and potential efficiency.

Consider an economy that produced two goods X_1 and X_2. Each of these goods has a production function and requires factor inputs of capital and labor.

$$X_i = X_i(K_i, L_i) \qquad i = 1, 2 \tag{12.1}$$

where

$$X_{iK}, X_{iL} > 0 \qquad \text{and} \qquad X_{iKK}, X_{iLL} < 0.$$

Real factor inputs are required in addition to provide financial intermediation services defined as the gathering of resources from surplus economic units and the investment of these resources with the deficit firms of both industries. The provision of financial intermediation services requires factor inputs, and this is true regardless of the technique, method, or channel of finance. Financial intermediation services could be performed by the production firm, which directly sells its primary securities to savers or assigns the financial task to a financial broker, underwriter, or claim-issuing financial intermediary. Financial services could also be performed by the saver seeking primary securities from the firm. In some of these instances, the financial technique has been called direct finance when it involves only primary securities and indirect finance when it involves a claim-issuing intermediary (whether the intermediary is a depository firm or not).[4]

However, the precise financial technique, with its accompanying financial institutions and financial instruments, is less important in this analysis than the fact that each financial technique uses real factor inputs, and this drain of factors away from final goods production has a real economic cost in terms of foregone output. This output loss will be assumed to be proportionate to the quantity of capital utilized by the industry, and these proportions are denoted c_1 and c_2 for the X_1 and X_2 industries. The c_i variables are the average production costs of finance per unit of capital, and it is assumed for this argument that perfect competition exists among the

---

[4] The terminology of direct and indirect finance is taken from John Gurley and Edward S. Shaw, *Money in a Theory of Finance* (Washington, D.C.: Brookings Institution, 1960).

financial firms, so there is no economic profit in financial intermediation. Then given a set of c_i, the real opportunity cost of finance in terms of units of X_1 and X_2 is $c_1 K_1$ and $c_2 K_2$, respectively. The production functions that reflect the real opportunity cost of finance are thus defined by Eq. (12.2) and will be referred to as the net production functions; that is, production net of financial resource costs:

$$X_i = X_i(K_i, L_i) - c_i K_i \qquad i = 1, 2. \tag{12.2}$$

Explicitly including financial costs in the analysis will affect not only output, but the returns to the owners of capital as well. From the production functions we see that the use of an additional unit of capital will yield output units equal to capital's marginal product less the financial production cost,[5] since the use of capital necessitates the deflection of resources into a financial sector:

$$X_{iK} - c_i. \tag{12.3}$$

Where firms in competitive commodity markets pay marginal value products to inputs, the period return to capital is then

$$P_i(X_{iK} - c_i). \tag{12.4}$$

Thus the c_i can be seen as financial costs affecting the net returns to capital. If we were to integrate Eq. (12.3) with respect to K_i, the real unit cost of financing capital translates into the real output costs reflected in the net production functions

$$\int (X_{iK}(K_i, L_i) - c_i)\, dK_i = X_i(K_i, L_i) - c_i K_i \tag{12.5}$$

for a given L_i. Thus, real financial costs can be seen either in the dimension of reducing the return to capital or of reducing output.

Given the net production functions and the existing total endowments of capital and labor, K and L, we can calculate production possibility frontiers that take into account real financial costs. The production possibility frontiers are calculated by forming the Lagrangian $\mathscr{L}$,

$$\mathscr{L} = X_1(K_1, L_1) - c_1 K_1 - \lambda(X_2 - X_2(K - K_1, L - L_1) + c_2(K - K_1)) \tag{12.6}$$

and setting the first-order conditions equal to 0. The allocation conditions

---

[5] This form of the net production function relates output loss to the use of financed capital without specifying the ratios of labor and total capital to the production of X and the production of financial services. This could be accomplished through a further suboptimization, which would add little substance to the present argument. For the details of capital and labor allocations to a financial sector in a single-good world, see Chapter 14.

for the financed economy are given by

$$X_{1K}(K_1, L_1) - c_1 = \lambda(X_{2K}(K - K_1, L - L_1) - c_2) \qquad (12.7)$$

and

$$X_{1L}(K_1, L_1) = \lambda(X_{2L}(K - K_1, L - L_1)), \qquad (12.8)$$

and the production possibility frontier can be derived from these equations which are depicted in Figure 12.1.

In the same way, a potential production possibility frontier could be calculated in the absence of financial costs by using the production functions of Eq. (12.1). The relative positions of the net financed frontier and potential frontier depend on several technological factors. The relative unit financial costs, the set of c_i, will influence the position of the net frontier, and this influence is most directly measured at the section of the axis where the entire difference between gross and net output is due to finan-

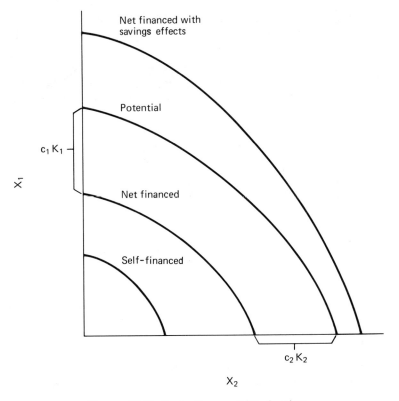

Figure 12.1 Production possibility frontiers.

cial costs. Within the interior, the relative shapes of the net and potential frontiers would depend on the sensitivity of factor input combinations to relative input prices, as the financial costs apply to capital inputs alone. Thus the elasticity of factor substitution of the underlying production functions will affect the relative position of the net financed frontier to the potential frontier.

12.4   FINANCE AND REAL ECONOMIC OUTPUT

The manner in which finance can affect real economic output will be analyzed in terms of the production possibility frontiers. The frontiers are affected by changes in capital resources or changes in efficiency. Efficiency is characterized as either financial, allocative, or potential.

Financial efficiency is meant to be technical efficiency in conducting financial intermediation. It is attained when the average production or financial costs per unit of capital, c_i, are the lowest obtainable from all the technically feasible methods of finance.[6] These financial costs are associated with the costs of obtaining resources from saving units and placing these resources into productive investments. The costs of placing resources would include the costs of finding, evaluating, and selecting investment opportunities and combining them into desired portfolios.[7]

There is a strong possibility that there is an association between a particular industry and the level of its financial costs. Financial costs across industries may differ because of the difference in costs of obtaining information or differences in the cost of appraising assets or income streams. In addition, the unique characteristics of an industry might also influence which financial channel is most efficient. An industry comprised of many small units could conceivably be more efficiently serviced by a specialized financial intermediary, whereas the industry giant might find the

---

[6] Technical efficiency in conducting financial intermediation implies that the unit financial costs are associated with the parameters of a financial production function. For an analysis of the problem along these lines, see Chapter 14.

[7] The unit financial costs have been related to the total capital stock. The incidence of financial cost would depend upon a number of factors. For example, if the maturity of the financial instruments were one period, financial intermediation input would be associated with the entire capital stock. If the maturity were two periods, then the financial system would be required to process half of the total capital stock certificates each period; thus, a shorter average maturity implies that financial intermediation inputs are more closely related to the total capital stock. If, in the extreme case of infinite maturity of all financial instruments, resource costs were related to only the new flow of savings, in a constant growth case this would also bear a direct relationship to the capital stock, as $\dot{K}$ is directly related to K by $\dot{K} = K/n$ where n is the natural growth rate.

direct financial channel to be more efficient. Thus the c_1 and c_2 variables need not be identical, nor need they refer to the same financial channel or involve the same combination of financial instruments.

The economics of the depository intermediary have been highlighted in Chapters 3–11. The prevalence of depository institutions in a financial system must rest to some degree on the possibilities of economies of scale in the financial intermediation process. However, it should be pointed out that the shape of the depository intermediary's average cost curve and the size of the most efficient intermediary is not as much an issue here as the level of unit financial costs when an intermediary is operating at minimum average unit cost.[8] Irrespective of which financial institution and which instruments are utilized in financial intermediation, a more efficient channel will utilize fewer resources and will shift out the net financed frontier of the economy, and this will be a Pareto movement.

In an economy in which capital is financed, optimal capital allocation is given by Eq. (12.7), which indicates that these allocations are made net of financial costs. Such an allocation could be made by any economic entity when information concerning net rates of return is provided on markets in which prices are an accurate reflection of all available information. Thus, allocative efficiency does not require the existence of depository or even nondepository financial insitutions, although there is a presumption that financial intermediaries help to achieve allocative efficiency, as the intermediaries gather information and compare a large number of investments in allocating the resources at their command.

Many conditions exist that might cause an economy to fail to achieve allocative efficiency and thus not attain its potential frontier. Indivisibilities of assets might exist. Considerations in portfolio selection will be given not only to net return, but such factors as risk and liquidity. Monopoly elements in financial markets might cause available market rates of return to diverge from the net rate of return, and market segmentation, regulatory or institutional, could further cause allocative distortions. In addition, the tendency for firms to reinvest retained earnings at lower rates of return has long been noted as a possible cause for a suboptimal allocation. Governments as well could bias allocative efficiency if market signals are given by regulatory-dictated rather than market-dictated rates, through usury laws or deposit and loan rate ceilings, for example. Governments can create further distortions by taxation of financial wealth either directly or through inflation. All these factors could cause a society to

---

[8] It is assumed that expansion of the financial sector is accomplished through the introduction of new financial intermediaries, each operating at minimum average cost. In this way the marginal expansion for the sector is accomplished at the level of the minimum average cost for the efficient intermediary.

fall within its potential frontier, and not only will they cause a redirection of resources, but they will likely affect the selection of financial channels.

Potential efficiency is a notion that the gross output reflected by the production functions of Eq. (12.1) results from a microeconomic organization of production, such that capital resources reach the most efficient producers, those with the most efficient techniques of production, or those who operate at the most efficient scale of operation. If, for example, all output was produced by individuals utilizing their own capital and their own production techniques, then that economy could be characterized by the self-financed frontier of Figure 12.1. The potential frontier is attained when both potential and allocative efficiency exists. That is, if there were no separation of the ownership and the use of capital, its use would be tied to the wealth-owner and to that individual's techniques, knowledge, and production know-how. Thus, potential efficiency refers to the change in output from changes in the organization of production at the level of the microproducing unit. When one compares the self-financed with the net financed frontier output possibilities are compared after financial costs, which are negligible in the case of self-finance. Thus, if the net financed frontier lies outside the self-financed frontiers, financed production is more desirable, even after allowances are made for the real financial costs. The financial system facilitates the transfer of resources by providing signals to wealth-owners that their resources would be more advantageously utilized elsewhere, and as a result, output levels are increased.

In addition to shifts in the frontier due to sources of technical and allocative efficiency, the financial system has also been purported to alter the production possibility frontier through changes in the total quantity of capital. Such an enlargement of the Edgeworth Box would result in a Pareto movement of the frontier because of an increase in the capital–labor ratio of the economy.

An increase in the economy's capital intensity rests on the presumptions that the financial system is able, through specialized financial instruments, to provide a more desirable form of wealth-owning than self-employment of capital and that wealth-owners respond to these incentives by increasing per capita wealth-owning. Depository institutions have been especially touted in this regard for their ability to stimulate saving by offering risk-diversified, liquid assets tailor-made to the needs of wealth-owners. In another view of the process, there is the possibility that the financial system will encourage accumulation of capital for ultimate investment by paying a rate of return on saving as it is being accumulated in sufficient scale for lumpy investment. Thus the financial system, by providing interim returns on saving, will raise the savings rate and capitalization of the economy.[9]

In the terms of the production frontier framework of this chapter, the financial system, if it succeeds in its role of raising the savings rates and capital intensity of an economy, will shift the financed frontiers outward. This effect is also shown in Figure 12.1 as the net financed frontier with savings effects.

12.5 THE DETERMINATION OF FINANCIAL STRUCTURE

The actual financial structure of the economy, the financial instruments and financial channels at a given point in time would depend upon the actual combinations of goods produced. Thus far we have developed production possibility frontiers that indicate the possible choices of goods, but now the issue is: Given this feasible set of outputs, what combination of goods is actually chosen? To determine this, we must broaden the analysis to include consumer choice.

From the total derivatives of the production functions, we can obtain an expression for the production possibility frontier

$$\frac{dX_1}{dX_2} = \frac{(X_{1K} - c_1)\, dK_1 + X_{1L}\, dL_1}{(X_{2K} - c_2)\, dK_2 + X_{2L}\, dL_2}. \tag{12.9}$$

Consider the following conditions: all markets are competitive and firms in each industry maximize profit by paying each factor a return equal to its marginal value product $w_i = P_i X_{iL}$ and $r_i = P_i(X_{iK} - c_i)$; laborers equate wage rates by their allocations $w_1 = w_2$; wealth-owners consider financial assets to be perfect substitutes $r_1 = r_2$; and full employment of factors exists $dL_1 = -dL_2$ and $dK_1 = -dK_2$. Then expression (12.9) reduces to

$$\frac{dX_1}{dX_2} = -\frac{P_2}{P_1}.$$

Thus, the general equilibrium solution is found where the slope of the production possibility frontier is equal to the commodity price ratio. The significance of that point is that it will determine not only the combination of goods produced, but, more importantly for the purpose of this analysis, it will simultaneously determine the structure of finance. This results from the fact that this combination of goods corresponds to a quantity of capital passing through each financial channel to each industry. Thus, implicit in this solution is the financial structure, institutions, and instruments employed in each channel, and the real cost of the financial system.[10]

The financial system can have real impacts on economic output, as is reflected by movements in the production possibility frontier. These shifts in the frontier can be due to changes in production techniques at the microeconomic producing level. This has been called potential efficiency. An efficient financial system, as measured by resource use, will minimize the output loss from the use of the financial system. This has been termed financial efficiency. The financial system, either through efficient financial markets or financial intermediaries, can help attain allocative efficiency and, in doing so, cause the economy to operate on the net financed frontier. Finally, the financial system, by offering saving instruments with more desirable features or greater services that result in an increase in the saving rate, will alter the capital intensity of the economy. In consequence, greater quantities of capital resources will move the frontier outward. Financial costs and benefits have been discussed in terms of the movement of production possibility frontiers. If one knew the prevailing commodity price ratios that would emerge in general equilibrium, it would be possible to measure these real costs and benefits in output units as the economy moves from a point on one frontier to a point on another frontier.

The financial system can influence the composition of goods produced. For example, an industry with high unit financial costs would reduce net returns to capital, which would tend to reduce the flow of capital to that industry. Conversely, a relatively small unit financial cost will tend to attract resources. The structural composition of financial instruments is part of the simultaneous determination of outputs and the distribution of inputs. The general equilibrium solution for combinations of goods and financial channels rests on the technologies of each industry and on the financial technology that most efficiently services the capital accumulation of each industry. Preferences of laborers will affect their allocations between sectors; preferences of wealth-owners will affect the distribution of capital between sectors; and preferences for goods will also direct resources between industries.

An efficient financial system (allocative, potential and financial) need not be accompanied by a complex structure of financial instruments, nor is a complex financial structure a clear indication of an efficient financial system. In fact, a complex financial structure might be indicative of regulatory distortions or other barriers to allocative efficiency, and a simple

---

[10] The quantity of capital can be read off the contract curve of an Edgeworth Box or from the first-order condition equations.

financial structure could also be indicative of regulatory-maintained market segmentation. Thus, examining the financial structure alone yields few clues to its efficiency or its contribution to economic development.

The evolution of a financial structure over time will depend on changes in any of the above considerations. Foremost of the systematic influences could be the potential for scale economies in financial institutions and financial markets. Such a factor would tend to account for the higher proportionate use of the indirect financial channel in more developed economies operating with larger scales of capital inputs. Mass production technologies common to more developed nations also might influence the financial structure in that the firms of industries using these technologies might find direct finance more economical then would those in industries composed of many smaller-sized firms. The diversity of goods demanded in a more developed county can also have a bearing on the diversity of financial structure as financial specialists are developed to efficiently handle the unique problems of each industry.

There is no simple way to measure from observed data the extent to which a financial system is providing the benefits discussed here. A large financial sector in terms of resource use might be indicative of financial inefficiency rather than the effectiveness of the financial system; a low proportion of financed capital accumulation might be indicative of highly productive self-financed industries rather than financial and potential inefficiency; differences in the marginal product of capital between industries might be indicative of differences in unit financial costs rather than allocative inefficiency; and a complex structure of financial instruments might be reflective of financial distortions rather than an economy that has achieved a higher capital intensity due to a diversity of financial savings instruments.

BIBLIOGRAPHY

Bennett, R. *The Financial Sector and Economic Development: The Mexican Case.* Baltimore: Johns Hopkins Press, 1965.

Boyd, John H., and Kwast, Myron L. *Bank Regulation and the Efficiency of Financial Intermediation.* Board of Governors, Federal Reserve System, Washington, D.C., April 1979.

Brimmer, Andrew F. "Central Banking and Economic Development," *Journal of Money, Credit and Banking,* **3,** November 1971.

Cohen, Jacob. "Integrating the Real and Financial via the Linkage of Financial Flow," *Journal of Finance,* **23,** March 1968.

Dutton, Dean S. "A Model of Self-Generating Inflation: The Argentine Case," *Journal of Money, Credit and Banking,* **3,** May 1971.

Engberg, Holger L. "The New African Central Banks and Monetary Management." In

Financial Development and Economic Growth, ed. Arthur W. Sametz. New York: New York Univ. Press, 1972.

Fand, David. "Financial Regulation and Allocative Efficiency of Our Capital Markets," *The National Banking Review,* **3,** September 1965.

Fei, John C. H., and Ranis, Gustav. "Foreign Assistance and Economic Development: Comment," *American Economic Review,* **58,** September 1968.

Fraser, Donald R., and Rose, Peter S. "More on Banking Structure and Performance: The Evidence from Texas, " *Journal of Financial and Quantitative Analysis,* **6,** January 1971.

Galbis, Vicente. "Financial Intermediation and Economic Growth in LDC's," *Journal of Developmental Studies,* **14,** January 1977.

Goldfeld, Stephen M. "Savings and Loan Associations and the Market for Savings: Aspects of Allocational Efficience," In *A Study of the Savings and Loan Industry,* Federal Home Loan Bank Board, Washington, D.C., 1969.

Goldsmith, Raymond, *The Financial Development of Mexico,* Paris: Organization for Economic Cooperation and Development, 1966.

Goldsmith, Raymond. *Financial Structure and Development,* New Haven, Conn.: Yale Univ. Press, 1969.

Gurley, John, and Shaw, Edward S. "Financial Aspects of Economic Development." *American Economic Review,* **45,** September 1955.

Gurley, John, and Shaw, Edward S. *Money in a Theory of Finance.* Washington D.C.: Brookings Institution, 1960.

Gurley, John, and Shaw, Edward S. "Financial Structure and Economic Development," *Economic Development and Cultural Change,* **15,** April 1967.

Hirshleifer, Jack. *Investment, Interest and Capital. Englewood Cliffs, N.J.:* Prentice-Hall, 1970.

Kane, Edward J. "Good Intentions and Unintended Evil: The Case Against Selective Credit Allocation," *Journal of Money, Credit and Banking,* **9,** February 1977.

Kindelberger, Charles. "International Financial Intermediation for Developing Countries." In *Money and Finance in Economic Growth and Development,* ed. Ronald McKinnon. New York: Marcel Dekker, 1976.

McKinnon, Ronald. *Money and Capital in Economic Development.* Washington, D.C.: Brookings Institution, 1973.

McKinnon, Ronald, ed. *Money and Finance in Economic Growth and Development.* New York: Marcel Dekker, 1976.

Ness, Walter L., Jr. "Some Effects of Inflation on Financing Investment in Argentina and Brazil." In *Financial Development and Economic Growth,* ed. Arthur W. Sametz. New York: New York Univ. Press, 1972.

Neufeld, E. *The Financial System of Canada.* New York: St. Martin's Press, 1972.

Papenek, Gustav F. "Aid, Foreign Private Investment, Savings, and Growth in Less Developed Countries," *Journal of Political Economy,* **81,** January–February 1973.

Papanek, Gustav F. "The Effects of Aid and Other Resource Transfers on Savings and Growth in Less Developed Countries," *Economic Journal,* **82,** September 1972.

Patrick, Hugh T. "Finance, Capital Markets and Economic Growth in Japan." In *Financial Development and Economic Growth,* ed. Arthur W. Sametz. New York: New York Univ. Press, 1972.

Penner, Rudolph G., and Silber, William L. "The Interaction Between Federal Credit Programs and the Allocation of Credit," Federal Home Loan Bank Board Invited Working Paper No. 2, Washington, D.C., February 1972.

Reynolds, Clark W. *The Use of the Flow of Funds Analysis in the Study of Latin American Capital Market Development.* OAS Workshop on Capital Market Development in Latin America, Mexico City, 1973.

Reynolds, Clark W., and Spellman, Lewis J. "Financial Intermediation as Seen Through the Flow of Funds Accounts." Mimeographed. Stanford, Calif: Stanford Univ. Food Research Institute, January 1975.

Sametz, Arnold W. *Financial Development and Economic Growth: The Economic Consequence of Underdeveloped Capital Markets.* New York: New York Univ. Press, 1972.

Sametz, Arnold W. "Financing U.S. Direct Foreign Investment in Europe: The Data, Causal Factors and Some Implications." In *Financial Development and Economic Growth,* ed. Arthur W. Sametz. New York: New York Univ. Press, 1972.

Schumpeter, Joseph A. *The Theory of Economic Development.* Cambridge, Mass.: Harvard Univ. Press, 1955.

Shaw, Edward S. *Financial Deepening in Economic Development.* London/New York: Oxford Univ. Press, 1973.

Stigler, George J. "Imperfections in the Capital Market," *Journal of Political Economy,* **75,** June, 1967.

Weisskopf, Thomas E. "An Econometric Test of Alternative Constraints on the Growth of Underdeveloped Countries," *Review of Economics and Statistics,* **54,** February 1972.

CHAPTER 13

Financial Policy and the Performance of the Aggregate Economy

13.1 The Aggregate Growth Model

In Chapter 12, the impact of the financial system on the economy's production possibility frontier was explored. This was an analysis of output possibilities and the allocation of capital resources at a given point in time. In this chapter, the way in which finance and financial policy influence capital accumulation and real growth over time are examined. To demonstrate this, some simplifying assumptions are made in order to focus on the relationship between the financial industry and the real variables of the economy. The analysis will be confined to the depository institution, and some of the analyses developed earlier will be utilized. The performance of the depository industry as it affects the savings rate, the capital intensity, the level of per capita output and consumption, and the economy's growth rate will be considered.

Depository institutions state deposit rates and then place λ percent of the deposit proceeds in loans, securities, or other earning assets. The leakage from deposits to earning assets λ is due to cash reserve requirements and is considered an exogenous constant. The recipients of the loans from the depository institutions are assumed to purchase and hold real physical capital. Competition in loan markets is assumed to prevail so that the loan rate is driven to be equal to the marginal product of capital in the economy. Regardless of the specific financial channel, financial instrument, or market used to accomplish the intermediation process from gathering deposits to placing loans, a real cost is incurred and is ultimately reflected in deposit rates. These real production costs per deposit will be denoted c. In a market unconstrained by deposit ceilings, rates paid to depositors r fall short of asset earning rates r_a by the sum the unit cost of deposits c and profit margins p per deposit unit. Hence,

$$r = r_a - c - p, \tag{13.1}$$

and one can see the influence of competition and efficiency in the financial sector on deposit rates acting through the variables c and p. The competitive and efficiency effects on the rate spread $r_a - r$ has, of course, been developed in Chapter 3.

Concerning aggregate wealth demands W, it will merely be assumed that all wealth is held in deposits and the desired real wealth level depends on the real deposit rate r and net real income Y. This, of course, abstracts from other assets and other forms of wealth-owning, so that this relationship could be considered the *ceteris paribus* relationship of deposit rate to deposit level:

$$W = W(r, Y). \tag{13.2}$$

Since it was assumed that λ percent of deposits finances real capital accumulation, or $K = \lambda D$, it will also be symmetrically assumed that r_a falls short of the marginal productivity of capital such that $r_a = \lambda Y_K$, since λ percent of assets are sterilized in nonearning cash.

From this, $K = \lambda W(r, Y)$, which is interpreted as a capital demand function, although it is a derived demand for physical capital arising from the wealth-owners' deposit demands. It is assumed that the function is linear homogeneous in income and can be written

$$K = \lambda W(r)Y, \qquad \infty > W_r > 0. \tag{13.3}$$

The desired stock of real deposits and hence capital increases with the deposit rate, which indicates that wealth-owners accumulate deposits relative to income as the incentive to hold deposits increases.

This aggregate deposit demand might also be viewed as the wealth-owners' desired ratio of their stock of capital to their flow of income. This desired capital–income ratio is interest-elastic:

$$K/Y = \lambda W(r). \tag{13.4}$$

13.2 THE DEPOSITORY INDUSTRY AND THE AGGREGATE SAVINGS RATE

The structural desired saving equation for the economy is obtained by differentiating the demand for capital (deposits) with respect to time

$$\dot{K} = \lambda W(r)\dot{Y} + \lambda Y W_r \dot{r}, \tag{13.5}$$

and the wealth-owners' desired saving proportion from current income s can be deducted by simply dividing (13.5) by Y

$$s = \dot{K}/Y = \lambda W(r)(\dot{Y}/Y) + \lambda W_r \dot{r}. \tag{13.6}$$

The desired proportion of income to be committed to capital accumulation through depository institutions is thus a function the parameters of which derive in turn from the parameters of the wealth demand function

$W(r)$, the level of r, and from the parameter λ. Since r depends on c and p, the desired saving ratio depends on productive efficiency and competition in the depository industries. Given this propensity to hold the deposits of financial institutions, it can be seen that when the deposit rate is in equilibrium and $\dot{r}$ becomes 0, the desired proportion of income devoted to real capital accumulation depends on the desired deposit–income ratio $W(r)$, the rate of growth of income, and the proportion of assets committed to cash reserves:

$$s = \lambda W(r)(\dot{Y}/Y). \tag{13.7}$$

Thus, higher income growth rates will tend to increase the desired saving proportion as wealth-owners strive to maintain their wealth portfolios in proportion to their higher income levels.

The role of interest rates in stimulating saving has long been a question in economic theory. In this model, the deposit rate influences desired saving proportions by both its level and changes in its level. *High* deposit rates induce larger desired deposit–income ratios; *increasing* deposit rates when not in equilibrium [as indicated by Eq. (13.6)] raise the desired saving proportion. Thus both high and rising deposit rates stimulate the desired saving proportion. As seen from Eq. (13.1), this can result from lower profit margins or greater technical efficiency in the depository industries or if a capital scarcity in the production sector increases the marginal product of capital and the loan rate.

Concerning output, the microeconomic technology is utilized efficiently by many atomistic producers and yields a marcoeconomic production function in which net output Y is linear homogeneous in the two substitutable factors, capital and labor (K and L, respectively):

$$\theta Y = Y(\theta K, \theta L). \tag{13.8}$$

The standard technological assumption of diminishing returns to each factor is made, where the marginal factor contributions are

$$Y_K, Y_L > 0, \qquad Y_{KK}, Y_{LL} < 0. \tag{13.9}$$

In the case of a linear homogeneous technology, the marginal products of capital and labor depend on the capital–labor ratio k only

$$Y_K = Y_K(k), \qquad Y_L = Y_L(k) \tag{13.10}$$

where

$$Y_{Kk} < 0 \qquad \text{and} \qquad Y_{Lk} > 0.$$

The labor force is assumed to grow at the natural rate of growth n

$$\dot{L}/L = n. \tag{13.11}$$

The labor force is inelastically supplied on the labor market and is thus fully employed at all times. Competition prevails and output is distributed according to the marginal contribution of each factor of production.[1]

13.3 THE CAPITAL–LABOR RATIO, THE INVESTMENT SHARE OF OUTPUT, AND PER CAPITA CONSUMPTION

The simultaneous solution to the model is obtained in the following way. From the preceding assumptions, Eq. (13.3) becomes

$$K = \lambda W(\lambda Y_k - c - p)Y, \tag{13.3}$$

which we shall immediately simplify by assuming λ is equal to unity. We then differentiate the production function and the capital demand function with respect to time:

$$\dot{Y} = Y_K \dot{K} + Y_L \dot{L} \tag{13.12}$$

$$\dot{K} = W(r)\dot{Y} + YW_r(\dot{Y}_K - \dot{c} - \dot{p}). \tag{13.13}$$

If we substitute Eq. (13.12) into Eq. (13.13) and solve for $\dot{K}$, we derive a simultaneous solution for net capital accumulation

$$\dot{K} = [W(r)Y_L/(1 - W(r)Y_K)]\dot{L} + [YW_r/(1 - W(r)Y_K)](\dot{Y}_K - \dot{c} - \dot{p}). \tag{13.14}$$

The capital growth process involves parameters relecting desired asset accumulations, the production technology, the efficiency and profitability of the depository institutions, and the exogenous growth of the labor force. In a growth equilibrium in which capital grows with labor, the capital–labor ratio of the production sector is constant, and thus the term reflecting changes in the marginal product becomes 0, as the marginal product of capital depends upon the capital–labor ratio only. This growth equilibrium also involves the depository industry. The depository production costs and the profit margin must be constant to yield a constant deposit rate. In balanced growth, capital accumulation is then a multiple of the increase in the labor force

$$\dot{K} = [W(r)Y_L/(1 - W(r)Y_K)]\dot{L}. \tag{13.15}$$

Then the growth rate of capital matches the natural growth rate of the labor force

$$\dot{K}/K = \dot{L}/L \quad \text{or} \quad k = \dot{K}/\dot{L}, \tag{13.16}$$

---

[1] These assumptions, with the exception of the interest elastic wealth demand curve, are standard to growth theory. See for example the classic article by Robert M. Solow, "A Contribution to the Theory of Economic Growth," *Quarterly Journal of Economics* **70** (February 1956).

where k is the capital–labor ratio or, more commonly, the capital intensity. Hence, from Eqs. (13.15) and (13.16), the equilibrium capital intensity is

$$k = W(r)Y_L/(1 - W(r)Y_K). \qquad (13.17)$$

And by implicit differentiation, the relationship between a change in r or its components Y_K, c, and p as expressed in Eq. (13.1), and the changes in k would be found to be negative.

$$\frac{\partial k}{\partial c} = \frac{-\left(\dfrac{Y_L W_r}{1 - W(r)Y_K} + \dfrac{W(r)Y_L Y_K W_r}{(1 - W(r)Y_K)^2}\right)}{1 - \left(\dfrac{W_r Y_{Kk} Y_L + W(r)Y_{Lk}}{1 - W(r)Y_K} + \dfrac{W(r)Y_L(W_r Y_{Kk} + W(r)Y_{Kk})}{(1 - W(r)Y_K)^2}\right)} < 0$$

$$(13.18)$$

Hence, a more technically efficient or more competitive depository industry (which lowers p) raises the economy's capital intensity. Similarly, as asset earning rates more nearly approach the marginal productivity of capital on competitive asset markets, the capital intensity is increased.

Furthermore, as the depository industries need to allocate fewer deposits to cash, capital intensities are increased. For $0 < \lambda \geq 1$ the equilibrium capital intensity is

$$k = (\lambda W(\lambda Y_K - c - p)Y_L)/(1 - \lambda W(Y_K - c - p)Y_K),$$

and higher levels of λ unambiguously increase capital intensities.

With natural growth rate of inputs and a linear homogeneous technology, the economic system produces natural growth rates of output as well.

Once the model has been solved for k, it is possible to solve for the investment share of output i in terms of k and n. The equilibrium ex post investment share of output is simply derived from Eq. (13.15) by dividing through by Y:

$$i = \dot{K}/Y = \{W(r)Y_L/[1 - W(r)Y_K]\}[\dot{L}/Y(K, L)]. \qquad (13.19)$$

By factoring L from the production function (which is permissible with a linear homogeneous production function so that $LY(k, 1) = Y(K, L)$, and substituting the value n for the population growth rate, the investment share becomes a function of n and k only:

$$i(n, k) = [n/Y(k, 1)]\{W(r)Y_L(k)/[1 - W(r)Y_K(k)]\}. \qquad (13.20)$$

Per capita output y in steady-state growth simply depends on k via $Y(k, 1)$, and per capita consumption c in steady-state growth is simply derived from per capita output less steady-state per capita investment requirements nk:[2]

$$c(n, k) = Y(k,1) - nk. \qquad (13.21)$$

It should be noted that the equilibrium capital intensity given by Eq. (13.20) depends on wealth demands and the parameters of the technologies of the production sector and depository industry. Furthermore, the capital intensity is independent of the population growth rate.

In order for the capital intensity and interest rate to be independent of the population growth rate, the investment share of income, as seen by Eq. (13.20), must be directly proportional to the population growth rate. As a result, if population growth rates increase and if all members of society maintain the same capital endowments, the investment share must increase in proportion to population growth rates. The converse is, of course, also true, and if a stationary population emerges, the capital intensity will be maintained, as the (net) investment share of output would fall to 0. Thus the independence of the capital intensity and interest rate from population growth rates is due to the responsiveness of the investment share to population growth rates.[3]

13.4 FINANCIAL POLICY AND REAL OUTPUT

The policy implication for an economy that behaved in the manner described in Section 13.3 is clear. Population control would not influence the capital intensity, interest rate, or per capita output, whereas in direct contrast, policies to increase desired capital–income ratios relative to the rate of interest would increase the capital intensity, the investment share, and would—during a transitory period—raise the income growth rate from one steady-state growth path to another. Thus, in an economy described by this model, the centerpiece of economic policy would be measures to stimulate wealth-owning by shifting the W curve. The payoff of such attributes as "confidence" or "financial stability" can then be seen to have important effects on the capital intensity if they shift the $W(r)$ function to the right. Furthermore, if financial regulation, deposit insurance, and/or the liquidity and solvency backing of a central bank are seen

[2] The per capita consumption and investment requirements in steady state growth have been discussed and developed by Edmund S. Phelps in *Golden Rules of Economic Growth: Studies of Efficient and Optimal Investment* (New York: Norton, 1966).

[3] The mechanisms that cause these adjustments to take place are somewhat indirect. An increase in the population growth rate increases the amount of labor relative to capital and thus lowers the capital intensity, which in turn raises the rate of return to wealth. As previously noted, the high and rising rate of return will increase desired saving proportions.

to reduce the risk of holding deposits, they will tend to reduce the liquidity level of the depository system and hence, by increasing λ, will tend to increase the capital intensity of the economy.

In addition, financial regulation, through its many avenues of influence on the financial system, can affect the capital growth process by influencing the efficiency and competitiveness of the depository market. Equation (3.18) has shown that a more technically efficient financial sector, with lower levels of c and/or a more competitive depository industry with lower levels of p, will raise the capital intensity. Furthermore, with a competitive loan market, in which asset earning rates of the depository institutions approach the marginal productivity of capital, the capital intensity is higher because the higher levels of revenues are passed on to depositors. Since all of these variables are affected by financial regulation and financial policy, they are important not only in their direct impact on the industry, but also because of the aggregate impacts on output and growth.

Technical change in the production sector represented by a shift in the Y_K function would also raise the desired saving proportion as seen in Eq. (13.6) by increasing the marginal product of capital and by causing a transitional increase in the income growth rate. Hence, technical change stimulates desired saving proportions, both through a rate effect and an income effect. Since the real variables in equilibrium growth are independent of the population growth rate, the model has the property that for any two economies that possess the same production technologies, financial production costs, level of competition, and predilections to accumulate capital, the same equilibrium capital intensity and equilibrium real deposit rate would be found. Thus we have a growth analog to the static Fisherian system in which the capital intensity and interest rate are determined by productivity and thrift alone.

13.5　A DIAGRAMMATIC SOLUTION

A diagrammatic interpretation of the model can be seen through Figure 13.1. Equations (13.1), (13.3), and (13.8) are represented by the r, Y_K, and W curves, respectively.

The Y_K curve represents the rate of return yielded by the production function at each $K:Y$ ratio. It is constructed from the production function. Since the production function is linear homogeneous, both sides of the equation can be divided through by K to obtain the output–capital ratio

$$Y/K = Y(1, L/K) = Y(1, 1/k).$$

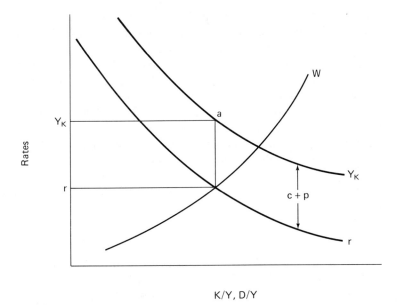

Figure 13.1 Equilibrium capital intensity, marginal productivity of capital, and deposit rate.

Thus, each capital–output ratio corresponds to a capital–labor ratio

$$K/Y = 1/Y(1, 1/k).$$

With the linear homogeneous technology, the level of the marginal product of capital also depends on the level of the capital–labor ratio as expressed in Eq. (13.10). Thus the Y_K curve is a locus of points each of which corresponds to a capital–labor ratio. From the preceding, it can be seen that as the capital–labor ratio increases, there is a correspondingly higher capital–output ratio and a lower marginal product of capital. Thus, the Y_K curve has a negative slope.[4]

With competition in loan markets, the Y_K curve is equal to r_a. The r curve represents the level of the deposit rate, which is capital's net yield to depositors at each capital—income ratio. It falls short of the loan rate by the sum of production costs and the profit margin. The W curve traces Eq. (13.3). It is the community's desired deposit (capital) holdings at each successive deposit rate. The intersection of the W and r curves determines the equilibrium deposit-rate and $K:Y$ ratio. A projection to point a

[4] A similar construction was employed by James Tobin in "Notes on Optimal Monetary Growth," *Journal of Political economy* **76** (July–August 1968).

indicates the level of the marginal product of capital at this capital–output ratio. This intersection also fixes the level of the capital intensity, as capital's marginal product is monotonically related to k.

This figure makes it clear that the more efficient the depository industry in terms of a lower value of c, the higher will be the r curve and the greater will be the equilibrium capital intensity. This in turn will raise per capita output. Further real effects on the capital intensity and output will also be felt if competitive pressures reduce profit margins and hence raise the equilibrium capital intensity. The magnitude of the impact on the capital intensity depends critically on the elasticity of the $W(r)$ curve. The more sensitive the deposit level to the deposit rate, the greater will be the real economic gains from technological and competitive changes in the depository industries.

13.6 RATE SPREADS AND PROFIT MARGINS IN UNITED STATES AND LATIN AMERICAN FINANCIAL SYSTEMS

From Figure 13.1 it is clear that the rate spread between asset and deposit rates is critical to an economy's capital intensity and real per capita output. In the absence of deposit ceilings, this rate spread, as developed in Chapter 3, depends only on production costs and the profit margin. When there are deposit ceilings, the rate spread depends on production costs, the profit margin, and the implicit deposit rate as developed in Chapter 7. In either case, the size of the wedge separating asset and deposit rates affects the capital intensity in the production sector. This section presents some empirical data from the financial systems of Colombia, Mexico, and Peru and compares these data to the experience of the United States between 1966 and 1973. These data from Latin America suggest there is sufficient leeway for gains in efficiency or for competitive gains that could lead to significantly higher real deposit rates and higher capital intensities.

The three Latin American financial systems studied have several common characteristics. In all three systems there was a segmentation in both deposit and asset markets by maturity, lending purpose, or both. This segmentation also extended to instances where certain intermediaries were created by the governments of these countries to service specific production sectors or perceived credit needs, or to compensate for previous discrimination regarding access to credit.

In all three systems are found essentially the same types of depository institutions: commercial banks, development banks, and mortgage lending banks, as well as other intermediaries that concentrate their lending activities in specific sectors. In the case of Mexico, observations were limited to the private financial depository sector and do not include data for government banks, which in 1970 represented approximately 26% of the banking systems' total deposits.

In all three countries there is extensive regulation and control. Regulation is implemented in all cases through two entities: the respective central banks and independent regulatory agencies.[5] The areas controlled by the regulatory agencies include reserve requirements, credit allocations, interest rate ceilings, entry, and general supervision.

Quantitative reserve requirements are specified in proportion to deposits with reserves held in cash or other types of authorized assets. Asset restrictions are imposed with the intent of specifically allocating certain proportions of the loan portfolio to predetermined economic sectors. The regulatory authorities impose deposit rate ceilings in all three countries, so implicit deposit rate competition may exist.[6] Demand deposits bear no interest, although as a point of interest, Peru authorized the payment of a 1% rate on these balances from 1962 to 1965. The regulatory authorities in all three systems must charter any new intermediaries, and thus they control access of new competitors to the market. Strict reporting requirements and supervision by regulatory authorities over the activity of the intermediaries are actively pursued in all three cases.

In contrast to the United States, banking regulation takes place only at the national level. The political subdivisions subjugate their local or regional objectives to national objectives. Another important similarity among these depository systems exists: national branching is prevalent. This contrasts, of course, radically with the case of the United States, where at this time interstate branching is prohibited.

Although there are indeed similarities and dissimilarities of asset and depository instruments, each system can be evaluated in terms of its operating costs and profit margins. Together these constitute the rate spread that characterizes the wedge between earnings and explicit deposit rates earned by depositors. These homogeneous comparisons are possible despite the different currency units, as all measures are stated as rates.

13.6.1 Operating Costs

The operating costs for each country's intermediaries were obtained by calculating the operating cost per deposit unit and computing a weighted

---

[5] The relevant authorities are Superintendencia Bancaria, Colombia, Banco de Mexico S.A., Superintendencia de Banca y Seguros, Peru.

[6] Deposit rates were indexed for a time for the Colombian *financieras* (savings banks).

average for the different intermediaries in which the weight was based on their share of total deposits. Table 13.1 indicates a wide difference between the United States intermediaries' operating costs and those of Mexico, Peru, and Colombia. The weighted average operating cost per deposit unit over the studied period for the United States was 2.21%, with a range of 1.89 to 2.56%. It was found that the same rank order prevailed for most years, with the Mexican system ranked next to that of the United States. On average for the years studied, the Mexican system experienced over 70% higher operating costs per deposit unit than the United States. Mexico's average operating cost for the 8-year period 1966–1973 was 3.79%, or 185 basis points lower than Peru, which ranked third. The Mexican system also appears to be the most stable, with a range of only 20 basis points separating the high and low years. Since operating costs for the United States depository institutions were increasing at this time, primarily as the result of increased implicit deposit rates, the gap between the United States and Mexican operating costs narrowed over the period: in 1966 average cost per deposit unit in Mexico was more than twice that of the United States, whereas in 1973 it was only 60% higher.

The Peruvian system ranked next in terms of operating costs, with an average operating cost per deposit unit over time of 5.64%, or 155% higher than that of the United States and 48% higher than Mexico's. From

TABLE 13.1

Aggregate Financial Intermediaries: Average Cost Per Deposit Unit[a]

Year	Colombia	Mexico	Peru	U.S.
1966	—	3.90	5.35	1.91
1967	5.71	3.66	5.20	1.89
1968	5.13	3.92	6.03	1.90
1969	5.08	3.72	6.43	2.33
1970	6.20	3.76	6.23	2.56
1971	6.76	3.81	5.73	2.43
1972	7.38	3.75	5.46	2.29
1973	7.07	3.83	5.08	2.38
Mean	6.19	3.79	5.64	2.21
Variance	.729	.006	.227	.063

[a] Expressed in percentages and computed as a weighted average of intermediaries' average cost per deposit unit, based on percentage of deposits held by each subsector. Source: Superintendencia Bancaria, Colombia; Banco de Mexico S.A.; Superintendencia de Banca y Seguros, Peru; *Annual Reports*, Federal Deposit Insurance Corporation; and *Combined Financial Statements*, Federal Home Loan Bank Board.

1967 to 1969 the Peruvian system's operating costs increased from 5.20 to 6.43%, a 23% increase. This trend was reversed in subsequent years, decreasing 21% to 5.08% in 1973. A very interesting fact should be highlighted in this regard: it was in 1970, at the end of this period of increasing costs, that the Peruvian government took an equity position in the banking system. The reversal of this trend also could have been a defensive reaction to avoid insolvency, as the acquired institutions were those with thin profit margins.

The highest cost levels are observed in the case of Colombia: the observed average cost per deposit unit for the 1967–1973 period was 6.9%, which was 175% higher than that of the United States, 60% higher than Mexico, and 9.8% higher than Peru. The Colombian system also had the largest fluctuation in operating costs, from 5.08 to 7.07%.

As has been previously pointed out, these financial systems often direct some of their depository institutions to the credit needs of a specific output sector. This could account for some degree of variance among the special-purpose depository intermediaries. However, commercial banks are essentially similar in all four countries, and more relevant comparisons can be made of these subsectors of the respective financial systems. The results of this comparison are shown in Table 13.2.

As would be expected, commercial banks exhibited higher costs than the aggregate system in all cases. These results are consistent with a priori expectations, as these institutions incur costs for the transfer of deposits and asset management of short-term portfolios, as well as the cost of cash management with more volatile demand deposits. Furthermore, with

TABLE 13.2

Commercial Banks: Average Cost Per Deposit Unit[a]

Year	Colombia	Mexico	Peru	U.S.
1966	—	6.35	5.42	2.34
1967	5.84	6.42	5.49	2.38
1968	5.31	6.63	5.96	2.39
1969	5.71	6.63	6.36	2.81
1970	6.97	7.27	6.57	3.29
1971	7.49	7.62	5.66	3.16
1972	8.12	7.43	6.15	3.01
1973	7.67	7.02	5.55	3.06
Mean	6.73	6.92	5.89	2.80
Variance	1.042	.203	.163	.129

[a] Expressed in percentages. Source: See Table 13.1.

interest rate prohibitions, these institutions would be expected to pay higher implicit deposit rates. When ranking the operating costs of the commercial banking sector alone we find that the United States has the lowest cost with an average of 2.80%, but both Peru and Colombia are closer to the United States than Mexico for this particular depository institution. The operating cost for the banking system of Mexico was 147% higher than the United States', 17% higher than Peru's, and 2.5% higher than the banking system of Colombia. In the Mexican system, where vertical integration of depository institutions exists, savings banks, or *financieras,* are not only owned, but often operate in concert with commercial banks. Given this organization structure, the allocation of costs becomes somewhat arbitrary.

In further disaggregation of the data, the most extreme case is perhaps that of the *Caja Agraria* (agricultural bank) in Colombia, as can be seen in Appendix Table C13.1. This depository intermediary, with its large branch system, penetrates many relatively remote and otherwise unserviced areas of the country. In 1973 its 741 offices provided the rural sector with more than just financial services; it provided technical assistance, certain types of insurance, and general social and economic assistance. As a result, the *Caja Agraria* consistently shows the highest cost of any sector examined in the countries studied. Its operating costs range from 10.3 to 14.4%, averaging 12.2%. It should be noted that this was the only case where an intermediary was found to provide a substantial service beyond the scope of financial intermediation. Given the relatively low proportion of the aggregate financial system's deposits held by the *Caja*

TABLE 13.3

Aggregate Financial Intermediaries: Profit Margin Per Deposit Unit[a]

Year	Colombia	Mexico	Peru	U.S.
1966	—	.97	.59	.69
1967	1.88	.72	.71	.66
1968	1.87	.86	.80	.86
1969	1.79	.78	.63	.77
1970	2.04	.71	.02	.72
1971	1.72	.67	1.04	.58
1972	1.73	.71	.82	.65
1973	1.71	.61	1.26	.79
Mean	1.82	.75	.73	.72
Variance	.01	.01	.12	.01

[a] Expressed in percentages. Source: See Table 13.1.

TABLE 13.4

Aggregate Financial Intermediaries: Rate Spreads and Their Distribution[a]

Year	Colombia			Mexico			Peru			U.S.		
	$r_a - r$	$c/r_a - r$	$p/r_a - r$	$r_a - r$	$c/r_a - r$	$p/r_a - r$	$r_a - r$	$c/r_a - r$	$p/r_a - r$	$r_a - r$	$c/r_a - r$	$p/r_a - r$
1966	—	—	—	4.87	.80	.20	5.94	.90	.10	2.6	.74	.26
1967	7.59	.75	.25	4.38	.84	.16	5.91	.88	.12	2.55	.74	.26
1968	7.00	.73	.27	4.78	.82	.18	6.84	.88	.12	2.76	.69	.31
1969	6.87	.74	.26	4.50	.83	.17	7.06	.91	.09	3.10	.75	.25
1970	8.28	.75	.25	4.47	.84	.16	6.25	.98	.02	3.28	.78	.22
1971	8.48	.80	.20	4.48	.85	.15	6.42	.84	.16	3.01	.81	.19
1972	9.11	.81	.19	4.46	.84	.16	6.28	.87	.13	2.99	.78	.22
1973	8.78	.81	.19	4.44	.86	.14	6.34	.80	.20	3.17	.75	.25

[a] Source: See Table 13.1.

Agraria, these services did not substantially increase the aggregate system's average cost per deposit unit. Despite the increase in costs from the additional services provided, profit margins were maintained.

13.6.2 Competition

The Colombian financial system was found to be operating with the highest profit margins, with these profit margins per deposit unit averaging 182 basis points for the period studied. The range for the Colombian system was 171–204 basis points. This level was more than twice the profit margin found in the other systems, which were surprisingly similar on the average, ranging from 72 basis points for the United States to 73 for Peru and 75 for Mexico. These data are contained in Table 13.3.

The behavior over time of these profit margins, however, was quite different. In Mexico there was a downtrend of from 90 basis points in 1966 to 61 basis points in 1973. One might suspect increasing competitive forces through entry. In Mexico there was no entry by new competitors, and in fact, the number of existing depository institutions decreased in that time span from 349 to 344. Offsetting this, however, was substantial branching activity, with the total number of depository offices increasing from 2720 in 1966 to 4058 by 1973.

In Peru we find a somewhat different picture; profit margins doubled in

TABLE 13.5

Aggregate Financial Intermediaries: Nominal and Real
Asset Earning and Deposit Rates[a]

	Colombia					Mexico				
	Nominal		Infla-tion rate	Real		Nominal		Infla-tion rate	Real	
Year	r_a	r		r_a	r	r_a	r		r_a	r
1966	—	—	—	—	—	10.85	5.98	4.34	6.51	1.64
1967	10.02	2.43	8.15	—	—	10.45	6.07	2.98	7.47	3.09
1968	9.51	2.51	5.83	3.66	−3.34	11.38	6.60	2.34	9.04	4.26
1969	9.56	2.69	10.11	−.55	−7.42	11.32	6.82	3.70	7.62	3.12
1970	10.93	2.65	6.83	4.10	−4.18	12.32	7.85	5.15	7.17	2.70
1971	11.45	2.97	9.00	2.45	−6.03	12.61	8.13	5.80	6.81	2.33
1972	12.47	3.36	14.31	−1.84	−10.95	11.92	7.46	4.15	7.77	3.31
1973	12.32	3.54	22.79	−10.47	−19.25	11.86	7.42	12.06	−.20	−4.64

[a] Source: Deposit and asset rate: See Table 13.1. Inflation rate is based on each country's consumer price index as reported by the International Monetary Fund in *International Financial Statistics*, Nov. 1971 and July 1975.

the 1966–1973 period from 59 to 126 basis points. In 1970, which was previously noted as the year the government took a competitive position in the financial system, the profit margins of the system were negligible, but in the 3 subsequent years they increased dramatically, suggesting that competition among institutions actually declined. This is substantiated by the fact that between 1968 and 1973 the number of existing institutions declined from 24 to 20, and total banking offices declined from 806 to 771. In Colombia, profit margins decreased slightly in the 7 years under study, as the total number of banking offices increased from 752 to 2200.

13.6.3 Potential Gains in Real Deposit Rates

While it is important in making these comparisons to keep in mind that the United States' financial system is not a standard of excellence, the contrasts provide evidence, however, that substantial gains can be made in real deposit rates in the Latin American financial systems through both reduced operating costs and reduced profit margins. In the case of Colombia, the potential leeway for gains in real deposit rates is in the neighborhood of 400 basis points, in Mexico about 150 basis points, and approximately 340 in the Peruvian case. It is clear from Tables 13.4 and 13.5 that gains of this magnitude could increase inflation-corrected deposit rates such that they would have been positive in many years.

To explain the high cost per deposit unit, one might look to the high fixed costs associated with the large-scale branching found in the Latin Amercian systems as shown in Table 13.6. In the literature concerning

TABLE 13.5 (Continued)

	Peru					U.S.				
	Nominal		Infla-tion rate	Real		Nominal		Infla-tion rate	Real	
Year	r_a	r		r_a	r	r_a	r		r_a	r
1966	8.22	2.28	9.44	−1.22	−7.16	5.08	1.83	2.91	2.17	−1.08
1967	7.92	2.01	9.83	−1.91	−7.02	5.18	1.97	2.83	2.35	−.86
1968	8.91	2.07	18.99	−10.08	−16.92	5.93	2.04	4.18	1.75	−2.14
1969	9.27	2.20	6.25	3.02	−4.05	6.06	2.20	5.35	.71	−3.15
1970	8.35	2.13	5.04	3.31	−2.91	6.37	2.38	5.93	.44	−3.65
1971	8.25	1.83	7.10	1.15	−5.27	6.08	2.39	4.30	1.78	−1.91
1972	8.06	1.78	6.90	1.16	−5.12	5.94	2.39	3.25	2.69	−.86
1973	8.11	1.77	9.51	−1.40	−7.79	6.86	3.05	6.22	.64	−3.17

TABLE 13.6

Branching and Deposit Distribution among Intermediaries, 1973[a]

Colombia

	Commercial banks	Caja Agraria[b]	Banco Central Hipotecario[c]	Corporaciones financieras[a]	Aggregate
Deposits	1,607	222	433	274	2,536
Average branches per intermediary	54	741	54	—	47
Average deposits per intermediary	62	222	433	14	54

Mexico

	Commercial banks	Financieras[a]	Mortgage banks	Aggregate private intermediaries
Deposits	6,057	7,764	1,991	15,812
Average branches per intermediary	18	>1	>1	12
Average deposits per intermediary	27	85	80	46

Peru

	Private commercial banks	Government commercial banks	Regional banks	Foreign banks	Private development banks	Savings banks	Aggregate
Deposits	919	539	64	53	39	68	1,148
Average branches per intermediary	83	111	10	4	2	27	39
Average deposits per intermediary	230	180	11	13	20	68	57

U.S.

	Commercial banks	Savings & loan associations	Mutual savings banks	Aggregate
Deposits	681,619	220,442	83,212	985,273
Average branches per intermediary	1.83	1.36	.30	1.73
Average deposits per intermediary	49	43	172	50

[a] Deposits and average deposits in millions of U.S. dollars. Exchange rate per U.S. dollar: Colombia 24.89, Mexico 12.50, Peru 38.70.
Source: See Table 13.1.
[b] Agricultural bank.
[c] Mortgage bank.
[d] Savings banks.

financial intermediary costs, there are several studies that indicate the relatively higher cost of expansion of the financial system through branching. An alternative hypothesis for these high costs might be that the Latin American systems failed to achieve the economies of scale that are reputedly achieved in financial intermediation. However, examination of Table 13.6 shows that the intermediaries of Colombia, Mexico, and Peru were surprisingly large compared with those of the United States. When deposits of these countries are converted to U.S. dollars at the prevailing rate of exchange, and a comparison is made of average deposits per intermediary in U.S. dollars, we find there are relatively small differences in the aggregate average deposits per institution in all four of the systems. Thus, despite the higher number of branches per intermediary in the Latin American systems, the difference in cost cannot be attributed to difference in size of institution.

It is also plausible that the relatively higher cost per deposit units in the Latin American system resulted from providing some additional services that are imposed on those intermediaries when the governments or the regulatory authorities expect them to perform some "social responsibility" functions. This would increase operating costs and cause these intermediaries to operate at higher costs than those of comparable intermediaries in the United States.

Nonrate competition as a cause of higher operating costs, of course, exists as a possibility. The level of the implicit deposit rate embedded in operating costs depends on competitive pressures. It is not possible to indicate clearly how much of these high operating costs were due to nonrate competitive costs, but the relatively higher profit margins of the Latin American system seem to indicate less competitive pressure to pay implicit deposit rates.

Whatever the reason for the high cost levels found in the Latin American Systems, there is a potential to achieve efficiencies that could translate into higher real deposit rates of as much as between 2 and 4% in real terms. With any reasonable response in the level of real deposits, this could result in sizable real gains to the capital intensity of an economy and thus higher levels of real per capita output.

BIBLIOGRAPHY

Bailey, Martin. "Savings and the Rate of Interest," *Journal of Political Economy,* **56,** August 1957.

Brothers, Dwight, and Solis, Leopoldo. *Mexican Financial Development*. Austin: The University of Texas Press, 1966.

Fry, Marshall J. "Money and Capital or Financial Deepening in Economic Development?", *Journal of Money, Credit and Banking,* **10,** November 1978.

Galbis, Vicente. "Structuralism and Financial Liberalization," *Finance and Development,* **13,** June 1976.

Gurley, John G. "The Savings–Investment Process and the Market for Loanable Funds." In *Money and Economic Activity,* ed. L. Ritter. Boston: Houghton, 1967.

Gurley, John G., and Shaw, Edward S. "Financial Intermediaries and the Saving–Investment Process, *Journal of Finance,* **11,** May 1965.

Leff, Nathaniel H., and Sato, Kazuo. "A Simultaneous Equations Model of Savings in Developing Countries," *Journal of Political Economy,* **83,** December 1975.

McKinnon, Ronald. *Money and Capital in Economic Development.* Washington, D.C.: Brookings Institution, 1973.

McNulty, James E. "A Re-Examination of the Problem of State Usury Ceilings: The Impact in the Mortgage Market," Federal Home Loan Bank Board, Invited Working Paper No. 21, March 1979.

Pflucker, Julio. *Profitability Competition and Efficiency in the Peruvian Banking System.* MBA Professional Report. Austin: University of Texas, May 1976.

Samuelson, Paul A. "An Analytical Evaluation of Interest Rate Ceiling for Savings and Loan Associations and Competitive Institutions." In *A Study of the Savings and Loan Industry.* Federal Home Loan Bank Board, Washington, D.C., 1969.

Shaw, Edward S. *Financial Deepening in Economic Development.* London/New York: Oxford Univ. Press, 1973.

Solow, Robert M. "A Contribution to the Theory of Economic Growth," *Quarterly Journal of Economics,* **70,** February 1956.

Solow, Robert J. *Growth Theory: An Exposition.* London/New York: Oxford Univ. Press, 1970.

Spellman, Lewis J. "Fixed and Flexible Saving Shares in Economic Growth," Graduate School of Business, Working Paper 72–337, Austin: University of Texas, 1972.

Spellman, Lewis J. "Financial Repression in a Model of Growth." In *Money and Finance in Economic Growth and Development,* ed. Ronald McKinnon. New York: Marcel Dekker, 1975.

Spellman, Lewis J., and Dieli, Robert F. "Intermediacion Financiera y Desarrollo Economic de Mexico, 1966–1973," *Centro de Estudios Monetarios Latinoamericanos. Boletin Bimensula,* **24,** March–April 1978.

Tobin, James. "Notes on Optimal Monetary Growth," *Journal of Political Economy,* **76,** July–August 1968.

Tobin, James. "A General Equilibrium Approach to Monetary Theory," *Journal of Money, Credit and Banking,* **1,** Febraury 1969.

Tobin, James. "Deposit Rate Ceilings as a Monetary Control," *Journal of Money, Credit and Banking,* **2,** February 1970.

CHAPTER 14

A Financial Sector in an Aggregate Growth Model

14.1 THE FINANCIAL SYSTEM AND THE TECHNOLOGY OF THE ECONOMY

The purpose of this chapter is to delve into the relationship of economic and financial growth. The linkage of finance to per capita consumption is through its ability to change the production technology of the economy. Finance is seen as a vehicle to accumulate sufficient capital to allow the adoption of a superior production technology—a technology that requires financial intermediation to match surplus and deficit units. The technology of the financed production sector must be able to yield higher per capita output levels even after the diversion of real factors of production into a financial sector is allowed for. This financed technology must generate higher per capita output and consumption for workers of both the production and financial sectors. It must also provide the private incentives for firms to finance their capital stock and for wealth-owners to hold financial instruments in their portfolios. It also examines how private incentives to accumulate capital are affected by usury and deposit ceilings and credit restrictions.

The building blocks of this chapter are the micro- and macroeconomic production functions. A financial technology, or a financial production function, is developed that relates the financial sector's inputs of capital and labor to its output. The influence of a production technology that requires the financing of its capital stock on the economywide capital–labor ratio, marginal product of capital, per capita output and consumption, and the rate of growth output is compared with the same aggregate measures for an economy using merely a self-financed technology. Finally, using the framework of the model of financed capital accumulation, an examination is made of the impact of financial intermediary regulation on the real variables of the economy. The effects of aggregate credit controls, deposit ceilings, and usury ceilings are examined for their real impacts. An optimal deposit rate that maximizes per capita consumption is derived. Finally, the use of monetary seigniorage as a subsidy to deposit holding and capital accumulation is analyzed.

In this chapter, all capital is assumed to be financed through a depository intermediary. This economy is described by a two-sector growth model with a production sector and a financial sector. The real physical capital of the economy is utilized by the business sector for the production of the homogeneous good and by the financial intermediary sector for the production of financial intermediary services. Providing financial services, in short, has a real resource cost. To focus on the real resource allocations and costs, we shall assume that perfect competition exists in both the business and financial sectors, yielding no profit beyond normal economic profit.

In this economy, the economic agent's currently earned share of a homogeneous good is allocated to consumption and to saving. The capital saved is deposited with the depository firm in return for a deposit certificate. The depository firm, in turn, places its capital deposits with a business firm in exchange for a capital certificate issued by the business firm. The wealth-owners of the economy have the option of providing capital for the intermediary's use in return for a capital certificate that is a claim on the intermediary's income. Consequently, the wealth-owners' portfolios consist of deposit certificates and the capital certificates of the financial intermediaries. Capital receives its marginal product, which accrues in this nonmonetary economy in units of the homogeneous good that is paid to the depository intermediary as holder of the business sector capital certificates. The intermediary in turn distributes its receipts of the homogeneous good to depositors and its labor force, and the residual is distributed to its capital certificate holders. This assumes no retained earnings by either type of firm.

The balance sheets that result from these trades are depicted in Figure 14.1.

The allocation of capital to the production and financial sectors and the resulting holdings of capital and financial certificates that are described by these balance sheets arise out of a specialization of function in this economy. The firms in the production sector only produce the homogeneous good, and the firms in the financial sector only produce financial intermediary services. The emergence of specialization in performing the financial services solely through intermediaries can be envisioned if economies of scale obtain in either the gathering or placing of savings. If such economies of scale do not exist, then it is entirely possible that the real resource inputs for matching surplus and deficit units could be conducted by households or business firms. This has been termed direct

Households		Financial sector			Business sector	
Deposit certificates		Business firms' capital certificates	Deposit certificates	K^P		Business firms' capital certificates
	Wealth					
Financial firm's capital certificates		K^F	Financial firm's capital certificates			

Figure 14.1 Sectoral balance sheets.

finance. Direct finance could eliminate the financial sector entirely, but could not eliminate the use of resources in performing financial intermediation service. Inasmuch as the use of resources in performing financial services is more easily described through a financial firm's production function, consideration will be given to the case of indirect finance in which all of the resource use in finance is conducted by the financial intermediary sector.

To explain a financed capital stock, reasons must be found for the economic agents' desire to seek resources beyond their current budgets and for economic agents' willingness to commit their resources to be used by others. In addition, the economic role of the financial middleman in the capital accumulation process must be understood. A clear picture of the inputs and the outputs of the financial firm and the unit price that it charges for its service must be obtained. At the macroeconomic level, it should be understood how the financial intermediary affects the economy's capital–labor ratio as well as per capita consumption and the growth rate of output. As this is a two-sector model, the allocation of resources to both sectors will be explored.

14.2 THE TECHNOLOGIES OF THE PRODUCTION AND FINANCIAL SECTORS

Many assumptions can be made that would give rise to private incentives for lending and borrowing. This model will focus solely on rate-of-return incentives available from two alternative technologies.[1]

---

[1] This assumption excludes reasons for consumption loans that might be due to differences in time preferences.

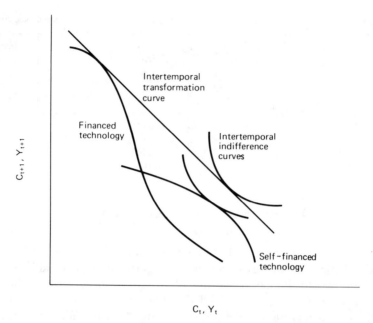

Figure 14.2   Income and consumption with financed and self-financed technologies.

14.2.1   The Microeconomic Technology

The financed production technology assumed in this chapter provides private incentive to wealth-owners to exchange capital for deposit certificates because the certificates' rates of return are more attractive than those that can be earned through the direct application of capital to the self-financed technology. Wealth-owners must work through the financial intermediary, since the superior returns are only available if large blocks of capital are applied to this process.

Such a technology is shown in Figure 14.2 for the simplest two-period Fisherian example for which income and consumption possibilities in each period are measured on the axes.[2] It can be seen in Figure 14.2 that the technology requiring finance provides superior returns to capital if a sufficient scale of capital is reached.

It could be argued that individual economic agents might seek to circumvent the financial intermediaries. One possibility would be to undertake direct finance, but this has previously been understood to be relatively inefficient in comparison with indirect finance. Another alternative for circumventing the financial intermediaries would arise from the possi-

[2] This diagram was suggested by Ronald McKinnon in *Money and Capital in Economic Development* (Washington, D.C.: Brookings Institution, 1973), p. 20.

bility of self-finance. Self-finance, however, is also undesirable in this model because rates of return lower than the deposit rate would accrue to the individual economic agent who attempted to self-finance either of the two possible production technologies.

Thus, superior returns and higher income levels in both time periods from pooled savings provide incentives for wealth-owners to lend capital and business firms to borrow capital; this gives rise to the financial certificates that are a by-product of these trades. The pooling of capital for the purpose of risk reduction is possible, but here we merely examine the incentives presented by the net output differences in a world of certainty.

14.2.2 The Macroeconomic Technology

On the macroeconomic level, the technology will be designated as

$$Y^f = Y^f(K, L), \tag{14.1}$$

with the superscript f signifying that this is a production technology that requires financing. In this process, expansion is also carried out by the addition of new firms, each producing at minimum average cost. The aggregate technology with finance is thus linear homogeneous.

It has been stipulated that the marginal returns to capital in the process requiring finance are equal to or exceed the returns to capital in the self-financed process. Yet, in order to maintain sufficient incentives to commit capital to the financed technology, the marginal return, net of financial costs, must still be greater than the return to self-financed capital. When there is no profit in financial intermediation and all net revenues per deposit unit are paid out, this condition can be stated as

$$Y^f_K(k) - c \geq Y^s_K(k) \tag{14.2}$$

for all k. Here c is the real factor cost of the financial sector per unit of capital and Y^s_K is the marginal product of capital in the self-financed sector. The unit cost of finance is the maximum yield differential between the technologies necessary to maintain incentives to funnel capital through a financial system. This minimum condition is shown in Figure 14.3.

If Eq. (14.2) is integrated with respect to K at all points in time,

$$\int_0^K Y^f_K \, dK - \int_0^K c \, dK \geq \int_0^K Y^s_K \, dK \tag{14.3}$$

or

$$Y^f(K, L) - cK \geq Y^s(K, L). \tag{14.4}$$

The output of the homogeneous good produced by the financed technology must be equal to or exceed the output of the homogeneous good pro-

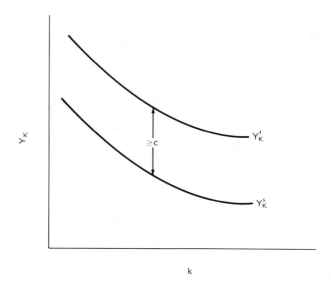

Figure 14.3   Marginal productivities differences.

duced by the self-financed technology by an amount cK. Therefore, the financed technology is superior not only on the basis of a rate of return to capital, but on an output basis as well.[3] This is shown in Figure 14.4. As will be discussed in a later section, this added amount of output is necessary to pay for the real resources employed by the financial sector.

14.2.3   The Micro-Level Financial Firm

The role of the financial firm in this model is that of a middleman gathering and allocating capital and distributing income to the factors of production in the financial sector and to depositors. The work required in the processing of capital can be conceptualized as a financial production function that relates the required factor inputs by the financial firm to the stock

---

[3] In this section, we discuss the private incentives that will lead to a shift in capital from the self-financed technology to the financed. From the point of view of the economic planner, the appropriate comparison might be in terms of the level of output from the financed technology that will be produced after recognizing the redirection of resources into the financial sector. That is, if $Y^f(K - K^f, L - L^f) > Y^s(K, L)$, where K^f and L^f are capital and labor committed to the financial sector, then the planner should switch to the financed technology and direct factors of production to the financial sector. A crucial determinant of whether the output of the self-financed technology will be greater than the financed technology rests on the factor requirements in finance for any given level of capital in the production sector. These factor requirements in finance will be set by the production function of the financial sector.

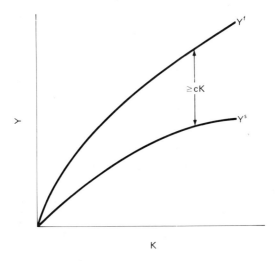

Figure 14.4   Output differences.

of capital that the financial firm places with the firms of the business sector. Thus, the unit of output of the financial firm is the capital stock that it places with producers. The production function for the ith financial firm can be written

$$K_i^p = K^p(K_i^f, L_i^f). \qquad (14.5)$$

For simplicity's sake, let it be assumed that the certificates have a maturity of one time period. In this case, the resource cost associated with financial intermediation derives from (1) the gathering of the total stock of capital from households, (2) the placement of this capital with business firms, (3) the liquidation of these capital loans to depositors at the end of the period, and (4) the distribution of the returns from production sector capital to depositors and to the factors employed in finance. All work—(1) through (4)—performed by the intermediary is related to the total production sector stock of capital. This production function would also be reasonable if any other fixed maturity date were assumed. For example, if a two-period maturity obtained, the work done in gathering capital and redistributing this capital to depositors would be performed every other period, and the work done in any single period would be related to one-half the stock of capital. With infinite maturities, resource cost would be related to new capital accumulation, which in steady state growth is also proportional to the stock of capital.[4]

Given the financial firm's production function, its isoquants and unit

---

[4] See footnote 7, Chapter 12.

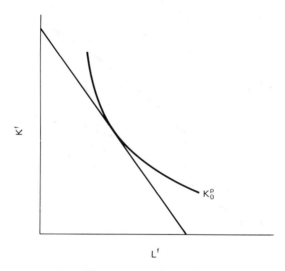

Figure 14.5 Financial firm isoquant.

cost curves can be conceptualized. An isoquant that would result from this production function is shown in Figure 14.5, where the isoquant represents the required capital and labor K^f and L^f employed by the depository intermediary to maintain a given level of capital in the production sector, denoted as K_0^p. This process might also be viewed simply as a requirement that the depository intermediary increase its capital and labor inputs as its deposit liability increases, or equivalently, as its assets increase. If the financial firm is operating efficiently, the choice of the input mix of capital and labor that minimizes cost depends on relative factor prices.

The financial firm, having a claim on the capital of the business sector, receives revenue per unit of capital. This unit revenue, or the unit price of output of the financial firm, is the marginal product of capital. This can also be looked at as a loan rate. It is the nonmonetary economy's equivalent of the asset earning rate of Chapters 3–11. This unit price must cover all costs of operation. The unit costs of the financial firm are the payments to both capital and labor factor inputs, which is denoted c, and a real deposit rate that the firm must pay to deposit holders for the use of their capital, denoted r.

The deposit rate under perfect competition in deposit markets is

$$r = Y_K - c. \qquad (14.6)$$

One could conceptualize revenues and costs on a per unit of output basis. The unit of output is the capital stock maintained in the production

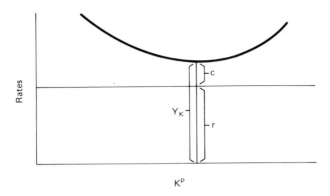

Figure 14.6 Average cost per unit of output.

sector, and the unit price of this output is the marginal product of capital, or the loan rate. The costs of financial intermediation are the deposit rate and the unit cost of finance; this is depicted by a U-shaped cost curve. The unit cost of finance is the average production cost per unit of capital processed by the financial firm. It is obviously the nonmonetary economy's equivalent to the average production cost of Chapters 3–11. If perfect competition prevails in the financial sector and all firms have the same technology, the revenues per unit will gravitate toward the low point of the firms' cost curve.

Another manner of describing the operation of financial intermediation is that the financial firm purchases capital as an intermediate input and at the unit cost of r. It then processes this capital and receives Y_K for the processed capital. The difference in the price between unprocessed capital and processed capital is c. This, then, can be looked upon as value added from the processing of capital. The value added is then distributed to factor inputs in financial intermediation.

Technical change in financial intermediation can be regarded as a shift in the financial production function, an inward shift in the isoquants, or a downward shift in the unit cost curve. Technical change, along with competition, will tend to cause c to diminish.

14.2.4 The Macro-Level Financial Sector

At the sectoral level, the financial production function is

$$K^p = K^p(K^f, L^f). \tag{14.7}$$

Here K^p is the aggregate capital stock of the production sector, and capital and labor inputs into financial intermediation are denoted as K^f and L^f. It is assumed at the aggregate level that this production function is linear homogeneous, as expansion is carried out by the introduction of new firms each operating efficiently. It is assumed that the marginal products of capital and labor are positive and diminishing:

$$K^p_{K'}, K^p_{L'} > 0, \qquad K^p_{K'K'}, K^p_{L'L'} < 0 \qquad (14.8)$$

14.3   THE DISTRIBUTION OF INCOME BETWEEN SECTORS

Income in this economy must be distributed to the factors of production in each sector. Inasmuch as the production sector is the only sector capable of producing final output, its product must be distributed to the factors of both sectors. Given the linear homogeneous macrotechnology by Euler's theorem, aggregate output can be expressed in the following way:

$$Y = Y_L L^p + Y_K K^p. \qquad (14.9)$$

Since the financial sector distributes its revenues Y_K to depositors and to factors in finance, by Eq. (14.6) this expression can be rewritten

$$Y = Y_L L^p + rK^p + cK^p. \qquad (14.10)$$

Furthermore, inasmuch as the financial production function is linear homogeneous, it, in turn, can be broken down in the following way:

$$K^p = K^p_{K'} K^f + K^p_{L'} L^f. \qquad (14.11)$$

Substituting (14.11) into (14.10) yields

$$Y = Y_L L^p + rK^p + cK^p_{K'} K^f + cK^p_{L'} L^f. \qquad (14.12)$$

If firms in both sectors maximize profits under competition, they will set the value of the marginal product of each factor equal to factor costs:

$$Y = w_p L^p + rK^p + w_f K^f + r_f L^f. \qquad (14.13)$$

This means that the value of the marginal product of capital and labor in finance is expressed as

$$cK^p_{K'} = r_f \quad \text{and} \quad cK^p_{L'} = w_f. \qquad (14.14)$$

Because there are no differences in risk in a certainty model, wealth-owners consider the certificates to be perfect substitutes, and because laborers consider employment in either sector to be perfect substitutes, their allocations drive the returns to each factor into equality. This implies

$$w_f = w_p = w \quad \text{and} \quad r = r_f. \qquad (14.15)$$

Making these substitutions into Eq. (14.13), the distribution of income between the factors of production in the two sectors can be written as

$$Y = wL^p + rK^p + wL^f + rK^f. \qquad (14.16)$$

Thus, the product is totally exhausted when competitive distribution is made to the factors of production to each sector.

14.4   OUTPUT, CONSUMPTION, AND ALLOCATION IN THE TWO-SECTOR MODEL

The two-sector model itself is described by the two-production functions[5]

$$Y = Y(K^p, L^p) \qquad (14.17)$$

and

$$K^p = K^p(K^f, L^f). \qquad (14.18)$$

The inputs to the production and financial sectors must add up to total factors at every point in time t so that

$$K^p(t) + K^f(t) = K(t) \qquad (14.19)$$

and

$$L^p(t) + L^f(t) = L(t). \qquad (14.20)$$

The labor force, as in Chapter 13, is assumed to grow at the natural rate n. All laborers seek work, no matter what the prevailing wage, and they allocate their services between sectors such that wage rates in the two sectors are equal.

The portfolio behavior of wealth-owners can be expressed as in Chapter 13. The demand for wealth is an increasing function of the rate of return to wealth and linear homogeneous in net real income. Wealth-owners allocate their capital between sectors such that rates of return are equal.

The demand for production sector capital (or, equivalently, the deposit certificates of the depository intermediary) depends on its rate of return. With the financed model, the return to production sector capital accrues as a deposit rate:

$$K^p = W(r)Y. \qquad (14.21)$$

Because the deposit rate is equal to the marginal product of capital less c

---

[5] The superscript of Y^f is assumed and will be dropped for the remainder of this chapter.

[the unit cost of finance by Eq. (14.6)], the demand for capital in the production sector can be rewritten

$$K^p = W(Y_K - c)Y. \qquad (14.22)$$

The model might be formalized into a simultaneous system of five equations and five unknowns. The unknowns are k, the overall capital–labor ratio; k^p and k^f, the sectoral capital labor ratios; c, the unit production cost of finance; and h, the proportion of the total labor force in the production sector.

The five equations can be derived as follows. As in Chapter 13 Eqs. (13.12) and (13.14), the production function equation (14.17) is combined with the deposit demand curve. With stable growth, this will yield an expression equivalent to Eq. (13.15), except that in this case, because of perfect competition, the profit margin p is 0 by assumption:

$$\dot{K}^p = [(W(Y_K - c)Y_K)/(1 - W(Y_K - c)Y_K)]\dot{L}^p. \qquad (14.23)$$

The capital–labor ratio of the production sector is again equivalent to Eq. (13.17):

$$k^p = (W(Y_k - c)Y_K)/(1 - W(Y_K - c)Y_K). \qquad (14.24)$$

From this equation, one of the primary interactions between the sectors can be clearly seen. The level of efficiency of the depository industry is reflected in the level of c. Forces that tend to lower c will tend to raise the deposit rate and tend to raise k^p.

Two equations can also be obtained from the private allocations that drive the returns to the factors into equality:

$$r = cK_{K'}^p \quad \text{or} \quad Y_K - c = cK_{K'}^p \qquad (14.25)$$

and

$$Y_L = cK_{L'}^p. \qquad (14.26)$$

The equality of the rates of return to capital, Eq. (14.25), can be written as

$$c = Y_K/(1 + K_{K'}^p) = (1/1 + K_{K'}^p)Y_K. \qquad (14.27)$$

In this form c, the equation for the unit cost of finance, has some intuitive appeal. If the technology of the economy is such that for each unit of capital in the production sector there is a requirement of a unit of capital in the financial sector, the marginal product of capital in the financial sector is equal to 1. Substituting this value into Eq. (14.27) yields

$$c = (1/2)Y_K, \qquad (14.28)$$

and substituting this into the equation for the deposit rate, we find that the deposit rate is equal to just one-half the marginal product of capital in the production sector:

$$r = Y_k - c = Y_K(1 - (1/2)) = .5Y_K. \qquad (14.29)$$

Consequently, as the capital requirements of this economy are doubled because this technology requires a unit of capital in the financial sector to gather resources, the return to capital via the deposit rate is reduced by one-half. Similarly, a marginal productivity of financial sector capital of two reduces the deposit rate by a third, etc.

Another equation of the model can be derived from the constraint equation (14.19), whereby the overall capital–labor ratio is equal to the weighted capital–labor ratios of each sector:

$$k = hk^p + (1 - h)k^f. \qquad (14.30)$$

The weight h, the proportion of labor in the production sector, is equal to

$$h = L^p/L. \qquad (14.31)$$

A fifth equation can be derived from the financial production function. If the financial production function were divided by L^f, we would arrive at

$$K^p/L^f = K^p(k^f, 1). \qquad (14.32)$$

The left-hand side of this equation can be written

$$(K^p/L^p)(L^p/L^f). \qquad (14.33)$$

By Eq. (14.20), the ratio of labor in the two sectors can be expressed

$$L^p/L^f = h/(1 - h), \qquad (14.34)$$

and the financial production function can be written as

$$k^p = ((1 - h)/h)K^p(k^f, 1). \qquad (14.35)$$

In summary then, the five-variable model can be simultaneously solved by use of the following five equations:

$$k^p = (W(Y_K(k^p) - c)Y_L(k^p))/(1 - W(Y_K(k^p) - c)Y_K(k^p)), \qquad (14.24)$$

$$Y_K(k^p) = c + cK_{\!K}^p(k^f), \qquad (14.25)$$

$$Y_L(k^p) = cK_{\!L}^p(k^f), \qquad (14.26)$$

$$k = hk^p + (1 - h)k^f, \qquad (14.30)$$

and

$$k^p = ((1 - h)/h)K^p(k^f, 1). \qquad (14.35)$$

Other aggregate measures can then be derived from the equilibrium capital–labor ratio. Output per capita in this system is

$$Y/L = (1/L)(L^p)Y(K^p/L^p), 1) = hY(k^p, 1). \qquad (14.36)$$

Notice that output per capita depends on the proportion of the labor force h directly engaged in the production of the homogeneous good. This is an explicit recognition that only production sector workers produce final-good output, which must be shared by workers of both sectors.

As in Chapter 13, Eq. (13.21) investment per capita is equal to kn in balanced growth. The investment requirement per capita is the sum of investment requirements for each industry. This k is an aggregate or weighted capital–labor ratio.

Consumption per capita is equal to the difference between output per capita and investment requirements per capita. It reflects the facts that only the production sector produces output and both sectors use part of the output as capital inputs:

$$c = hY(k^p, 1) - nk. \qquad (14.37)$$

From this formulation it is clear that the greater the equilibrium proportion of labor in the production sector, the higher will be per capita consumption. In a state of balanced growth with equilibrium capital–labor ratios, and with a linear homogeneous technology, the growth rate of this system is equal to n.

14.5   THE REAL ECONOMIC IMPACT OF FINANCE: A COMPARISON OF MODELS

A comparison of the self-financed economy and the financed economy can be made from the assumptions regarding the technology developed in Section 14.2. There it was assumed that the financed production technology must yield higher returns to capital, even after the real production cost of finance is deducted. This is necessary to provide incentives to wealth-owners so that they direct their capital to this technology through the depository intermediaries. In this way, the returns to capital from the financed technology in the form of a deposit rate [by Eq. (14.6) the marginal product of capital less the unit production cost of finance] exceed the returns to capital from the self-financed economy for any given capital–labor ratio.

This condition is stated in Eq. (14.2) in which the returns to the financed technology must exceed the return to the self-financed technol-

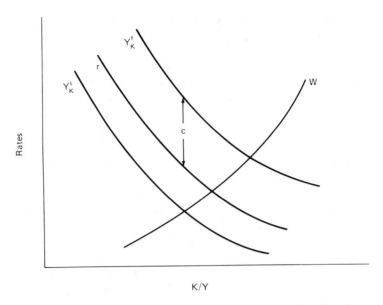

Figure 14.7   Net yields from financed and self-financed technologies.

ogy by an amount c:[6]

$$Y_K^f(k) - c \geq Y_K^s(k). \qquad (14.2)$$

The impact of this assumed condition can be examined through the use
of Figure 14.7, which shows the net yield curves for both the financed and
self-financed technologies. These net yield curves, which relate yield to
the capital–output ratio, have been developed in Chapter 13. With the assumed difference in the return to capital, the net yield curve for the
financed economy lies above the net yield of the self-financed economy.
The net yield of the self-financed economy is simply the marginal product
of capital, and the net yield of the financed economy is the marginal product of production sector capital less the unit cost of finance.

Figure 14.7 indicates that for the same wealth preferences, the equilibrium rate of return to wealth-owning for the financed economy will exceed

[6] To facilitate comparisons between the models, the notation of Section 14.2 has been
adopted; the superscripts f and s refer to the financed or the self-financed production technology, and the terms k^p and k^f refer to the capital–labor ratios of the production sector and
the financial sector of the financed model. The aggregate capital–labor ratio is simply referred to as k, which in the self-financed model is also the capital–labor ratio of the production sector. For the self-financed technology, k or k^p are used interchangeably.

the return to capital in the self-financed economy. The equilibrium capital–output and capital–labor ratios will also be higher for the financed economy.

The crucial comparison of the models in welfare terms can be made in an examination of per capita consumption from the two models. Per capita consumption for the self-financed technology is obtained in the same way as for the financed technology. From Eq. (14.37) we have

$$c^f = h Y^f(k^p, 1) - nk \quad \text{and} \quad c^s = Y^s(k, 1) - nk. \quad (14.38)$$

Any differences in the two are reflected in differences in the first term, which is per capita output. That is, if $h Y^f(k^p, 1)$ exceeds $Y^s(k, 1)$, then per capital consumption from the financed technology exceeds that of the self-financed technology. It is possible to make the comparison of per capita output from assumptions previously made. The output comparison of the two technologies is given by Eq. (14.4) in which $Y^f(K, L) - cK \geq Y^s(K, L)$. In this form, the output of the financed technology is stated in terms of applying all of the economy's capital and labor to the financed technology and then deducting the real cost of the output of the homogeneous good because of the necessity of diverting resources to the financial sector. The output loss from operating the financial sector is proportional to the capital stock, but despite this loss, net output is greater than the output of the self-financed technology:

$$Y^f(K, L) - cK = Y^f(K^p, L^p) \geq Y^s(K, L). \quad (14.39)$$

In terms of per capita output, the comparison is stated as

$$Y^f(k, 1) - ck = h Y^f(k^p, 1) \geq Y^s(k, 1). \quad (14.40)$$

The difference in per capita output for the two technologies can be seen in Figure 14.8 for any k. Thus, per capita output for workers of both sectors is higher under the financed technology even after resources are deflected away from production.

To derive the difference between the two economies in terms of per capita consumption, the per capita consumption expression (14.37) is rewritten with the use of Eq. (14.40):

$$c^f = Y^f(k, 1) - ck - nk. \quad (14.41)$$

The difference in per capita consumption is shown in Figure 14.9 for any level of k.

The difference is positive by Eq. (14.40) and an increasing function of k by Eq. (14.2). Thus, a higher capital–labor ratio for the financed technology along with a superior technology will ensure a higher level of per capita consumption. This is true whether the equilibrium capital–labor ratio

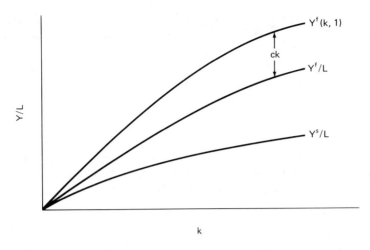

Figure 14.8   Per capita output from financed and self-financed technologies.

of the self-financed model lies to the left (undercapitalized) or to the right (overcapitalized) of the capital–labor ratio corresponding to the maximum level of per capita consumption.

In addition to the technological differences between the two regimes, it is also possible that the financed technology could lead to higher per capita consumption through possible differences in the demand for wealth in financial form, as compared to the direct capital holdings of the self-financed model. If the certainty assumptions of this model were relaxed and the possibility of the intermediary reducing risk through diversification were introduced, the demand for financial intermediary deposit certificates would shift for any given rate of return. Other possible factors such as divisibility or liquidity might also account for a greater demand for

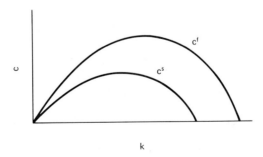

Figure 14.9   Per capita consumption from financed and self-financed technologies.

capital holdings through the deposit certificates than was present under self-financed capital holdings. These possibilities would result in a shift to the right for the W curve and lead to a higher capital–labor ratio and a lower deposit rate. (See Figure 14.11.) A higher capital–labor ratio would result in movement along the c^f curve.

14.6 THE OPTIMUM DEPOSIT RATE

A standard criterion for optimality—the maximization of per capita consumption—can be utilized to derive an optimum deposit rate.

For the self-financed economy, c^s from Eq. (14.38) is maximized with respect to k:

$$c^s = Y^s(k, 1) - nk. \tag{14.42}$$

The condition for a maximum is

$$Y^s_k(k) = n, \tag{14.43}$$

which indicates that the capital–labor ratio should be selected that equates the marginal product of capital to the population growth rate—a standard result of growth theory.

For the financed economy, c^f from Eq. (14.41) is maximized with respect to k.[7] The condition for a maximum is

$$Y^f_k(k) = n + c. \tag{14.44}$$

Since $c > 0$, the optimum marginal product of capital for the financed model economy is higher than for the self-financed economy. Diagrammatically, this is shown in Figure 14.10.

Since the deposit rate from Eq. (14.6) is equal to the marginal product of production sector capital less the unit cost of finance, $r = Y^f_k(k^p) - c$, and when the production sector capital intensity k^p is equal to the overall capital intensity, the optimum deposit rate r^* reduces to the population

---

[7] The maximum per capita consumption can also be derived with respect to the sectoral capital–labor ratios. By Eq. (14.37), per capita consumption can be written $c^f = hY^f(k^p, 1) - nk$. Substituting Eq. (14.30) for k, the expression becomes

$$c^f = hY^f(k^p, 1) - n(hk^p + (1 - h)k^f).$$

Where the sectors' capital intensities are the same, c^f can be maximized with respect to k^p. In this case, the maximum per capita consumption for the financed technology is found, where

$$Y^f_k(k^p) = (1/h)n.$$

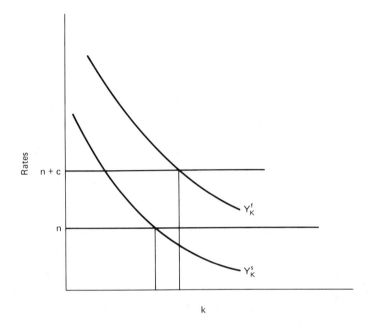

Figure 14.10   Optimum capital intensity.

growth rate:

$$r^* = n + c - c = n. \tag{14.45}$$

Thus the wealth-owner obtains the same yield at the margin on his savings, but the marginal product of capital, the capital intensity, and per capita output and consumption are higher in the financed economy.

14.7   THE REAL ECONOMIC IMPACT OF FINANCIAL REGULATION: A COST–BENEFIT ANALYSIS

It is possible to use the model to analyze the costs and benefits of financial regulation and to also examine their aggregate economic effects. Regulation will be assumed to have the effect of increasing c, the unit cost of finance. This can occur from cost increases to the depository firm because of required reports, examinations, or any other means that would cause the depository firm to use real resources and thus shift its cost curve. Such an effect might also occur through a more indirect manner, such as the establishment of a regulatory agency that uses real resources itself.

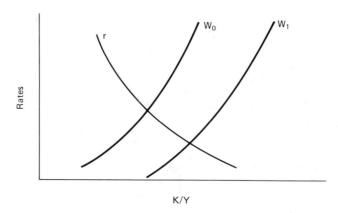

Figure 14.11   Real effects from financial stability.

This can be interpreted as a downward shift in the net yield curve as an increase in c is experienced. As indicated in Chapter 13, an increase in c will lower the capital–labor ratio. In an economy that is not overcapitalized, this will lower per capita consumption.

The benefits of financial regulation or deposit insurance can be realized through a shift in the demand for financial wealth in the form of deposit certificates. This would occur if wealth-owners were to perceive deposit

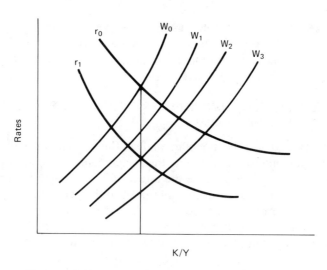

Figure 14.12   Costs and benefits of financial regulation.

certificates as more desirable at given deposit rates because of the exist-ence of a regulatory body backing or stabilizing the industry.

This shift in the W curve results in a lower deposit rate, a higher capital intensity, and higher levels of per capita consumption for the undercapital-ized economy. This is shown in Figure 14.11.

A balanced appraisal of the effects of financial regulation results from weighing the costs against the benefits of regulation. As indicated above, the cost of regulation will shift the r curve downward, and the regulation, if effective, will shift the W curve to the right. The impact on the deposit rate is clearly in the direction of reducing it. The impact on the capital–output ratio and thus other aggregate measures is less clear. A relatively weak shift in the W_o curve to W_1 will produce a lower capital output ratio; a shift to W_2 will produce no change in this ratio; and a strong shift to W_3 will result in an increase. These possibilities are shown in Figure 14.12.

14.8 FINANCIAL AND ECONOMIC REPRESSION FROM DEPOSIT AND LOAN RATE CEILINGS AND CREDIT RESTRICTIONS

A simple extension of the framework allows the analysis of the real eco-nomic and financial impacts of an imposed loan or deposit rate ceiling. Both cases are shown in Figure 14.13. If a loan rate or usury ceiling is im-

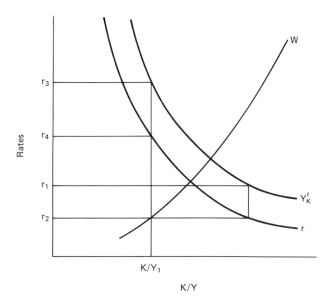

Figure 14.13 Usury and deposit rate ceilings and capital–output ratios.

posed at the rate level r_1, the depository firm must cover its unit costs and is then only able to pay a deposit rate amounting to r_2. At this deposit rate, the financial sector will only attract a capital–income ratio of K/Y_1. Since the intermediary can only charge r_1 for its capital, there is an excess demand for capital by firms. This scarce capital must then be rationed by the financial intermediary. If the amount of capital K/Y_1 is available for investment and is allocated to its highest use, it will earn a marginal product equal to r_3 for which firms pay r_1, and the differential would accrue to the business firm. This differential would undoubtedly give rise to efforts on the part of firms to secure the rationed capital, as it could be usefully employed in all projects for which the marginal productivity exceeds or is equal to r_1. Since there are many applications for which capital will earn more than r_1 but less than r_3, it is plausible that capital might not earn its highest rate. Thus, loan rate ceilings not only cause an undercapitalization, but present the possibility of a misallocation of scarce capital resources. The same results occur for aggregate credit restrictions at, for instance, K/Y_1. The depository industry becomes the recipient of an increased rate spread and profit, and the economy suffers from undercapitalization and a possible misallocation of scarce capital resources.

If the deposit rate ceiling were imposed at r_2, this rate would again only attract a deposit–income ratio of K/Y_1. As before, this amount of capital would be allocated to business firms, and with no loan rate ceiling, the intermediary could charge r_3 and earn r_4 after its factor costs were covered. Thus, it would be possible for the financial firm to earn regulatory rents amounting to the difference between r_4 and r_2. The disposition of this surplus could take many forms. If competition prevails in the depository industry, the nonrate competitive responses described in Chapter 7 will result.

In summary, both cases of interest rate ceilings are similar in that they tend to result in a lower deposit rate, a repressed financial system, a lower capital intensity, and an increased rate spread between capital's marginal product in production and the real deposit rates paid to wealth-owners. Hence, as deposit rates do not accurately reflect the scarcity of capital, a state of undercapitalization prevails in the economy.

It should also be noted that the result, particularly for the case of the loan rate ceiling, is decidedly the converse of what someone with Keynesian reflexes would anticipate. *Depressed loan rates caused by a ceiling are not consistent with a high capital intensity and a high investment level.*

In addition to a low capital intensity, another far-reaching impact from deposit and loan rate ceilings might occur. If the rate of return received by wealth-owners is less than their possible earnings under self-finance, one might expect not only a reduction in the size of the financial sector but, a return to self-financed techniques.

14.9 MONETARY SEIGNIORAGE AND PRIVATE CAPITAL FORMATION

Monetary seigniorage has been utilized by governments in a variety of ways that were described in Chapter 12. In this section the use of money issue as a stimulant to private capital formation through the depository system will be considered. This is accomplished when seigniorage proceeds are allocated to depositors at depository institutions in order to augment real deposit rates and hence attract higher levels of wealth-owning. This signifies an intention to stimulate private savings and capital formation through financial intermediaries that can attract and direct resources to the highest yielding investments.

Total real monetary growth per period is given by

$$\dot{M}/P \equiv m(\dot{M}/M), \tag{14.46}$$

where M is nominal outside money, P is the price level, and m is real outside money balances.[8]

Real monetary growth per real unit of financial intermediary deposits d is then

$$(m/d)(\dot{M}/M). \tag{14.47}$$

Where this monetary subsidy per unit of real financial wealth is passed on to depositors, either by the financial intermediary or directly by government, the real deposit rate then becomes

$$r = Y_K^f - c + (m/d)(\dot{M}/M). \tag{14.48}$$

It should be noted that the real deposit rate includes the current proceeds of the investments of the depository firm net of real unit costs as well as the per deposit share of the seigniorage revenues. In most instances of seigniorage, banks collect the seigniorage revenue from inside money issue by paying a zero deposit rate and thus do not pass on to depositors the current proceeds Y_K^f from real investment, except perhaps through the implicit deposit rate. In this scheme, the investment proceeds, however, are passed on to depositors, and thus the depositor is the recipient of the flow of net real income from *both* private capital formation and from outside monetary creation.

[8] The concept of inside and outside money is, of course, from John Gurley and Edward S. Shaw, *Money in a Theory of Finance* (Washington, D.C.: Brookings Institution, 1960).

When seigniorage revenues from outside money issue are shifted to the depositors of the financial system to stimulate private capital formation, this constitutes an upward shift in the net yield curve r discussed in the previous sections. The quantitative impact of this policy would depend on the magnitude of the real deposit rate increase and the elasticity of the demand for deposits with respect to that rate.

A final evaluation of the policy rests on a comparison of the gains to private capital formation with the opportunity cost of the gain in public capital formation when the seigniorage revenues are utilized by the state in other ways. However, such a quantitative comparison alone is incomplete, as one does not know if public capital formation will take place at the highest rates of return, whereas there is a strong presumption that a competitive private financial system will more efficiently allocate these funds.

Finally, it should be noted that a policy of monetary subsidy in conjunction with deposit rate ceilings could be even more depressing than was noted in the previous section, as real deposit rates will only increase if the intermediary is free to pass on fully to depositors the monetary premiums, as they will surely suffer the inflation tax on deposits. A deposit rate ceiling along with inflation could lower real deposit rates and thus lower private savings, even if the intention of the monetary issue was to shift the seigniorage revenues to the depositors.

14.10   SUMMARY

This chapter attempted to identify clearly one variable that could be responsible for the existence of a financed capital stock. This inducement for finance is the availability of a production technology that affords superior rates of return to wealth if savings are pooled. The gains that result from financing the capital stock and utilizing the economies-of-scale production technology can ultimately be measured in terms of consumption per capita. A comparison between the models of the self-financed technology and the financed technology also indicates higher rates of return to capital and a higher capital–labor ratio for the financed technology. The comparison between the models does not indicate, however, that the financing of the capital stock would necessarily lead to higher per capita consumption levels. Rather, a precondition in the form of a superior production technology and an efficient financial technology must exist to realize per capita consumption gains. The superior production technology must be attainable only through the pooling of savings, and the financial technology must be efficient enough not to reduce the rate of return to capital below that which might exist from alternatively self-financed projects.

The real cost of providing financial services can be calculated in terms of the reduced rate of return per unit of capital c or in terms of the opportunity cost of commodities foregone through the necessity of diverting factors of production to the financial sector. This opportunity cost in terms of final output is cK. The real cost of finance can also be viewed in terms of required factor inputs to the financial sector. These factor inputs are specified by the financial production function for any level of the production sector capital stock. Financial intermediary regulation has both costs and potential benefits. The costs add to the unit cost of finance, and the benefits accrue through increases in wealth-holding in financial form. The impact of financial intermediary regulation can ultimately be measured in terms of the capital stock and output per capita.

BIBLIOGRAPHY

Cathcart, Charles D. "Monetary Dynamics, Growth, and the Efficiency of Inflationary Finance," *Journal of Money, Credit and Banking,* **6,** May 1974.

Friedman, Milton. "Government Revenue from Inflation," *Journal of Political Economy,* **79,** July–August 1971.

Johnson, Harry G. "Inside Money, Outside Money, Income, Wealth and Welfare in Monetary Theory," *Journal of Money, Credit and Banking,* **1,** February 1969.

Miller, Randall J. "The Manpower Cost of Bank Examination." In *State and Federal Regulation of Commercial Banks,* vol. II. Federal Deposit Insurance Corporation, Washington, D.C.

Patinkin, Don. "Inside Money, Monopoly Bank Profits, and Real-Balance Effect, A Comment," *Journal of Money, Credit and Banking,* **3,** May 1971.

Phelps, Edmund S. *Golden Rules of Economic Growth: Studies of Efficient and Optimal Investment,* New York: Norton, 1966.

Solow, Robert M. "A Contribution to the Theory of Economic Growth," *Quarterly Journal of Economics,* **70,** February 1956.

Spellman, Lewis J. "Finance as an Industry: A Model of Growth." Ph.D. dissertation, Stanford University, 1971.

PART IV

Summary

CHAPTER 15

Regulation and Deregulation: The Forces at Work

15.1 RECAPITULATION

This study has examined the depository institutions and the financial intermediation process as they evolved in the United States. An alternative set of historical pressures would no doubt have resulted in a different configuration of financial instruments, depository institutions, and regulatory controls. What shapes this nation's or any nation's historical record are the powerful market forces affecting financial intermediation. Market forces create the opportunities for private individuals to profitably connect surplus and deficit units.

There are a variety of circumstances that would cause an economy to move to a system of financial claims that joins surplus and deficit units. If the optimal firm size in the industrial sector provides incentives for large-scale or lumpy capital accumulation, those firms will attract capital if its earning rate exceeds the potential returns to capital in self-financed production. When there is a gap in the marginal productivities, capital will flow in order to reconstitute production.

Another force giving rise to financial intermediation is gaps in net rates and in net risks in different uses of capital. One possibility often presented is the existence of rate differentials on securities of different maturities. The differential in rates along a yield curve allows financial institutions to purchase higher yielding long-term assets and attract deposit funds in competition with lower yielding short-term rates. Other incentives for financial intermediation come when gaps are presented not only by arbitraging rates between maturities, firms, and geographic locations, but also through a bundling of assets in a way that reduces the variability of earnings or increases liquidity. Each of these gaps must be large enough to generate revenues that will more than cover the resource cost of financial intermediation.

There are a variety of financial firms that could step into the role of providing financial services between lenders and borrowers. The depository

343

firm is a common response to that market gap. The deposit claim is quite divisible, can be liquid, can exploit economies of scale in production, and generally keeps transaction costs for the depositor to a minimum. The exact form of the depository claim and its contractual terms can be quite flexible. The return, maturity, amount, and even the risks can be varied so that numerous depository claims exist and their exact terms follow market demands.

The description of the basic forces affecting the depository firm is contained in the model developed in Chapter 3. The depository firm is characterized as one that maximizes profit and in so doing selects a deposit rate suitable for that deposit market. That deposit rate depends on the earning capacity of the portfolio, the marginal costs of production, and the competitiveness of the deposit market. The depository firm sets a deposit rate, and the market's wealth-owners respond by selecting a deposit level consistent with their incomes and alternative market yields. In that model, the depository firm was free to place its deposit inflows into both interest-yielding earning assets and cash. The optimal cash position in a regulatory-free environment was examined in Chapter 6 by evaluating the expected costs from holding either too much or too little idle cash. Here the existence of liquidity facilities and their borrowing rates were important determinants of the cash position, as were the mean and the variance of the growth of the deposit market.

The effects on the depository firm of the competitiveness of the asset markets were explored in Chapter 4. In general, it was found that if asset markets are imperfectly competitive, the spread between asset and deposit rate and the profit margin tends to increase. The effects of economies of scale in production on the deposit rate and deposit size were also explored in Chapter 4. Here it was found that scale economies *ceteris parabis* would tend to cause larger firm size, but firm size would ultimately be constrained even with economies in production, since it was reasonable to expect that the marginal and average interest costs would rise and more than offset any economies in production. The unregulated depository firm's motivations for holding equity capital were explored in Chapter 5. Incentives to hold capital exist because not only is capital a buffer against the risk of insolvency, but it serves to gain deposits at more attractive terms.

In all these models of the regulatory-free deposit firm, the force of competition determined the distribution of net revenues between the depositor and the equity position. The income distribution was dependent upon the forces of competition, and the forces of competition in turn were sensitive to the number of firms in the deposit market and other regulatory constraints, particularly deposit ceilings. In Chapters 8 and 9 the distribution of income was examined in both a deposit-free environment and under a deposit ceiling regime. In either environment not only does the number of firms matter in this distribution, but as was indicated in Chapters 10 and 11, the branching structure and interdepository competition between banks and thrifts affects profit margins and income distribution.

This study examined not only the depository firm and industry in a regulatory-free environment, but also the influence of regulatory interposition in the depository process in a number of instances. The possible effects of regulatory constraints that imposed market segmentation in asset markets were seen as influencing the elasticity of asset rates with respect to the quantity of funds a depository firm places in the market. This asset rate elasticity was seen as affecting rate spreads, profit margins, and the firm's deposit size. The marginal costs of production were seen as being influenced by regulatory actions, since the industry structure resulting from those actions influences production costs. Asset restrictions, whether they be cash reserve requirements, usury ceilings, or various quantity constraints on asset categories, were seen as affecting the asset earning rate and ultimately the deposit rate, profit margin, and firm size. Tax considerations and their effect on the deposit rate were addressed in Chapter 5, along with the equity capital constraint. A regulatory-required minimum equity–deposit ratio, the provision of federal deposit insurance, and a stockholder-required minimum target rate of return were seen to affect deposit rates and firm size. The firm and industry adjustments to deposit ceilings were studied in Chapter 7, with empirical estimates of implicit deposit rates, elasticities, and regulatory rent included in Chapter 8.

The aggregate economic effects of deposit or usury ceilings, quantity credit controls and financial stability were examined in Chapters 13 and 14. Depository regulation not only influences rates, profit margins and deposit levels at the firm level, but the regulation of rates also tends to hinder the accumulation of capital, affect its allocation, and ultimately reduce per capita output and consumption. Financial regulation is not merely of interest because of the way it shapes the depository industry, but because it is an important determinant of aggregate economic output and income and thus affects individuals and firms outside the depository orbit. The real resource cost of the financial conduit affects not only financial channels but also the distribution of income between the financial and production sectors. In Chapter 12, the financial process was seen as one that was capable in a static sense of shifting the economy's production possibility frontier and influencing the equilibrium position on that frontier. Thus, finance and its regulation could easily affect resource allocation in the industrial sector as well as aggregate capital accumulation and consumption.

15.2 REGULATION AND FINANCIAL POLICY: PRESENT AND FUTURE

Although affecting these critical economic variables, depository regulations have rarely, if ever, been introduced with that purpose in mind. Rather, these impositions have generally been ad hoc reactions to shocks associated with economic depression, financial panic, national emergencies, or pressing social goals. With these alternative motivations for regulation, it is little wonder that regulatory forces have been subject to varying philosophies and pressures to deal with a series of short-term emergencies. Once the regulatory structures are put into place, they are not resilient to change—until the next crisis.

Arising out of a variety of motivations, depository regulation has often been pointed toward conflicting goals, and hence, the objectives of regulation have never been clearly defined. Should regulation be directed at preserving the depository firm and industry or should it stimulate the delivery of services to depositors or borrowers? Should regulation preserve safety and soundness at the expense of cutting off the flow of venture capital to industry? If regulatory decisions affect rates of return to equity capital in the depository industry and if these decisions affect the risk of committing that equity capital, what then is the proper rate of return and amount of risk for the depository firms? Furthermore, how much should the interests of the institutions and the depositors and borrowers be subordinated to more compelling national interests such as the need for wartime finance, economic stability, or the attainment of pressing social objectives?

Regulators are caught in the middle; they must determine the public's need for services and the private need for profit. They must make uncomfortable decisions that set "fair" standards, "fair" rates and "fair" policies. Regulators are not only in the uncomfortable position of mediating between the industry and the borrower, and the industry and the depositor, but through such devices as deposit ceiling differentials and policies regarding entry and branching, the regulators must mediate among the different depository firms within an industry as well as among the different depository industries.

The regulatory authorities have viewed their mission as the pursuit of the goals of ensuring safety, preserving competition, protecting con-

sumers in their dealings with the depository institutions, allocating credit
to favored sectors (such as housing or small businesses), and promoting
efficiency in the delivery of financial services. Decision making, in this
contentious environment, is clearly a very tall order. It is no wonder that
policy is often determined on a very short-run, ad hoc, and pragmatic
basis, with the point of least resistance in these multifaceted arenas often
determining the direction of change.

There is, however, an underlying force that directs gradual change in
regulation. Since it is the reflex of the depository institutions to move in
the direction of market opportunities, and since it is the reflex of the regulatory agencies to yield only gradually to cumulative pressure, the depository institutions are made to walk at a rather cautious pace along a rather
narrow path circumscribed by the regulatory authority. When the market
changes direction, the path changes direction, whether the new profitable
opportunities result from changes in the geographic location of economic
development, the kinds of economic development, the location and types
of deposit or other liability markets, the technology of the delivery of
financial services, or the desired scale of financial resources. Any of these
will tend to affect asset and liability instruments, market size, and industrial structure, and to cause the firm to strain at the regulatory leash.

Since some regulatory authorities insure deposits, they have a vested
interest in safety and soundness and an aversion to firm failure. As a result, they tend to proceed cautiously in allowing any innovation or in allowing new competitors to enter a market. If the agencies attempt to tip
the competitive balance by allowing fewer competitors, this in turn will
tend to elevate rates of return for those quasi-monopolies or oligopolies
that have already gained entry. It is possible to adjust returns through taxation or other policy levers, but the restraint of free competition tends to
bestow regulatory rent on the existing competitors. Regulatory rent will
invite an excess demand for entry and a high value for a new charter will
exist. This induces charter shopping as potential new entrants seek the
least resistance to entry among the different state and federal thrift and
banking agencies. Thus, policies regarding industrial structure are generally the result of not only some notation of optimum firm size, market
shares, and convenience and needs of depositors, but are also pragmati-
cally governed by differential rates of return.

All the forces of the market push and pull at the regulatory constric-
tions. If the authorities, through inertia, respond by inaction, opportunity
is then created for financial intermediation to be performed by firms that
are not subject to regulatory constraints. When financial intermediation
moves to the nonregulated sector, often at a higher resource cost, this redirection of financial activity tends to alter market shares, with the regu-

lated industries tending to be reduced in relative size. This mechanism continually invites competition from outside the established industries. In this event, the system is faced with the options of extending restrictions to all nonchartered competitors, providing the depository firms with some form of subsidy to offset losses incurred as their market shares diminished, or relaxing regulatory constraints to allow firms to gradually participate in new market opportunities. If the regulatory agencies resist the market forces and extend the scope of regulation, they often create new problems and new side effects. There is a further hardening of the arteries of the financial system, and even if it were conceivable to extend regulation to all firms, the aggregate side effects of lower capital–labor ratios, lower per capita income, and lower levels of output, as outlined in Chapter 14, would result. As an alternative, the economy could be pushed back to self-finance, or financial intermediation could be pushed offshore and handled by a foreign financial entity.

This history of regulatory change has indicated that financial firms have responded to the market whether the response is a new asset or liability, a change in the size or scope of operation, or a change in the contractual terms of financial instruments. Ultimately those charged with financial regulation must recognize that the market determines the direction of movement and that barriers that impede this movement will either eliminate the importance of the industry, reduce its profit, or necessitate subsidies. Even if the extension of regulation to all firms in the financial intermediary process were conceivable, the perverse aggregate side effects do not warrant short-run gains to industry safety, stability, or prosperity.

Not all regulatory change has been a slow response to market pressures. The most sweeping changes were reactions, perhaps overreactions, to the two great crises that faced the depository institutions in this century. Both the great liquidity crisis and the economic depression of the 1930s as well as the inflation shock beginning in mid-1960s and extending through the 1970s threatened the existence of the depository institutions. Although the crisis of the 1930s centered more on banking and the inflation shock of the 1960s and 1970s most affected thrifts, there were similar elements in the problems, although a great dissimilarity in the solutions.

The institutions similarly suffered deposit loss and declining market asset prices in both the depression and the inflation shock eras. The loss of deposits in the contraction of the 1930s sprang from a cumulative financial panic, and the thrift disintermediation of the inflation era was the result of depositors seeking higher market rates. Nevertheless, the outflow of deposits, coupled with declining asset prices in the depository institutions' portfolios, created this situation: not only were current profits threatened because of high illiquidity costs, but the decline in asset values without a similar decline in liability values dissolved the capital buffer that was needed to offset current losses.

Despite charges of over-banking in the 1920s, the historical analysis of commercial bank profit margins in Chapter 9 indicates reasonable earning rates for commercial banks in the late 1920s. A pinch in earnings resulted from rising illiquidity costs, but insolvencies occurred when deposits were run and assets went into total default or were reduced in value in the marketplace. The large-scale failures of the 1930s caused massive federal intervention in the depository environment. This growing federal involvement, recounted in Chapter 2, resulted in improvements in liquidity facilities for the commercial banks at the Federal Reserve and for the savings and loan associations at the Federal Home Loan Banks. In addition, deposit ceilings and various other forms of indirect subsidization, such as through low borrowing rates and relatively inexpensive deposit insurance, were applied to commercial banking deposits. While these federal responses were helpful, the most fundamental and long-run response to the crises of the 1930s was the segmentation of both asset and deposit markets so that individual institutions were granted quasi-monopolies by type of instrument and by geographic territory.

In the inflation shock of the 1970s, the thrift institutions suffered far more than the commercial banks. The late-1960s and early-1970s were a period of moderate prosperity in real economic terms, but an ever-rising inflation rate put pressure on the depository institutions laboring in a regulatory framework designed to alleviate the problems of the 1930s. As inflation rates began to increase in 1966 and continued to rise in an erratic path through 1980, this in turn caused market interest rates in the unregulated market to rise as inflation premiums were incorporated into the interest rate structure. The incorporation of inflation premiums into market interest rates caused these rates to far exceed those that could be earned at the depository institutions. The depository institutions were unable to pay comparable rates because of insufficient earnings. The mutual savings banks and the savings and loan associations were constrained in some cases by usury ceilings on their loans, but also because they held portfolios in which the assets were of a vintage that accorded yields reflecting considerably lower inflation rates. The savings and loan association with a large proportion of its assets invested in older mortgages had limited ability to purchase new high-yielding mortgages because of net deposit outflows. The thrifts were simply not in a position to pay competitive open-market rates for deposits.

As a first line of defense, Congress in the 1960s authorized the extension of deposit ceilings to thrift institutions. This, however, turned out to be a mixed blessing. While deposit ceilings for a period of time reduced competition among the depository institutions and did elevate profit margins, the open-market rates continued to move upward, especially during the periods of tight money that occurred in 1968, 1969–1970, 1974, and in the period beginning in late-1979. At these particular times, not only were market rates higher, but an inversion of the yield curve occurred such that short-term rates exceeded long-term rates. The deposit ceilings exacerbated the disintermediation problem, and distintermediation adversely affected earnings, as the depository institutions were faced with rising illiquidity costs. In an attempt to reduce the high illiquidity costs, the money market certificate was introduced in 1978 as a means of keeping deposits from fleeing the depository institutions. The money market certificate, tied to short-term open market rates, attracted deposits but did not help the institutions' earnings, since higher deposit costs were incurred. The money market certificate merely substituted deposit costs for illiquidity costs with much the same impact on earnings.

Working the yield curve was a profitable and successful strategy during much of the postwar period, as long as the financial markets were free of rising inflation and there were few periods of tight money. However, with rising and variable interest rates when yesterday's long-term rates fall below today's short-term rates, the thrift institutions found themselves in a vulnerable position.

In the regulatory view of the problem, the depository institutions were faced with a maturity structure "mismatch." They were incapable of dealing with periods of rising interest rates and yield curve inversions. A correction for this vulnerability to inflation was offered; if the thrift institutions, like the banks, could adjust the maturity structures of their assets and liabilities to eliminate maturity difference, they could then successfully defend their earning positions with any inflation rate. To do this, both asset and liability authority was expanded to allow depository firms to bring their maturity structures into balance by adjusting both sides of their balance sheets. Those institutions that specialized in long-term assets were given authority to purchase assets with short-term maturities and vice versa. On the liability side of the balance sheet, a large variety of alternative maturity instruments came into being. Not only was the vulnerability to inflation to be checked by more flexible borrowing and lending authority, but in addition, the vulnerability to inflation was reduced when usury ceilings were eliminated on many important asset categories.

The elimination of maturity mismatch was an important short-run adjustment, but in so vigorously attempting to reduce the thrifts' vulnerability to rising interest rates, the expansion of asset and liability authority ironically removed the market segmentations set up by the regulatory

movement of the 1930s. The quasi-monopolies or the oligopolies by territory and by type of asset and liability were struck down. As a result, the
competitiveness of all asset and deposit markets will undoubtedly be increased. Furthermore, in the zeal to protect the thrifts from disintermediation, ceilings on deposit rates were knocked down.

15.3 FUTURE INDUSTRY ADJUSTMENTS

Without deposit ceilings, the depository institutions will again have to
engage in explicit rate competition rather than nonrate competition to attract deposits. The empirical work of Chapters 8–11 clearly indicates that
under explicit rate competition there are lower profit retention rates and
lower profit margins than is the case under implicit rate competition. The
regulatory rent from the deposit ceilings, or the shifting of revenues to the
depository institutions, was eliminated with apparently little thought to
the change in income distribution that results under rate competition, in
which the explicit deposit elasticities and pass-through proportions are increased.

Not only were the protective market segmentations and deposit ceilings
eliminated; the extension of transaction accounts to all depository institutions further adds to the procompetitive thrust. The reduction of liability
segmentation between thrifts and banks further promotes deposit rate
competition now that a very large number of firms are able to offer
transaction-type accounts.

The result of the broadening of authority was not only to increase rate
competition; these regulatory changes also tended to homogenize depository institutions. With the NOW account authority and with mandatory
cash reserves on transactions accounts at the Federal Reserve, distinctions between commercial banks and nonbank thrift institutions have
melted away, leaving only the differences in asset authorities. However,
since all depository institutions must pay essentially similar deposit rates,
they will all eventually need similar asset authority to generate the same
net revenues per deposit dollar. Significant differences still exist among
depository institutions in asset authority, although mutual savings banks
and savings and loan associations have made considerable inroads into
what were the traditional commercial banking markets. With approximately 20,000 thrift institutions having liability authority similar to that of
the 14,000 commercial banks, the number of depository institutions
directly competing with banks is more than doubled. If one also were to
take account of the very substantial growth in the number of savings and
loan branches as well as commercial bank branches during the 1960s and

1970s, one could only anticipate that these large numbers of institutions and offices will be competing in highly rate-sensitive deposit markets. Since the number of competitors affects the deposit elasticity and since the elasticity in turn affects the profit margins and income distribution, one could then predict substantially lower profit margins and a larger income share for the depositor.

The end of nonrate competition and the reemergence of rate competition will bring more benefits to the depositors. The benefits of depository deregulation will likely be reaped by depositors both through higher deposit rates and from the aggregate effects of higher capitalization rates and output per capita, as outlined in Chapters 13 and 14. The end of regulatory segmentation can produce benefits in higher savings and investment levels, higher capital–labor ratios, and higher per capita output.

It is very curious that the regulatory reactions to deposit withdrawals and asset value losses in the 1930s and the 1970s were quite the opposite in terms of competition. The reaction of the 1930s was to reduce competition, protect markets, and set ceiling asset and deposit rates, whereas the 1970s reaction was to expand asset and liability flexibility and eliminate rate ceilings. The procompetitive response of the 1970s in an already crowded market could well give rise to yet another great regulatory response to preserve and protect depository institutions. The depository institutions, in the highly competitive environment they will face in the 1980s, will attempt to respond by more carefully selecting markets in which they have comparative advantages and by placing great emphasis on cost efficiency. Not only will the nonrate competitive costs be substantially reduced, but the pressure of a more competitive environment will no doubt cause the depository institutions to reduce production costs. This would likely result in the closing of branches and in mergers, both of which tend to reduce cost and which reduce competition. If these private adjustments are insufficient, we could also anticipate a new round of emergency assistance for the depository industries. The ebb and flow of deregulation and reregulation will perhaps always be present as the regulatory process first underreacts to economic pressures and then overreacts to the crises engendered by their cumulative neglect.

PART V

Appendixes

Additional Tables for Chapter 9

TABLE A9.1

Federal Reserve Member Banks—Assets[a]

Year	Total assets	Cash[b]	Total securities[c]	Loans	Bank premises, furniture, and fixtures[d]	Treasury items[e]	Reserves[f]	Cash items[g]	Risk assets[h]	Financial assets[i]	Average financial assets[j]
1914	11,444	1,071	2,079	6,419	273	760	1,005	2,500	8,184	11,171	—
1915	13,741	1,436	2,239	7,622	288	742	1,309	3,413	9,586	13,453	12,312
1916	15,850	1,407	2,561	8,714	304	690	1,646	4,013	11,147	15,546	14,500
1917	23,546	1,839	4,580	12,316	376	1,759	2,125	5,465	16,322	23,170	19,358
1918	28,152	2,324	6,368	14,224	429	3,472	2,330	6,173	18,507	27,723	25,447
1919	33,701	2,927	6,630	18,149	483	3,324	2,595	7,350	23,027	33,218	30,471
1920	32,985	2,278	5,976	19,555	566	2,619	2,441	5,618	24,748	32,419	32,819
1921	30,025	1,839	6,088	17,394	643	2,581	2,236	5,047	22,397	29,382	30,901
1922	33,732	2,721	7,649	17,930	712	3,754	2,501	6,466	23,512	33,020	31,201
1923	35,029	3,077	7,645	18,842	787	3,603	2,461	6,801	24,625	34,242	33,631
1924	38,738	3,391	8,813	19,933	861	3,874	2,825	7,958	26,906	37,887	36,065
1925	41,146	3,755	8,888	21,996	927	3,728	2,813	8,148	29,270	40,219	39,053
1926	41,775	3,592	8,990	22,652	998	3,389	2,733	7,868	30,518	40,777	40,498
1927	44,456	3,016	10,361	23,886	1,067	3,978	3,037	7,740	32,738	43,389	42,083
1928	48,258	5,229	10,529	25,155	1,107	4,312	2,973	9,762	34,184	47,151	45,270
1929	48,108	4,454	9,784	26,150	1,190	3,863	2,932	8,996	35,249	46,918	47,035
1930	46,395	3,519	10,989	23,870	1,240	4,125	3,068	8,450	33,820	45,155	46,037
1931	39,378	2,618	11,314	19,261	1,175	5,319	2,498	6,255	27,804	38,203	41,679
1932	36,245	1,545	12,265	15,204	1,150	6,540	2,934	6,472	23,233	35,095	36,649
1933	33,830	1,603	12,386	12,833	981	7,254	3,149	6,312	20,264	32,849	33,972
1934	40,075	2,512	16,122	12,028	1,001	10,895	4,691	9,743	19,437	39,074	35,962
1935	44,111	2,920	17,810	12,175	992	12,268	6,238	12,269	19,574	43,119	41,137
1936	48,708	3,230	19,640	13,360	982	13,546	7,269	13,868	21,295	47,726	45,623
1937	46,744	2,848	17,794	13,958	971	12,372	7,594	13,267	21,105	45,773	46,750

Year											
1938	49,330	2,505	18,863	13,208	945	13,223	9,440	15,439	20,668	48,385	47,079
1939	55,361	2,648	19,979	13,962	924	14,328	12,445	19,758	21,275	54,437	51,411
1940	62,658	3,775	21,805	15,321	914	15,823	14,983	23,952	22,883	61,744	58,091
1941	68,121	4,470	25,500	18,021	911	19,539	13,483	23,112	25,470	67,210	64,477
1942	84,917	4,030	43,175	16,088	904	37,546	14,091	24,268	23,103	84,013	75,612
1943	99,372	4,353	57,970	16,288	861	52,948	13,967	23,770	22,654	98,511	91,262
1944	118,706	3,958	72,893	18,676	817	67,685	15,532	25,844	25,177	117,889	108,200
1945	138,304	5,456	84,408	22,775	788	78,338	17,249	29,822	30,144	137,516	127,703
1946	127,241	6,005	69,666	26,696	789	63,042	17,591	29,532	34,667	126,452	131,984
1947	132,060	7,081	65,218	32,628	820	57,914	19,469	32,820	41,326	131,240	128,846
1948	131,392	6,608	59,556	36,060	872	52,154	21,892	34,174	45,064	130,520	130,880
1949	134,431	7,133	65,297	36,230	907	56,883	17,950	31,277	46,271	133,524	132,022
1950	144,660	9,413	64,736	44,705	957	52,365	19,102	35,383	56,912	143,703	138,614
1951	153,439	9,767	62,687	49,561	1,023	51,621	21,975	39,204	62,614	152,416	148,060
1952	160,826	9,911	64,514	55,034	1,100	52,763	21,891	39,180	68,883	159,726	156,071
1953	163,983	9,897	64,660	57,762	1,179	52,603	21,867	39,318	72,062	162,804	161,265
1954	172,242	9,767	71,352	60,250	1,292	57,809	20,578	37,958	76,475	170,950	166,877
1955	179,414	12,965	64,377	70,982	1,444	50,697	20,741	41,318	87,399	177,970	174,460
1956	184,874	13,529	60,734	78,034	1,604	47,575	21,194	42,847	94,452	183,270	180,620
1957	188,828	13,355	61,403	80,950	1,770	47,079	21,509	42,670	99,079	187,058	185,164
1958	202,017	14,230	70,804	84,061	1,955	54,299	20,869	43,076	104,642	200,062	193,560
1959	205,726	15,715	63,100	94,779	2,208	46,813	20,154	43,401	115,512	203,518	201,790
1960	216,577	17,799	65,685	99,933	2,266	49,106	19,238	45,619	121,852	214,311	208,915
1961	235,112	20,880	73,366	106,232	2,608	54,058	19,731	49,335	131,719	232,504	223,408
1962	249,488	18,361	77,061	118,637	2,839	52,968	20,943	47,201	149,319	246,649	239,577
1963	261,469	16,468	78,415	131,712	3,325	49,342	20,281	44,108	168,019	258,144	252,397
1964	289,142	22,327	80,807	147,690	3,980	48,717	21,071	52,455	187,970	285,162	271,653
1965	313,384	21,864	81,777	169,800	4,269	44,992	21,749	52,570	215,822	309,115	297,139
1966	335,500	27,783	80,884	183,743	4,659	41,924	23,318	60,501	233,075	330,846	319,981
1967	374,562	33,208	96,271	197,827	4,969	49,956	24,921	68,679	255,927	369,593	350,220
1968	413,479	35,360	104,802	221,222	5,490	47,881	26,864	73,503	292,095	407,989	388,791

(Continued)

TABLE A9.1 (Continued)

Year	Total assets	Cash[b]	Total securities[c]	Loans	Bank premises, furniture, and fixtures[d]	Treasury items[e]	Reserves[f]	Cash items[g]	Risk assets[h]	Financial assets[i]	Average financial assets[j]
1969	433,146	39,691	94,618	242,995	6,571	39,833	27,125	78,747	314,566	426,575	417,282
1970	466,225	38,673	112,004	254,516	7,353	45,399	28,764	81,181	339,645	458,872	442,724
1971	511,835	43,374	127,371	262,826	8,476	47,633	33,256	85,745	378,457	503,359	481,116
1972	585,506	50,498	136,239	309,969	9,338	48,715	32,652	95,963	440,828	576,168	539,764
1973	656,250	51,245	137,092	365,257	10,188	41,494	35,958	99,501	515,255	646,062	611,115
1974	715,890	54,434	138,995	399,963	11,374	38,921	35,955	105,830	571,139	704,516	657,816
1975	733,780	54,773	162,194	387,439	13,061	61,519	36,019	106,121	566,140	720,719	712,618
1976	—	—	—	—	—	—	—	106,783	—	—	—
1977	—	—	—	—	—	—	—	131,357	—	—	—
1978	—	—	—	—	—	—	—	144,826	—	—	—

[a] In millions of dollars. Source: All basic data from: *Banking and Monetary Statistics 1914–1941*, pp. 72–75; *Banking and Monetary Statistics 1941–1970*, pp. 60–62; and *Annual Statistical Digest of 1971*, pp. 62–81. Board of Governors, Federal Reserve System, Washington, D.C.

[b] Includes cash in vault as well as cash items in process of collection.

[c] Includes U.S. government obligations and other securities.

[d] Reported jointly with other real estate from 1964 to June 1967.

[e] Until March 5, 1934 included only bills, certificates, notes and bonds of the U.S. government. In 1934, another class of U.S. government securities was added, obligations fully guaranteed by U.S., which were first issued in the latter part of 1933.

[f] Does not include interbank balances.

[g] Includes interbank balances.

[h] Total assets minus cash and treasury items.

[i] Total assets minus bank premises, furniture, and fixtures.

[j] An average of year-end values.

358

TABLE A9.2

Federal Reserve Member Banks—Liabilities[a]

Year	Total liabilities and capital	Total deposits	IPC demand[b]	IPC time[c]	Total time deposits[a]	Other liabilities	Borrowed money	Capital accounts[e]	Rediscounts and other borrowed money	Average deposits[f]
1914	11,444	8,305	4,793	1,198	1,234	913	133	2,093	.1	—
1915	13,741	10,636	5,793	1,457	1,506	848	99	2,126	.1	9,471
1916	15,850	12,661	6,847	1,902	1,983	754	95	2,231	.2	11,649
1917	23,546	18,668	10,010	3,057	3,156	937	783	2,807	1.1	15,665
1918	28,152	21,457	11,709	3,732	3,835	1,118	1,876	3,220	2.4	20,063
1919	33,701	26,139	13,859	5,217	5,304	1,032	2,347	3,542	3.0	23,798
1920	32,985	24,220	13,053	6,146	6,188	1,016	3,036	4,120	3.6	25,180
1921	30,025	23,247	12,296	6,406	6,450	952	1,364	4,093	1.7	23,734
1922	33,732	27,288	13,569	7,587	7,645	954	727	4,364	1.1	25,268
1923	35,029	28,507	13,628	8,586	8,651	910	808	4,378	1.2	27,898
1924	38,738	32,384	15,038	9,707	9,805	917	408	4,532	.9	30,446
1925	41,146	34,250	15,943	10,557	10,653	938	740	4,678	1.3	33,317
1926	41,775	34,528	15,783	11,340	11,440	959	792	4,944	1.4	34,389
1927	44,456	36,657	16,590	12,658	12,765	1,018	696	5,341	1.4	35,593
1928	48,258	39,067	17,604	12,794	13,453	1,024	1,296	3,899	2.3	37,862
1929	48,108	37,981	17,526	12,267	13,233	1,097	1,015	6,709	2.3	38,524
1930	46,395	37,029	16,139	12,503	13,546	1,106	513	6,593	1.7	37,505
1931	39,378	30,711	13,652	10,376	11,316	1,000	921	5,999	1.7	33,870
1932	36,245	28,690	12,273	9,411	10,550	1,117	592	5,409	1.1	29,701
1933	33,830	27,167	12,109	7,957	9,125	1,054	155	4,962	.6	27,929
1934	40,075	33,848	14,951	9,020	9,908	891	19	5,054	.3	30,508
1935	44,111	38,454	18,035	9,680	10,414	300	14	5,145	.2	36,151

(Continued)

359

TABLE A9.2 (Continued)

Year	Total liabilities and capital	Total deposits	IPC demand[b]	IPC time[c]	Total time deposits[d]	Other liabilities	Borrowed money	Capital accounts[e]	Rediscounts and other borrowed money[f]	Average deposits[f]
1936	48,708	42,885	20,970	10,429	10,989	329	17	5,275	.2	40,670
1937	46,744	40,839	19,747	10,806	11,522	346	15	5,371	.2	41,862
1938	49,330	43,363	21,119	10,846	11,510	398	6	5,424	.1	42,101
1939	55,361	49,340	24,604	11,215	11,852	372	3	5,522	.1	46,352
1940	62,658	56,430	29,576	11,687	12,319	430	3	5,698	.1	52,885
1941	68,121	61,717	33,061	11,878	12,487	426	4	5,886	.1	59,074
1942	84,917	78,277	42,139	12,366	12,841	488	5	6,101	.1	69,997
1943	99,372	92,262	51,820	14,822	15,330	540	39	6,475	.1	85,270
1944	118,706	110,917	56,270	18,807	19,317	638	111	6,968	.2	101,590
1945	138,304	129,670	62,950	23,712	24,274	761	208	7,589	.3	120,294
1946	127,241	118,170	69,127	26,525	27,253	814	30	8,095	.2	123,920
1947	132,060	122,528	72,704	27,542	28,390	850	54	8,464	.2	120,349
1948	131,392	121,362	70,947	27,801	28,902	982	45	8,801	.2	121,945
1949	134,431	123,885	71,589	27,934	29,324	1,163	11	9,174	.2	122,624
1950	144,660	133,089	78,659	28,032	29,677	1,558	79	9,695	.3	128,487
1951	153,439	141,015	83,240	29,128	31,045	1,827	26	10,218	.4	137,052
1952	160,826	147,527	85,680	31,266	33,482	2,030	165	10,761	.5	144,271
1953	163,983	150,164	85,711	33,311	36,234	2,059	43	11,316	.4	148,846
1954	172,242	157,252	88,859	35,650	39,425	2,156	15	12,210	.6	153,708
1955	179,414	163,757	93,687	36,972	40,518	2,286	137	12,783	.6	160,505
1956	188,874	167,906	95,163	38,769	42,197	2,531	48	13,655	.8	165,832
1957	188,828	170,637	93,804	42,845	46,537	2,558	57	14,554	1.1	169,272
1958	202,017	182,816	98,133	48,004	53,319	2,809	54	15,460	1.0	176,727
1959	205,726	184,716	98,532	50,185	54,165	3,380	581	16,264	1.3	183,766
1960	216,577	193,029	104,803	53,477	58,910	4,595	130	17,398	1.6	188,873

Year										
1961	235,112	209,630	104,803	60,352	67,460	4,746	438	18,638	2.1	201,330
1962	249,488	219,468	103,929	71,891	80,074	4,994	3,550	19,854	5.2	214,549
1963	261,469	229,376	103,296	81,293	91,311	5,954	3,499	21,054	5.1	224,422
1964	289,142	255,724	112,060	91,557	104,340	6,369	2,481	22,901	4.1	242,550
1965	313,384	275,517	115,023	105,874	121,042	6,875	4,234	24,926	6.1	265,621
1966	335,500	292,004	119,556	114,395	130,565	10,436	4,618	26,278	6.8	283,761
1967	374,562	327,012	131,318	130,237	149,589	11,770	5,370	28,098	5.7	309,508
1968	413,479	356,351	141,621	142,874	164,603	16,206	8,458	30,060	10.9	341,682
1969	433,146	350,759	145,082	133,988	151,055	29,699	17,395	32,047	20.6	353,555
1970	466,225	385,176	146,580	156,457	181,542	24,713	18,578	34,100	22.2	367,968
1971	511,835	425,862	152,060	180,857	212,438	13,924	1,312	37,279	5.1	405,519
1972	585,506	482,505	173,887	205,077	243,706	15,297	3,682	41,228	7.1	454,184
1973	656,250	527,188	179,044	234,461	281,569	17,451	6,879	44,741	11.1	504,847
1974	715,890	575,838	180,792	268,491	327,390	20,426	4,501	48,240	15.4	551,513
1975	733,780	590,999	187,632	283,823	339,350	20,206	4,342	52,074	13.3	583,419
1976	—	—	—	—	—	—	—	—	—	—
1977	—	—	—	—	—	—	—	—	—	—
1978	—	—	—	—	—	—	6,054	—	—	—

^{a} In millions of dollars. Source: All basic data from: *Banking and Monetary Statistics 1914–1941*, pp. 72–75; *Banking and Monetary Statistics 1941–1970*, pp. 62–64, 70–72; and *Annual Statistical Digest of 1971–1975*, pp. 62–81. Board of Governors, Federal Reserve System, Washington, D.C.

^{b} Reported as "Demand Deposits Adjusted" before 1928. They are not strictly comparable since "Demand Deposits Adjusted" is merely a statistical measure of the aggregate net balances in the checking accounts of individuals, partnerships, and corporations after allowing for checks outstanding for these accounts. It comprises the excess of gross demand deposits, other than interbank and U.S. government deposits, over cash items in process of collection ("float"). It is the closest measure of IPC demand available before 1928.

^{c} Statistically estimated similarly to IPC demand for years preceding 1928.

^{d} Does not include postal savings deposits at national banks, only prior to 1928. Thereafter, they are included.

^{e} Includes reserves for contingencies.

^{f} A simple average of year-end values.

TABLE A9.3

Federal Reserve Member Banks—Revenues, Expenses, and Income[a]

Year	Gross operating income[b,c,e]	Total operating costs[b,d,e,f]	Officers' salaries[b,g,h]	Wages and other compensation[b,g,h]	Office occupancy expense[e,f,i]	Depreciation expense[b]	Interest and dividends[b,f,j]	Interest on borrowed funds[b,f]	Other operating expenses[b,k]	Net income before taxes	Net income after taxes
1914	—	—	—	—	—	—	—	—	—	214.2	214.2
1915	—	—	—	—	—	—	—	—	—	205.5	205.5
1916	—	—	—	—	—	—	—	—	—	219.7	219.7
1917	—	—	—	—	—	—	—	—	—	256.7	256.7
1918	—	—	—	—	—	—	—	—	—	303.8	303.8
1919	1331.6	369.2	224.1	—	—	28.0	422.5	85.2	145.1	351.5	351.5
1920	1687.9	481.6	291.3	—	—	33.1	468.8	161.0	190.2	396.4	396.4
1921	1616.3	493.7	307.3	—	—	31.3	468.1	120.9	186.4	293.4	293.4
1922	1553.4	500.8	314.0	—	—	30.6	508.5	37.7	186.8	349.2	349.2
1923	1617.2	540.1	335.8	—	—	27.7	548.0	42.2	204.3	337.1	337.1
1924	1689.7	564.2	355.2	—	—	31.1	594.6	24.7	209.1	361.5	361.5
1925	1816.3	596.0	372.9	—	—	29.2	643.3	26.0	223.1	419.7	419.7
1926	1921.9	631.6	396.8	—	—	46.7	672.9	31.4	234.8	431.5	431.5
1927	1903.8	668.4	420.1	—	—	27.2	631.4	24.5	248.2	447.0	447.0
1928	2080.3	701.9	440.0	—	—	31.8	674.3	48.4	261.9	503.9	503.9
1929	2286.5	747.7	463.8	—	—	33.2	691.1	65.3	283.9	556.5	556.5
1930	2044.5	719.9	451.8	—	—	36.6	676.2	22.0	268.1	306.5	306.5
1931	1755.1	649.0	412.5	—	—	29.1	528.0	19.1	236.4	12.3	12.3
1932	1486.5	603.2	356.6	—	—	21.4	399.8	38.8	246.6	-254.9	-254.9
1933	1178.8	477.5	306.0	—	—	35.8	274.6	15.2	192.1	-355.8	-355.8
1934	1181.6	512.5	327.4	—	—	39.4	239.9	3.6	212.7	-224.5	-224.5
1935	1143.0	523.5	334.5	—	—	33.6	205.8	1.2	224.7	211.9	211.9
1936	1236.9	566.5	135.5	216.2	—	38.7	182.3	.6	247.9	465.3	465.3
1937	1287.1	589.8	142.8	229.3	—	36.9	179.1	.6	255.7	336.6	336.6

Year											
1938	265.5	265.5	249.3	.3	171.0	42.1	—	233.4	146.5	585.9	1239.8
1939	337.5	337.5	254.6	.2	159.1	38.0	—	237.8	150.1	595.6	1261.0
1940	349.1	349.1	265.0	.1	147.5	45.5	—	244.8	155.5	613.8	1288.6
1941	389.8	389.8	284.8	.1	139.9	47.6	—	262.6	163.3	654.0	1384.2
1942	383.1	450.6	404.1	.1	128.3	—	—	290.6	169.9	805.0	1486.7
1943	557.3	672.7	419.0	.4	123.7	—	—	312.1	174.9	838.3	1650.2
1944	649.3	833.0	447.2	1.0	144.1	—	—	337.4	187.5	896.2	1873.8
1945	788.4	1058.5	492.1	2.3	182.9	—	—	371.4	208.2	995.0	2102.2
1946	757.8	1042.8	542.9	2.2	211.6	—	—	457.0	242.4	1155.1	2402.5
1947	653.0	909.5	600.9	2.5	235.9	—	—	527.5	269.5	1292.3	2578.6
1948	620.9	854.5	650.9	3.1	250.5	—	—	578.5	297.3	1400.5	2828.3
1949	686.3	961.3	682.3	3.3	261.1	—	—	607.9	318.2	1466.5	2985.6
1950	780.8	1149.9	727.5	3.9	271.0	—	—	655.2	344.8	1572.3	3264.7
1951	755.6	1246.5	772.8	9.1	305.5	—	—	750.0	375.3	1730.5	3668.7
1952	829.3	1437.2	851.6	19.8	364.5	—	—	835.3	408.3	1919.0	4119.6
1953	865.3	1557.5	938.9	22.7	424.7	—	—	924.3	447.1	2115.3	4590.2
1954	1096.1	1900.3	1008.6	8.0	493.6	—	—	983.8	478.9	2244.6	4826.1
1955	985.2	1676.0	1101.5	22.0	543.1	—	—	1059.7	511.7	2426.0	5342.6
1956	1026.6	1744.3	1222.1	43.8	649.7	—	—	1181.9	553.3	2676.3	6078.2
1957	1168.9	2063.5	1339.2	47.9	927.2	—	—	1284.9	592.4	2893.1	6771.0
1958	1457.2	2605.6	1456.6	23.2	1123.4	—	—	1349.2	632.1	3081.8	7126.6
1959	1256.9	2031.5	1631.1	75.9	1279.7	—	—	1438.3	680.1	3362.3	8074.9
1960	1688.8	2929.4	1810.6	84.2	1434.3	—	423.6	1557.2	731.5	3672.5	8927.9
1961	1712.0	2962.5	980.4	36.4	1720.4	—	458.6	1585.0	778.4	3822.2	9216.8
1962	1694.9	2804.7	1038.7	62.5	2358.1	—	500.6	1671.1	830.3	4088.3	10153.6
1963	1831.1	2909.9	1116.7	104.1	2857.6	—	549.8	1768.2	892.6	4401.6	11169.5
1964	1923.1	2920.7	1236.3	122.1	3383.5	—	598.2	1871.9	968.4	4781.8	12385.8
1965	2102.9	2982.9	1355.8	183.7	4214.1	—	653.8	1976.6	1047.4	5155.3	13841.8
1966	2208.8	3084.5	1560.8	293.9	5213.4	—	708.7	2141.5	1148.5	5729.2	16071.6
1967	2608.9	3616.1	1750.6	259.0	6091.4	—	783.1	2389.6	1258.6	6399.5	17859.3
1968	2805.1	3859.1	2052.4	516.2	7108.1	—	783.1	2701.6	1395.3	7330.0	20818.9
1969	3449.8	5466.6	3336.2	561.8	7059.2	—	866.8	—	4689.7	9421.3	24991.2

(Continued)

TABLE A9.3 (Continued)

Year	Gross operating income[b,c,e]	Total operating costs[b,d,e,f]	Officers' salaries[b,g,h]	Wages and other compensation[b,g,h]	Office occupancy expense[e,f,i]	Depreciation expense[b]	Interest and dividends[b,f,j]	Interest on borrowed funds[b,f]	Other operating expenses[b,k]	Net income before taxes	Net income after taxes
1970	27912.7	10545.4	5282.0	—	1012.5	—	8138.8	444.0	3727.9	5720.0	3822.6
1971	28670.2	11019.7	5666.1	—	1130.5	—	9425.7	126.6	3348.1	5324.7	4116.9
1972	31334.5	11782.0	6020.3	—	1259.4	—	10512.9	102.1	3485.8	5695.6	4399.9
1973	41707.9	13275.0	6571.3	—	1407.6	—	15376.9	473.5	4077.7	6680.7	5011.8
1974	53827.5	15317.9	7425.9	—	1602.8	—	21805.8	871.7	4869.2	7021.3	5364.4
1975	51355.6	16754.7	8061.2	—	1791.5	—	19793.9	335.8	5273.4	6957.5	5545.5
1976	63640.6	19922.0	—	—	—	—	—	—	—	—	—
1977	70513.6	22067.2	—	—	—	—	—	—	—	—	—
1978	—	—	—	—	—	—	—	—	—	—	—

[a] In millions of dollars. Source: All basic data from: *Banking and Monetary Statistics 1914–1941*, pp. 262–263; *Banking and Monetary Statistics 1941–1970*, pp. 378–373; and *Annual Statistics Digest 1971–1975*, pp. 286–295. Board of Governors, Federal Reserve System, Washington, D.C.

[b] First year for which detailed information of earnings and expense figures was available is 1919. Before that, only net income figures are available.

[c] Includes profits on securities sold, until 1926.

[d] Service charges on deposit accounts, which are not reported until 1933, were deducted from the reported revenue figures and were netted out of total operating expenses *oc*.

[e] Real estate taxes and other taxes were deducted from total operating expenses and were netted out of gross operating income (the asset earning rate).

[f] Interest on demand deposits (which was paid until 1938), on time deposits, and on borrowed money were deducted from total operating expenses *oc* and are used instead in the calculation of the effective deposit rate *r* and the effective rate on borrowed money r_b.

[g] Salaries of officers and other salaries and wages are reported together from 1919 to 1935 inclusive and from 1969 to 1975 inclusive.

[h] Includes officer and employee benefits from 1961 on.

[i] Occupancy expense is not reported until 1961.

[j] Through 1926, interest on time and demand deposits as well as interbank deposits reported jointly. Beginning with 1938, interest on time deposits comprises all interest on deposits.

[k] Depreciation expense not reported separately from 1942 on. It is included in general operating expenses but not detailed from 1941 to 1960. From 1961 on it is reported under occupancy expense.

TABLE A9.4

Federal Reserve Member Banks—Selected Ratios[a]

Year	NIBT/ capital account	NIAT/ capital account	(α) Capital account/ average deposits	(β) Bank premises, furniture, & fixtures/ capital account	Profit/ capital account	Capital account/ risk assets	Reserves/ average deposits	Cash items/ average deposits	IPC demand/ average IPC total deposits	Office occupancy expense/ average deposits[b]	Salaries and wages/ average deposits
1914	10.2	10.2	—	13.0	—	25.5	12.1	30.1	80.0	—	—
1915	9.6	9.6	22.4	13.5	—	22.1	12.3	32.0	79.9	—	—
1916	9.8	9.8	19.1	13.6	—	20.0	13.0	31.6	78.2	—	—
1917	9.1	9.1	17.9	13.3	—	17.1	11.3	29.2	76.6	—	—
1918	9.4	9.4	16.0	13.3	—	17.3	10.8	28.7	64.8	—	—
1919	9.9	9.9	14.8	13.6	7.0	15.3	9.9	28.1	72.6	—	.9
1920	9.6	9.6	16.3	13.7	8.3	16.6	10.0	23.1	67.9	—	1.1
1921	7.1	7.1	17.2	15.7	6.8	18.2	9.6	21.7	65.7	—	1.2
1922	8.0	8.0	17.2	16.3	5.7	18.5	9.1	23.6	64.1	—	1.2
1923	7.7	7.7	15.6	17.9	5.4	17.7	8.6	23.8	61.3	—	1.2
1924	7.9	7.9	14.8	18.9	5.9	16.8	8.7	24.5	60.7	—	1.1
1925	8.9	8.9	14.0	19.8	6.6	15.9	8.2	23.7	60.1	—	1.1
1926	8.7	8.7	14.3	20.1	6.6	16.2	7.9	22.7	58.1	—	1.1
1927	8.3	8.3	15.0	19.9	5.8	16.3	8.2	21.1	56.7	—	1.1
1928	8.5	8.5	15.5	18.7	5.8	17.2	7.6	24.9	57.9	—	1.1
1929	8.2	8.2	17.4	17.7	6.4	19.0	7.7	23.6	58.8	—	1.2
1930	4.6	4.6	17.5	18.8	4.0	19.4	8.2	22.8	56.3	—	1.2
1931	.2	.2	17.7	19.5	4.1	21.5	8.1	20.3	51.0	—	1.2
1932	-4.7	-4.7	18.2	21.2	3.7	23.2	10.2	22.5	56.5	—	1.2

(Continued)

Year	NIBT/ capital account	NIAT/ capital account	(α) Capital account/ average deposits	(β) Bank premises, furniture, & fixtures/ capital account	Profit/ capital account	Capital account/ risk assets	Reserves/ average deposits	Cash items/ average deposits	IPC demand/ average IPC total deposits	Office occupancy expense/ average deposits[b]	Salaries and wages/ average deposits
1933	−7.1	−7.1	17.7	19.7	4.3	24.4	11.5	23.2	60.3	—	1.0
1934	−4.4	−4.4	16.5	19.8	4.9	26.0	13.8	28.7	62.3	—	1.0
1935	4.1	4.1	14.2	19.2	5.3	26.2	16.2	31.9	65.0	—	.9
1936	8.8	8.8	12.9	18.6	6.7	24.7	16.9	32.3	66.7	—	.8
1937	6.2	6.2	12.8	18.0	7.1	25.4	18.5	32.4	64.6	—	.8
1938	4.8	4.8	12.8	17.4	6.4	26.2	21.7	35.6	66.0	—	.9
1939	6.1	6.1	11.9	16.7	6.9	25.9	25.2	40.0	68.6	—	.8
1940	6.1	6.1	10.7	16.0	7.2	24.9	26.5	42.4	71.6	—	.7
1941	6.6	6.6	9.9	15.4	8.0	23.1	21.8	37.4	73.5	—	.7
1942	7.3	6.2	8.7	14.8	7.2	26.4	18.0	31.0	77.3	—	.6
1943	10.3	8.6	7.5	13.2	8.9	28.5	15.1	25.7	77.7	—	.5
1944	11.9	9.3	6.8	11.7	10.3	27.6	14.0	23.3	74.9	—	.5
1945	13.9	10.3	6.3	10.3	10.5	25.1	13.3	22.9	72.6	—	.4
1946	12.8	9.3	6.5	9.7	10.9	23.3	14.8	24.9	72.2	—	.5
1947	10.7	7.7	7.0	9.6	10.3	20.4	15.8	26.7	72.5	—	.6
1948	9.7	7.0	7.2	9.9	11.1	19.5	18.0	28.1	71.8	—	.7
1949	10.4	7.4	7.4	9.8	11.3	19.8	14.4	25.2	71.9	—	.7
1950	11.8	8.0	7.5	9.8	12.1	17.0	14.3	26.5	73.7	—	.7
1951	12.1	7.3	7.4	10.0	13.3	16.3	15.5	27.8	74.0	—	.8
1952	13.3	7.7	7.4	10.2	14.1	15.6	14.8	26.5	73.2	—	.8

Year											
1953	13.7	7.6	7.6	10.4	14.9	15.7	14.5	26.1	72.0	—	.9
1954	15.5	8.9	7.9	10.5	13.9	15.9	13.0	24.1	71.3	—	.9
1955	13.1	7.7	7.9	11.2	15.2	14.6	12.6	25.2	71.7	—	.9
1956	12.7	7.5	8.2	11.7	16.5	14.4	12.6	25.5	71.0	—	1.0
1957	14.1	8.0	8.5	12.1	16.2	14.6	12.6	25.0	68.6	—	1.1
1958	16.8	9.4	8.7	12.6	14.8	14.7	11.4	23.5	67.1	—	1.1
1959	12.4	7.7	8.8	13.5	17.3	14.0	10.9	23.4	66.2	—	1.1
1960	16.8	9.7	9.2	13.0	17.0	14.2	9.9	23.6	64.9	—	1.2
1961	15.8	9.1	9.2	13.9	13.9	14.1	9.4	23.5	63.4	.2	1.1
1962	14.1	8.5	9.2	14.2	13.3	13.2	9.5	21.5	59.1	.2	1.1
1963	13.8	8.6	9.3	15.7	12.6	12.5	8.8	19.2	55.9	.2	1.1
1964	12.7	8.3	9.4	17.3	12.6	12.1	8.2	20.5	55.0	.2	1.1
1965	11.9	8.4	9.3	17.1	11.4	11.5	7.8	19.0	52.0	.2	1.1
1966	11.7	8.4	9.2	17.7	12.6	11.2	7.9	20.7	51.1	.2	1.1
1967	12.8	9.2	9.0	17.6	11.7	10.9	7.6	21.0	50.2	.2	1.1
1968	12.8	9.3	8.7	18.2	12.8	10.2	7.5	20.6	49.7	.2	1.1
1969	17.0	10.7	9.0	20.5	14.6	10.1	7.7	22.4	51.9	.2	1.3
1970	16.7	11.2	9.2	21.5	13.2	10.0	7.4	21.0	48.3	.2	1.4
1971	14.2	11.0	9.1	22.7	9.9	9.8	7.8	20.1	45.6	.2	1.3
1972	13.8	10.6	9.0	22.6	9.8	9.3	6.7	19.8	45.8	.2	1.3
1973	14.9	11.2	8.8	22.7	12.9	8.6	6.8	18.8	43.2	.2	1.3
1974	14.5	11.1	8.7	23.5	16.6	8.4	6.2	18.3	40.2	.2	1.3
1975	13.3	10.6	8.9	25.0	10.5	9.1	6.0	17.9	39.7	.3	1.3
1976	—	—	—	—	—	—	—	—	—	—	—
1977	—	—	—	—	—	—	—	—	—	—	—
1978	—	—	—	—	—	—	—	—	—	—	—

[a] Expressed in percentages. Source: Tables A9.1–A9.3.
[b] Not reported until 1961.

367

TABLE A9.5

FDIC Commercial Banks—Assets[a]

Year	Total assets	Cash[b]	Total securities[c,e]	Loans[d,e,f]	Bank premises, furniture, and fixtures[g]	Treasury items[h]	Reserves[i]	Risk assets[j]	Financial assets[k]	Average financial assets[l]
1934	46,448	11,202	18,172	14,614	1,212	11,713	4,875	23,533	45,236	—
1935	50,927	13,851	20,116	14,719	1,196	13,275	6,443	23,801	49,731	47,484
1936	56,210	15,731	22,307	15,965	1,178	14,750	7,489	25,729	55,032	52,382
1937	54,212	14,931	20,477	16,750	1,161	13,669	7,795	25,612	53,051	54,042
1938	56,800	17,176	21,451	16,024	1,123	14,507	9,644	25,117	55,677	54,364
1939	63,147	21,876	22,428	16,866	1,091	15,566	12,671	25,705	62,056	58,867
1940	70,720	26,291	24,163	18,397	1,071	17,064	15,227	27,366	69,649	65,853
1941	76,827	25,793	28,032	21,262	1,061	21,047	13,755	29,987	75,766	72,708
1942	95,459	27,593	47,344	18,906	1,048	40,712	14,379	27,154	94,411	85,089
1943	112,246	27,191	64,678	18,843	994	58,694	14,281	26,361	111,252	102,832
1944	134,613	29,746	82,053	21,355	940	75,896	15,886	28,971	133,673	122,463
1945	152,582	34,303	96,067	25,769	903	88,933	17,642	29,346	151,679	142,676
1946	147,365	33,704	81,468	30,740	902	73,575	18,028	40,086	146,463	149,071
1947	152,773	36,936	76,712	37,592	936	67,960	19,944	47,877	157,210	151,837
1948	152,163	38,097	70,339	41,979	999	61,407	22,345	52,659	145,790	151,500
1949	155,319	35,222	75,824	42,499	1,046	54,847	18,416	54,250	159,646	152,718
1950	166,792	39,865	73,198	51,809	1,109	61,047	19,623	65,880	160,309	159,978
1951	177,449	44,242	73,673	57,371	1,193	60,599	22,597	72,608	181,630	170,970
1952	186,682	44,299	76,280	63,824	1,291	62,408	22,559	79,975	180,018	180,824
1953	191,063	44,478	76,852	67,266	1,392	62,743	22,503	84,111	195,044	187,531
1954	200,588	43,235	84,142	70,341	1,523	68,121	21,205	89,232	193,692	194,368
1955	209,145	46,560	77,240	82,360	1,700	60,877	21,405	101,708	212,819	203,255
1956	216,145	48,444	73,947	90,143	1,894	57,958	21,976	109,743	208,878	210,848
1957	221,534	48,219	75,330	93,801	2,096	57,686	22,318	115,629	224,812	216,845
1958	237,473	48,792	86,056	98,132	2,322	65,789	21,685	122,892	229,777	227,295
1959	243,423	49,212	78,582	110,695	2,625	58,391	20,941	135,820	246,172	237,975
1960	256,323	51,902	81,020	117,522	2,829	60,522	20,067	143,899	248,120	247,146

Year										
1961	277,374	56,182	89,662	124,807	3,102	66,091	20,611	155,102	279,646	263,883
1962	295,983	53,799	94,913	140,023	3,404	54,966	21,939	176,218	287,205	283,426
1963	311,791	50,446	97,472	155,933	3,946	62,812	21,203	198,533	313,219	300,212
1964	345,130	60,033	100,960	175,096	4,754	52,588	22,133	222,509	335,003	324,111
1965	375,394	60,437	103,651	201,114	5,144	59,210	22,858	255,747	375,624	355,313
1966	402,946	68,652	104,286	218,456	5,620	55,904	24,526	278,390	391,952	383,788
1967	450,713	77,533	123,264	236,710	6,290	62,229	26,228	310,951	449,797	420,875
1968	500,238	83,270	135,242	265,982	6,980	64,171	28,446	352,797	487,884	468,840
1969	530,715	89,335	125,385	295,464	8,070	54,330	28,800	386,850	528,018	507,951
1970	576,351	93,048	147,219	314,142	9,143	61,617	30,409	421,686	561,834	544,926
1971	639,903	98,691	169,167	347,869	10,285	64,647	35,007	476,566	634,992	598,413
1972	737,699	111,844	183,761	414,537	11,525	66,750	34,710	559,105	720,801	677,896
1973	832,658	116,939	188,230	494,136	12,789	57,961	38,498	657,758	825,243	773,022
1974	912,529	126,081	185,919	553,300	14,297	54,132	38,742	732,316	892,858	859,051
1975	938,888	129,023	227,832	502,282	15,598	81,008	39,134	728,857	923,290	908,074
1976	1,011,274	130,210	249,965	537,558	16,703	96,884	38,155	784,180	994,571	958,930
1977	1,137,795	160,382	258,405	612,726	18,345	95,961	43,341	881,451	1,119,450	1,057,010
1978	1,273,189	178,327	268,778	708,308	20,551	89,699	49,969	1,005,163	1,252,638	1,186,044

^a In millions of dollars. Source: All basic data from: "Tables of Assets and Liabilities of Insured Commercial Banks in the U.S.," *Annual Report of the F.D.I.C.*, Board of Directors of the F.D.I.C., Washington, D.C., 1934–1978.

^b Includes cash in vault, reserves, interbank balances, and cash items in the process of collection.

^c Includes all U.S. government obligations and all other securities. Excludes corporate stocks (other than Federal Reserve bank stock) of National Banks, as of Dec. 31, 1965; reported with "Other Assets." As of Dec. 30, 1967, also includes securities purchased under agreements to resell.

^d Includes all loans, discounts, and overdrafts, including rediscounts.

^e Amount of loans and securities from 1938 on are not entirely comparable with prior dates because "investments and other assets (chiefly loans) indirectly representing bank premises and other real estate" are now reported separately.

^f Loan items are reported gross as of Dec. 31, 1948, and are therefore not strictly comparable with amounts for previous years, which were reported on a net basis.

^g Reported net of mortgages and other liens as of Dec. 31, 1965; previously included with "Other Liabilities."

^h Includes bills, certificates, notes, bonds, and obligations fully guaranteed by the U.S. government.

ⁱ Does not include interbank balances.

^j Total assets minus cash minus treasury items.

^k Total assets minus bank premises, furniture, and fixtures.

^l An average of year-end values.

TABLE A9.6
FDIC Commercial Banks—Liabilities[a]

Year	Total liabilities and capital	Total deposits[b]	IPC demand[b]	IPC time[b]	Total time deposits[b]	Other liabilities[c]	Borrowed money[d]	Capital account[e]	Rediscounts and other borrowed money[c]	Average deposits[f]
1934	46,448	39,015	16,976	11,374	12,245	1,282	79	6,152	79	—
1935	50,927	44,147	20,561	12,411	13,136	569	46	6,210	46	41,581
1936	56,210	49,283	24,372	13,218	13,987	598	39	6,329	39	46,715
1937	54,212	47,224	25,915	14,189	14,835	584	35	6,404	35	48,254
1938	56,800	49,779	25,003	14,358	14,860	586	27	6,435	27	48,502
1939	63,147	46,076	27,197	14,471	15,237	546	16	6,524	14	52,928
1940	70,720	63,469	32,401	15,001	15,753	576	14	6,673	12	59,773
1941	76,827	69,421	36,547	15,152	15,860	564	10	6,842	10	66,445
1942	95,459	87,820	47,128	15,706	16,261	582	10	7,056	10	78,621
1943	112,246	104,116	58,346	18,575	19,160	677	46	7,454	46	95,968
1944	134,613	125,752	64,149	23,361	23,958	872	122	7,990	122	114,934
1945	152,582	147,811	72,606	29,295	29,964	1,099	215	8,672	215	136,782
1946	147,365	137,029	79,903	32,761	33,613	1,047	39	9,288	39	142,420
1947	152,773	141,887	83,738	33,963	34,954	1,149	61	9,736	61	141,887
1948	152,163	140,683	81,699	34,262	35,528	1,320	54	10,161	54	141,285
1949	155,319	143,194	82,129	34,462	36,049	1,476	14	10,649	14	141,938
1950	166,792	153,498	89,993	34,582	36,491	2,013	87	11,281	87	148,346
1951	177,449	163,172	95,701	36,057	38,292	2,354	38	11,923	38	158,335
1952	186,682	171,357	98,898	38,795	41,365	2,740	189	12,585	189	167,265
1953	191,063	175,084	99,196	41,484	44,794	2,715	59	13,265	59	173,220
1954	200,588	183,309	102,715	44,276	48,527	3,000	23	14,279	23	179,196
1955	209,145	190,989	108,326	45,891	49,951	3,147	150	15,009	150	187,149
1956	216,145	196,507	110,483	48,113	52,122	3,618	63	16,020	63	193,748
1957	221,534	200,485	109,186	53,325	57,658	3,963	69	17,086	69	198,496

1958	237,473	215,169	114,645	59,570	65,681	4,114	70	18,191	70	207,827
1959	243,423	219,012	115,672	62,697	67,473	5,180	609	19,232	609	217,090
1960	256,323	228,993	116,606	66,834	73,284	6,671	152	20,658	152	224,002
1961	277,374	247,905	123,490	74,561	82,812	7,346	462	22,123	462	238,449
1962	295,983	261,444	123,297	88,678	98,227	10,787	3,584	23,752	3,584	254,674
1963	311,791	274,647	123,561	100,033	111,695	11,822	3,577	25,322	3,577	268,045
1964	345,130	306,230	134,301	112,805	127,539	11,462	2,591	27,438	2,591	290,439
1965	375,394	331,513	139,078	130,195	147,676	13,977	4,337	29,905	4,337	318,872
1966	402,946	352,840	144,324	142,261	161,103	18,413	4,729	31,693	4,729	342,177
1967	450,713	395,796	158,491	162,728	185,339	20,911	5,549	34,006	5,549	374,318
1968	500,238	454,652	172,007	180,506	205,927	28,958	8,683	36,628	8,683	425,224
1969	530,715	436,990	178,186	176,241	196,859	47,967	10,852	39,576	10,852	445,821
1970	576,351	482,514	181,897	204,927	235,343	44,968	19,182	42,566	19,182	459,752
1971	639,903	539,184	191,776	237,931	276,905	47,367	25,643	46,905	25,643	510,849
1972	737,699	616,908	221,205	271,827	320,517	61,509	37,651	33,731	37,651	578,046
1973	832,658	681,619	231,957	312,333	372,513	85,386	57,661	57,839	57,661	649,264
1974	912,529	746,413	235,985	358,274	430,996	94,147	56,020	63,287	56,020	714,016
1975	938,888	780,747	247,869	388,345	459,326	87,787	101,918	65,956	30,217	763,580
1976	1,011,274	830,927	256,807	428,873	496,958	102,976	105,648	72,249	26,792	805,837
1977	1,137,795	929,274	287,844	475,094	550,518	123,501	125,239	79,280	32,816	880,100
1978	1,273,189	1,016,385	309,348	532,650	616,099	163,522	156,087	87,418	47,404	972,829

[a] In millions of dollars. Source: See Table A9.5.

[b] Total Time Deposits and therefore Total Deposits and IPC Time include postal savings deposits after 1973.

[c] Revised for call dates prior to Dec. 31, 1938 to exclude "acceptance of other banks and bills sold with endorsement" now treated as contingent liabilities. As of Dec. 30, 1967, also includes securities sold under agreements to repurchase, which were previously reported under "Rediscounts and Other Borrowed Money."

[d] Prior to Dec. 31, 1965, "Federal Funds Purchased" were included. Since then, they are reported separately.

[e] Includes "Capital Notes and Debentures" as well as "Reserve for Contingencies and Other Capital Reserves." (These are not the same as "Reserves for Bad Debt Losses on Loans" and/or "Reserves on Securities." They are reported separately.)

[f] An average of year-end values.

TABLE A9.7

FDIC Commercial Banks—Revenues, Expenses, and Income[a]

Year	Gross operating income[b]	Total operating costs[c]	Officers' salaries[d]	Wages and other compensation[d]	Office occupancy expense[e]	Depreciation expense	Interest and dividends[f]	Interest on borrowed funds	Other operating expenses	Net income before taxes	Net income after taxes
1934	1518.4	759.5	168.2	233.8	—	47.7	302.6	7.3	280.4	−340.0	−340.0
1935	1486.1	778.4	171.1	239.9	—	39.9	262.2	2.6	288.1	207.4	207.4
1936	1566.7	835.0	177.4	249.6	—	52.2	237.2	1.6	299.7	526.6	524.2
1937	1633.6	878.6	187.0	265.1	—	51.5	235.4	1.3	307.6	385.5	380.6
1938	1584.4	871.9	192.0	270.0	—	56.4	229.6	.9	294.9	304.6	300.3
1939	1605.5	890.4	196.4	274.9	—	53.6	215.2	.6	299.8	393.3	388.7
1940	1631.1	929.9	202.4	282.8	—	61.8	200.8	.5	309.5	406.8	401.1
1941	1729.9	1025.1	211.3	302.6	—	64.4	190.3	.4	330.3	504.6	454.6
1942	1790.7	1047.2	219.4	333.2	—	39.9	174.7	.3	346.0	520.2	440.7
1943	1959.5	1091.6	225.1	357.0	—	40.0	163.9	.5	357.8	765.8	639.0
1944	2214.9	1168.8	240.4	386.3	—	41.8	186.8	1.1	390.0	954.1	751.2
1945	2482.3	1287.1	266.0	424.9	—	40.3	233.3	2.4	442.5	1204.7	905.9
1946	2862.9	1491.6	309.2	521.7	—	40.9	268.6	2.4	506.6	1225.7	902.3
1947	3097.7	1680.8	344.8	602.3	—	42.3	298.3	2.7	569.0	1083.6	781.4
1948	3403.6	1843.5	381.8	662.7	—	48.3	316.6	3.4	623.8	1020.8	745.3
1949	3606.9	1952.1	410.7	700.1	—	54.0	328.0	3.6	651.2	1156.5	831.4
1950	3930.7	2097.2	446.0	755.7	—	59.5	343.0	4.3	683.2	1364.7	936.9
1951	4395.4	2306.3	486.3	864.5	—	65.8	385.3	9.7	726.7	1467.6	908.2
1952	4931.7	2549.6	530.0	965.2	—	75.0	458.1	20.9	809.3	1684.8	989.9
1953	5484.0	2816.9	582.4	1069.9	—	84.1	534.5	24.2	897.1	1812.5	1026.0
1954	5773.8	3011.2	622.9	1139.0	—	94.7	618.3	8.6	950.9	2214.6	1307.0
1955	6377.7	3258.9	666.2	1229.8	—	108.3	678.2	23.1	1038.2	1950.0	1156.2
1956	7231.9	3605.9	720.9	1372.3	—	128.1	805.9	45.4	1154.6	2031.4	1216.7
1957	8050.4	3928.0	773.8	1493.8	—	146.3	1141.7	49.5	1262.8	2372.2	1373.8

Year											
1958	8500.9	4207.9	827.1	1573.3	—	168.4	1380.6	24.2	1369.3	2973.1	1701.7
1959	9669.4	4587.5	892.7	1684.2	—	191.4	1580.3	78.4	1532.7	2372.5	1488.1
1960	10723.5	5060.3	966.6	1831.3	—	212.5	1785.1	87.4	1707.8	3387.1	2002.7
1961	11069.6	5295.9	1028.9	1870.0	510.7	224.9	2106.6	38.0	1224.2	3401.8	1995.7
1962	12219.0	5679.6	1098.1	1975.4	555.7	267.9	2845.3	64.3	1300.1	3260.2	2003.8
1963	13509.7	6144.2	1183.3	2101.1	608.5	311.5	3464.3	106.5	1415.3	3379.5	2152.8
1964	15024.5	6682.1	1284.1	2234.9	670.2	362.3	4088.1	127.3	1567.6	3431.8	2283.6
1965	16817.2	7225.9	1392.8	2369.3	731.6	411.9	5070.8	189.5	1717.5	3543.9	2514.7
1966	19508.4	8000.7	4095.7	—	802.1	458.7	6259.4	301.8	2045.3	3714.2	2684.3
1967	21781.6	8907.2	4537.9	—	873.5	533.8	7379.9	266.5	2294.7	4319.0	3141.9
1968	25478.4	10142.5	4101.8	—	970.0	631.6	8681.7	530.0	2684.4	4693.0	3427.9
1969	30806.8	12547.3	5878.8	—	1073.3	773.1	9789.9	1739.6	3397.5	5839.9	4334.6
1970	34716.4	15134.7	6656.9	—	1254.5	909.1	10483.8	1970.1	4550.9	6701.1	4837.3
1971	36364.0	16145.7	7203.0	—	1410.2	1018.1	12218.0	1287.3	4365.0	6888.0	5236.2
1972	40247.6	17394.7	7754.8	—	1583.5	1097.8	13844.0	1757.9	4664.8	7253.3	5654.4
1973	53063.4	19837.6	8574.7	—	1783.0	1201.2	19834.8	4657.4	5460.9	8294.6	6579.2
1974	68160.8	23834.9	9797.7	—	2052.3	1360.7	27888.8	7186.3	6549.3	8851.0	7091.3
1975	66558.5	27341.8	12686.7	—	2324.6	1532.7	26245.9	3994.3	7185.3	8976.5	7183.8
1976	76845.5	31927.8	14752.3	—	2764.8	1721.4	26254.3	4323.9	8492.5	9913.7	7622.9
1977	86142.3	35764.4	16346.1	—	3049.1	1904.2	28596.0	5753.4	9599.3	11566.0	8734.1
1978	108595.3	43281.0	18743.8	—	5584.8	2085.7	35654.6	9170.4	11243.7	15101.3	10139.2

a In millions of dollars. Source: All basic data from the respective tables of income, earnings, and expenses of insured commercial banks in the U.S., Annual Report of the F.D.I.C., 1934–1978.

b "Service Charges on Deposit Accounts" were deducted from the reported revenue figures and were also netted out of total operating costs.

c Real estate taxes and other taxes were deducted from total operating costs and were netted out of gross operating income as well, as it is thought this better reflects the nature of the accounts. Interest on demand deposits (which was paid until 1938) and on time deposits were also deducted from total operating costs and instead are used in the calculation of the effective deposit rate r. Interest on borrowed money was also deducted from total operating costs and instead is used in the calculation of the effective rate on borrowed money.

d Officers' salaries and wages and other compensation are reported jointly as of Dec. 31, 1966.

e Not reported until 1961.

f Beginning with 1938, interest on time deposits comprises all interest (dividends) on deposits.

TABLE A9.8

Mutual Savings Banks—Assets[a]

Year	Total assets	Cash[b]	Total securities[c]	Loans[d]	Bank premises, furniture, and fixtures	Treasury items[e]	Risk assets[f]	Financial assets[g]	Average financial assets[h]
1934	1,177	60	478	555	13	160	957	1,161	—
1935	1,108	68	463	489	12	179	861	1,096	1,129
1936	1,132	70	498	469	11	237	825	1,121	1,109
1937	1,141	72	496	472	11	251	818	1,130	1,126
1938	1,137	71	511	461	11	280	786	1,126	1,128
1939	1,566	133	724	605	18	422	1,011	1,548	1,337
1940	1,984	202	1,018	637	25	548	1,234	1,959	1,754
1941	1,958	151	1,050	642	24	629	1,178	1,934	1,947
1942	2,254	130	1,267	740	27	861	1,263	2,227	2,081
1943	8,364	559	4,452	3,073	77	3,844	3,961	8,287	5,257
1944	9,827	400	6,113	3,110	76	5,509	3,918	9,751	9,019
1945	11,424	429	7,765	3,081	71	7,160	3,835	11,353	10,552
1946	12,637	612	8,641	3,250	70	7,946	4,079	12,567	11,960
1947	13,499	675	9,123	3,560	78	8,165	4,659	13,421	12,994
1948	14,150	684	9,202	4,109	82	7,795	5,671	14,068	13,745
1949	15,060	682	9,394	4,814	82	7,832	6,546	14,978	14,523
1950	15,907	617	9,015	6,086	88	7,487	7,803	15,819	15,399
1951	17,129	695	8,668	7,523	93	6,921	9,513	17,036	16,428
1952	18,612	732	8,930	8,691	103	6,593	11,287	18,509	17,773
1953	20,334	799	9,236	10,016	114	6,476	13,059	20,220	19,365
1954	21,981	832	9,179	11,651	129	6,117	15,032	21,852	21,036
1955	23,458	785	8,768	13,563	139	5,858	16,815	23,319	22,586
1956	25,282	739	8,628	15,542	152	5,518	19,025	25,130	24,225
1957	27,671	719	9,341	17,194	167	5,404	21,548	27,504	26,317

In millions of dollars. Source: "Assets and Liabilities and Income of Insured Mutual Savings Banks," *Annual Report of the F.D.I.C.*, 1934–1978.

Year									
1958	30,189	752	9,800	19,180	183	5,215	24,222	30,006	28,755
1959	31,743	686	9,638	20,942	200	5,016	26,041	31,543	30,775
1960	35,092	766	9,942	23,852	227	4,787	29,542	34,865	33,204
1961	37,065	828	9,848	25,812	247	4,690	31,547	36,818	35,842
1962	39,951	784	9,819	28,778	269	4,639	34,528	39,682	38,250
1963	43,019	722	9,365	32,300	290	4,324	37,973	42,729	41,206
1964	47,044	893	9,125	36,233	343	4,110	42,041	46,701	44,715
1965	50,500	904	8,770	39,964	381	3,760	45,836	50,119	48,410
1966	53,049	848	8,676	42,593	415	3,324	48,877	52,634	51,377
1967	57,867	882	10,447	45,492	429	3,111	53,874	57,438	55,036
1968	62,123	883	11,803	48,287	470	2,855	58,385	61,653	59,546
1969	64,634	780	11,844	50,829	497	2,446	61,408	64,137	62,895
1970	78,995	1,270	16,224	60,030	529	2,354	75,371	78,466	71,302
1971	89,581	1,389	21,688	64,794	590	3,268	84,924	88,991	83,728
1972	100,593	1,644	26,289	70,542	661	3,510	95,439	99,932	94,461
1973	106,651	1,968	25,266	77,102	760	2,957	101,726	105,891	102,911
1974	109,550	2,167	26,035	78,703	858	2,555	104,828	108,692	107,291
1975	121,056	2,330	34,277	81,224	964	4,777	113,949	120,035	114,364
1976	135,462	2,316	48,812	86,492	1,064	7,147	125,999	134,398	127,217
1977	147,006	2,339	46,217	94,045	1,162	9,023	135,644	145,844	140,121
1978	157,592	3,712	47,608	101,687	1,267	10,637	143,243	156,325	151,085

[b] Includes cash in vault, interbank balances, and cash items in the process of collection.

[c] Includes all U.S. government obligations and all other securities.

[d] Includes all loans, discounts, overdrafts, and rediscounts.

[e] Includes bills, certificates, notes, bonds, and obligations fully guaranteed by the U.S. government.

[f] Total assets minus cash minus treasury items.

[g] Total assets minus bank premises, furniture, and fixtures.

[h] The average of year-end balances.

TABLE A9.9

Mutual Savings Banks—Liabilities[a]

Year	Total liabilities and capital	Total deposits	Other liabil- ities[b]	Capital account	Borrowed money[c]	Average deposits[d]
1934	1,177	1,045	2	128	2	—
1935	1,108	978	3	126	1	1,012
1936	1,132	998	3	132	3	988
1937	1,141	1,004	3	133	3	1,001
1938	1,137	1,012	3	122	3	1,008
1939	1,566	1,409	4	153	4	1,211
1940	1,984	1,818	5	161	5	1,614
1941	1,958	1,789	6	164	6	1,804
1942	2,254	2,048	5	201	5	1,919
1943	8,364	7,534	22	808	22	4,791
1944	9,827	8,910	25	892	25	8,222
1945	11,424	10,363	26	1,034	26	9,637
1946	12,637	11,428	36	1,173	36	10,896
1947	13,499	12,207	40	1,252	40	11,818
1948	14,150	12,772	44	1,334	44	12,490
1949	15,060	13,592	49	1,420	49	13,182
1950	15,907	14,320	74	1,513	74	13,956
1951	17,129	15,368	83	1,678	83	14,844
1952	18,612	16,785	96	1,730	96	16,077
1953	20,334	18,383	133	1,819	—	17,584
1954	21,981	19,885	176	1,920	—	19,134
1955	23,458	21,237	215	2,006	—	20,561
1956	25,282	22,886	267	2,130	—	22,062
1957	27,671	25,022	340	2,309	—	23,954
1958	30,189	27,277	440	2,473	—	26,150
1959	31,743	28,577	512	2,654	—	27,927
1960	35,092	31,502	592	2,998	—	30,040
1961	37,065	33,400	474	3,191	—	32,451
1962	39,951	36,104	504	3,343	—	34,752
1963	43,019	38,657	790	3,572	38	37,381
1964	47,044	42,751	562	3,731	20	40,704
1965	50,500	45,887	655	3,957	91	44,319
1966	53,049	48,256	654	4,140	69	47,072
1967	57,867	52,913	717	4,238	68	50,585
1968	62,123	56,861	781	4,481	71	54,887
1969	64,634	58,868	1,068	4,698	382	57,865
1970	78,995	71,580	1,690	4,857	252	65,224
1971	89,581	81,440	1,810	5,405	100	76,510
1972	100,593	91,613	2,024	5,904	99	86,527
1973	106,651	96,496	2,566	6,398	446	94,055
1974	109,550	98,701	2,888	6,653	667	97,599

TABLE A9.9 (Continued)

Year	Total liabilities and capital	Total deposits	Other liabil- ities[b]	Capital account	Borrowed money[c]	Average deposits[d]
1975	121,056	109,783	2,755	7,149	465	104,249
1976	135,462	122,729	2,812	7,975	356	116,301
1977	147,006	132,959	2,951	8,809	483	127,844
1978	157,592	141,336	3,418	9,652	1,025	137,148

[a] In millions of dollars. Source: See Table A9.8.

[b] As of Dec. 30, 1967, includes securities sold under agreements to repurchase, which were previously reported under "Other Borrowed Money."

[c] Figures not reported separately from 1953 until 1962, inclusive.

[d] A simple arithmetic average of year-end values.

TABLE A9.10

Mutual Savings Banks—Revenues, Expenses, and Income[a]

Year	Gross operating income[b,c]	Total operating costs[b,c]	Officers' salaries[d]	Wages and other compensation[d]	Office occupancy	Interest and dividends	Interest on borrowed funds[e]	Other operating costs	Net income before taxes	Net income after taxes
1934	47.8	11.9	3.5	—	.1	26.7	1.600	5.4	3.6	2.0
1935	42.7	12.9	3.2	—	.1	22.1	0	6.6	5.9	5.9
1936	41.4	14.3	1.4	1.9	.6	19.6	.018	7.3	7.1	7.1
1937	42.0	15.8	1.6	2.0	.8	19.3	.034	7.6	1.8	1.8
1938	44.5	16.3	1.6	2.1	.7	19.3	.004	7.8	−11.5	−11.5
1939	57.0	19.7	2.0	3.4	.9	26.6	0	8.6	−1.8	−1.8
1940	71.0	22.5	2.4	4.8	1.5	31.4	0	8.3	−19.0	−18.9
1941	69.5	23.3	2.5	5.1	.7	29.7	.300	9.6	4.7	4.2
1942	76.3	24.5	3.1	5.9	.7	33.2	.300	9.7	4.2	3.8
1943	273.5	87.8	11.2	19.8	3.0	118.1	.300	36.8	28.0	27.3
1944	295.7	86.6	12.1	20.7	3.4	132.4	.500	35.7	64.5	63.9
1945	322.8	77.7	11.4	22.2	2.6	143.4	.300	33.0	148.0	145.6
1946	351.1	85.5	13.1	26.9	2.6	160.1	.300	35.8	149.5	143.5
1947	375.6	93.6	14.4	31.2	2.6	181.2	.200	38.5	88.3	82.1
1948	403.2	100.8	15.5	34.2	2.7	196.1	.200	42.0	89.4	84.6
1949	436.9	104.2	16.5	35.8	3.1	235.8	.200	42.3	86.5	82.0
1950	478.7	115.5	18.1	38.5	2.9	257.8	.200	49.0	96.5	91.2
1951	513.8	106.7	19.9	37.7	11.6	282.2	—	20.3	124.9	118.8
1952	568.5	116.8	21.4	41.0	12.2	365.5	—	23.0	86.3	77.1
1953	647.1	127.3	23.4	44.4	13.5	415.0	—	25.2	104.8	96.2
1954	721.3	140.0	25.4	48.1	15.0	466.1	—	28.5	115.3	104.6
1955	801.7	147.7	26.9	50.9	15.1	536.3	—	30.5	117.7	108.7
1956	898.4	158.3	28.7	54.0	17.5	609.3	—	32.1	130.8	121.8

1957	1026.3	174.8	31.6	58.3	19.3	716.4	—	36.4	135.2	126.1
1958	1149.6	187.8	33.3	61.8	20.9	812.3	—	39.7	149.6	139.3
1959	1280.4	201.4	35.4	64.4	22.7	897.5	—	43.1	181.5	169.8
1960	1461.8	224.8	40.3	71.3	25.3	1073.5	—	48.8	163.4	149.8
1961	1595.2	241.7	42.2	75.3	27.4	1147.8	—	54.5	205.7	189.7
1962	1755.6	253.0	44.6	79.2	29.3	1334.0	—	56.3	168.6	150.6
1963	1946.8	274.5	47.2	84.5	32.2	1481.9	—	63.0	190.4	167.8
1964	2164.1	290.5	50.1	89.5	34.7	1653.8	—	64.9	219.9	193.9
1965	2391.8	311.8	53.2	93.7	37.2	1809.4	—	71.4	270.6	241.2
1966	2606.0	334.5	56.9	98.4	38.9	2087.1	—	78.1	184.5	147.0
1967	2884.8	354.0	60.5	105.6	42.4	2395.8	2.900	99.4	135.1	97.4
1968	3238.7	386.7	175.3	—	47.2	2612.6	4.000	109.7	242.6	194.9
1969	3581.6	433.2	193.6	—	52.5	2808.1	9.900	124.6	270.9	209.0
1970	3874.9	500.5	217.5	—	60.7	2987.2	20.300	151.3	245.4	167.0
1971	4529.0	573.8	243.4	—	71.1	3418.8	7.900	171.6	470.2	343.6
1972	5295.4	665.1	270.4	—	82.8	3943.2	6.700	211.3	665.5	479.2
1973	6064.9	782.8	307.0	—	96.1	4480.9	28.900	261.0	680.0	478.2
1974	6483.7	872.6	344.3	—	114.2	4916.7	66.100	276.9	479.4	317.5
1975	7179.3	1028.0	388.1	—	135.8	5495.8	55.200	331.6	536.9	365.4
1976	8312.7	1265.6	440.3	—	158.0	6288.0	45.400	411.9	734.1	507.0
1977	9405.6	1418.4	497.6	—	172.1	6997.5	46.800	476.3	961.4	681.1
1978	10638.7	1636.4	570.8	—	189.5	7706.7	122.400	530.4	1119.7	808.7

[a] In millions of dollars. Source: See Table A9.8.

[b] *Gross Operating Income* — Service charges on deposit accounts were deducted from the reported revenue figures. These service charges are reported as a negative cost and were netted out of total operating costs.

[c] Real estate taxes and other taxes were netted out of Gross Operating Income and total operating costs to reflect net portfolio revenues. Interest on deposits were also deducted from total operating costs to reflect only administrative costs. Interest on borrowed money was also deducted from total operating costs, and is used instead in the calculation of the effective rate on borrowed money.

[d] Officers' salaries and wages and other compensation are reported jointly in 1934 and 1935 as well as from 1968 to the present.

[e] Not available for 1951–1966.

379

TABLE A9.11

Savings and Loan Associations—Assets[a]

Year	Mortgage loans	Total assets	Government securities	Office building	Cash	Other loans	Cash and investments	Real estate	Office real estate	Other assets	Average total financial assets	Total financial assets
1942	3989.5	5025.5	259.7	30.5	336.3	9.2	1042.2	3.4	38.0	5.8	4592.162	4719.605
1943	4047.7	5538.6	736.6	34.8	387.2	14.8	1269.3	4.5	41.5	6.4	4947.763	5175.921
1944	4273.7	6422.7	1490.7	42.1	347.3	16.2	1680.5	5.8	50.1	7.9	5640.053	6104.184
1945	4823.4	7681.5	2181.2	50.5	383.9	18.7	1969.9	7.1	60.3	8.2	6764.155	7424.126
1946	6487.3	9017.2	1779.5	59.2	466.7	20.0	2354.5	8.0	72.0	10.4	8188.629	8953.132
1947	8073.6	10427.5	1533.3	71.4	502.2	33.5	2064.7	7.1	78.0	11.9	9780.914	9854.000
1948	9438.5	11733.4	1295.5	84.7	609.8	53.6	1955.6	8.0	95.7	14.1	10990.829	11080.500
1949	10682.7	13278.3	1319.8	103.1	822.6	88.9	2185.8	10.4	117.1	16.1	12396.177	12505.900
1950	12660.7	15468.5	1364.4	123.7	890.5	118.9	2289.2	13.6	143.0	17.0	14239.409	14373.400
1951	14600.3	17857.6	1513.6	159.0	1018.2	138.3	2591.4	11.3	185.3	20.1	16489.474	16663.100
1952	17409.6	21257.6	1697.6	198.3	1248.5	188.6	3023.1	18.0	234.1	24.9	19338.248	19557.600
1953	20859.4	25216.3	1831.7	247.0	1438.9	247.6	3354.9	17.7	293.9	26.7	22961.616	23237.000
1954	24955.6	30030.9	1903.9	298.4	1888.6	304.5	3882.8	22.6	355.9	32.8	27290.122	27623.600
1955	30201.3	36023.6	2236.6	367.8	2015.7	363.8	4392.8	30.7	437.0	38.1	32617.831	33027.300
1956	34495.4	41179.8	2650.7	452.2	2046.2	443.1	4971.6	39.8	534.2	39.1	38101.155	38601.700
1957	38685.7	46369.4	3064.2	546.5	2087.8	527.9	5665.9	48.7	644.5	42.2	43170.704	43774.600

Year												
1958	44129.7	53206.7	3686.3	641.2	2482.6	649.6	6700.4	71.1	752.1	51.1	49083.382	49788.100
1959	51528.2	61507.1	4384.3	748.6	2126.6	802.7	7159.1	100.1	875.0	66.3	56537.025	57356.900
1960	58391.5	69330.1	4510.5	858.9	2582.6	888.7	7692.5	154.8	1014.6	72.0	64467.920	65418.600
1961	67111.4	79889.2	5107.5	1009.2	3248.4	967.9	9002.7	286.3	1192.6	91.0	73492.324	74609.700
1962	77325.5	91664.8	5486.2	1179.3	3862.1	962.7	10017.6	398.7	1387.8	270.0	84476.631	85777.000
1963	89375.1	105457.7	6300.4	1389.6	3918.7	1080.5	10989.0	562.0	1613.1	474.5	97049.825	98561.300
1964	99960.5	117383.0	6812.4	1542.2	3926.9	1102.9	11547.3	792.8	1778.7	758.7	109753.758	111420.400
1965	108463.3	127473.8	7255.9	1667.6	3788.5	1162.6	11902.2	1054.9	1929.6	1047.4	120359.065	122167.100
1966	112079.5	131854.6	7618.5	1746.5	3279.3	1209.7	11865.7	1258.5	2020.9	1263.9	127522.217	129415.800
1967	119184.0	141378.6	9076.2	1814.4	3360.1	1268.3	13722.1	1319.4	2099.5	1412.3	134311.868	136279.100
1968	127881.6	150522.2	9411.6	1886.3	2882.4	1418.4	13816.2	1007.0	2182.7	1685.3	143580.110	145625.300
1969	136514.8	158731.7	583.0	1993.4	2356.7	1627.0	12939.7	805.7	2306.6	1952.5	151947.516	154108.800
1970	146193.5	171986.0	2090.9	2147.6	3002.7	1947.6	16021.9	727.5	2485.1	2016.1	162675.061	165003.600
1971	169709.7	199841.4	4891.3	2388.9	2492.3	2813.1	21771.9	744.1	2764.3	2175.9	183323.551	185913.700
1972	200054.0	236195.6	6479.9	2743.5	2630.4	3899.4	22663.9	752.1	3174.6	2418.2	215043.900	218018.500
1973	225739.4	264364.8	5705.3	3182.6	2633.8	4996.8	22283.4	882.9	3682.7	2724.0	246829.510	250280.200
1974	243130.4	287583.3	6679.3	3727.5	2735.4	5697.5	24824.2	1187.0	4313.2	3076.6	271932.632	275974.100
1975	271320.7	329015.4	—	4498.2	3004.0	6606.3	32506.2	1622.7	4917.4	3509.5	300036.100	324098.000
1976	315288.0	381671.2	—	4979.5	3736.8	8062.0	37245.7	1884.0	5458.1	3646.8	350155.600	376213.100
1977	372434.4	447871.6	—	5438.6	3384.2	10236.8	41268.1	1755.5	5967.8	3954.1	409058.500	441903.800
1978	423544.4	510753.5		5918.4	2769.9	11469.2	47320.0	1684.0	6517.6	4519.7	473069.900	504235.900

a In millions of dollars. Source: *Combined Financial Statements, FSLIC-Insured Savings and Loan Associations,* Federal Home Loan Bank Board, Washington, D.C.: U.S. Govt. Printing Office, 1941–1980.

TABLE A9.12

Savings and Loan Associations—Liabilities[a]

Year	Average savings accounts	Year-end savings accounts	Total borrowed funds	FHLB advances	Other borrowings	Debentures	Total liabilities	Net worth
1942	4123.5	4285.7	142.7	120.6	30.1	—	4656.6	368.9
1943	4478.6	4671.5	127.8	123.2	49.3	—	5112.9	425.7
1944	4987.8	5304.1	190.4	178.7	61.2	—	5931.5	491.2
1945	5815.3	6326.5	324.7	306.1	62.8	—	7114.7	566.8
1946	6933.8	7541.1	378.5	322.6	83.4	—	8363.1	654.1
1947	8226.1	8745.1	512.3	425.8	86.5	—	9769.3	758.2
1948	9334.0	9922.9	562.2	500.2	62.0	—	10866.6	866.0
1949	10650.3	11377.6	470.0	423.9	46.1	—	12277.6	1164.0
1950	12119.6	12861.6	849.2	788.8	60.4	—	14303.7	1164.0
1951	13943.6	15025.5	848.5	788.9	59.6	—	16493.0	1364.0
1952	16550.2	18074.9	903.4	844.7	58.7	—	19691.3	1566.0
1953	19850.3	21627.5	984.8	931.7	53.1	—	23416.8	1799.0
1954	23794.6	25961.7	905.8	847.4	58.4	—	27946.4	2084.0
1955	28387.3	30812.9	1494.0	1386.9	107.1	—	33511.1	2452.0
1956	33272.6	35732.2	1312.2	1220.5	91.7	—	38348.0	2831.8
1957	38089.4	40446.6	1340.5	1212.2	88.3	—	43126.9	3242.0
1958	43411.0	46375.3	1399.7	1278.6	121.1	—	49482.0	3724.0
1959	49639.7	52904.1	2308.8	2092.7	216.1	—	57227.3	4279.0
1960	56614.1	60333.6	2143.8	1964.6	179.2	—	64481.6	4848.0
1961	64748.9	69036.7	2803.9	2640.1	163.8	—	74318.3	5570.0
1962	73923.7	78633.8	3573.0	3444.6	128.4	—	85233.4	6431.4
1963	84138.1	89591.1	4956.5	4740.8	215.7	—	98389.1	7068.0
1964	94638.8	100296.6	5576.6	5328.1	248.5	—	109474.3	7908.0
1965	104289.6	108703.9	6374.4	5970.8	403.6	—	118789.0	8684.0
1966	110320.0	112354.7	7337.8	6902.9	434.9	—	122644.2	9210.0
1967	117280.5	122768.7	4665.1	4373.8	291.3	—	131708.2	9670.0
1968	125968.9	129722.1	5582.3	5213.6	368.7	—	140126.4	10395.0
1969	130771.5	132739.0	9601.6	9161.3	440.3	—	147450.6	11281.0
1970	137502.9	142881.5	10829.7	10487.7	342.0	—	159981.1	12004.0
1971	155958.7	169035.8	8926.0	7910.4	993.8	—	186773.6	13067.0
1972	184986.3	200936.8	9722.8	7948.1	1744.4	—	221516.0	14679.0
1973	210690.0	200442.9	17019.1	14483.8	2077.1	—	247899.3	16465.0
1974	228229.1	236015.3	24468.2	21332.1	3021.8	—	269770.7	17812.0
1975	256844.7	277674.1	20474.3	17430.4	2920.4	123.5	309913.8	19101.7
1976	302182.7	326691.2	18989.4	15726.9	3146.2	116.3	360391.7	21279.2
1977	351996.5	377301.7	26976.7	19509.9	7296.4	170.4	423444.8	24425.9
1978	398842.2	420382.6	41941.7	31620.4	10129.7	191.5	482617.6	28136.1

[a] In millions of dollars. Source: See Table A9.11.

TABLE A9.13

Savings and Loan Associations—Revenues, Expenses, and Income[a]

Year	Gross operating income	Wages and other compensation	Office occupancy expense	Advertising	Total operating expenses	Interest and dividends	Interest on borrowed funds	Net income before taxes	Net income after taxes
1942	188.64	24.71	3.54	3.58	50.55	90.63	1.90	—	—
1943	208.45	28.14	4.03	3.54	56.69	101.57	2.40	—	—
1944	233.05	32.16	4.79	4.19	65.72	114.07	2.70	—	—
1945	288.67	40.13	5.93	5.48	83.71	134.97	4.10	—	—
1946	353.84	50.42	7.18	6.85	105.21	167.45	4.90	—	—
1947	415.50	59.40	10.30	8.60	121.80	195.30	6.80	29.5	295.00
1948	487.00	67.80	11.90	11.10	140.50	227.80	9.80	33.8	338.10
1949	558.40	75.90	13.30	13.30	157.80	268.10	8.30	3.97	395.80
1950	660.20	87.70	14.90	16.00	180.10	35.80	11.10	4.73	470.60
1951	764.60	101.90	13.90	19.80	209.00	361.90	17.80	5.40	540.30
1952	902.40	117.80	23.60	24.50	244.90	446.60	18.00	6.41	637.80
1953	1097.40	138.50	26.90	29.20	286.50	557.80	20.50	7.93	788.90
1954	1324.70	162.30	32.00	34.10	338.50	684.70	20.00	9.74	968.80
1955	1618.80	190.30	36.80	41.20	398.30	835.40	28.40	119.6	1190.90
1956	1903.10	217.60	43.30	52.60	463.50	1009.40	40.50	140.1	1396.10
1957	2222.50	244.20	50.80	60.60	527.90	1243.70	42.40	165.5	1651.50
1958	2570.60	272.60	59.30	65.40	598.50	1467.40	35.10	164.9	1943.70
1959	3069.00	313.90	68.40	78.60	696.90	1754.60	61.60	231.0	2305.00
1960	3601.90	349.50	77.80	91.10	787.30	2183.50	79.30	274.7	2743.00
1961	4165.80	395.30	90.10	103.20	894.30	2495.00	67.40	322.2	3218.60
1962	4937.10	441.60	100.70	112.20	1002.60	3054.20	91.40	388.6	3883.00
1963	5603.70	508.70	121.10	132.30	1198.80	3505.20	130.60	428.1	4187.40

(Continued)

TABLE A9.13 (Continued)

Year	Gross operating income	Wages and other compensation	Office occupancy expense	Advertising	Total operating expenses	Interest and dividends	Interest on borrowed funds	Net income before taxes	Net income after taxes
1964	6369.30	589.00	142.60	122.50	1269.90	3965.50	192.20	490.2	4769.40
1965	6972.60	628.70	159.50	128.60	1345.10	4415.90	243.20	537.9	5225.50
1966	7453.20	646.30	171.60	136.50	1396.50	4910.70	373.60	567.0	5555.00
1967	7944.60	670.10	185.30	128.00	1448.80	5477.60	285.90	621.4	6105.60
1968	8760.60	724.40	198.70	140.70	1574.40	5891.80	285.60	693.2	6765.90
1969	9721.30	791.70	216.80	168.40	1733.30	6282.90	455.90	750.0	7328.20
1970	10763.10	872.00	236.90	193.70	1918.00	6956.60	765.30	813.1	7888.90
1971	12593.30	993.60	240.40	195.40	2105.00	8274.30	603.40	1002.2	9587.90
1972	15128.70	1156.90	245.20	236.80	2451.80	9966.60	478.90	1228.3	11654.10
1973	18187.80	1370.90	289.60	308.50	2944.60	11688.50	916.90	1434.3	13585.40
1974	20893.20	1584.40	349.70	348.20	3405.10	13646.10	1671.00	1578.9	15128.70
1975	23719.00	1817.40	425.90	352.40	3949.40	16019.80	1599.80	208.2	1448.40
1976	28217.30	2317.30	503.20	344.90	4581.90	19089.60	1392.60	321.8	2249.80
1977	33890.50	2511.80	576.50	381.10	5327.60	22546.80	1506.00	461.0	3198.20
1978	40589.10	2936.20	653.10	481.50	6177.40	26024.30	2666.60	571.6	3198.10

[a] In millions of dollars. Source: See Table A9.11.

Additional Tables for Chapter 10

TABLE B10.1

Market Shares of Savings Deposits[a]

Year	Commercial banks	Mutual savings banks	Savings & loan associations	Credit unions
1942	48.1	32.1	14.8	.9
1943	49.0	31.1	14.6	.9
1944	50.6	29.7	14.1	.8
1945	52.8	27.9	13.3	.7
1946	54.0	26.9	13.2	.7
1947	53.4	26.6	14.0	.8
1948	52.4	26.5	15.2	.9
1949	51.2	26.6	16.5	1.0
1950	49.8	26.8	18.0	1.2
1951	48.5	28.8	19.6	1.4
1952	47.6	26.3	21.3	1.6
1953	46.5	25.9	23.1	1.9
1954	45.5	25.3	24.9	2.0
1955	43.8	24.9	27.1	2.2
1956	42.2	24.6	29.3	2.5
1957	41.7	23.9	30.6	2.6
1958	42.7	22.8	31.0	2.7
1959	41.9	22.0	32.6	2.8
1960	40.3	21.3	34.9	3.0
1961	41.9	19.8	35.0	3.0
1962	43.0	18.6	35.1	3.0
1963	43.7	17.8	35.4	3.0
1964	44.1	17.3	35.5	3.0
1965	45.3	16.7	34.8	3.0
1966	46.9	16.2	33.8	3.1
1967	48.0	16.0	32.9	3.1
1968	48.4	16.0	32.5	3.1
1969	48.3	16.0	32.4	3.3
1970	47.8	16.1	32.5	3.6
1971	50.6	15.1	30.1	3.6
1972	50.3	14.7	31.4	3.7
1973	51.6	13.8	31.0	3.6
1974	53.6	12.8	30.0	3.6
1975	53.0	12.4	30.1	3.9
1976	51.1	12.4	32.3	4.2
1977	49.9	12.2	33.5	4.4
1978	50.1	11.6	33.8	4.5

[a] Expressed in percentages. Entries do not necessarily total 100.00 because a small amount of nondepository savings is excluded. Source: 1945–1965: Jack R. Vernon, "Competition for Savings Deposits: The Recent Experience," *National Bank Review*, **3**, December 1966. 1966–1976: (1) Board of Governors of the Federal Reserve System, *Flow of Funds, Assets and Liabilities*, 1945–1976; (2) F.D.I.C., *Annual Report*, various years.

TABLE B10.2

Market Share of Total Deposits[a]

Year	Commercial banks	Mutual savings banks	Savings & loan associations	Credit unions
1942	78.8	13.1	6.0	.4
1943	80.6	11.8	5.5	.3
1944	80.5	11.7	5.6	.3
1945	80.4	11.6	5.5	.3
1946	80.2	11.5	5.7	.4
1947	79.6	11.7	6.1	.4
1948	78.3	12.1	6.9	.4
1949	77.4	12.3	7.7	.5
1950	77.4	12.1	8.1	.5
1951	77.2	11.9	8.7	.6
1952	76.1	12.0	9.7	.7
1953	74.4	12.4	11.0	.9
1954	73.1	12.5	12.3	1.0
1955	71.8	12.5	13.6	1.1
1956	70.1	12.7	15.1	1.3
1957	68.5	12.9	16.5	1.4
1958	68.1	12.7	17.3	1.5
1959	66.6	12.6	18.7	1.6
1960	64.9	12.5	20.5	1.8
1961	64.9	11.9	21.2	1.8
1962	63.9	11.8	22.3	1.9
1963	62.7	11.8	23.4	2.0
1964	62.6	11.5	23.7	2.0
1965	62.5	11.5	23.9	2.1
1966	63.0	11.3	23.5	2.1
1967	63.9	11.1	22.9	2.1
1968	64.1	11.1	22.6	2.2
1969	63.9	11.2	22.6	2.3
1970	63.4	11.3	22.8	2.5
1971	63.6	11.1	22.6	2.7
1972	62.5	11.1	23.7	2.8
1973	63.5	10.4	23.4	2.7
1974	64.5	9.8	22.9	2.8
1975	63.7	9.6	23.6	3.0
1976	61.6	9.7	25.4	3.3
1977	60.7	9.5	26.3	3.5
1978	60.4	9.2	6.8	3.6

[a] Expressed in percentages. Source: See Table B10.1.

TABLE B10.3

Household Savings in Commercial Banks[a]

Year	Percent of household savings in banks	Change in percentage in banks	Return to savers at savings & loans	Return to savers at banks	Rate spread
1945	78.55				
1946[b]	78.12	−0.43	.0240	.0084	.0156
1947	76.50	−1.62	.0230	.0087	.0143
1948	74.54	−1.96	.0229	.0090	.0139
1949	72.10	−2.44	.0234	.0091	.0143
1950	69.76	−2.34	.0252	.0094	.0158
1951	67.67	−2.09	.0258	.0103	.0155
1952	65.47	−2.20	.0269	.0115	.0154
1953	63.05	−2.42	.0281	.0124	.0157
1954	60.26	−2.79	.0287	.0132	.0155
1955	57.31	−2.95	.0294	.0138	.0156
1956	54.98	−2.43	.0303	.0158	.0145
1957	54.65	−0.33	.0326	.0208	.0118
1958	53.76	−0.89	.0338	.0221	.0117
1959	52.11	−1.65	.0353	.0236	.0117
1960	50.04	−2.07	.0386	.0256	.0130
1961	49.10	−0.94	.0390	.0271	.0119
1962	49.53	+0.43	.0408	.0318	.0090
1963	48.68	−0.85	.0417	.0331	.0086
1964	48.22	−0.46	.0419	.0342	.0077
1965	49.08	+0.86	.0423	.0369	.0054
1966[b]	53.43	+4.35	.0445	.0404	.0041
1967	54.55	+1.12	.0467	.0424	.0043
1968	56.01	+1.46	.0468	.0448	.0020
1969	55.41	−0.6	.0480	.0487	−.0007
1970	57.16	+1.75	.0506	.0495	.0011
1971	56.21	−0.95	.0531	.0478	.0053
1972	54.65	−1.56	.0539	.0466	.0073
1973	55.98	+1.35	.0555	.0571	−.0016
1974	57.22	+1.24	.0598	.0693	−.0095
1975	55.07	−2.15	.0624	.0592	.0032
1976	53.71	−1.36	.0632	.0553	.0079

[a] Source: See Table B10.1.
[b] Excluded from calculations.

Additional Table for Chapter 13

TABLE C13.1

Deposits, Average Deposit Rates, Average Cost per Deposit Unit and Average Profit Margin per Deposit Unit, by Selected Subsectors, 1966–1973[a]

Country and subsector	Year	Deposits[b]	Average deposit rate	Average cost per deposit unit	Average profit margin per deposit unit
Colombia					
Commercial banks	1967	11,330	2.18	5.84	1.95
	1968	13,598	2.07	5.31	1.75
	1969	16,801	1.96	5.72	1.92
	1970	20,705	1.64	6.97	2.06
	1971	25,049	1.63	7.49	1.83
	1972	30,749	2.08	8.12	1.79
	1973	40,007	2.16	7.67	1.72
Caja Agraria	1967	1,512	2.38	10.38	.99
	1968	1,808	2.16	11.28	1.11
	1969	2,206	2.63	10.34	1.41
	1970	2,708	2.51	11.45	.74
	1971	3,224	2.88	14.08	.93
	1972	4,241	3.98	14.36	.14
	1973	5,480	3.98	13.47	.24
Banco Central Hipotecario	1967	2,360	2.88	1.91	.25
	1968	3,685	3.15	1.19	.27
	1969	5,397	3.59	.91	.24
	1970	6,903	3.71	1.41	.81
	1971	8,950	4.16	1.06	1.02
	1972	10,956	3.63	1.32	.77
	1973	10,772	4.28	1.76	.46

(Continued)

TABLE C13.1 (Continued)

Country and subsector	Year	Deposits[b]	Average deposit rate	Average cost per deposit unit	Average profit margin per deposit unit
Corporaciones financieras	1967	458	1.68[b]	6.40[c]	11.46
	1968	1,111	6.53[b]	5.75[c]	9.99
	1969	1,654	7.22[b]	5.37[c]	11.03
	1970	2,942	7.39	7.48	6.05
	1971	3,943	8.86	9.09	3.25
	1972	4,860	10.32	8.59	4.92
	1973	6,813	10.10	6.87	4.77
Mexico					
Commercial banks	1966	30,059	8.38	6.35	1.20
	1967	33,820	2.52	6.42	.81
	1968	37,829	2.66	6.63	.76
	1969	43,666	2.81	6.63	.66
	1970	47,841	3.53	7.27	.79
	1971	52,483	3.81	7.62	.76
	1972	60,199	3.34	7.43	.88
	1973	75,710	3.29	7.02	.80
Financieras	1966	27,163	8.87	1.56	.50
	1967	37,888	8.40	1.41	.72
	1968	40,722	9.58	1.66	.79
	1969	52,614	9.65	1.57	.66
	1970	66,630	10.66	1.57	.60
	1971	78,663	10.85	1.67	.60
	1972	90,760	9.91	1.73	.57
	1973	97,050	10.27	1.82	.44
Mortgage banks	1966	7,242	10.06	2.45	1.78
	1967	8,622	9.73	2.73	1.60
	1968	10,133	9.33	2.85	1.48
	1969	12,035	8.99	2.58	1.16
	1970	14,420	9.14	2.26	.95
	1971	17,893	8.85	2.07	.76
	1972	21,875	8.58	2.00	.79
	1973	24,888	9.01	1.94	.65
Peru[d]					
Private commercial banks	1966	24,010	2.31	5.42	.49
	1968	34,697	1.96	5.96	.74
	1972	30,482	1.80	6.15	.60
	1973	35,482	1.671	5.55	1.12

TABLE C13.1 (Continued)

Country and subsector	Year	Deposits[b]	Average deposit rate	Average cost per deposit unit	Average profit margin per deposit unit
Regional banks	1966	956	3.61	6.27	1.03
	1968	1,085	3.31	8.16	.34
	1972	1,830	2.87	6.54	.62
	1973	2,469	3.13	6.04	.26
Foreign banks	1966	840	.80	4.35	.67
	1968	1,147	.53	5.87	1.84
	1972	1,747	.63	5.14	1.59
	1973	2,039	.60	5.03	2.10
Private development banks	1966	195	2.87	6.30	.80
	1968	264	5.16	5.40	.69
	1972	754	4.79	4.26	.60
	1973	833	4.35	4.16	.93
Savings banks	1966	589	4.36	2.87	3.64
	1968	631	4.36	4.32	3.31
	1972	1,876	6.08	2.56	2.55
	1973	2,634	6.63	2.21	1.99

[a] Source: See Table 13.1.
[b] In millions of local currency.
[c] Estimated.
[d] Years for which data were unavailable are omitted.

Index